Airline Service Marketing

AIRLINE SERVICE MARKETING

Dr. Sharad Goel, Ed.

PENTAGON PRESS

Airline Service Marketing / Dr. Sharad Goel, Ed.

ISBN 978-81-8274-404-2

First Indian Edition 2009

Published by

PENTAGON PRESS
206, Peacock Lane, Shahpur Jat, New Delhi-110049
Phones: 011-64706243, 26491568
Telefax: 011-26490600
email: rajan@pentagon-press.com
website: www.pentagon-press.com

Printed at
Syndicate Binders
A-20, Hosiery Complex, Noida Phase-II Extn., Noida-201305, U.P.

Preface

This book is designed to offer a truly international perceptive on Airlines Marketing in the diverse field of Air travel, Airport and Cargo marketing. It examines the principles of marketing and demonstrates the ways in which these principles can be applied to today's airline industry. It is not simply meant to be a description of the situation in individual countries. Instead it is an attempt to take a supranational view of the subject for we believe Airlines Marketing is now a truly global phenomenon. This edition emphasizes the global airline industry and discusses airline passenger marketing, Airport and Cargo Marketing. Why we believe there is a need for a book on Airline Marketing, in the first place.

Firstly, Why Airlines? This industry, if single industry it is, has grown dramatically in recent decades. Airlines services has been in the vanguard of the development of the modern customer society.

Secondly, Why Marketing? Because marketing is the "Buzz Word" of modern management theory and practice, in both the public and private sectors, across the world. The concept of marketing has been broadened to the point where it is now appears to encompass most aspect of corporate life. It is particularly appropriate to talk a marketing approach when one is looking at services industries like Airlines, Airport and Cargo for it is in such largely modern industries where staff and customers interact on a face to face basis, that many modern innovations in marketing have been born.

An initial review of the structure of the air transport market and the industry marketing environment is followed by detailed chapters examining airline business and marketing strategies, product design and management, pricing and revenue management, distribution channels and selling and advertising policies.

The text is intended and designed to be both, valuable and hopefully stimulating for a variety of readers including:

1. Undergraduate and Post-graduate students on Business Courses, who have interest in Airlines Marketing and Services industries Courses.

2. Students following short term and vocational courses, training related to Airlines, Aviation and Air transport programs.
3. Persons working for Travel business, Airlines Services.
4. Faculty delivering courses on Airlines Business related areas.

The readers will benefit from the clear explanation of both marketing and airline industry jargon and from the knowledge obtained of the significant strategic challenges facing aviation at the present time.

The text is split into a numbers of chapters as follows:

Chapter one provides the context for the book and explains the overview of Airlines industry. This also include a discussion of the meaning of the terms Marketing, Marketing Mix, Marketing Environment and about Airline Customer.

Chapter two set out the international dimension of Airline Segmentation, Target and Positioning in terms of Air Passenger Market, Business Travel Market, Leisure Travel Market, Airline Market Segmentation and Segmentation Air freight market.

Chapter three explains about the Airlines Business and Marketing Strategies and focused on strategic analysis, Cost Leadership Strategies, Differentiation Strategies, Focused Strategies and Strategic Alliance

Chapter four tell us about the concepts of Airlines marketing Mix and explaining the role of all the components of Marketing Mix applied in the Airline Service marketing.

Chapter five highlights the importance of Airport Marketing and explains about non-aviation related revenue generation areas.

Finally, Chapter six has been added here to bring clarity on Cargo Marketing as another important marketing activity in the Airline Business and requires equal importance while discussing about Airlines Service Marketing.

Through out the book, the points made are illustrated by a wide range of examples taken from the sources available on the public domain. The book is edited in a straightforward, easy-to-read style and is full of up-to-date and relevant examples drawn from the world-wide aviation industry.

Dr. Sharad Goel

Contents

CHAPTER 1

Overview of Airline Industry

ABOUT AIRLINES

Air travel remains a large and growing industry. It facilitates economic growth, world trade, international investment and tourism and is therefore central to the globalization taking place in many other industries.

In the past decade, air travel has grown by 7% per year. Travel for both business and leisure purposes grew strongly worldwide. Scheduled airlines carried 1.5 billion passengers last year. In the leisure market, the availability of large aircraft such as the Boeing 747 made it convenient and affordable for people to travel further to new and exotic destinations. Governments in developing countries realized the benefits of tourism to their national economies and spurred the development of resorts and infrastructure to lure tourists from the prosperous countries in Western Europe and North America. As the economies of developing countries grow, their own citizens are already becoming the new international tourists of the future.

Business travel has also grown as companies become increasingly international in terms of their investments, their supply and production chains and their customers. The rapid growth of world trade in goods and services and international direct investment have also contributed to growth in business travel.

Worldwide, IATA, International Air Transport Association, forecasts international air travel to grow by an average 6.6% a year to the end of the decade and over 5% a year from 2000 to 2010. These rates are similar to those of the past ten years. In Europe and North America, where the air travel market is already highly developed, slower growth of 4%-6% is expected. The most dynamic growth is centered on the Asia/Pacific region, where fast-growing trade and investment are coupled with rising domestic prosperity. Air travel for the region has been rising by up to 9% a year and is forecast to continue to grow rapidly, although the Asian financial crisis in 1997 and 1998 will put the brakes on growth for a year or two. In terms of total passenger trips, however, the main air travel markets of the future will continue to be in and between Europe, North America and Asia.

Airlines' profitability is closely tied to economic growth and trade. During the first half of the 1990s, the industry suffered not only from world recession but travel was further depressed by the Gulf War. In 1991 the number of international passengers dropped for the first time. The financial difficulties were exacerbated by airlines over-ordering aircraft in the boom years of the late 1980s, leading to significant excess capacity in the market. IATA's member airlines suffered cumulative net losses of $20.4bn in the years from 1990 to 1994.

Since then, airlines have had to recognize the need for radical change to ensure their survival and prosperity. Many have tried to cut costs aggressively, to reduce capacity growth and to increase load factors. At a time of renewed economic growth, such actions have returned the industry as a whole to profitability: IATA airlines' profits were $5bn in 1996, less than 2% of total revenues. This is below the level IATA believes is necessary for airlines to reduce their debt, build reserves and sustain investment levels. In addition, many airlines remain unprofitable.

To meet the requirements of their increasingly discerning customers, some airlines are having to invest heavily in the quality of service that they offer, both on the ground and in the air. Ticketless travel, new interactive entertainment systems, and more comfortable seating are just some of the product enhancements being introduced to attract and retain customers.

A number of factors are forcing airlines to become more efficient. In Europe, the European Union (EU) has ruled that governments should not be allowed to subsidize their loss-making airlines. Elsewhere too, governments' concerns over their own finances and a recognition of the benefits of privatization have led to a gradual transfer of ownership of airlines from the state to the private sector. In order to appeal to prospective shareholders, the airlines are having to become more efficient and competitive.

Deregulation is also stimulating competition, such as that from small, low-cost carriers. The US led the way in 1978 and Europe and India is following suit. The EU's final stage of deregulation took effect in April 1997, allowing an airline from one member state to fly passengers within another member's domestic market. Beyond Europe too, 'open skies' agreements are beginning to dismantle some of the regulations governing which carriers can fly on certain routes. Nevertheless, the aviation industry is characterized by strong nationalist sentiments towards domestic 'flag carriers'. In many parts of the world, airlines will therefore continue to face limitations on where they can fly and restrictions on their ownership of foreign carriers.

Despite this, the airline industry has proceeded along the path towards globalization and consolidation, characteristics associated with the normal development of many other industries. It has done this through the establishment of alliances and partnerships between airlines, linking their networks to expand access to their customers. Hundreds of airlines have entered into alliances, ranging from marketing agreements and code-shares to franchises and equity transfers.

The Indian outlook for the air travel industry is one of strong growth. Forecasts suggest that the number of passengers will double by 2010. For airlines, the future will hold many challenges. Successful airlines will be those that continue to tackle their costs and improve their products, thereby securing a strong presence in the key world aviation markets.

Today Flying has become the most popular form of public transportation. Now air transportation is as much a part of life as telephone or computer. Speed, efficiency, comfort and safety—these are the symbols of both modern civilisation and modern air transportation. If you want to get there in a hurry, and most businesses do, because time means money, then fly. Air transportation has enabled employees of business and government organisations to reach any point in the world within hours. As airports were flooded by more and more passengers it became more and more obvious that only the technology of the integrated information systems can be the way leading to the future.

As airlines look forward, *innovation and a unique relationship* with passengers and the air transport industry will continue to be key to the future. Innovation and partnership will have to play a major role in airlines' strategy, which focuses on Internet Protocol technologies, end-to-end services to the desktop and airport integration. Airlines will have to continue development such as on-line distribution, ticketless travel, self-service ticketing and smart cards. There is a great opportunity for the integration of airport and airline systems, along with new applications for biometric security, electronic passports, wireless bag tracing and much more.

An **airline** provides air transport services for passengers or freight, generally with a recognized operating certificate or license. Airlines lease or own their aircraft with which to supply these services and may form partnerships or alliances with other airlines for mutual benefit.

Airlines vary from those with a single airplane carrying mail or cargo, through full-service international airlines operating many hundreds of airplanes. Airline services can be categorized as being intercontinental, intra continental, or domestic and may be operated as scheduled services or charters.

Patterns

The pattern of ownership has gone from government owned or supported to independent, for-profit public companies. This occurs as regulators permit greater freedom and non-government ownership, in steps that are usually decades apart. This pattern is not seen for all airlines in all regions.

The demand for air travel services depends on: business needs for cargo shipments, business passenger demand, leisure passenger demand, all influenced by economic activity. The overall trend of demand has been consistently increasing. In the 1950s and 1960s, annual growth rates of 15% or more were common. Annual growth of 5-6% persisted through the 1980s and 1990s.

Growth rates are not consistent in all regions, but countries with a de-regulated airline industry have more competition and greater pricing freedom.

This results in lower fares and sometimes dramatic spurts in traffic growth. The U.S., Australia, Japan, Brazil, Mexico,India and other markets exhibit this trend. The industry is cyclical. Four or five years of poor performance precede five or six years of improved performance. But profitability in the good years is generally low, in the range of 2-3% net profit after interest and tax. In times of profit, airlines lease new generations of airplanes and upgrade services in response to higher demand.

Since 1980, the industry has not earned back the cost of capital during the best of times. Conversely, in bad times losses can be dramatically worse. Warren Buffett once said that despite all the money that has been invested in all airlines, the net profit is less than zero.

He believes it is one of the hardest businesses to manage. As in many mature industries, consolidation is a trend. Airline groupings may consist of limited bilateral partnerships, long-term, multi-faceted alliances between carriers, equity arrangements, mergers, or takeovers.

Since governments often restrict ownership and merger between companies in different countries, most consolidation takes place within a country. In the U.S., over 200 airlines have merged, been taken over, or gone out of business since deregulation in 1978. Many international airline managers are lobbying their governments to permit greater consolidation to achieve higher economy and efficiency.

World's First Airline

DELAG, *Deutsche Luftschiffahrts-Aktiengesellschaft* (German: acronym for "German Airship Transport Corporation") was the world's first airline. It was founded on November 16, 1909 with government assistance, and operated airships manufactured by Zeppelin Corporation. Its headquarters were in Frankfurt. The four oldest non-dirigible airlines are Netherland's KLM, Colombia's Avianca, Australia's Qantas, and Mexico's Mexicana. KLM first flew in May 1920 while Qantas (for the Queensland and Northern Territory Aerial Services Limited) was founded in Queensland, Australia in late 1920.

Development of Airlines in the U.S.

Tony Jannus conducted the United State's first scheduled commercial airline flight on 1 January 1914 for the St. Petersburg-Tampa Airboat Line. The 23 minute flight traveled between St. Petersburg, Florida and Tampa, Florida, passing some 50 feet above Tampa Bay in Jannus' Benoist XIV biplane flying boat. Chalk's Airlines (now Chalk's International Airlines) began service between Miami and Bimini in the Bahamas in February 1919. Now based in Ft. Lauderdale, Chalk's claims to be the oldest continuously operating airline in the United States.

Following World War I, the United States found itself swamped with aviators. Many decided to take their war-surplus aircraft on barnstorming campaigns, performing acrobatic maneuvers to woo crowds. In 1918, the United

States Postal Service won the financial backing of Congress to begin experimenting with air mail service, initially using Curtiss Jenny aircraft that had been procured by the United States Army for reconnaissance missions on the Western Front. Private operators were the first to fly the mail but due to numerous accidents the US Army was tasked with mail delivery. During the course of the Army's involvement they proved to be too unreliable and lost their air mail duties. By the mid-1920s, the Postal Service had developed its own air mail network, based on a transcontinental backbone between New York and San Francisco. To supplant this service, they offered twelve contracts for spur routes to independent bidders: the carriers that won these routes would, through time and mergers, evolve into Delta Air Lines, Braniff Airways, American Airlines, United Airlines (originally a division of Boeing), Trans World Airlines, Northwest Airlines, and Eastern Air Lines, to name a few.

Airline Before World War II

Passenger service during the early 1920s was sporadic: most airlines at the time were focused on carrying bags of mail. In 1925, however, the Ford Motor Company bought out the Stout Aircraft Company and began construction of the all-metal Ford Trimotor, which became the first successful American airliner. With a 12-passenger capacity, the Trimotor made passenger service potentially profitable. Air service was seen as a supplement to rail service in the American transportation network.

At the same time, Juan Trippe began a crusade to create an air network that would link America to the world, and he achieved this goal through his airline, Pan American World Airways, with a fleet of flying boats that linked Los Angeles to Shanghai and Boston to London. Pan Am was the only U.S. airline to go international before the 1940s.

With the introduction of the Boeing 247 and Douglas DC-3 in the 1930s, the U.S. airline industry was generally profitable, even during the Great Depression. This trend continued until the beginning of World War II.

Development of Airlines in Europe

The first countries in Europe to embrace air transport were Finland, France, Germany and the Netherlands.

KLM, the oldest carrier still operating under its original name, was founded in 1919. The first flight transported two English passengers to Schiphol, Amsterdam from London in 1920. Like other major European airlines of the time (see France and the UK below), KLM's early growth depended heavily on the needs to service links with far-flung colonial possessions (Dutch Indies). It is only after the loss of the Dutch Empire that KLM found itself based at a small country with few potential passengers, depending heavily on transfer traffic, and was one of the first to introduce the hub-system to facilitate easy connections.

France began an air mail service to Morocco in 1919 that was bought out in 1927, renamed Aéropostale, and injected with capital to become a major international carrier. In 1933, Aéropostale went bankrupt, was nationalized and merged with several other airlines into what became Air France.

In Finland, the charter establishing Aero O/Y (now Finnair, one of the oldest still-operating airlines in the world) was signed in the city of Helsinki on 12 September 1923. Junkers F 13 D-335 became the first aircraft of the company, when Aero took delivery of it on 14 March 1924. The first flight was between Helsinki and Tallinn, capital of Estonia, and it took place on 20 March 1924, one week later.

Germany's Lufthansa began in 1926. Lufthansa, unlike most other airlines at the time, became a major investor in airlines outside of Europe, providing capital to Varig and Avianca. German airliners built by Junkers, Dornier, and Fokker were the most advanced in the world at the time. The peak of German air travel came in the mid-1930s, when Nazi propaganda ministers approved the start of commercial zeppelin service: the big airships were a symbol of industrial might, but the fact that they used flammable hydrogen gas raised safety concerns that culminated with the Hindenburg disaster of 1937. The reason they used hydrogen instead of the not-flammable helium gas was a United States military embargo on helium.

The United Kingdom's flag carrier during this period was Imperial Airways, which became BOAC (British Overseas Airlines Co.) in 1939. Imperial Airways used huge Handley-Page biplanes for routes between London, the Middle East, and India: images of Imperial aircraft in the middle of the Rub'al Khali, being maintained by Bedouins, are among the most famous pictures from the heyday of the British Empire.

Development of Airlines in Asia

The First country in Asia to embrace air transport was the Philippines. Philippine Airlines was founded on February 26, 1941, making it Asia's oldest carrier still operating under its current name. The airline was started by a group of businessmen led by Andres Soriano, hailed as one of the Philippines' leading industrialists at the time. The airline's first flight was made on March 15, 1941 with a single Beech Model 18 NPC-54 aircraft, which started its daily services between Manila (from Nielson Field) and Baguio, later to expand with larger aircraft such as the DC-3 and Vickers Viscount. Notably Philippine Airlines leased Japan Airlines their first aircraft, a DC-3 named "Kinsei".

Neighbouring countries soon embraced air transport, notably with Cathay Pacific founded in 1946, Singapore Airlines and Malaysian Airlines in 1947 *(as Malayan Airways)*, Garuda Indonesia in 1949 and Japan Airlines founded in 1951. With the outbreak of World War Two, the airline presence in Asia came to a relative halt, with many new flag carriers donating their aircraft for military aid and other uses.

Development of Airlines Post-1945

As governments met to set the standards and scope for an emergent civil air industry toward the end of the war, it was no surprise that the U.S. took a position of maximum operating freedom. After all, U.S. airline companies were not devastated by the war, as European companies and the few Asian companies had been. This preference for "open skies" operating regimes continues, within limitations, to this day.

World War II, like World War I, brought new life to the airline industry. Many airlines in the Allied countries were flush from lease contracts to the military, and foresaw a future explosive demand for civil air transport, for both passengers and cargo. They were eager to invest in the newly emerging flagships of air travel such as the Boeing Stratocruiser, Lockheed Constellation, and Douglas DC-6. Most of these new aircraft were based on American bombers such as the B-29, which had spearheaded research into new technologies such as pressurization. Most offered increased efficiency from both added speed and greater payload.

In the 1950s, the De Havilland Comet, Boeing 707, Douglas DC-8, and Sud Aviation Caravelle became the first flagships of the Jet Age in the West, while the Soviet Union bloc countered with the Tupolev Tu-104 and Tupolev Tu-124 in the fleets of state-owned carriers such as Aeroflot and Interflug. The Vickers Viscount and Lockheed L-188 Electra inaugurated turboprop transport.

The next big boost for the airlines would come in the 1970s, when the Boeing 747, McDonnell Douglas DC-10, and Lockheed L-1011 inaugurated widebody ("jumbo jet") service, which is still the standard in international travel. The Tupolev Tu-144 and its Western counterpart, Concorde, made supersonic travel a reality. In 1972, Airbus began producing Europe's most commercially successful line of airliners to date. The added efficiencies for these aircraft were often not in speed, but in passenger capacity, payload, and range.

1978's U.S. airline industry deregulation lowered barriers for new airlines. In this period, new start-ups entered during downturns in the normal 8-10 year business cycle. At that time, they find aircraft, are financed, contract hangar and maintenance services, train new employees, and recruit laid off staff from other airlines.

As the business cycle returned to normalcy, major airlines dominated their routes through aggressive pricing and additional capacity offerings, often swamping new startups. Only America West Airlines (which has since merged with US Airways) remained a significant survivor from this new entrant era, as dozens, even hundreds, have gone under.

In many ways, the biggest winner in the deregulated environment was the air passenger. Indeed, the U.S. witnessed an explosive growth in demand for air travel, as many millions who had never or rarely flown before became regular fliers, even joining frequent flyer loyalty programs and receiving free flights and other benefits from their flying. New services and higher frequencies meant that business fliers could fly to another city, do business, and return the same day, for almost any point in the country. Air travel's advantages put intercity bus lines under pressure, and most have withered away.

By the 1980s, almost half of the total flying in the world took place in the U.S., and today the domestic industry operates over 10,000 daily departures nationwide.

Toward the end of the century, a new style of low cost airline emerged, offering a no-frills product at a lower price. Southwest Airlines, JetBlue, AirTran Airways, Skybus Airlines and other low-cost carriers represent a serious challenge to today's legacy airlines, as do their low-cost counterparts in Europe, Canada, and Asia. Their commercial viability represents a serious competitive threat to the legacy carriers.

Thus the last 50 years of the airline industry have varied from reasonably profitable, to devastatingly depressed. As the first major market to deregulate the industry in 1978, U.S. airlines have experienced more turbulence than almost any other country or region.

Regulatory Considerations

Government Regulation

Many countries have national airlines that the government owns and operates. Even fully private airlines are subject to a great deal of government regulation for economic, political, and safety concerns. For instance, the government often intervenes to halt airline labour actions in order to protect the free flow of people, communications, and goods between different regions without compromising safety.

The United States, Australia, and to a lesser extent Brazil, Mexico, the United Kingdom, India and Japan have "deregulated" their airlines. In the past, these governments dictated airfares, route networks, and other operational requirements for each airline. Since deregulation, airlines have been largely free to negotiate their own operating arrangements with different airports, enter and exit routes easily, and to levy airfares and supply flights according to market demand.

The entry barriers for new airlines are lower in a deregulated market, and so the U.S. has seen hundreds of airlines start up (sometimes for only a brief operating period). This has produced far greater competition than before deregulation in most markets, and average fares tend to drop 20% or more. The added competition, together with pricing freedom, means that new entrants often take market share with highly reduced rates that, to a limited degree, full service airlines must match. This is a major constraint on profitability for established carriers, which tend to have a higher cost base.

As a result, profitability in a deregulated market is uneven for most airlines. These forces have caused some major airlines to go out of business, in addition to most of the poorly established new entrants.

International Regulation

Groups such as the International Civil Aviation Organization establish worldwide standards for safety and other vital concerns. Most international air traffic is regulated by bilateral agreements between countries, which designate specific carriers to operate on specific routes. The model of such an agreement was the Bermuda Agreement between the US and UK following World War II, which designated airports to be used for transatlantic flights and gave each government the authority to nominate carriers to operate routes.

Bilateral agreements are based on the "freedoms of the air," a group of generalized traffic rights ranging from the freedom to overfly a country to the freedom to provide domestic flights within a country (a very rarely granted right known as cabotage). Most agreements permit airlines to fly from their home country to designated airports in the other country: some also extend the freedom to provide continuing service to a third country, or to another destination in the other country while carrying passengers from overseas.

In the 1990s, "open skies" agreements became more common. These agreements take many of these regulatory powers from state governments and open up international routes to further competition. Open skies agreements have met some criticism, particularly within the European Union, whose airlines would be at a comparative disadvantage with the United States' because of cabotage restrictions.

Economic Considerations

Historically, air travel has survived largely through state support, whether in the form of equity or subsidies. The airline industry as a whole has made a cumulative loss during its 120-year history, once the costs include subsidies for aircraft development and airport construction.

One argument is that positive externalities, such as higher growth due to global mobility, outweigh the microeconomic losses and justify continuing government. A historically high level of government intervention in the airline industry can be seen as part of a wider political consensus on strategic forms of transport, such as highways and railways, both of which receive public funding in most parts of the world. Profitability is likely to improve in the future as privatization continues and more competitive low-cost carriers proliferate.

Although many countries continue to operate state-owned or parastatal airlines, many large airlines today are privately owned and are therefore governed by microeconomic principles in order to maximize shareholder profit.

Ticket Revenue

Airlines assign prices to their services in an attempt to maximize profitability. The pricing of airline tickets has become increasingly complicated over the years and is now largely determined by computerized yield management systems.

Because of the complications in scheduling flights and maintaining profitability, airlines have many loopholes that can be used by the knowledgable traveler. Many of these airfare secrets are becoming more and more known to the general public, so airlines are forced to make constant adjustments.

Most airlines use differentiated pricing, a form of price discrimination, in order to sell air services at varying prices simultaneously to different segments. Factors influencing the price include the days remaining until departure, the current booked load factor, the forecast of total demand by price point, competitive pricing in force, and variations by day of week of departure and by time of day. Carriers often accomplish this by dividing each cabin of the aircraft (first, business and economy) into a number of travel classes for pricing purposes.

A complicating factor is that of origin-destination control ("O&D control"). Someone purchasing a ticket from Delhi to Mumbai (as an example) for Rs. 4000 is competing with someone else who wants to fly Delhi to Goa through Mumbai on the same flight, and who is willing to pay Rs. 9000. Should the airline prefer the Rs. 9000 passenger, or the Rs. 4000 passenger plus a possible Mumbai-Goa passenger willing to pay Rs. 6000? Airlines have to make hundreds of thousands of similar pricing decisions daily.

The advent of advanced computerized reservations systems in the late 1970s, allowed airlines to easily perform cost-benefit analyses on different pricing structures, leading to almost perfect price discrimination in some cases (that is, filling each seat on an aircraft at the highest price that can be charged without driving the consumer elsewhere). The intense nature of airfare pricing has led to the term "fare war" to describe efforts by airlines to under cut other airlines on competitive routes. Through computers, new airfares can be published quickly and efficiently to the airlines' sales channels. For this purpose the airlines use the Airline Tariff Publishing Company (ATPCO), who distribute latest fares for more than 500 airlines to Computer Reservation Systems across the world.

The extent of these pricing phenomena is strongest in "legacy" carriers. In contrast, low fare carriers usually offer preannounced and simplified price structure, and often quote prices for each leg of a trip separately.

Computers also allow airlines to predict, with some accuracy, how many passengers will actually fly after making a reservation to fly. This allows airlines to overbook their flights enough to fill the aircraft while accounting for "no-shows," but not enough (in most cases) to force paying passengers off the aircraft for lack of seats. Since an average of all seats are flown empty, stimulative pricing for low demand flights coupled with overbooking on high demand flights can help reduce this figure.

Operating Costs

Full-service airlines have a high level of fixed and operating costs in order to establish and maintain air services: labour, fuel, airplanes, engines, spares and parts, IT services and networks, airport equipment, airport handling services, sales distribution, catering, training, Aviation insurance and other costs. Thus all but a small percentage of the income from ticket sales is paid out to a wide variety of external providers or internal cost centers.

Moreover, the industry is structured so that airlines often act as tax collectors. Airline fuel is untaxed, however, due to a series of treaties existing between countries. Ticket prices include a number of fees, taxes, and surcharges they have little or no control over, and these are passed through to various providers. Airlines are also responsible for enforcing government regulations. If airlines carry passengers without proper documentation on an international flight, they are responsible for returning them back to the originating country.

Analysis of the 1992-1996 period shows that every player in the air transport chain is far more profitable than the airlines, who collect and pass through fees and revenues to them from ticket sales. While airlines as a whole earned 6% return on capital employed (2-3.5% less than the cost of capital), airports earned 10%, catering companies 10-13%, handling companies 11-14%, aircraft lessors 15%, aircraft manufacturers 16%, and global distribution companies more than 30%. (Source: Spinetta, 2000, quoted in Doganis, 2002)

In contrast, Southwest Airlines has been the most profitable of airline companies since 1970. Indeed, some sources have calculated Southwest to be the best performing stock over the period, outperforming Microsoft and many other high performing companies. The chief reasons for this are their product consistency and cost control.

The widespread entrance of a new breed of low cost airlines beginning at the turn of the century has accelerated the demand that full service carriers control costs. Many of these low cost companies emulate Air Deccan in various respects, and like Southwest, they are able to eke out profit throughout all phases of the business cycle.

As a result, a shakeout of airlines is occurring in the U.S. and elsewhere. United Airlines, US Airways (twice), Delta Air Lines, and Northwest Airlines have all declared bankruptcy, and American has barely avoided doing so. Alitalia, Scandinavian Airlines System, SABENA, Swissair, Japan Air System, Viasa, Air Canada, Ansett Australia, and others have flirted with or declared bankruptcy since 1995, as low cost entrants enter their home markets as well. Some argue that it would be far better for the industry as a whole if a wave of actual closures were to reduce the number of "undead" airlines competing with healthy airlines while being artificially protected from creditors via bankruptcy law. On the other hand, some have pointed out that the reduction in capacity would be short lived given that there would be large quantities of relatively new aircraft that bankruptcies would want to get rid of and would re-enter the market either as increased fleets for the survivors or the basis of cheap planes for new startups.

Where an airline has established an engineering base at an airport then there may be considerable economic advantages in using that same airport as a preferred focus (or "hub") for its scheduled flights.

Assets and Financing

Airline financing is quite complex, since airlines are highly leveraged operations. Not only must they purchase (or lease) new airliner bodies and engines regularly, they must make major long-term fleet decisions with the goal of meeting the demands of their markets while producing a fleet that is relatively economical to operate and maintain. Compare Southwest Airlines and their reliance on a single airplane type (the Boeing 737 and derivatives), with the now defunct Eastern Air Lines which operated 17 different aircraft types, each with varying pilot, engine, maintenance, and support needs.

A second financial issue is that of hedging oil and fuel purchases, which are usually second only to labour in its relative cost to the company. However, with the current high fuel prices it has become the largest cost to an airline. While hedging instruments can be expensive, they can easily pay for themselves many times over in periods of increasing fuel costs, such as in the 2000-2005 period.

In view of the congestion apparent at many international airports, the ownership of slots at certain airports (the right to take-off or land an aircraft at a particular time of day or night) has become a significant tradable asset for many airlines. Clearly take-off slots at popular times of the day can be critical in attracting the more profitable business traveler to a given airline's flight and in establishing a competitive advantage against a competing airline. If a particular city has two or more airports, market forces will tend to attract the less profitable routes, or those on which competition is weakest, to the less congested airport, where slots are likely to be more available and therefore cheaper. Other factors, such as surface transport facilities and onward connections, will also affect the relative appeal of different airports and some long distance flights may need to operate from the one with the longest runway.

Airline Partnerships

Code sharing is the most common type of airline partnership; it involves one airline selling tickets for another airline's flights under its own airline code. An early example of this was Japan Airlines' code sharing partnership with Aeroflot in the 1960s on flights from Tokyo to Moscow: Aeroflot operated the flights using Aeroflot aircraft, but JAL sold tickets for the flights as if they were JAL flights. This practice allows airlines to expand their operations, at least on paper, into parts of the world where they cannot afford to establish bases or purchase aircraft. Another example was the Austrian-Sabena partnership on the Vienna-Brussels-New York JFK route during the late 60's, using a Sabena Boeing 707 with Austrian colors.

Since airline reservation requests are often made by city-pair (such as "show me flights from Chicago to Düsseldorf"), an airline who is able to code share with another airline for a variety of routes might be able to be listed as indeed offering a Chicago-Düsseldorf flight. The passenger is advised however, that Airline 1 operates the flight from say Chicago to Amsterdam, and Airline

2 operates the continuing flight (on a different airplane, sometimes from another terminal) to Düsseldorf. Thus the primary rationale for code sharing is to expand one's service offerings in city-pair terms so as to increase sales.

A more recent development is the airline alliance, which became prevalent in the 1990s. These alliances can act as virtual mergers to get around government restrictions. Groups of airlines such as the Star Alliance, Oneworld, and SkyTeam coordinate their passenger service programs (such as lounges and frequent flyer programs), offer special interline tickets, and often engage in extensive codesharing (sometimes systemwide). These are increasingly integrated business combinations—sometimes including cross-equity arrangements—in which products, service standards, schedules, and airport facilities are standardized and combined for higher efficiency. One of the first airlines to start an alliance with another airline was KLM, who partnered with Northwest Airlines. Both airlines later entered the SkyTeam alliance after the fusion of KLM and Air France in 2004.

Often the companies combine IT operations, buy fuel, or purchase airplanes as a bloc in order to achieve higher bargaining power. However, the alliances have been most successful at purchasing invisible supplies and services, such as fuel. Airlines usually prefer to purchase items visible to their passengers to differentiate themselves from local competitors. If an airline's main domestic competitor flies Boeing airliners, then the airline may prefer to use Airbus aircraft regardless of what the rest of the alliance chooses.

Customers and Conventions

Each operator of a scheduled or charter flight uses a distinct airline call sign when communicating with airports or air traffic control centers. Most of these call-signs are derived from the airline's trade name, but for reasons of history, marketing, or the need to reduce ambiguity in spoken English (so that pilots do not mistakenly make navigational decisions based on instructions issued to a different aircraft), some airlines and air forces use call-signs less obviously connected with their trading name. For example, British Airways uses a *Speedbird* call-sign, named after the logo of its predecessor, BOAC while America West used *Cactus* reflecting that company's home in the state of Arizona and to differentiate itself from numerous other airlines using *America* and *West* in their call signs.

New Technological Areas in the Airline Industry

Carriers have been able to add more functionality, especially in customer service areas ranging from check-in desks upwards. Furthermore, airlines have also been able to integrate internal systems. This relatively under-developed area may have the strongest potential for future growth. The drastic effect in the year 2001 on airline ticket sales forced carriers to reappraise their distribution systems, focusing sharply on e-commerce. Online services can be configured to include specialist applications such as:

- content management, for example—to make the site easier to navigate and use;
- Business intelligence tools—for in-depth management information;
- Personalization software—that will allow the site to be customized for each individual user.

This kind of solution is increasingly integrated with other processes which, if not underway already, are certainly under development by many airlines today, intending delivering effective online customer services at the lowest cost. For example, online sales can be backed up with streamlined fulfillment procedures that simplify the administration of high-volume, high-value transactions on which the air travel industry increasingly depends. Automating time-consuming manual processes improves efficiency, contains costs and frees staff for more profitable activities. It also plays an important role in enhancing business knowledge, collecting data as transactions are processed and delivering valuable management information that can help airlines shape their marketing strategy. Other areas of airline operation can also benefit from some of the same processes and e-commerce integration expertise. Airline catering, for instance, requires rapid, streamlined communication with business partners.

Internet Technology

Internet Technology has become recognized as a major enabler for aviation to work effectively and safely, while achieving substantial cost savings. If Internet Technology plays a critical role in determining how the airlines compete with one another, there is also a need for it to serve common purposes. At present carriers have two main strategic goals: to get closer to their customers and to reduce costs. And they are looking to Internet Protocol to deliver both. It is clear that strategy-planning horizons have been falling as the speed of technology change increases. Nowadays airports are at the very early stages of leveraging the power of the Web. The first initiative airports can take is to improve their websites. Three pieces of information most travellers require are the local weather, the local time and the exchange rate. Few airport websites currently provide this information. The initial stages of using information technology involve attempting to replicate the physical world in cyberspace. Accordingly, airports are trying to move merchandising to the Web but it is highly unlikely that the current variants are proving to be successful. The devil, however, is in the details. The race between VHS and Betamax home video formats showed us that superior technology alone was not enough to get ahead. For example, pre-ordering foreign currency and duty-free items is useful in that it saves the time one might spend browsing at duty free shops. Pre-ordering currency is a valuable service only if the currency one requires is expected to be in short supply. This is unlikely to be an attractive service for those embarking from countries with international currencies. Moreover, consumers will unlikely pay for currency using credit or charge cards due to the high interest rates associated with cash advances.

Through closely monitoring and collecting information on their stakeholders, airports can provide data on the local community to visitors and vice-versa. For example, it is possible for a first time visitor to a particular city to obtain a list of good restaurants from websites. But in order to make it more valuable, that information has to be cross-referenced from other sources to determine if the best restaurants are located within a convenient distance from the hotel they are staying at. How airports use the Internet is likely to reflect how airports view themselves.

A very minimalist view would be that an airport is an infrastructure supplier or a supplier of an intermediate input in providing air transportation services. What else do airports do? They provide some facilities, either themselves or through tenants, for the passengers they serve. The facilities vary considerably with airports, however, most if not all airports have health facilities, currency exchange booths, duty-free shops and restaurants. Other tenants could provide travel-related services such as rental cars, hotel services, tour operators etc. In addition airports provide parking facilities, ground transportation links through cars, taxicabs, buses and rail. Airports also provide a variety of services to airlines, including air-traffic control, baggage and cargo handling, catering, aircraft maintenance and land for cargo handling terminals and hangers. Lastly, they provide facilities to Government departments for immigration, customs and possibly health services. Although IT has been long at the heart of every airline operation the truth is that now it is time to reorganize the future of the industry. This future will be characterized by three critical success factors—lower costs, increased profitability and improved levels of customer service.

S-Travel Initiative to Increase Security of Global Aviation

Major air transport organizations have teamed up with world leading smart card and biometrics integration companies to develop and trial a *'secure-travel'* initiative. The s-Travel project aims to achieve the highest level of identity verification for frequent travellers and to contribute to a secure global air transport system. The European Commission and a Swiss-funded consortium will undertake trials in Europe, with a view to expanding the initiative globally s-Travel will include digital authentication to enable secure access to airport facilities for frequent air travellers. The project team will develop and implement systems to authenticate passengers at both check-in and boarding stages. The solution will also enable effective control of airport and airline employees' access to restricted areas, as well as electronic access to computer systems. To ensure the provision of an interoperable global solution, IATA and SITA will lead the agreement of standards. The s-Travel system will combine a certification authority, smart-cards technology and biometrics technology integration. To ensure that the s-Travel system does not infringe upon the privacy of frequent travellers, the consortium will work closely with the EC and relevant data commissioners to resolve confidentiality issues. Both EC and

Swiss funding, subject to final contract negotiations, were awarded as part of their programme to foster research and development on a pan-European scale.

Security Solutions

The most notable change will emerge in the relationship between the passenger and the airline. Travellers will accept new security requirements. But they will also be capable. They'll accept positive bag matching, but increasingly they won't accept lengthy delays and irritations. The air travel industry has to make flying safer while speeding up the process of getting on a flight. In the near future, we can expect to see secure integrated networks within airports by pulling together existing capabilities, such as baggage reconciliation or border control with third party technology in areas like biometrics and explosive detection devices. In spite of some improvement at the turn of the year, it has become clear that the air transport industry will not bounce back in terms of growth and profitability as quickly as it fell into trouble. Improved *security* has become a vital factor in efforts to revive the fortunes of the air transport industry. Vendors have responded to last September's terrorist attacks in the US with the launch of Intelligent Aviation Security Solution—a robust platform for governments, airlines, airports and cargo agents that is available now. Pick up any information technology magazine in the past couple of months and you will see that the emphasis has been firmly on security. Airlines need to know exactly who gets on aircraft and must be sure, that along with their baggage, they have been properly screened.

Common use security equipment will allow shared biometric devices in airport common use areas to be accessed by different agencies and airlines to serve their own security applications. The resultant shared environment for airport, airline, security and handling agents would be a secure, common platform. One of the major requirements of the new legislation is *baggage screening*.

This effort is designed to prevent the loading of unaccompanied baggage on aircraft. Every checked bag on every flight must be either screened for explosives—by machines, specially trained dogs, or manual searches—or each piece must be matched to a passenger on the plane. The issue is global, and for reasons of costs and time, the best option is the existing technology that matches baggage with passengers, but as procedures for baggage handling—including screening, reconciliation and tracking at the airport—are evaluated, it is important to reassess Positive Passenger Bag Match (PPBM) based on today's environment. PPBM saves airlines millions of dollars in mishandled baggage costs and improves customer service.

Inconvenience to passengers would be minimal to none. The scanning technology knows exactly where bags are loaded on the aircraft, so if a bag must be removed because its owner does not fly, that retrieval can be done in a matter of minutes. Without this technology handlers would need to off-load each bag and inspect the tags to find any orphan luggage, taking almost an hour. There is no question that airports and airlines can make this an effective solution and avoid long delays searching for unaccompanied baggage.

Possible Choices for Improving Air Transport Information Systems

Many vendor companies are currently re-organizing and investing strongly in technologies focused on improving customer service changing—from self-service kiosks to check-in via mobile phone services, to baggage and airport management services, to electronic visas and in-flight e-mail. For the airlines, the prime objective remains: optimising revenues while maximizing customer relationships. What has changed is the variety and scope of channels available for distribution that the airlines want to control. Online electronic ticketing must be integrated with frequent flyer programmes and yield management will continue to develop as passenger demands for price competitiveness and transparency increase.

Simplify Passenger Check-in

One possible goal is to simplify the check-in process. Through the use of a Common Language Front-end to host check-in systems, agents and staff see the same screens no matter what host system they access. Agents sign in only once, after which hosts are accessed by simply entering the flight number associated with that host. Built around open systems standards, vendors offer a platform for additional integration and customisation. Using system-wide information available from each centralised check-in host and easy-to-use presentation, the staff will have automation that is dedicated to customer service. Latest Check-in solutions incorporate the latest PC capabilities to help airport staff perform both simple and difficult passenger check-in transactions. For example, graphical windows-style presentations simplify passenger check-in. User prompts, color-coded screens, drop-down menus and dialogue boxes allow agents with minimal training to quickly complete passenger check-in. Edit checks at the PC level prevent wasted typing and considerably reduce transaction costs. Within seconds, data is displayed on the screen, and agents can verify passenger requests for special services. In this way passenger and baggage check-in is quick and requires minimal agent interaction.

Increase Agent Productivity while Better Serving Customers

Airport staffs are the customer representatives. And a customer's perception of an airport can be strongly influenced by the service they receive. Service that is personalised and efficient wins loyalty for operation and helps recurring business. A good information system enables airport staff to provide the utmost in customer service. Onscreen user guide, customised workflow design, and other easy-to-use features:

- Allow experienced agents to spend more time to important personal contact with passengers, because routine check-in activity is performed quickly;

- Enable new agents to become proficient quickly, without lengthy on-the-job training;
- Reduce initial and refresher training for new and experienced agents;
- Open new avenues of sales, based on improved customer service and accessibility of pertinent passenger data.

We have to know that improving customer service while increasing staff productivity is impossible without the right tools.

Empower Airport Staff

Latest Check-in solutions provide staff with much more versatility than ever before. The graphical screens let airport staff customise screens to best fit its check-in and operational environment. Changes can be made quickly and easily and can beadapted to one location or all locations, depending on the needs of each airport. As an airline, airport operator, or independent company supplying ground handling support for other airlines, wants to provide the best service possible, vendors provide the capability for airport staff to focus on customer service. They no longer need to concentrate on the computer processing aspects of their job, but the system provides additional information, special promotions, and personalized service to customers. Internet, intranet and e-business solutions play an increasingly crucial role in transportation. Migration to network computing and Internet Protocol solutions are critical to the air transport industry. In this field, vendors have achieved a position as recognized leaders for the industry, providing the infrastructure for IP-based services like e-business and e-commerce, high-speed connectivity and integrated data, voice and video.

As the air transport industry evolves, its applications are increasingly integrated within an IP environment. Vendors' range of integrated industry solutions and applications covers every step of the journey. This includes reservations and bookings; freight movement; airport check-in, departure control and baggage management; flight management and operations; and aircraft maintenance and engineering. Offering IP access, these value-added solutions improve the passenger experience, streamline and integrate airline and airport operations, and enable efficient communications to support aircraft maintenance, safety and security processes. Airports systems integration capability brings together existing airport products and third-party products in order to provide vendor-independent, best-in-class solutions. These enable airports to benefit from greater efficiency and effectiveness, including improvements in productivity, cash flow and profitability, as well as safety and service.

For catering logistics management, vendors have developed a new solution extending an airline's catering supply applications over an extranet, helping to improve catering management efficiency and reducing costs through the use of Internet technologies. Vendors provide a range of aircraft data, voice and fax communications solutions for aircrew, systems and passengers as well.

The air transport, information and telecommunications industries have come a long way. The airline of 2000 has at its fingertips sophisticated desktop and Internet technology, in the form of powerful personal computers and connection to a wealth of information on corporate intranets, through e-mail and the Internet. In the airport industry, circumstances have changed in recent years in a way that suggests that nowcompetition is more important. In travel industry, the pressure to provide better customer service has never been greater. Yet the pressure to reduce operating costs is equally strong. Airport automation can play a key role in attaining these goals, and today many innovative solutions are available to assist. To meet these challenges, there are plenty of software solutions that help airports, airlines and ground handling companies distinguish themselves by making travel both convenient and easy.

A good information technology enables operation to run efficiently, while emphasising customer service. Technology has the potential to answer the demands of politicians and the travelling public—increasing the level of security, without creating excessive time delays and without adding significantly to the cost of travel. No doubt, the research on these topics will go on as the industry continues to evolve in the future.

CONCEPT OF MARKETING

What is marketing? Almost every marketing textbook has a different definition of the term "marketing." The American Marketing Association (AMA) uses the following: "The process of planning and executing the conception, pricing, promotion, and distribution of ideas, goods, and services to create exchanges that satisfy individual and organizational objectives." From this definition, we see that:

Marketing involves an ongoing process. The environment is "dynamic." This means that the market tends to change—what customers want today is not necessarily what they want tomorrow. For example, sales of beef are declining in the United States because consumers have become health oriented. Similarly, Tupperware parties are less popular today than they once were because there are fewer housewives who do not work outside the home.

- This process involves both planning and implementing (executing) the plan.
- Some of the main issues involved include:
  - Marketers help design products, finding out what customers want and what can practically be made available given technology and price constraints.
  - Marketers distribute products—there must be some efficient way to get the products from the factory to the end-consumer.
  - Marketers also promote products, and this is perhaps what we tend to think of first when we think of marketing. Promotion involves advertising—and much more. Other tools to promote

products include trade promotion (store sales, coupons, and rebates), obtaining favorable and visible shelf-space, and obtaining favorable press coverage.

- Marketers also price products to "move" them. We know from economics that, in most cases, sales correlate negatively with price—the higher the price, the lower the quantity demanded. In some cases, however, price may provide the customer with a "signal" of quality. Thus, the marketer needs to price the product to (1) maximize profit and (2) communicate a desired image of the product.
- Marketing is applicable to services and ideas as well as to tangible products. For example, accountants may need to market their tax preparation services to consumers.

Several definitions have been proposed for the term marketing. Each tends to emphasize different issues. Memorizing a definition is unlikely to be useful; ultimately, it makes more sense to thinking of ways to benefit from creating customer value in the most effective way, subject to ethical and other constraints that one may have. The 2006 and 2007 definitions offered by the American Marketing Association are relatively similar, with the 2007 appearing a bit more concise. Note that the definitions make several points:

- A main objective of marketing is to create customer value.
- Marketing usually involves an exchange between buyers and sellers or between other parties.
- Marketing has an impact on the firm, its suppliers, its customers, and others affected by the firm's choices.
- Marketing frequently involves enduring relationships between buyers, sellers, and other parties.
- Processes involved include "creating, communicating, delivering, and exchanging offerings."

Delivering customer value. The central idea behind marketing is the idea that a firm or other entity will create something of value to one or more customers who, in turn, are willing to pay enough (or contribute other forms of value) to make the venture worthwhile considering opportunity costs. Value can be created in a number of different ways. Some firms manufacture basic products (e.g., bricks) but provide relatively little value above that. Other firms make products whose tangible value is supplemented by services (e.g., a computer manufacturer provides a computer loaded with software and provides a warranty, technical support, and software updates). It is not necessary for a firm to physically handle a product to add value—e.g., online airline reservation systems add value by:

(1) Compiling information about available flight connections and fares,
(2) Allowing the customer to buy a ticket,
(3) Forwarding billing information to the airline, and

(4) Forwarding reservation information to the customer.

It should be noted that value must be examined from the point of view of the customer. Some customer segments value certain product attributes more than others. A very expensive product—relative to others in the category—may, in fact, represent great value to a particular customer segment because the benefits received are seen as even greater than the sacrifice made (usually in terms of money). Some segments have very unique and specific desires, and may value what—to some individuals—may seem a "lower quality" item—very highly.

Some forms of customer value. The marketing process involves ways that value can be created for the customer.

Form utility involves the idea that the product is made available to the consumer in some form that is more useful than any commodities that are used to create it. A customer buys a chair, for example, rather than the wood and other components used to create the chair. Thus, the customer benefits from the specialization that allows the manufacturer to more efficiently create a chair than the customer could do himself or herself.

Place utility refers to the idea that a product made available to the customer at a preferred location is worth more than one at the place of manufacture. It is much more convenient for the customer to be able to buy food items in a supermarket in his or her neighborhood than it is to pick up these from the farmer.

Time utility involves the idea of having the product made available when needed by the customer. The customer may buy a turkey a few days before Thanksgiving without having to plan to have it available. Intermediaries take care of the logistics to have the turkeys—which are easily perishable and bulky to store in a freezer—available when customers demand them.

Possession utility involves the idea that the consumer can go to one store and obtain a large assortment of goods from different manufacturers during one shopping occasion. Supermarkets combine food and other household items from a number of different suppliers in one place. Certain "superstores" such as the European hypermarkets and the Wal-Mart "super centers" combine even more items into one setting.

Reasons for studying marketing. There are several good reasons for studying marketing. First of all, marketing issues are important in all areas of the organization—customers are the reasons why businesses exist! In fact, marketing efforts (including such services as promotion and distribution) often account for more than half of the price of a product. As an added benefit, studying marketing often helps us become more savvy consumers. We will learn, for instance, that the per unit price of a bigger package is frequently higher than that of a smaller one, and that more expensive products are frequently not better in quality.

Criteria that must be met for marketing to occur. Several criteria must be met for marketing to occur:

- There must be two parties, each with unsatisfied needs or wants. This want, of course, could be money for the seller.
- Each must have something to offer. Marketing involves voluntary "exchange" relationships where both sides must be willing parties. Thus, a consumer who buys a soft drink in a vending machine for 60¢ must value the soft drink, available at that time and place, more than the money. Conversely, the vendor must value the money more. (It is interesting to note that money is, strictly speaking, not necessary for this exchange to take place. It is possible, albeit a bit cumbersome, to exchange two ducks for a pair of shoes.)
- The parties must be able to communicate. This could be through a display in a store, an infomercial, or a posting on eBay.

One of the greatest needs of managers of business is to understand and develop marketing programs for their products and services. Business success is based on the ability to build a growing body of satisfied customers. Modern marketing programs are built around the "marketing concept," which directs managers to focus their efforts on identifying and satisfying customer needs—at a profit.

The Marketing Concept

The marketing concept rests on the importance of customers to a firm and states that:

- All company policies and activities should be aimed at satisfying customer needs, and
- Profitable sales volume is a better company goal than maximum sales volume.

To use the marketing concept, businesses should:

- Determine the needs of their customers (Market Research);
- Analyze their competitive advantages (Market Strategy);
- Select specific markets to serve (Target Marketing), and;
- Determine how to satisfy those needs (Market Mix).

Market Research

In order to manage the marketing function successfully, good information about the market is necessary. Frequently, a small market research program, based on a questionnaire given to present customers and/or prospective customers, can disclose problems and areas of dissatisfaction that can be easily remedied, or new products or services that could be offered successfully.

Marketing Strategy

Marketing strategy encompasses identifying customer groups (Target

Markets), which a small business can serve better than its larger competitors, and tailoring its product offerings, prices, distribution, promotional efforts and services towards that particular market segment (Managing the Market Mix). A good strategy implies that a business cannot be all things to all people and must analyze its markets and its own capabilities so as to focus on a target market it can serve best.

Target Marketing

Owners of small businesses have limited resources to spend on marketing activities. Concentrating their marketing efforts on one or a few key market segments is the basis of target marketing. The major ways to segment a market are:

- *Geographical segmentation*—developing a loyal group of consumers in the home geographical territory before expanding into new territories.
- *Product segmentation*—extensively promoting existing best-selling products and services before introducing a lot of new products.
- *Customer segmentation*—identifying and promoting to those groups of people most likely to buy the product. In other words, selling to heavy users before trying to develop new users.

Managing the Market Mix

There are four key marketing decision areas in a marketing program. They are:

- Products and Services,
- Promotion,
- Distribution, and
- Pricing.

The marketing mix is used to describe how owner-managers combine these four areas into an overall marketing program.

Products and Services

Effective product strategies for a business may include concentrating on a narrow product line, developing a highly specialized product containing an unusual amount of service.

Promotion

This marketing decision area includes advertising, salesmanship and other promotional activities. In general, high quality salesmanship is a must for small businesses due to their limited ability to advertise heavily. Good yellow-page advertising is a must for small retailers. Direct mail is an effective, low-cost medium of advertising available to small businesses.

Price

Determining price levels and/or pricing policies (including credit policy) is the major factor affecting total revenue. Generally, higher prices mean lower volume and vice-versa, however, small businesses can often command higher prices due to the personalized service they can offer.

Distribution

The manufacturer and wholesaler must decide how to distribute their products. Working through established distributors or manufacturers' agents generally is most feasible for small manufacturers. retailers should consider cost and traffic flow as two major factors in location site selection, especially since advertising and rent can be reciprocal. In other words, low-cost, low-traffic location means you must spend more on advertising to build traffic.

Marketing Performance

After marketing program decisions are made, owner-managers need to evaluate how well decisions have turned out. Standards of performance need to be set up so results can be evaluated against them. Sound data on industry norms and past performance provide the basis for comparing against present performance.

Owner-managers should audit their company's performance at least quarterly. The key questions to ask are:

- Is the company doing all it can to be customer-orientated?
- Do the employees make sure the customer's needs are truly satisfied and leave them with the feeling that they would enjoy coming back?
- Is it easy for the customer to find what he or she wants and at a competitive price?

The marketing vs. the selling concept. Two approaches to marketing exist. The traditional selling concept emphasizes selling existing products. The philosophy here is that if a product is not selling, more aggressive measures must be taken to sell it—e.g., cutting price, advertising more, or hiring more aggressive (and obnoxious) sales-people. When the railroads started to lose business due to the advent of more effective trucks that could deliver goods right to the customer's door, the railroads cut prices instead of recognizing that the customers ultimately wanted transportation of goods, not necessarily railroad transportation. Smith Corona, a manufacturer of typewriters, was too slow to realize that consumers wanted the ability to process documents and not typewriters per se. The marketing concept, in contrast, focuses on getting consumers what they seek, regardless of whether this entails coming up with entirely new products.

The four Ps—*product*, *place* (distribution), *promotion*, and *price*—represent the variables that are within the control of the firm (at least in the medium to long run). In contrast, the firm is faced with uncertainty from the environment.

THE ROLE OF MARKETING

An **airline** provides air transport services for passengers or freight. Airlines lease or own their aircraft with which to supply these services and may form partnerships or alliances with other airlines for mutual benefit.

In basic terms, the role of Marketing has always been to satisfy consumer demand at a profit. In order to fulfill this role, the Marketing Process must ensure that the organization's products or services meet the needs and wants of consumers, and that these products or services are delivered at the right price, in the right place, and at the right time.

At the same time, Marketing must create consumer awareness of the benefits of these products or services, in order to motivate purchase.

Marketing must also anticipate change to make sure that the organization adapts to future market conditions.

It is clear from this introduction to the role of Marketing that it covers a very wide range of activities. Peter Drucker was the first leading authority on Marketing to recognize how fundamental Marketing really is, and he defined it as follows:

Marketing is so basic that it cannot be considered a separate function. It is the whole business seen from the point of its final result, that is, from the customer's point of view."

Drunker was saying two things here. Firstly, he points out that "Marketing really is the business". Secondly, he says that what Marketing needs to create in the business is Customer Focus—that is using the customer's viewpoint to drive decision-making—as this is the "recipe for success".

Recognition of this modem role of Marketing became widespread in the last 30 years of the 20th Century. The Marketing function developed rapidly during this period, taking responsibility for all of the following:

- Being the "eyes and the ears" of organizations in relation to their customers, the competition and the many trends and issues that may affect the future.
- Playing the lead role in specifying what needs to be produced, how much it is to be sold for, and how it is to be distributed.
- Acting as the "voice" of the company through responsibility for advertising, promotion and new media like direct mail and the Internet.

It is important to understand how this increased responsibility occurred and what the implications are for modern Marketing management, and to illustrate this we will look at a diagram that is quite easy to remember. (Fig. 1)

The circle around this triangle represents the environment Developments in the technological, regulatory and socio-economic environment of any industry will influence the rate of change. Taking the airline industry as an example:

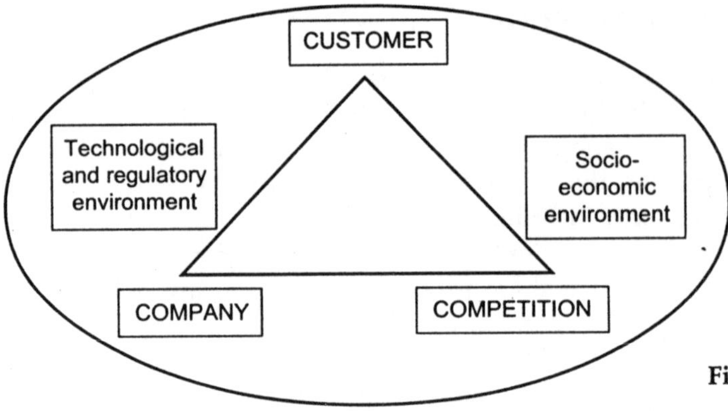

Fig. 1

- Technology has vastly influenced the airline business by providing larger and more economic aircraft.
- Deregulation has revolutionized what was once a very stable framework. For example, an "open skies" environment allows easier access to the market, greater competition, and low fares.
- Socio-economic developments, such as increased incomes and desire to travel, have produced the basis for a broader and more varied market of consumers.

Marketing in the airline business has had to keep pace with these factors by enabling the airline concerned to understand the changing relationships among their customers, the company and the competition.

This triangle of relationships is "eternal" because it will always hold the key to success and failure. If you can change the shape of the triangle by finding out how to get closer to customers than the competition can manage to do, you win; if you allow your competitors to get closer, you lose. As the environment changes more rapidly, the need to constantly re-evaluate what is needed to "win" increases.

All of this has produced the broader role for Marketing just described, and it explains why "customer focus"—getting close to customers in order to understand and satisfy their needs and wants in a highly competitive environment—has become the essence of today's approach to Marketing.

The "Eternal Triangle" is a useful concept to remember as you learn and apply Marketing. It acts as a checklist for gathering market information and as a template or agenda for discussing marketing issues with people from other parts of your airline. It also serves as a constant reminder of the forces at play in your market, helping you to assess your market position and plan accordingly.

MARKETING MIX

The marketing mix consists of the types and amounts of controllable mai.keting-decision variables that a company uses over a particular time period. Commonly referred to as the "four Ps," these variables are:

1. **Product:** The right product (or service) must be developed for the target market.
2. **Price:** A price that gives good value to the customer and adequate revenue to the carrier must be set for the product.
3. **Promotion:** Personal selling and advertising must be used, both to communicate information about the product to the customer and to facilitate sales.
4. **Place:** Appropriate channels of distribution must be found to ensure that the product reaches the target market at the right time and in the right place.

These four elements are the controllable marketing factors that should be used to reach the target market. Thus, any discussion of the business activities that direct the flow of services to customers must stress the four Ps. Because all four elements are present to some degree in any marketing situation, the airline marketer's task is not to decide whether to use a particular element, but rather to determine the relative emphasis to place on each element in the final marketing program. It must be recognized that the marketer must contend with certain uncontrollable variables. Unfortunately, the marketing team does not work in a vacuum. Its actions and strategies will be affected by some or all of the following variables:

1. ***Cultural and social differences:*** These are the traditions and values of various ethnic groups that represent potential customers. Such traits as eating habits can vary considerably in different parts of our own country, to say nothing of different countries.

2. ***Political and regulatory environment:*** Political climates are constantly changing. New levels of taxation and government spending can affect marketing strategies set by the carriers. Regulatory requirements, such as allocations of landing quotas at certain airports because of extreme peaking in the number of flights, can undermine the best of marketing plans.

3. ***Economic environment:*** A good marketing program might be a flop if economy is going through a recession or rapid business downturn. Airlines are very sensitive to changes in the economy.

4. ***Existing competitive structure:*** The number and types of competitors; marketing team must face in its target markets may vary considerably

5. ***Resources and objectives of the company:*** Top management really controls these variables, and the marketing team must work within the restraints-imposed on them. For example, if management has placed great emphasis on short-term profits and less emphasis on long-term market share a particular route, the marketing team must develop a strategy consists with the company's goal. Although the marketing team can do little or nothing about these uncontrollable variables; it certainly must recognize them and be in a position to respond to them by altering its marketing strategy. The term *marketing strategy* is used to describe the process by which the marketing mix is changed.

Service's Marketing

Airlines are often providing services, rather than physically distinct products. Marketing experts acknowledge that marketing a service is more difficult than marketing a tangible product. They identify the following as being characteristic of services:

- **Intangibility** the service cannot be touched or viewed, so it is difficult for clients to tell in advance what they will be getting;
- **Inseparability of production and consumption** the service is being produced at the same time that the client is receiving it (e.g. during an online search, or a legal consultation);
- **Perishibility** unused capacity cannot be stored for future use. For example, spare seats on one aeroplane cannot be transferred to the next flight, and query-free times at the reference desk cannot be saved up until there is a busy period.
- **Heterogeneity** (or **variability**): services involve people, and people are all different. There is a strong possibility that the same enquiry would be answered slightly differently by different people (or even by the same person at different times). It is important to minimise the differences in performance (through training, standard-setting and quality assurance).

The Service marketing mix involves analysing the 7'p of marketing involving, Product, Price, Place, Promotion, Physical Evidence, Process and People.

To certain extent managing services are more complicated then managing products, products can be standardised, to standardise a service is far more difficult as there are more input factors i e. people, physical evidence, process to manage then with a product.

So far we have used the term *product* which basically means a "bundle of attributes" that fulfils consumer needs. We have also covered the "4 p's" that have been developed to describe all marketing activity. When it comes to marketing services like airline travel, however, we need to make a greater differentiation for the following reasons:

- Products are tangible (can be seen and felt) whereas services are intangible (cannot be seen, and lack physical substance)
- Products are homogeneous or stable (always the same), whereas services are variable or for example they can vary in quality from time to time
- Most products have a very long shelf life (imperishable) whereas services are highly perishable

What do airlines sell? They sell services that are intangible, perishable, variable, and highly dependent on the people who deliver them.

Three Additional "P's" in the Service Marketing Mix

Due to these important and unique attributes, service marketing calls for a slightly different approach and emphasis, and this is where the additional three "P's" or marketing mix elements come in:

People

Unlike products that are promoted and sold on the basis of their own quality and physical attributes (a smooth-running car or a reliable computer, for example), the quality of services is highly dependant on the *people* who sell and deliver them.

For example, the attitude and efficiency of an airline's reservations check-in and cabin staff will define the quality of the overall purchase experience, as well as determine whether or not the customer returns to the agency for repeat business.

It is for this reason that many customer-focused (and award-winning) service firms focus on hiring the right staff and providing comprehensive customer service training. Some even take on the slogan "our people are our product" as testimony to the importance of people as an ingredient of their success.

Process

In light of the intangible nature of services, some service companies also consider the process by which their services are made available or supported as being important enough to give them a competitive edge. For example, American Express promises to replace a lost or stolen credit card within 24 hours, whereas Embassy Suites promises "100% satisfaction or your money back". An airline that promises a "24-hour emergency hotline" would offer a process that is important to both corporate and leisure travelers.

Physical Possession

Where is the service being delivered? Physical Evidence is the element of the service mix which allows the consumer again to make judgements on the organisation. If you walk into a restaurant your expectations are of a clean, friendly environment. On an aircraft if you travel first class you expect enough room to be able to lay down.Physical evidence is an essential ingredient of the service mix, consumers will make perceptions based on their sight of the service provision which will have an impact on the organisations perceptual plan of the service.

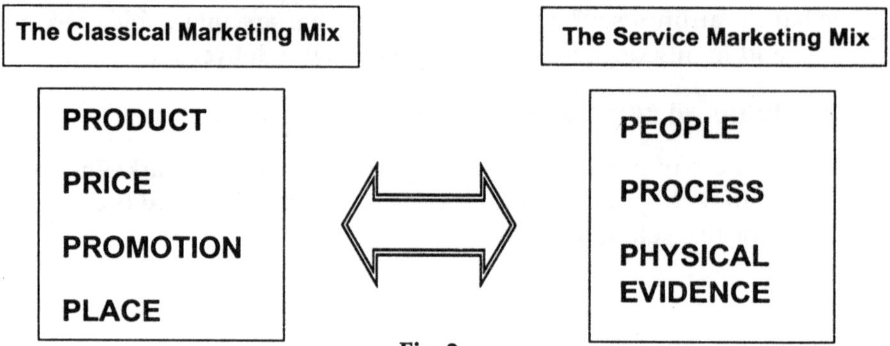

Fig. 2

The Expanded Marketing Mix

If we added these three additional "Ps" to our process of marketing of services, our marketing mix would look like the illustration in Fig. 2.

In manufacturing industry, the people and processes used to create the product are remote from the customer. In the airline industry, these people and processes form a major part of the customer's direct experience of each carrier—the quality of your front line staff and the way in which they go about their tasks therefore make a deep impression on the customer.

Managing the Marketing Mix

We have just referred to the schedule of initiatives, activity and results contained in Marketing Plans. These describe how all elements of the Marketing Mix—The "Four P's" of Product, Price, Promotion and Place, and in addition "Physical evidence," "People" and "Process"—will be managed to satisfy the needs and wants of customers at a profit. Two key features about Managing the Marketing Mix that you need to understand from the start are that:

- The elements involved such as product and price need to be put together to form offerings that are delivered as "complete customer propositions."
- Every proposition will inevitably involve you in considering alternatives and making trade-offs in order to "strike the right balance" between different requirements, such as delivering customer value and achieving profit.

If all we had to do as Marketers was say that we needed more of everything—more products, more low prices, more advertising budgets and more agents on more commission—in order to deliver results, then life would be very easy.

But this is not how Marketing works—we constantly have to make trade-offs involving having more of one of these things at the expense of another in order to be successful. This is less easy, but more exciting. so welcome to the first rule of Marketing—in return for "less easy" you get "more exciting"!

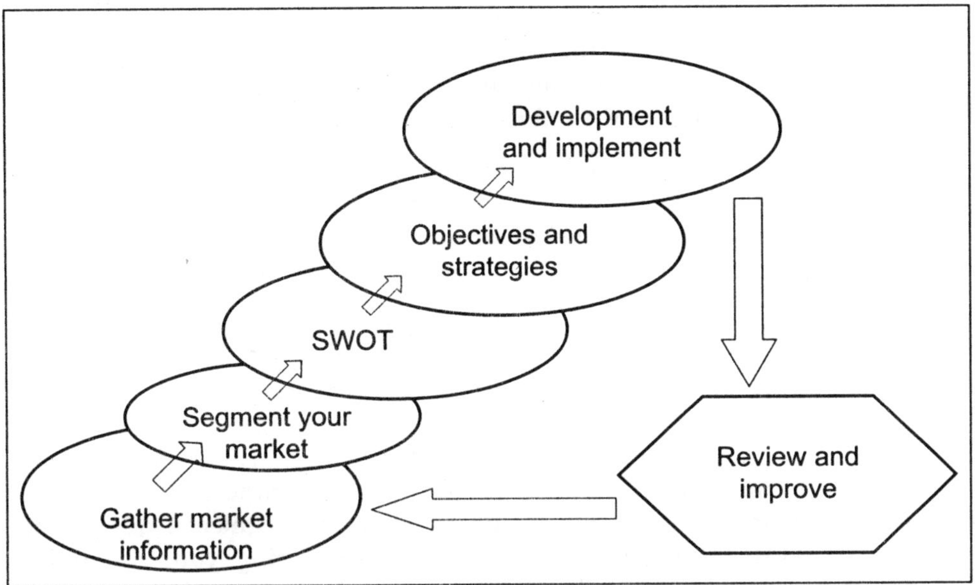

Fig. 3

Marketing Process

The Fig. 3 illustrates the key stages involved in a properly organized process for planning and executing Marketing activity:

In building up to the steps at the top of the diagram—the formulation of objectives and strategies, and the development of marketing plans.

We need to start by gathering market information. This first stage is sometimes referred to as a "Marketing Audit", and it involves gathering and analyzing all the information relevant to a Marketing Plan. Remember from the "eternal triangle" discussed earlier that this must cover all of the following areas of information:

- **The environment**—what key trends in your airline's environment are evident and what is their likely impact? For example, will there be a trend towards de-regulation leading to more competition, increased capacity and a downward pressure on prices?
- **The customers**—what data do you have on your customers' motivations and how often they travel? In addition, what do you know about your prospects (your competitors' customers)?
- **The competition**—What key product and service advantages does each competitor have compared to your airline? What feedback are you getting from your salespeople and agents about competitor activity?
- **Your company**—What key product and service advantages does your company have? How are these being used?

The next major step is to segment your market, that is to divide it into different "customer groups" that are distinct from one another. As we have seen, one useful way of segmenting your market is to use purpose for travel. Using this, you could have the following segments:

- Business travelers seeking convenience and comfort.
- Holiday travelers who require reasonably-priced ground accommodation as well as air travel.
- VFR (Visiting Friends and Relatives) travelers looking for the cheapest form of air travel.

The important insight that customer focus gives you is the ability to easily recognize and act on the different needs and wants of each of these three simple segments.

Once your market segmentation is completed, you need to rank each segment in terms of its future importance to your airline and focus your attention on your market position in the top two or three segments. This is done using a "SWOT" analysis, which involves considering your Strengths, Weaknesses, Opportunities and Threats in each segment in relation to your competitors.

When this is done, you will have the strong foundation that you need to build realistic objectives and sound strategies upon. These objectives and strategies will then need to be broken down into a Marketing Plan that highlights the schedule of initiatives, activity and results foreseen usually over a 3-year time scale.

As this plan is implemented, a program of reviews will be necessary to monitor performance and analyses events. This provides the new information required to create a process where new plans are made based on the experience of implementing old ones.

Marketing involves a circular process, whereby new strategies and plans are based on the results of implementing previous strategies and plans. This means that the process will become easier and more refined as time goes on.

Stages in the Application of Marketing Principles to Airline Management

The "7Ps" model is a powerful one, and describes much of what an airline must do if it is to apply the principles of marketing in order to achieve business success. It does not, though, give a complete description. Here it will be suggested that the application of marketing consists of even interlinked stages:

1. The Customer

The cornerstone of successful marketing activity is that fIrms should obtain full knowledge of their current and potential customers. This knowledge needs to encompass information about market size, demographics, customer requirements and attitudes. There also needs to be an ability to forecast the future size of the market, and any possible future changes in customer needs. The processes whereby airlines seek this information will be those of market research and market analysis.

2. The Marketing Environment

The nature of sound marketing policies will clearly vary according to the constraints and opportunities provided by the external environment.

In analysing a flrm's marketing environment it is usual to use the model known as PESTE analysis. This model categorises the factors in the marketing environment under the flve headings of Political, Economic, Social, Technological and Environmental. The analyst's task is to isolate those factors in the external environment which will have a signiflcant impact on the formulation of sound marketing policies and to assess their implications.

3. Strategy Formulation

Clearly, it will not be possible to deflne marketing policies witho,ut the marketing input being a crucial one in the deflnition of a flrm's overall strategic direction. This strategic direction must identify the flrm's goals and objectives, the markets in which it will participate and the methods it will employ to ensure successful exploitation of market potential.

4. Product Design and Development

5. Pricing and Revenue Management

6. Distribution Channel Selection and Control

Once an overall strategy has been selected, these stages should follow on logically. Today's aviation industry offers airlines many possible routes to success (and, interestingly, many different ways in which they can fail). What matters is that a clear strategy is selected and pursued steadily over the long-term. Each possible strategic option will result in a requirement for a linked set of product, pricing and distribution decisions.

7. Selling, Advertising and Promotional Policies

A common mistake is to assume that the words "marketing" and "selling" are synonymous. They are not. The term "marketing", as we have seen, describes a total philosophy for running an entire business. "Selling" is the concluding stage of a correctly-applied marketing process, whereby customers are persuaded to buy the firm's products.

"Marketing" ought to make "selling" easier. It is likely to be a great deal easier to sell something to someone which is available in response to a well-researched and well-understood customer need. Indeed, one of the traditional faults of industry in the past has been a so-called production orientation whereby firms made what they liked making, or found it easiest to make, and then tried to persuade reluctant customers through high-pressure selling to buy these less-than-ideal products. It should not be thought, though, that "marketing" will make the skills of selling obsolete. In today's competitive markets, customers will usually have plenty of choice open to them. Persuading them to exercise this choice in a particular way will require the use of professional skills of a high order.

AIRLINE MARKETING ENVIRONMENT

The marketing *environment* involves factors that, for the most part, are beyond the control of the company. Thus, the company must *adapt* to these factors. It is important to observe how the environment changes so that a firm can adapt its strategies appropriately. Consider these environmental forces:

- *Competition*: Competitors often "creep" in and threaten to take away markets from firms. For example, Japanese auto manufacturers became a serious threat to American car makers in the late 1970s and early 1980s. Similarly, the Lotus Corporation, maker of one of the first commercially successful spreadsheets, soon faced competition from other software firms. Note that while competition may be frustrating for the firm, it is good for consumers. Note that competition today is increasingly global in scope. It is important to recognize that competition can happen at different "levels." At the brand level, two firms compete in providing a very similar product or service. Coca Cola and Pepsi, for example, compete for the cola drink market, and Kingfisher and Tetair compete for the passenger air transportation market. Firms also face less direct—but frequently very serious—competition at the product level. For example, cola drinks compete against bottled water. Products or services can serve as substitutes for each other even though they are very different in form. Teleconferencing facilities, for example, are very different from airline passenger transportation, but both can "bring together" people for a "meeting." At the budget level, different products or services provide very different benefits, but buyers have to make choices as to what they will buy when they cannot afford—or are unwilling to spend on—both. For example, a family may decide between buying a new car or a high definition television set. The family may also have to choose between going on a foreign vacation or remodeling its kitchen. Firms, too, may have to make choices. The firm has the cash flow either to remodel its offices or install a more energy efficient climate control system; or the firm can choose either to invest in new product development or in a promotional campaign to increase awareness of its brand among consumers.
- *Economics*: Two economic forces strongly affect firms and their customers:
  - *Economic Cycles.* Some firms in particular are extremely vulnerable

to changes in the economy. Consumers tend to put off travelling by air, buying a new car, going out to eat, or building new homes in bad times. In contrast, in good times, firms serving those needs may have difficulty keeping up with demand. One important point to realize is that different industries are affected to different degrees by changes in the economy. Although families can cut down on their travels plans—going with lower priced brands, for example—there are limits to the savings that can be made without greatly affecting the living standard of the family. On the other hand, it is often much easier to put off the purchase of a new car for a year or hold off on remodeling the family home. If need, Airlines can keep the current computers—even though they are getting a bit slow—when sales are down. The economy goes through cycles. Currently, the economy fluctuates between increasing strength, stagnation, or slight decline. Many Airlines face consequences of economic downturns. Airline makers, for example, have seen declining profit margins (and even losses) as they have had to cut prices and offer low air fares. Generally, in good economic times, there is a great deal of demand, but this introduces a fear of possible inflation. This makes businesses less willing to invest, and as a result, people tend to make less money. During a recession, unemployment tends to rise, causing consumers to spend less. This may result in a "bad circle," with more people losing their jobs due to lowered demands. Some businesses, however, may take this opportunity to invest in growth now that things can be bought more cheaply.

- *Inflation.* Over time, most economies experience some level of inflation. Therefore, it is useful to explicitly state whether a reference to money over time involves the actual dollar (or other currency) amount exchanged at any point (e.g., one Rupee spent in 1960 and one dollar in 2007) or an "inflation adjusted" figure that "anchors" a given amount of money to the value of that money at some point in time. It is important to note that inflation is uneven. Some goods and services—such as health care travel and Tourism and education—are currently increasing in cost much higher than the average rate of inflation.

• ***Political***: Businesses are very vulnerable to changes in the political situation. For example, because consumer groups lobbied Congress, more stringent rules were made on the terms of Aircraft leases. The liquor and tobacco industry is currently the target of much negative attention from government and public interest groups. Currently, the desire to avoid aiding the enemy may result in laws that make it more difficult for domestic firms to export goods to other countries. Many industries have a strong economic interest in policies that benefit the industry may have a negative impact on the nation as a whole but enhance profits for the industry. However, the interests of the industry are much more concentrated. The industry can rally its stockholders, unions and employees, and suppliers together to lobby for their special interests. In turn, the industry can join forces with other agricultural interests which each support each other's programs.

- ***Legal***: Airlines are very vulnerable to changing laws and changing interpretations by the courts. Airlines in the U.S. are very vulnerable to lawsuits. McDonald's, for example, is currently being sued by people who claim that eating the chain's hamburgers caused them to get fat. Firms are significantly limited in what they can do by various laws—some laws, for example, require that disclosures be made to consumers on the effective interest rates they pay on products bought on installment. A particularly interesting group of laws relate to antitrust. These laws basically exist to promote fair competition among firms. We will consider such laws when we cover pricing later in the term.
- ***Technological***: Changes in technology may significantly influence the demand for a product. For example, the advent of the fax machine was bad news for Federal Express. The Internet is a major threat to travel agents. Many record stores have been wiped out of business by the trend toward downloading songs. Although technological change eliminates or at least greatly diminishes some markets, it creates opportunities for others. For example, although Federal Express has lost a considerable amount of business from documents that can now be faxed or sent by the Internet rather than having to be physically shipped, there has been a large increase in demand for packages to be delivered overnight or "second day air." Just-in-time manufacturing techniques, in addition to online sales, have dramatically increased the market for such shipments. Online sites such as eBay now makes it possible to sell specialty products that, in the old days, would have been difficult to distribute. Although it has been possible for more than a hundred years to sell merchandise by catalog, buyers of these specialty products often had no easy access to the catalogs.
- ***Social***: Changes in customs or demographics greatly influence firms. Most middle class travellers are born resulting in a increased demand for Airlines tickets. More women work outside the home today, so there is a greater demand for travelling needs and prepared foods. There are more unmarried singles today. This provides opportunities for some firms (e.g., fast food restaurants) but creates problems for others (e.g., manufacturers of high quality furniture that many people put off buying until marriage). Today, there are more "blended" families that result as parents remarry after divorce. These families are often strapped for money but may require "duplicate" items for children at each parent's residence.

- Companies are significantly limited in what they can do by various laws—some laws, for example, require that disclosures be made to consumers on the effective interest rates they pay on products bought on installment. A particularly interesting group of laws relate to antitrust. These laws basically exist to promote fair competition among firms. Some principles involved here include:
  - *Collusion*: Companies may not "conspire" to fix prices (agree that they will not sell below an agreed upon price) or reduce services.
  - *Predation*: Companies may not sell their products below their cost of production for the purpose of driving competitors out of business so that they, themselves, can raise prices when competition is reduced.
  - *Market share*: Companies which have an unacceptably large market share may be "broken" up by court order so that many smaller firms will be around to compete. (This is what happened to AT&T, and at times, IBM has been worried about this prospect).
  - *Tying*: A firm that controls a valuable product may not require the consumer to buy a more commonplace one to get the scarce product. For example, Intel controls many of the newest microprocessors (e.g., Pentium IV). Intel also makes motherboards for computers; however, motherboards are made by a lot of firms. Intel would be thought to abuse its effective monopoly power if it required consumers to buy a motherboard in order to get its newest chips.

Marketing Environment Model

The literature on marketing provides one, particularly useful, model for the study of a firm's marketing environment. This model proposes that the relevant factors should be divided into the categories of Political, Economic, Social, Technological and Environmental known as PESTE Analysis.

It should of course be born in mind that the categories are not mutually exclusive, and that it might be appropriate to discuss a particular issue under more than one heading. However, the model is still a powerful one especially in the airline industry. Airlines can not develop sound marketing policies independently of a range of political decisions. The industry has always been, and remains, intensely political. The fortunes of the world economy will also have substantial impact, with marketing policies needing to ensure that the favourable economics trends are exploited, and unfavourable one countered. Social issues such as those relating to demographic trends will also be significant especially at the present time. Technology provides both extining opportunities and difficult challenges today, whilst problems associated with the environment may threaten the whole future of the industry.

We will now explore in turn each component of the PESTE model in an airline context.

POLITICAL FACTORS

1. Terrorism Fears/Political Instability

The years at the beginning of the new millennium are turning out to be some of the most difficult that the aviation industry has ever faced.

The industry undoubtedly heading for challenging times in any case, but there can be no doubt that the events of September 11, 2001 caused an unprecedented crisis. Armed hijackerers seized four air craft in the USA, and use these to attack the World Trade Centre in New York and the Pentagon in Washington. Many thousands of people lost their lives.

The effects on the airline industry were catas trophic. For four days, the airspace over the eastern USA was closed, resulting in direct losses to airlines (for which, admittedly, they have mostly been compensated). More seriously still, the fear of further terrorism attacks caused a step decline demand, both in the USA, on international routes to and from the US, and to a lesser extent elsewhere.

The time since the September 11 attacks has seen little improvement. Further vary serious terrorist attacks have occurred in places as far apart as Mombasa and Bali. The second Gulf War fought in March and April 2003 seems to have fanned the flames of international terrorism rather than causing the improvement in the situation which it was presumably intended to bring about.

Assessing the longer term impact of the fear of terrorist attack aon the size of the aviation market is very difficult. It is of course, important to keep personal political opinions out of any any analysis as far as possible. A terrorism threat can only be addressed by seeking to understand and address the underlying grievances, which caused the terrorist movement to arise in the first place.

This lead to a thoroughly depressing conclusion. We may have to accept that periodic attacks by the Al-Qaeda organization, and others that will grow up around it will be a long-term feature. Worse still, the aviation industry will probably be peculiarly vulnerable to these attacks because airlines are often strongly identified with a particular nation. It is also a very high profile activity, meeting the terrorist group's desire for widespread publicity for their course.

Perhaps the best that can be hoped for is that September 11 2001 will turn out to be an extreme case. New security measure will make the task of terrorist groups a harder one, so they may target aircraft less frequently. There will still be an effect on the aviation industry, though because a terrorist outrage in a particular city will greatly reduce demand, at least for a time, on routes to and from it.

We can now reach an overall, difficult conclusion for airline marketing. In a very real sense, airline do not have any control over the size of the markets they have available to them because wars and terrorist attacks—or the threat of them—can have sudden, strong and negative impact. Given the growing instabilities in the world political scene, it is unlikely that this fact will change significantly in the industry's favour.

2. Deregulation and "Open Skies"

Throughout its history, the airline industry has been constrained by decisions made by politicians and governments. Governments have controlled where airlines can fly freely, and aspects of their product planning and pricing policies. They have also had a major involvement in the industry through the ownership of airlines. Finally, political decisions have often affected the extent, nature and geographical distribution of demand. We will consider each of these aspects in turn.

Almost from the inception of the commercial aviation industry, governments regulated airlines. They have always had a role in regulating airline safety standards, a role that remains important and, in principle, relatively non-controversial. Government regulation, though traditionally went very much further than this. For many years, and in almost all aviation markets, governments controlled airlines' route entry and capacity and frequency decisions. Very commonly too, and astonishingly by today's standards, governments intervened to stop airlines engaging in price competition.

In recent years, substantial regulatory reform has taken place, giving carriers the challenge and opportunity of responding to a freer economic environment. We need to look now at exactly what has happened, and the issues which change poses for marketing policies.

In describing the environment. We need to look now at exactly what has happened, and the issues which change poses for marketing policies.

In describing the system of economic regulation of the airline industry, a fundamental distinction has always been between the regulation of domestic services, which are solely under the control of one government, and international services, which require the agreement of at least two.

Until relatively recently, almost all domestic travel markets were highly regulated. An extreme case was the USA. Despite the United States supposedly being the home of free market thinking, airlines' commercial freedom was constrained by what now seems a very burdensome system of economic regulation. Between the passing of the Federal Aviation Act in 1938 and the Airline Deregulation Act in 1978, carriers could only enter new routes by going through a cumbersome and extremely slow bureaucratic procedure. A similar process was needed before service could be withdrawn from an unprofitable route. At the same time, regulatory approval was needed before fares could be raised or lowered. The actions of the regulatory body concerned—the Civil Aeronautics Board—ensured that where two airlines competed on a particular route, their fares were generally identical.

Another extreme case of a highly regulated domestic market was that of Australia. For many years prior to 1990, Australia pursued a so-called "Two

Airline" policy. Under this, only two airlines were granted access to Australian domestic trunk routes, Ansett Airlines and Trans-Australia Airlines (later renamed Australian Airlines). Even though these carriers were supposed to compete with each other, in practice almost all the areas where competition might have occurred were regulated, including the question of price levels.

The situation with regard to domestic aviation markets today has undergone substantial change, though in one very important sense we are still (with one exception) very far from true "deregulation".

In terms of regulatory change, the USA led the way with the passing of the Airline Deregulation Act in 1978. This allowed for much greater freedom for airlines to enter new markets and to exploit them free of constraints on capacity or pricing policies. However, one important regulatory limitation remained—that of ownership. Still today, it is necessary for 75% of the voting shares of an airline to be owned by United States citizens before that airline is allowed to fly domestic routes in the USA. This means that foreign-owned carriers are still denied the much prized "Cabotage" rights to fly internal routes in the US.

Regulatory reform in the United States has been followed by a similar pattern in many other countries. Today, many countries would claim to have "deregulated" their domestic aviation industries. Still, though, rules on ownership provide a highly significant constraint on the extent of airlines' true commercial freedom of action. At the time of writing, Australia and New Zealand provide rare exceptions to the general rule that foreign-owned airlines are not allowed domestic rights. One of the major players in the Australian domestic market, Virgin Blue, is still dominantly owned by a non-Australian—the British businessman Sir Richard Branson.

With domestic aviation, the European Union now provides an interesting case study. By a progressive process of liberalization (completed in 1997), the countries of the European Union effectively set up a Single Aviation Market which freed airlines to make their own decisions regarding market access, capacity and fares.

The situation regarding regulatory change in international markets has inevitably been more fragmented and diffuses, but even here, the state-of-play is significantly different from the one which prevailed only a few years ago. On the horizon, we can now see the possibility for radical regulatory reform, which could transform the structure of the entire international airline industry.

For more than fifty years, international aviation has generally been very tightly regulated indeed. Early attempts were made by the USA to establish a liberal environment at the so-called Chicago Convention of 1944. These were decisively rejected and in the ensuing compromise, the world fell back on a system of controls through intergovernmental Air Services Agreements. Working on a bilateral basis between pairs of governments, these Agreements have limited market entry, controlled capacity and interfered (though now, to a much reduced extent) with airlines' freedom-of-action over pricing policy. As a particularly severe constraint, the Air Services Agreement system has limited the exercising of traffic rights to airlines which are owned and controlled by nationals of the two countries which have signed a particular agreement. This has made nationality of ownership as important a constraint in international aviation as it has been in domestic services.

Given the all-embracing nature of the Air Services Agreement system, it is almost impossible to exaggerate its significance as a constraint on airlines' marketing and commercial policies. In almost every other industry, it is possible for firms to trade on a global basis. They widely do so, by entering foreign markets and by engaging in cross-border merger and take-over activity. Airlines are denied such freedom. Their route networks(the cornerstone, of course, of the product they offer) largely begin and end in the countries in which they are based. Any wider global presence can only be secured by the unsatisfactory and second-best solution of signing alliance agreements with other airlines.

Few would disagree with the general proposition that the regulatory system facing airlines today is many years out-of-date and in need of root- and-branch reform. So far, though, efforts at reform have produced results which are fragmented, piecemeal and unsatisfactory.

As we have seen, the "deregulation" of many domestic markets has left the constraint that foreign-owned airlines are prevented from competing in almost all domestic markets. We will not have true free trade in aviation services until these constraints are removed.

In international aviation, the United States began a process, which it presumably regarded as a reforming one during the 1990s. Beginning with the government of the Netherlands in 1993, the US has signed with foreign governments what it has described as "Open Skies" agreements. At the time of writing, more than fifty of these agreements are in place. They do change the regulatory landscapes significantly in the markets where they apply, in that they allow each side to designate as many airlines as they choose, with these airlines then being able to fly to any number of gateway points with no limitations on their capacity and pricing decisions. They do not, however, break free of question of ownership and control. Entry is still confined to airlines which are owned and effectively controlled by nationals of the two countries. Nor do they concede access to internal routes by foreign airlines. In that sense, to describe these agreements as representing "Open Skies" is nonsense.

At the time of the preparation of this new edition (the summer of 2003), we may have seen the development which, by a long tortuous process, may finally bring about the long overdue process of true regulatory reform. In November 2002, the European Court published a complex, but possibly historic judgment. In this, the Court ruled that individual member governments of the European Union offended against EU law if they signed Air Services Agreements with other countries which limited the use of traffic rights purely to airlines which are owned and controlled by their citizens. Such rights had potentially to be available to all EU airlines. If they are not, such discrimination is an infringement against the Treaty of Rome.

Following on from this judgment, it is just possible to conceive of the present system continuing, with individual governments removing the now-illegal discrimination in favor of their own airlines. This would almost certainly prove to be impractical. A more likely outcome is a completely new system, whereby the European Commission will take over the negotiation of external aviation relationships with other countries, on behalf of all EU member states. If this happens—it will not be at all easy to sort out the "who does what" question amongst the different European Commission departments—it is already clear that the United States will be the first country with which the Commission will expect to open negotiations. Its aim will be the eventual setting up, through a stepped process of reform, a so-called Transatlantic Common Aviation Area or TCAA.

There are variations in the specific thinking of the different parties involved, but all their ideas have common themes. The United States (perhaps also including the NAFf A countries of Canada and Mexico) and the European Union would be declared a single aviation market. (Of course, by then, it is very likely that the EU will have been extended by the granting of membership to a number of additional countries.) In this market, it would be possible for any airline to provide service, which could satisfy appropriate safety and financial fitness requirements, between any city pair and with no regulatory constraints on capacity, frequency and fares and rates. This would, of course, imply the granting of full cabotage rights and, effectively, the ending of nationality of ownership as a constraint to airline marketing and commercial freedom of action.

If a Transatlantic Common Aviation Area can be set up, it is unlikely that the rest of the world could stand aside. Liberally-minded aviation nations such as Australia and Singapore would join in and as they did so there would be more and more pressure for other countries to do likewise.

The question of the future regulatory scene which will face airlines, is still an uncertain one. It is clear, though, that the trend will be towards an increasingly deregulated marketplace. This will in turn require a response in terms of the business and marketing strategies that carriers pursue.

3. Marketing Policies for a Deregulated Environment

In many aviation markets today, airline managers are facing the challenge of change and adaptation. They were formerly able to enjoy the reassurance of regulated conditions, with limited competition and only a very slow pace of change. Today, deregulation is giving new opportunities which must be exploited if success is to be achieved. It also brings new threats which must be countered effectively.

Given the nature of the challenges facing airlines, it would be naive in the extreme to assume that these do not impinge on the marketing area of an airline's activities. They most certainly do, with sound marketing policies for a deregulated market being quite different for those which might be appropriate for a regulated one.

Above all other considerations, a deregulated situation requires that systems s ould be in place to enable decisions to be made quickly. New opportunities to enter routes will arise at short notice, and may disappear equally rapidly if another airline is able to react faster and take advantage of the potential first. Equally, it may be necessary to change the specification of the product quickly, if a competitor offers customers better value-for-money. Also, pricing policies will have to be adjusted frequently, with changes often being required on a daily basis or sometimes even more frequently than this. A feature of regulated markets used to be that all airlines charged the same fares, and fares only changed infrequently, following an often tortuous set of procedures which needed to be undertaken in order to gain regulatory approval.

The situation in today's deregulated markets is in strong contrast. The combination of the ending of regulatory controls on pricing and the advent of the ability to disseminate fares information instantaneously, through the spread of so-called Global Distribution Systems and over the Internet has meant that millions of fares now often change overnight at times of active price competition. No airline can now afford the luxury of a slow response at such a time.

If airlines are to make decisions quickly, certain conditions must be met. Decision-making processes must be streamlined, with flat organizational structures and, often, a degree of autocracy prevailing in the most successful carriers. Where possible, too, decision-making must be decentralized to the managers of small profit centers, where people will have a better understanding of the detail of local market conditions.

Up-to-date and accurate commercial information will also be needed. In a regulated market, little damage will result from a situation where details of financial performance do not emerge for months, or where such information is of dubious accuracy. In a deregulated market, it almost certainly will. Inaccurate or late information will cause opportunities to be lost and problems to go undetected until it is too late. Not only must information be accurate and timely, it must also incorporate a forecasting capability which allows the state of forward bookings to be monitored and corrective action to be taken where appropriate.

Besides having the flexibility to ensure that opportunities are exploited as they become available, marketing policies for a deregulated environment need to have a defensive component, to enable airlines to fend off potential competitors. Many-carriers, particularly in the USA, have based their strategies for success under deregulation on the so-called "hub-and-spoke" principle, whereby an airline has set out to dominate as high a percentage as possible of the destinations served and the frequencies provided at a particular airport. High frequencies in themselves give a protection against the attacks of competitors because they rninirnise the gaps available for rivals to mount an attractive schedule.

The question of the control of distribution channels is of prime importance in defining marketing policies for deregulated markets. The firms which are successful in establishing and maintaining control will be those that achieve "Super-Profits", over and above the levels necessary to keep them in business. The instability characteristic of a deregulated market will give many opportunities for the control of distribution channels to be contested and to change. Any airline seeking to be successful must maintain control of distribution.

In a deregulated market, carriers often have to change the basis of their advertising and promotional policies. Regulation means a slow pace of change. Promotional activities can therefore be focused on long-term aims through corporate and brand-building advertising. In deregulated markets, however, a greater proportion of promotional spending must deal with tactical messages such as those announcing entry into new markets, changes to the product specification or fare reductions. It follows, therefore, that a different set of skills may be needed by the advertising agencies that airlines employ.

A final, but crucial, requirement for marketing success in a deregulated environment is a low cost base. As we have seen, competition under deregulation focuses to a large degree on the question of price. Low cost airlines can base their marketing strategy on the offer of attractive lower fares, and still be profitable. A high cost airline which matches or undercuts these fares will lose money as a result.

The need for low costs poses a special problem for mature, long-established airlines. These carriers had the luxury of developing their operations under regulated conditions, where price competition was either muted or absent. They therefore did not have a great deal of incentive to control their costs effectively. The result has often been that such airlines have carried an inappropriately high cost structure into the era of deregulation. Some have then successfully carried out the necessary changes. Others have taken on the appearance of dinosaurs, earning for themselves the unflattering title of "Legacy" airlines.

Privatisation

Historically, state ownership has always been important in the airline industry. Many governments have regarded the existence of a national airline as an essential requirement for nationhood. Besides questions of prestige, an airline may bring benefits as a back-up for national defense capability, in employment, and in terms of balance-of-payments and tourism income.

During the early years of the industry's development, it was often felt that public, rather than private ownership was appropriate. Public ownership allowed governments to insist that their airlines sometimes worked to a wider set of objectives than those associated with the attempt to achieve profits. These wider objectives were designed to ensure that the airline maximized the contribution it made to the advancement of the national interest. It also gave governments the reassurance that their airline would survive, despite the threat of competition from better-established rivals.

Until the mid-1980s, almost all the world's major airlines, with the exception of those from the USA, were state-owned. The Brazilian carrier V ARIG and the Korean-based Korean Air were rare exceptions to this general rule.

Since then, the situation has been transformed. The fashion in political and economic thinking has turned full circle, with the emphasis now on the benefits in efficiency likely to result from private rather than public ownership. At the same time, the airline industry has matured. It has become impossible to argue that a global industry such as aviation, now operating on a massive scale, is an infant one in need of the protection of widespread state ownership.

Many formerly state-owned airlines have now been fully privatized. British Airways, Lufthansa, Qantas, and Air Canada are examples. Many others have seen the proportion of their ownership which is state-controlled substantially reduced, to the point where only a minority of the shareholding is government-owned. KLM illustrates this latter change.

For marketing managers, airline privatization brings both problems and opportunities. For those who work for a carrier that has undergone privatization, their task is in many senses an easier one. They need have only one objective, to assist their airline in achieving satisfactory profits for shareholders. Often, under government ownership, objectives to cover costs had in practice to be combined with such requirements as ensuring that domestic air fares remained low or that services were maintained on socially-necessary but financially-unremunerative routes. Also, beyond argument, privatization has often been accompanied by substantial improvements in efficiency and the elimination of the bureaucracy stemming from political interference in decision-making.

For other airlines, privatization has changed the competitive scene substantially. Competition with a state-owned airline has always been a different proposition from that with a privately-owned carrier. State ownership has always been a virtual guarantee that an airline will not be allowed to go out of business, with state subsidy being used to cover operating losses. State-owned airlines may, therefore, have been able to take greater risks in defining their business and marketing strategies, a factor which has made it more difficult for privately-owned firms to compete effectively. At the same time, though, state-ownership has brought real problems. Government airlines often suffer from a poor image associated with subsidy and bureaucracy. They also sometimes have poorly-motivated staff, making it very difficult for them to implement changes designed to improve service to customers.

It should be noted that in the crisis that has faced the industry since the terrorist attacks of September 2001, we have seen the first reversal of the trend towards airline privatization. Two' airlines, Air New Zealand and Malaysia Airlines, have effectively been taken back into public ownership. In both cases, it is highly likely that the airlines would have collapsed if they had not been renationalized.

This illustrates a very important feature of the relationship between governments and airlines—that many governments seem committed to maintaining an airline as a "national carrier", and that they will use taxpayers' money where necessary to ensure their airline's survival.

"State Aid"

The question of political support given by governments to airlines in the form of subsidies has been a controversial one in recent years.

Following on from the events of September 11, 2001, many governments paid compensation to airlines for the losses incurred during the four days after the attacks when United States airspace was closed to all commercial airliners. However, the US government's attitude regarding aid to the American airline industry went very much further than this. Large direct subsidies were paid to all the US major carriers. These were intended to cover not only the immediate losses due to the airspace closure, but also to compensate airlines for the effect of the severe and long-lasting traffic downturn which followed. As a further piece of state aid, US carriers have been offered government loan guarantees of significant value. These have allowed struggling US carriers to borrow money at much lower interest rates than they would otherwise have had to pay.

Given the nature of these arrangements, there have been accusations made in Europe that they have given US carriers a freedom to behave in a cavalier commercial manner.

In Europe, State Aid questions have a much longer history. When agreement was reached to set up the Single Aviation Market of the European Union in 1993, it. was argued—entirely correctly—that government subsidies were incompatible with the concept. It was impossible for competition to take place on a level playing field when some government-owned airlines were receiving subsidies whilst, privately owned carriers were not.

Since then, the European Commission has attempted to police state aid. In doing so, it has followed two principles. Firstly, that when state aid is given to an airline, it should be possible to argue that the government that pays it is conforming to the so-called Economic Market Investor Principle. This means that a credible argument must be made that the government is offering additional equity capital, which a rational private investor would also have been willing to provide. In practice, the interpretation of this Principle has been that any fresh government investment in an airline must be matched by private sector investors on a 50/50 basis.

The other requirement in state aid cases has been that additional state funding must not just be there to fund continuing operating losses. It must provide a breathing space for an airline so carry out much needed reforms so that it will be able to survive in the future without additional government support. The history of Air France illustrates this idea. The airline received very large injections of new equity from the French government during the middle 1990s on a "one last time" basis. Within a few years, the airline had emerged much stronger, and in recent times has been one of the more successful of the older-established European carriers.

The market downturn in 2000 and 2001 and especially the after-effects of September 11 2001 brought the question of state aid for European Union carriers into sharp focus once again. In the aftermath of September 11, one European Union airline—Sabena of Belgium—collapsed because it was not possible under the rules for the Belgian government bail it out to the extent that would have been necessary to ensure its survival. Several others—notably TAP Portugal and Olympic—may find such survival difficult or impossible given the combination of economic circumstances and increasing competition which confronts them, and the non-availability of further support from taxpayers.

Airport Slot Allocation

The schedule that an airline offers will clearly be one of the cornerstones of the product that it offers. In turn, it will be the question—clearly a political one—of the ways in which airport slots are allocated which will decide on the schedule which can be planned, both in terms of the frequency of flights and their timings. At the time of writing, slot allocation is both complex and controversial.

The difficulties begin with the apparently straightforward question of agreeing what a slot is. A slot can be defined as "a pre-agreed time for a takeoff or landing to take place at a particular airport". This hides, though, a number of complexities. For a landing slot to have meaning, four different capacity constraints must be satisfied. Firstly, there must be capacity in the air traffic control system, to allow the aircraft to approach the destination airport. Runway space must be available, to permit the aircraft to land. There must be parking and apron space, so that turnaround procedures can be completed. Finally, terminal-processing capacity must be sufficient to enable passengers to pass through immigration and collect their bags in reasonable time.

Of course, for a departure, these capacity requirements must be satisfied in reverse. Also, for a departure slot to have meaning, the relevant arrival slot at the destination airport must be obtained, as must a further departure slot for the return journey once turnaround procedures have been completed.

All this brings us to the question of the methods by which slots at airports are awarded. It might be assumed that because airport operators are responsible for the provision of the terminal, apron and runway capacity which allow slots to exist, they will also be able to decide which airlines use these slots. This is not the case. The only role of the airport operator is to define (in liaison, of course, with the relevant air traffic control authority), the maximum capacity of a given airport. In this way, the number of slots available for distribution is decided.

Once it has been, the actual distribution of slots is carried out by a "Slot Co-coordinator". In the past, it has been traditional for the largest airline operator at a particular airport to carry out the slot co-ordination function. This is still the situation that prevails at many airports today. It is, though, a totally unsatisfactory one. It reflects a past time when slot allocation was essentially an administrative function, where there were generally plenty of slots available in relation to the demand for them. Today, the situation could not be more different, with many airports suffering from a shortage of peak-time slots and some, such as London's Heathrow, virtually full throughout the day. The pressure is on for slot coordination to be carried out by more neutral and transparent bodies, and at many European airports in particular, multi-owned airline consortia have been set up to co-ordinate airport slot allocation. In the UK, the company that does this is called Airport Co-ordination Ltd. It is a consortium owned by a total of 13 different airlines.

Whatever system is adopted to allocate slots, the fundamental principle which should be followed is not in doubt. Slot Co-coordinators are required to award slots under what is known as the "Grandfather Rights" concept. The year is divided into two traffic seasons, "Summer" (in the Northern Hemisphere) from 1 April to 31 October, and "Winter" from 1 November to 31 March. Slots are awarded separately for each season, reflecting different demand patterns.

Once an airline has been awarded a slot, the requirement is that they should use it on a minimum of 80% of the occasions when it is available to them during the season in question. Provided that they do, they will automatically receive the same slot for the next equivalent season. As reputable airlines normally have no difficulty in meeting the 80% rule, it effectively means that slots are awarded to them on an "in perpetuity" basis. It should also be noted that no payment is made following an initial award of a slot. They have been given away free of charge.

The Grandfather rights principle has many defenders, particularly, as one would expect, from the long-established airlines who benefit most from it. These carriers argue that airlines have a particularly long planning cycle. Once an order for new aircraft has been placed with a manufacturer, two or three years may elapse before the aircraft are actually delivered (at least at times of buoyant demand). Once they have been, modern aircraft may stay in an airline's fleet for a period of 25-28 years. It would be impossible (so the argument goes), to justify risking shareholders' funds on such costly assets, if it was feared that the most crucial requirement of all needed to allow the asset to produce profits for shareholders—the airport slot—could be taken away before the completion of the full operating life of the aircraft.

Though such arguments are powerful ones, they do not, of course, represent the only point-of-view. It is possible to say that Grandfather Rights represent a major distortion of competition in the industry. This is because they give opportunity to long-established (and perhaps undeserving) airlines, and deny such opportunity for fresh, innovative carriers, who might be able to deliver substantially better value-for-money to consumers.

Because of these criticisms, a great deal of thought has been given to the question of alternatives to Grandfather Rights in recent years, particularly by the European Commission. There is, however, little progress to report. An initial Directive on Slot Allocation was adopted by the European Union as long ago as 1993. This was intended to cover a three-year period, to allow time for a final Directive to be agreed. At the time of writing in the summer of 2003, no new agreement is in place and attempts continue, to secure a consensus on what it should contain.

There has, however, been one major recent development in slot allocation principles. In 1999, the High Court in the UK gave what has turned out to be a historic judgement about the question of the buying and selling of slots. It has always been possible for airlines to barter the slots on which they hold Grandfather Rights. The 1999 judgement confirmed the legality of taking this one step further, by an airline with a less attractive slot time being able to pay money to another carrier with a more attractive time, to encourage the second airline to undertake a slot exchange.

This judgement has been taken by airlines, within the European Union at least, as a green light to openly buy and sell slots (there can be little doubt that such activity had been taking place on an under-the-counter basis for several years beforehand).

The open buying and selling of slots is being accompanied by yet more controversy. It amounts to the shareholders of airlines benefiting from the sale of assets which they certainly do not own, and which were originally given to them for nothing. It could be argued that airport operators should gain from the sale of the slots that they have created. More convincingly, it could be said that airport slots should be regarded as a national asset. If they are, the proceeds of any sales could go to the government and through. this, hopefully, benefit everyone. This is exactly the policy that many governments have adopted in selling off third generation mobile phone licenses.

The other risk with the buying and selling of slots is that a greater and greater proportion of the available slots will come into the hands of a small number of giant airlines. We already have a situation today where at many hub airports, a high proportion of the slots are held by just one airline. This is the case, for example, with Lufthansa at Frankfurt, Air France at Paris, KLM at Schiphol and (admittedly, to a lesser degree) British Airways at London Heathrow. It is highly likely that, in the future, these airlines will be able to outbid smaller, new entrant carriers for any slots that do become available. If they can, they will be able to further cement their dominance of these major airports, to the detriment of competition and the consumer interest.

Despite these concerns, the movement towards a slot allocation system based on the buying and selling of slots, and with airlines pocketing the money from the slots whose Grandfather Rights they sell, now appears unstoppable. In marketing terms, this will undoubtedly give opportunities for airlines to grow their route networks and increase frequencies which would not have been possible had the old, purely administrative system for slot allocation continued. However, these possibilities will be bought at a high price.

Economic Factors

If there is a clear and important interplay between the world of politics and airline marketing, there is a relationship of equal or even greater importance with economic change and development.

Economic Growth and the Trade Cycle

The demand for air travel is characterized by a very high income elasticity. Therefore, as the world economy grows, so the demand for air travel can be expected to increase too.

This continuing growth gives both enormous opportunities and great challenges to the airline industry. The opportunities come with the chance to exploit a growing market, something which would be the envy of managers in many other industries. The challenges are to accommodate the growth through suitable infrastructure development and without unacceptable environmental consequences and to exploit the demand whilst achieving the stable profits which the industry has so often found elusive.

Besides a clear pattern of growth, growth rates are uneven through time. Just as one would expect, air transport industry growth rates are tied closely to those in the world economy. If growth in the economy is rapid in a particular year, so is the increase in air travel demand. Periods of economic stagnation see a significant slowing of the rate of increase in demand.

This pattern has immense strategic and marketing implications. It is not sufficient for carriers to implement policies which allow for profits during prosperous periods if these same policies result in heavy losses or bankruptcy during the downturns in the trade cycle.

Unfortunately, the industry's past record is not encouraging. Too often, periods of buoyant demand have seen airlines over-invest in additional capacity. They have also commonly given too much emphasis to the First and Business Class market, a market which tends to be very strong when times are good, but which suffers particularly severely during a downturn when firms require their executives to travel in Economy/Coach Class to save money. A final problem often is that in upswing periods, insufficient attention may be given to the control of costs, particularly labour costs. Pay increases that can easily be financed in good times may turn out to be a crippling burden when in a downturn, yields are forced down because of an overcapacity situation, to levels which do not allow costs to be covered.

The upswing of the middle and late 1990s illustrated all these shortcomings. Large orders for new aircraft were placed with the aircraft manufacturers, with many of these planes actually delivered in 2000 and 200 I" when market conditions were much less favorable. Labor costs were allowed to rise, with some airlines—notably so United Airlines–leading the industry by granting unprecedented increases in wages and salaries to a number of their work groups. Finally, some airlines changed their entire business strategy during 1997 and 1998, to focus very heavily on the booming market of so-called "Premium" travelers in First and Business Class. The flaws in this strategy became very obvious in 2000 and 2001, when recession ended the growth in this market and made its exceptional growth rates in the late 1990s look very much an aberration, far above any sustainable long-term level. British Airways is an example of an airline that appeared to make this serious strategic mistake.

Since September 11 2001, there has been a tendency to blame the severe financial problems being experienced by many airlines on the New York and Washington terrorist attacks and their aftermath. The impact of these was undoubtedly severe but they merely substantially increased the extent of serious problems which already existed. These problems can be traced to the fundamental error of failure to take adequate account of the trade cycle in setting business and marketing strategies.

Social Factors

Trends in social factors will have widespread consequences for airline marketing—indeed, in some senses, this is the most significant component of the PESTE analysis model as far as marketing policies are concerned.

The Ageing Population

In Europe and North America in particular, the average age of the population is now increasing steadily. Fewer babies are being born, and improving medical provision is allowing more people to live longer. (It should be born in mind, of course, that an ageing population is not yet at all characteristic of most countries in the Third World.)

The ageing of the population has some obvious, and some more subtle implications for airline marketing. Clearly, the product that airlines offer will have to evolve, with more provision being made for disabled passengers and those needing help at airports, and medical care services will have to be improved. There may also be opportunities for specialist brands to be launched, reflecting the needs and aspirations of older people. In the UK, the SAGA brand is already a good example of this.

In terms of subtler changes, the travel industry may have to adjust its promotional policies. In advertising to promote leisure air travel, the industry still overwhelmingly focuses on images of fun-loving younger people. The very fact that such advertising implies that a resort area is likely to be popular with such people is likely to discourage many older people from visiting it.

Changing Family Structures

Just as the population is ageing, so in many Western societies, the traditional structure of the family is also changing. The rise in divorce and an increase in the number of one-parent families are well-established trends, which the travel industry has so far done little to accommodate. Still, holiday brochures overwhelmingly feature on their front cover a "traditional" family of a man, woman and two children. The truth is that there are very important sub-segments to the market, such as those consisting of singles, gays or one-parent families, whose particular requirements from a holiday should be reflected in promotional and product-planning policies.

Changing Tastes and Fashions in Holidays

Partly, but not exclusively, reflecting trends in age and family structures, the modern travel industry is having to adjust to a marked broadening in the range of requirements of vacationers. When holidays by air first began to become popular in the 1960s, most people wanted little more than a relaxing opportunity to sunbathe by a hotel swimming pool. This is not so today. Better education, growing experience of air travel and fears about the health risks of excessive exposure to the sun are all meaning that to a greater and greater degree, holidays must reflect a lifestyle based on individual choice. People expect to be able to pursue their hobbies while they are on holiday, with skiing, golf, history and trekking holidays all now well-established sub-segments of the market. They expect to be able to take holidays of different lengths in order to fit in with their available vacation time. They also require opportunities to visit new and interesting, often long-haul, destinations.

Overall, the trend in the holiday market is often, and appropriately, described as "repackaging the package". People increasingly want a holiday experience which reflects their own individual requirements. They do not expect to be treated as part of a herd of cattle, to suit the convenience of the travel provider. We shall return to this theme in Chapter Nine, dealing with the subject of Relationship Marketing.

The Uncertain, Deregulated Labor Market

Of all the social trends occurring in the 1980s and 1990s, none was of greater significance than the transformation which took place in the world of work. Before this, in many societies most jobs were seen as being secure for a lifetime. Today, the situation could not be more different. Redundancy and job seeking occurs—perhaps several times—in many people's careers. At the same time, pressures at work are far greater as people battle to keep their jobs, often with far less administrative support than they once had.

The changes in the job market have consequences for airline marketing policies, in both the business travel and leisure travel segments of demand. In business travel, the fact that people are under greater and greater time pressure means that issues such as the ability to make a day-return trip, rather than take two days, is becoming more important still in short-haul markets. On long-haul routes, for many executives, it is now a thing of the past to expect to take a day off on arrival to recover from tiredness and jet lag. They are now expected to arrive at a destination in the morning and step off the plane into a busy day of meetings. This places a premium on their ability to sleep on board the aircraft, and on facilities for them to shower and freshen up on arrival.

More subtly, greater work pressures are changing business travellers' perception of the role of air travel. Many now see a flight as a haven of peace in an otherwise over-demanding schedule. Issues such as in-flight entertainment are thus assuming greater importance.

For those who lose their jobs, or who perhaps voluntarily decide to take a greater control of their lives, self-employment or working for a small, independent firm are often options to be considered. In the UK, the proportion of the working population which is self-employed has more than doubled since 1980.

Self-employment has lead to the emergence of the so-called "Independent" sub-segment of business travel demand, where customer requirements are different from those of the corporate traveler.

The deregulated labour market also has implications for the leisure air travel market. In the 1970s some extravagant, and, with the benefit of hindsight, absurd promises were made that by the 1990s a utopia would have arrived. This was expected to result from the growing automation of industrial processes through the micro-chip, cheap computing power and developments in robotics. The outcome was supposed to be a dream world of increases in leisure time through a shorter day, a shorter working week, longer holidays and earlier, more prosperous retirement.

Now that the 1990s have passed, we can certainly see that the micro-chip has had a dramatic impact, but not in the way these forecasters had predicted. There has certainly been a growth in the aggregate amount of so-called leisure, but this has been unevenly and unsatisfactorily distributed.

For people who have a job, their working lives are now busier than ever before. Working hours are often longer rather than shorter, with working at home commonplace in the evenings and at weekends. Also, whilst holiday entitlements have often risen in principle, many people are reluctant to take their full allowances because of a "presenteeism" philosophy of trying to seem indispensable to the firms that employ them.

At the opposite end of the spectrum, we see people who have large amounts of leisure, but who lack the financial resources to be able to enjoy it to the full. The young unemployed are a clear example of this, as are those who, often despite their qualifications and experience can only find poorly-paid, often part-time work. Particular issues surround those who have retired from work. In the past it has been fashionable to regard the trend towards earlier and earlier retirement as a very positive one from the point-of-view of the airline industry. It would, we were told, result in a larger and larger group of people with both the time and the inclination, to travel by air a great deal. Present trends are sometimes leading to people retiring earlier (often reluctantly, because they cannot find work), and living longer. The result is that a bigger and bigger retired population is relying on a smaller and smaller working one to maintain the value of their post-retirement incomes. Sooner rather than later, it seems inevitable that the trends will reverse, with living standards for the retired population starting to fall. If they do, this will be disappointing rather than encouraging news for air travel demand.

The Female Business Traveler

Until now, the business travel market has been overwhelmingly dominated! by men. In the USA, still more than 80% of business travelers are men whilst in many European countries the percentage is near to 90%.

Today, the role of women in the workplace is changing dramatically in many cultures. It is now usual for women to return to work after childbirth, and to expect to build a career alongside their male colleagues. Because of this, it is certain that the proportion of business travelers who are female will steadily increase. It is expected that a third of the North American business travel market will consist of women by the year 2010.

This is a change which is forcing airlines to re-think a number of components' of their marketing. The most obvious areas are in aspects of product detail. For example, most airlines give toilet bags to their First Class and Business Class travelers. Only recently has it become common for separate bags made up for female as well as male travelers to be offered. Also, it has been shown that women are far more likely than their male colleagues to check in hold baggage, and less likely to carry large amounts of baggage on board on aircraft. Increasingly numbers of female travelers suggest changes in the demands made on baggage handling systems.

More fundamental are issues associated with airline advertising. In the past, much airline advertising has had sexist undertones, with pictures of beautiful young girls ministering to the needs of men. In many cultures, such approaches will be less and less acceptable in the future.

Technological Factors

Video-conferencing

The conclusion reached was that it posed a significant long-term threat. It is unlikely to lead to a decline in the demand for air travel. It will, though, result in future growth rates for business air travel growth which are disappointing by historic standards. Business travel growth will tend to be below the growth rates for GDP rather then above them as has commonly been the case in the past. It will also increase the airline industry's already very substantial vulnerability to downturns in the trade cycle.

Given the nature of the threat, a progressively greater response will be required from airlines in their marketing policies. In terms of the product which is offered to the customer, greater and greater emphasis will be required on convenience to enable business travelers to fly with the minimum impact on their working time, allowing the benefits of a face-to-face meeting to outweigh the time required to travel to such a meeting. Issues such as a high frequency of direct flights with the right timings to allow for day return trips will become still more important.

Airline advertising approaches will also have to change. In the past, most airlines have simply concentrated on promoting the merits of their services against those of rival airlines. In the future, they will have to accept telecommunications companies as being amongst their most formidable competitors. Advertising will be needed which promotes the benefits of face-to-face meetings as opposed to conducting these meetings via video-conferencing.

The Internet

The mid-1990s saw the beginnings of airline interest in the marketing possibilities opened up by the Internet. At the time of writing almost all major airlines have websites which they use for promotional purposes, with these sites supplying timetable and product information and also often having an interactive component which allows people make bookings. Sites are also being used as a way of increasing the attractiveness of an airline's frequent flyer programme by permitting programme members to check on their mileage accounts and also by giving the availability of flights with the surplus seats available for redemption. In the field of air freight, firms such as UPS and Federal Express allow customers to track their consignments as they move through the system using the Internet.

The greatest debates about the future role of the Internet in airline marketing concern its use as a distribution channel. Full attention will be given to the many controversies which currently affect the subject of distribution in the airline industry in Chapter Seven. For the moment though, it is worthwhile to note two issues in particular. Firstly, in recent years airlines have become more and more concerned about the amount of commission they are paying to travel agents and other marketing intermediaries. Secondly, they have had to face the escalating costs associated with the booking fees charged to them by Global Distribution Systems (GDS) companies. Anger at these fees has been especially marked amongst airlines which do not have a shareholding in a GDS, and which do not therefore have the prospect of dividends on their investment compensating them for the booking fees they pay.

The Internet is now alleviating both these problems. If individuals or firms make bookings direct with the airlines through a personal computer, substantial reductions in both commissions and booking fees are now possible.

Surface Transport Investment

Today, many countries have seen a resurgence of interest in surface—especially railway—transport investment. Railway operators have largely won the battle to be viewed as the most environmentally acceptable form of transport. Investment is taking place in both new railways to provide fast city-centre to city-centre links, and in the tunnels to enable railway operators to extend their networks. This investment was especially notable in Europe, where during the 1990s as a whole, investment in railway infrastructure was more than three times as great as that in infrastructure for the aviation industry.

Surface transport investment provides both problems and opportunities in airline marketing. The problems come from the fact that, beyond question, railway investment can have a significant negative impact on the demand for air transport. The evidence from countries such as France, where new railway developments compete alongside formerly busy air routes, is that once rail can offer a city-centre to city-centre journey time of less than three hours, the effect on the air market will be a substantial one. Worse still, the traffic that is lost tends to be the so-called point-to-point demand. Those who have been using air services to connect onto a long-haul flight at a hub will continue to do so. The pricing practices adopted by airlines almost always mean that point-to-point traffic gives a much higher yield in terms of revenue per kilometer than connecting traffic does. The effect on the profitability of an airline's short-haul routes can therefore be even greater than the decline in demand would suggest.

The opportunities provided by surface transport come with the options which it opens up for airlines to co-operate rather than compete, with railway operators. As will be discussed in the next section, the future growth of the airline industry is now being jeopardised by growing shortages of runway and passenger handling capacity. Also, for most airlines, short-haul services tend only to be marginally profitable. The high incidence of fixed costs such as landing fees has always made it difficult to achieve satisfactory profits on these routes. On the other hand, most long-haul routes tend to be more profitable.

The opportunity of surface transport developments is for airlines to lobby for improved public transport links to major airports. If these come about, they will enable train operators to deliver long-haul passengers to airline hubs, thus freeing valuable airport slots for further long-haul services.

Environmental Factors

It might be thought that environmental factors would pose broadly strategic questions for airlines, rather than ones with a specific marketing component to them. However, in a number of areas, environmental issues will affect both the nature and characteristics of airline demand. They will therefore have an impact on marketing activities.

Global Warming

Concerns about global warming are very controversial, with arguments continuing about the likely future extent of the current warming trend and its consequences. It does, though, seem to be a reasonable conclusion that in the future, average temperatures will continue to rise, with warmer climatic zones being progressively displaced towards the Poles.

If this happens, the effect on both the extent and patterns of air transport demand could be a substantial one. For example, in the UK, the summer of

1995 was exceptionally warm and settled. The months of May through to September were characterized by almost unbroken hot, sunny weather. Though welcome no doubt to many British people, this turned out to be unhelpful to the air transport industry. In 1995, demand for air-based packaged holidays to Mediterranean resorts fell by nearly 10%. It was widely assumed that this was because many people who had left booking their holiday to the last minute (a trend increasingly characteristic of the market generally) decided to take a holiday at home instead of enduring the sometimes doubtful pleasures of a long flight by air.

Shortages of Infrastructure Capacity

Over the last three decades, the airline industry has made important progress in ensuring that its activities have become more environmentally acceptable. In particular, aircraft have become very much quieter during this time. Unfortunately, the result has not been an easing of the environmental pressures opposing aviation infrastructure investment. The lobby groups responsible for these pressures have become more vociferous and better organized. At the same time, the issue of atmospheric pollution has arisen alongside that of noise pollution and threatens soon to supersede it in importance.

The result of these pressures is that it is not possible, and probably never will be possible, for the aviation industry's infrastructure to be expanded at the pace, and in the locations, that airlines would ideally like. This may mean that some of the industry's growth plans cannot be brought to fruition. In many other cases, compromise and adaptation will be necessary in the face of growing shortages of infrastructure capacity.

"Tourism Saturation"

All tourism receiving areas have a finite capacity. This may be due to factors such as the limited amount of accommodation that can be provided. More importantly, though, over-exploitation of a tourism area can mean that the reasons for people going there are often destroyed. These reasons may include prestige and status through the exclusivity of a resort, natural resources such as wildlife, or un-crowded access to sites of historic importance.

The so-called "Tourism Saturation" effects of over-exploitation may not affect the total amount of air travel undertaken for leisure purposes. They will, though, have a substantial effect on its geographical distribution, and provide a challenge for all managers of resort areas.

Overall, the marketing environment of the airline industry provides a crucial background against which airline managers must develop their marketing policies. These policies clearly cannot be formulated in isolation. Instead, they must reflect the background factors illustrated by the PESTE analysis model.

AIRLINE CUSTOMER

Who is the "Customer"?

We now turn to the task of addressing one of the most fundamental and commonest mistakes made in airline marketing—failure to make a proper distinction between the "consumer" and the "customer."

To begin with definitions, "consumers" are those people who actually travel. They are therefore easy to identify and analyze. They make their existence clear by reporting for fights and their requirements and preferences can be analyzed using questionnaires. They are therefore usually given a great deal of attention by marketers in the airline business. Unfortunately they may not be decision-makers are defined as "Customers".

There are at least four customer decisions which must be analyzed:

1. Will a trip be made at all? For many firms today the cost of travel is a major item of corporate expense. In a recessionary period, firms will attempts to reduce expenditure in order to minimize the effect recession on corporate profitability, or in extreme case s, to stave off bankruptcy. In business trip should be undertaken, only to find that the necessary expenditure is not sanctioned. Instead they are told to use, say, the phone email or video-conferencing as away of conducting the business in question. In such a situation the true customer for the airlines might be the firm's CEO or VP-Finance.

2. What mode of transport will be selected? As we mentioned in the least section, it is likely that the future will be see a significant increase inn the amount completion that airline face from surface transport operators, especially railways. On short-haul routes railways are capable of giving superior door-to-door journey times and, arguably, a better quality of service than the airlines. Carriers will face a significant challenge for the business travel policies in order to minimize the adverse effect on their traffic.

For leisure travelers, the impact of surface transport competition to be even greater. Besides competition of service quality surface operators will be able to challenge airlines on price, with both train and bus services likely to become increasingly significant. The "customer" in such a situation might be the family member who has most influence in travel decisions.

3. *For air trips, what class of service will be purchased?* With many airlines passengers have a choice of flying first Class (at least on long-haul routes), business travel Market, the person who travels will have little or no say in the decision as to which class will be purchased. Almost all firms have a corporate travel policy whereby very senior executives are allowed to travel First Class, those of middle rank in Business Class, whilst junior. Interestingly during recessionary periods periods almost al firms have have downgurding policy in order to save money with, in particular much First Class and Business Class travel being eliminated.

In order to maximize the amount of high yielding traffic available to them, carriers will have to target those who make decisions about corporate travel policies. They will in particular have to persude these people that the benefits of buying travel in the premium cabins of the aircraft—for example that this cabins allow better opportunities for rest or work-outweigh the very substantially higher prices that are charged for access to them.

4. Which airline will be selected? It has been agreed that a particular journey will be made by air, the question of the choice of airline is obviously a crucial one. In the past, many business travelers did have the choice to make this decision themselves. It was a major trend of the 1990s that this became so in fewer cases. During that time more and more companies centralized travels purchasing in order to gain access to corporate discounts from airlines. Such policies narrowed the choice which the individual traveler could exercise, even if they were not restricted to using a single airline.

In leisure travel, the market is still largely a wholesale one. Many airlines still confine themselves to selling blocks of seats to tour operators and consolidators. The individuals who travel will therefore have very little say in the airline lines that they fly with.

Given the importance of these four decisions, there is a crucial need to take account of them properly if effective marketing policies are to be established. In particular the mistakes of assuming that the "customer" is the same person who boards the aircraft must be avoided.

Having just described "customer focus" as the essence of modem marketing, it is time for us to focus on some underlying aspects of customer behavior. We need to explore the following areas to provide you with the fundamental concepts necessary for a more sound understanding later on in this book, and in your airline careers.

- Defining the customer
- Consumer motivation
- The customer's decision-making roles and processes

In looking at any market, the most fundamental distinction to make is between "customers" and "prospects". A customer is defined as someone who has already made a purchase from your organization, whereas a prospect is someone who buys this product or service from someone else, and might make such a purchase from you in the future your customers are therefore counted as prospects by your competitors, while their customers are your prospects.

All customers and prospects are not the same. One simple classification of behavioral types is as follows:

- "Cold prospect": someone in your market with whom you have had no previous contact.
- "Warm prospect": someone with whom you have had previous contact indicating a possible future purchase.
- "First-time customer": someone who is buying from you for the first time.

- "Repeat customer": someone who is buying from you for the second time.
- "Regular customer": someone who buys from you frequently.
- "Solus customer" or "loyalist": someone who only buys from you.
- "Advocate": someone who recommends you to others on the basis of their experience of using your product or service.

This simple classification is very useful for guiding marketing action. Consider for a moment any two types, for example "warm prospect" and "repeat customer"; clearly, you would need to treat these two groups differently when marketing your product or service for reasons such as the following:

- Warm prospects have no experience of your product or service, and you would need to give them basic information about it that repeat customers would not require in order to make a purchase
- Your objective with repeat customers should be to encourage them to continue buying from you; this objective is premature for warm prospects

Consumer Behaviour

It involves the psychological processes that consumers go through in recognizing needs, finding ways to solve these needs, making purchase decisions (e.g., whether or not to purchase a product and, if so, which brand and where), interpret information, make plans, and implement these plans (e.g., by engaging in comparison shopping or actually purchasing a product).

Customer Decision-making Roles and Processes

One model of consumer decision making involves several steps. (See Fig. 4) The first one is *problem recognition*—you realize that something is not as it should be. Perhaps, for example, your car is getting more difficult to start and is not accelerating well. The second step *is information search*—what are some alternative ways of solving the problem? You might buy a new car, buy a used car, take your car in for repair, ride the bus, ride a taxi, or ride a skateboard to work. The third step involves *evaluation of alternatives.* A skateboard is inexpensive, but may be ill-suited for long distances and for rainy days. Finally, we have the *purchase* stage, and sometimes a post-purchase stage (e.g., you return a product to the store because you did not find it satisfactory). In reality, people may go back and forth between the stages. For example, a person may resume alternative identification during while evaluating already known alternatives.

Consumer *involvement* will tend to vary dramatically depending on the type of product. In general, consumer involvement will be higher for products that are very expensive (e.g., a home, a car) or are highly significant in the consumer's life in some other way (e.g., a word processing program).

It is important to consider the consumer's motivation for buying products. To achieve this goal, we can use the Means-End chain, wherein we consider a logical progression of consequences of product use that eventually lead to desired end benefit. Thus, for example, a consumer may see that a car has a large engine, leading to fast acceleration, leading to a feeling of performance, leading to a feeling of power, which ultimately improves the consumer's self-esteem. A handgun may aim bullets with precision, which enables the user to kill an intruder, which means that the intruder will not be able to harm the consumer's family, which achieves the desired end-state of security. In advertising, it is important to portray the desired end-states. Focusing on the large motor will do less good than portraying a successful person driving the car.

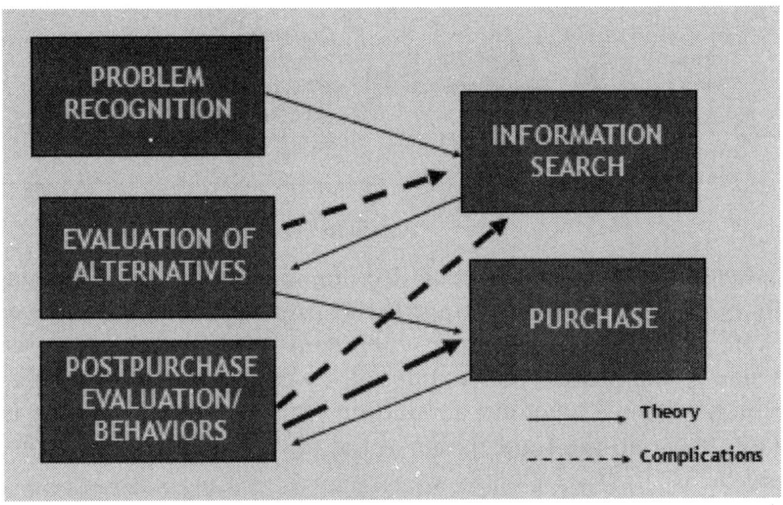

Fig. 4

Think about your office environment; let's book a ticket, for example an airline ticket. Most of the people are traveling and are booking their tickets, and it will be one that someone else chose, and perhaps a purchase that someone else approved. In other words, the person who wants to travel, the person who book the ticket, and the person who approved the travelling are different people. This illustrates three of the major roles in a decision-making process:

- "Specifier": the person or group of people who decide to pick a particular organization to deliver a product or service
- "User": the person or group of people who use or consume that product or service.
- "Influencer": the person or group that influences or approves the purchase. A travel agent or company controller, for example.

In the airline business, the traveler often performs all of these roles. This is certainly true for most leisure travel.

However, a company may specify that its staff cannot fly First Class on business, meaning that the company concerned is making at least one decision about purchasing air travel. The same company mayor may not specify which airline(s) can be used for business flights,

Indeed in most cases this decision is left to the traveler or user. Knowing who the decision-maker is will be crucial for successful Marketing; for example, there is little point in trying to persuade the users of airline services to fly First Class in a company that does not permit this!

It is also important to understand the decision-making process that leads to the purchase of air travel. Let us consider a holiday trip; a simple decision-making process for such a trip may look something like in Fig. 5:

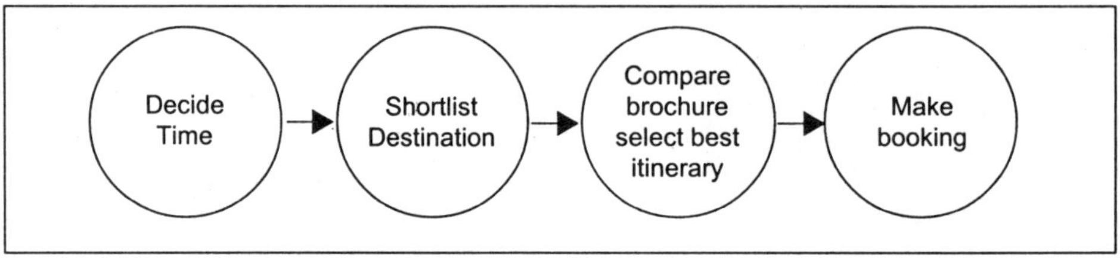

Fig. 5

Knowing the nature of customer decision-making processes is a major step towards more effective Marketing; for example, promoting your airline's holiday destinations will be ideal when consumers are about to reach the second step in the process above, but will be much less effective afterwards. Successful Marketing is not just about doing the right things. Timing is just as important. If we do the right things at the right time then success is almost guaranteed.

Consumer Motivation

As we have seen, marketing is primarily about *satisfying customer's needs and wants* with products and services. Consumer motivation is based on these "needs" and "wants", and we therefore "need" to understand them!

Customer Needs—"Apparent" and "True Needs"

In analyzing customer decision-making, all firms need to understand the factors that their customers take into account in making up their minds. In order to do so, the obvious method is to ask them to describe the factors in a properly constructed and administered market research survey.

The problem for the analyst is that what people say may not be the truth. Rather, it may perhaps reflect what they regard as an acceptable answer, rather than an accurate description of the factors they really take into account. This difference between the claim and the truth is known in marketing as the difference between "Apparent" and "True" needs.

To illustrate the point, a corporate business travelers asked to describe the factors that they take into account kin choosing their airline might give a series of responsible answers, all reflecting the service features which permitted them to use their time as effectively as possible up their employer's interest. If they did, issues such as flight frequency (to allow for travel flexibility), punctuality and a roomy cabin (to permit working during flight) might figure prominently. The truth might be rather different. Today many business travelers base their choice of airline decisions on their wish to support an airline on as many occasions as possible because this will maximize the personal benefits available to them (bought using their employer's money) through that airline's frequent flyer programme. This benefits will of course, feed the true need of greed.

As anther example, almost all airlines attempting to exploit the business travel market that, in order to do so, they must pander to the pride and ego of those who fly. Such features as separate reservations phone lines, a separate check-in-desk (ideally with a piece of red carpet in front of it) and separate cabins ion board the aircraft do, admittedly, sometimes have a practical purpose, of allowing the business traveler access to business benefits. However, of equal or probably greater, importance is that they massage the travelers ego.

"True needs" is marketing can cover other aspects as well. Some customers might, for example, be lazy and prefer to keep purchasing from an existing supplier rather than make the effort to change even if such a change might result in better value for money. Others might be better but which also might go disastrously wrong.

"True needs" are at the heart of successful marketing. In many ways they reflect the weakness of the human personality. They are also relatively constant in their importance through time. No-one who is concerned to make a success of an airline's marketing activities should make the mistake of assuming that a declared customer requirements actually a true description of what is motivating purchasing decisions.

Essentially, a need is a person's conscious feeling of deprivation. In other words, it is something that a customer requires in order to experience satisfaction. For example, in the case of a business air traveler, the reliability and convenience of a service are good examples of what constitutes key needs. An airline failing to provide a high standard of reliability and convenience would lose this business traveler to its competitors.

Customer Wants

A want is a need after culture, society and an individual's personality, have influenced it. There are two kinds of wants: a tangible want and a psychological want a tangible want may be to have familiar food available when you travel, and a psychological want could be to be able to communicate in your own language when travelling.

An airline that therefore offers its Japanese customers the option of Japanese cuisine on its flights and provides cabin crew who can speak Japanese is catering for the tangible and psychological wants of these customers. The airline is satisfying the tangible want for a particular type of food and the psychological want for ease of communication.

In the diagram overleaf, we can see the different needs of an airline's business and leisure travelers. We will see later how we use these different sets of needs to identify and develop groups of travelers called segments.

Short-Haul Business-Travellers	Long-Haul Business-Travellers	Leisure Travellers
1. Safety	1. Safety	1. Safety
2. Punctuality	2. Comfort	2. Price
3. Convenience	3. Punctuality	3. Culture Comfort
4. Price	4. Convenience	4. In-flight Service
5. Comfort	5. In-flight Service	5. Punctuality
6. In-flight Service	6. Loyalty Schemes	6. Loyalty Schemes
7. Loyalty Schemes	7. Facilities	7. Convenience

Fig. 6

In summary, the distinction between needs and wants is that a "need" is something a customer requires, whereas a "want" is something a customer *desires*. In light of the many different types of travelers that airlines carry on any given day, they must be able to distinguish between needs and wants and how they affect purchase decisions. As we will learn later, this crucial theme of satisfying needs and wants will become a cornerstone for our marketing strategies and plans that we develop throughout this module.

The customer in the Business Air Travel Market

It is hoped that enough has been said to show that that correctly identifying and targeting "Customer" rather than mere "Consumers" is cornerstone of successful marketing in the airline industry. This lead to the question of the identify of different customers and their "True" needs which should be taken into account in order to ensure accurate targeting.

We have already seen that, in the business travel market there will still be occasions when the person who travels has an absolute right to select the airline they will fly with. For example someone running their own small business will presumably have this right, whilst even in large corporations there are still cases where companies leave these choices to individuals.

Even where someone is able to claim that they have the right to choose the airline they fly with themselves, it may not actually be the case that they exercise this choice. For example, a busy business executive might trust their secretary to select airlines, and make the necessary bookings. There can be no doubt that executive secretaries make up an important group of "customers" in the business air travel market.

In making a choice-of-airline decision, a secretary will presumably not select an airline which they know their boss hates. They will also dke account of requirements such as preferred departure airport, flight timings etc. However, from the point-of-view of airline marketing, there will presumably be occasions where two or more airlines both have a sound reputation, and offer an equivalent product in terms of timings. Here, the secretary will be able to exercise choice. As with all marketing decisions, they will have a set of true needs which must be understood. For example, they will have understandable preference for the easy solution. It is unlikely that they will be prepared to wait for twenty minutes for an airline reservations department to answer the phone, when they know from experience that its rival will always respond instantly. They will also get to know which airline is pleasant to deal with in tenns of a wann and caring attitude from its customer contact staff.

Secretaries will also often have a true need of greed, in that they may well prefer to deal with airlines that offer them an incentive. Thus many airlines have clubs for executive secretaries which provides a database to allow them to target secretaries with offers of corporate entertainment and discounted travel in return for loyalty.

Another example of a possible customer in the business travel market is the travel agent. A business traveller may have the right to choose the airline they fly with themselves, but may leave the choice to their travel agent on the grounds that, perhaps, they are too busy to worry or that they regard the travel agent as an expert whose advice they should accept.

The role of the travel agent is a controversial one in airline marketing and there will be repeated references to it throughout the book. It is easy to isolate the proportion of bookings which come through agents today. In many markets, still something over 80% of the bookings that traditional airlines receive come through agents. In tenns of the subject of this section of the book, though, this does not mean that the travel agent is necessarily a "customer" for them on such a high proportion of occasions. If someone specifies to the agent that one particular airline is the only one that is acceptable to them, the agent does not make a choice as a customer, they merely take an order. The agent is a customer, though, in any situation where, as described above, the person who travels leaves the choice-of-airline decision to them.

In terms of true needs, senior agency managers will be motivated by greed, in that they will be predisposed to recommend the airline offering the highest rates of commission. They do not have complete freedom to merely consider commissions, because if they recommend airlines that the person who travels finds unacceptable they run the risk that they will lose the account to a rival, and presumably more trustworthy, agency. There are, though, now a good number of respectable airlines where a recommendation for one giving better commissions would not arouse Suspicion.

In the world of travel agency operations, airlines also have to take account of another set of customers. There are the travel clerks who actually make bookings and issue tickets. Generally, senior agency managers do not carry out this work. Equally, they rarely pass on to their staff the financial benefits of additional commission payments. In many countries, travel agency staff are poorly rewarded financially. Because of this, travel agency clerks often have true needs similar to those noted above for executive secretaries. They will prefer airlines that are easy and convenient to contact. They will also welcome the offer of incentives—particularly free travel opportunities on so-called educational or familiarisation visits arranged by airlines.

The final example of a "customer" in the business air travel market has I already been referred to in the last section. This is where a firm appoints someone to be responsible for corporate dealing with carriers. Under such an arrangement, freedom-of-action will be denied to the executives who actually fly. Instead, they will be required to choose from one or a small number of airlines. In turn carriers will be approached to offer substantial discounts in order to be one of the favoured airlines. In a large organisation, the management of business travel might be given to one executive with a job title such as Corporate Travel Manager. In a smaller one, it might be a task carried out by a senior manager from the Finance or Purchasing department.

As we have discussed, the growth of corporate dealing was one of the major trends in business air travel marketing during the 1990s. The years of severe recession from 1991-94 in particular saw firms attempting to reduce their costs. Rationalising the purchase of business air travel was a significant way in which many attempted to do so. Renewed recessionary conditions from 1999-2003 again saw severe pressure being placed on travel budgets in many markets.

Today, the question of correctly identifying and targeting "customers" in the business air travel market is a vital one for airlines, and one that is causing increasing controversy. The problem is that it is very difficult to be certain exactly who is making the relevant decision. The normal expedient adopted by many airlines of simply asking the person who flies the question as to who was responsible for their choice-of-airline decision is unlikely to yield much enlightenment, striking as is does at the heart of questions about corporate status and privilege.

Because of this difficulty, many airlines today follow the policy of incentivising everyone, whether or not the person in question is actually able to influence the amount of business obtained. Thus, today almost all airlines offer individual travellers incentives through a frequent flyer programme. They may also give the firms that these people work for substantial corporate discounts. Finally, the travel agents that these firms use are still sometimes incentivised through the offer of override commissions, though the extent of this practice has declined in recent years.

The results of such profligacy is that selling costs have been the fastest rising cost of doing business for many traditional airlines. Indeed, the escalation of such costs has stood in sharp contrast to carriers' success in reducing many other costs. It will be a major challenge in the future to better identify "customers" and to ensure that promotional spending is more effectively targeted. This is especially so because it is a mistake many of the newer "Cost Leader" airlines have avoided.

The "Customer" in the Leisure Air Travel Market

Identifying the "customer" is just as difficult, and just as important, in the leisure air travel market. when airlines are bidding for business f om the holiday or vacation traveller, they are competing for the person's disposable time and disposable income. They must also ensure that, if it is decided to spend time and money on a holiday, an air-based vacation will be selected. The airline must then ensure that the holiday is taken at a destination which it serves, and that people travel to the destination on its flights, rather than on those of a rival carrier.

In analysing this complex set of decisions, it should first of all be born in mind that a great deal of holiday travel is undertaken in family groups. The question of how travel decisions are made within the family is thus a crucial one which should, for example, decide the creative content of advertising and promotional work, and the media buying decisions which are made.

Within the family, children can have an important influence on travel buying decisions made by their parents. For very young children, parents may deliberately choose an airline where they believe that facilities available for the care of babies are good. For older children, such factors as the availability of video games in an airline's in-flight entertainment system might be significant. For older children too, the choice of vacation destination may be made by their parents, but parents will take into account their children's preferences.

This is something which is has been recognised in the creative strategies adopted by a number of vacation destinations, such as Disney resorts, in their advertising.

It is also a crucial issue as to whether or not men or women have a greater influence on holiday decision-making. Here, cultural influences assume great importance. Some societies are traditionally matriarchal, where women are dominant in family life. Others are patriarchal, where men dominate. In the UK, it is recognised that women are extremely. influential in holiday planning, and the creative strategies adopted by airlines and tour operators increasingly reflect this.

With other possible "customers" in the leisure air travel market, it must be recognised that the travel agent is important, being in fact more sc than is the case for business travel. In the leisure market, the question of the destination for a vacation is a significant one, where people will often accept the advice of their travel agent. Of course, with business air travel the destination will have been decided prior to contact with the agent.

Another difference between business and leisure travel market is that, the business travel market is a concentrated one. It consists of a relatively small number of people who each travel a great deal. Indeed, the average number of air trips made per year by a business traveller averages more than ten in many markets. The leisure market, on the other hand, has far fewer frequent travellers. Some leisure travellers are making their only trip of a lifetime. Many more take only one air trip a year, for their annual holiday. Given, therefore, that they are relatively inexperienced, they may have to turn to someone for advice on such aspects as the making of bookings, visa applications etc. The natural place for them to look is to their travel agent. The result is that it is possible to argue about the importance of the travel agent as a "customer" for airlines in the business travel market. No such argument should occur with leisure travel. Travel agents are extremely important, and airlines must cultivate their loyalty if they are to obtain a proper share of this market. They will do so through the traditional so-called offline agents, but will increasingly have to sell over the Internet to the rapidly developing on-line travel agency industry.

A further feature of the leisure market as far as airlines are concerned is that, it is largely a wholesale market. Few airlines have a substantial retail presence in the leisure market. Instead they rely on wholesaling blocks of seats to organisations known generically as tour operators (or travel organisers) and "consolidators".

The difference between a tour operator and a consolidator is becoming more and more difficult to define, given that many firms now combine both functions. In principle, though, the difference is that the tour operators are value-adders, in the sense that they take airline seats, accommodation, surface transfers and add-ons such as tours, sports opportunities etc to make up packaged holidays. A "consolidator" is simply a dealer in discounted air tickets. More popularly known as "bucket shops", they provide an outlet whereby airlines can wholesale blocks of seats for a very low cost-of-sale. The problem, of course, is that because of the consolidators' bargaining power, prices and yields can be extremely low.

In targeting the leisure air traveller, airlines must regard the senior managers and product managers of major tour operators as very important customers. They will have no hope of success in this market unless they can persuade tour operators to feature the destinations they serve in their brochures, and, when they do, to buy their seats to serve these destinations from the airline in question.

With the role of the consolidator, airlines have difficult decisions to make. Reliance on consolidators as a significant channel of distribution, will result in a straightforward selling task, in that an airline will be able to act purely as a wholesaler. There is a grave risk though, of the carrier losing control of its distribution channels, with potentially disastrous financial consequences. If, though, a decision is made to make significant use of the consolidator channel, then the owners of the major consolidators must be regarded as highly significant "customers."

The "Customer" in the Air Freight Market

The focus of this book is mainly on the passenger side of the airline business. A full study of the application of marketing principles to the air freight business is available elsewhere.5 It is nonetheless important that everyone who works for an airline should have an understanding of the air freight business, because the nature of the airline industry is such that frequent liaison will be necessary between passenger and freight departments. Air freight also gives another excellent illustration of the ways in which the application of marketing principles can make the difference between success and failure. No apology is therefore made for the inclusion of coverage of the air freight industry in this book.

In looking at the question of the "customer" in the air freight market, it should first of all be born in mind that there are marked differences between the passenger and freight businesses.

In air freight, marketing intermediaries known as air freight forwarders are extremely important to most airlines. Few carriers have a significant commitment to retail marketing. Instead, more than 90% of their traffic is typically provided by forwarders. There is every possible reason to regard the forwarder as a significant customer, more important still than the travel agent on the passenger side of the business. There seems to be a much greater degree of willingness on the part of freight customers to allow forwarders to make routing and carrier selection decisions than is the case with travel agents. Also, a considerable proportion of air freight traffic is sent under the "consolidation" principle. Here, a forwarder will gather together a large number of small packages from individual shippers and present them to the airline as one large consignment. In return, the airline charges a much lower rate per kilo, and the forwarder passes on some of this saving to the shippers who generate the small consignments.

By definition, when shippers allow their consignments to be sent as part of a consolidation, they are accepting that they will have no right to decide the airline that will be used to carry them. Instead, the decision as to which carrier will be given the traffic will be made by the senior management of the air freight forwarder, and all airlines must regard such managers as "customers."

In the individual shipment, non-consolidated market, airlines will have another set of customers—the clerks who work for freight forwarding companies. A great deal of air freight moves at night, and is dealt with by an army of shift-working clerks. A considerable proportion of air freight moves as emergency shipments with no prior notice of the need to move goods being possible. In such a situation, routeing and carrier selection decisions will be made by clerks, late at night, when the senior managers of a forwarder are at home in bed. Airlines therefore have the task of building and maintaining a relationship with forwarder clerks as a significant customer group.

As has been noted above, many airlines only attempt to market their air freight services through air freight forwarders. For those that try and do more than this, a very much broader base of "customers" appears.

It should first of all be born in mind that in air freight there is a true "retail" market of non-expert users. For example, a secretary may find that their boss tells them to send a small, urgent package of papers or samples. It is a major success of the so-called "Integrators" that they have been able to simplify their processes to such an extent, and to design and administer a retail marketing organisation, so that their services are easily accessible to all customers.

A way from the small shipment market, a limited number of airlines (notably, at the time of writing, KLM) have taken this retail marketing philosophy in another direction, in that they have chosen to deal with the firms who produce freight, rather than merely rely on traffic offered to them by air freight forwarders. To say that such policies have proved controversial would be an understatement. For the moment, though, it is important to note that such a strategy requires a completely different view to be taken regarding the identity of the "customer".

In bidding for business from the true originators of traffic, airlines will be facing two different situations. Firstly, they will have to attempt to obtain a good share of existing air freight flows. In order to do so, they will normally contact the Shipping Manager or some similarly-titled executive. Whether the correct person to approach is with the exporting firm or with the firm carrying out the importing activity will depend on the terms of trade under which a consignment is moving. Secondly, any cargo-orientate airline will also need to develop new air freight traffic by arguing that firms should use air freight in order to exploit new marketing opportunities, or to improve on the efficiency of existing logistics systems based on surface transport.

The exact arguments which should be used to do so are complex ones for the moment, though, it should be noted that air freight can only be justified as part of a logistics philosophy in which higher transport expenses are traded off against cost savings and marketing benefits achieved elsewhere. In most firms, Shipping Managers are comparatively junior executives who do not have the authority to make these tradeoffs as they have no say over issues such as inventory and warehousing policy. In order to achieve a favourable outcome, airline salespeople will often need to target their message at a much higher level in the management hierarchy. In some firms, the Managing Director or President will be the right person to approach. In others, which take an integrated view of the management of the logistics function, there may be an Executive Vice-President or Board Director in place whose responsibilities include all the sub-functions of logistics. If there is, this person should clearly be targeted in a sales campaign.

CHAPTER 2

Airline Segmentation, Targeting, and Positioning

Segmentation, targeting, and positioning together comprise a three stage process. We first:

(1) Determine which kinds of customers exist, then
(2) Select which ones we are best off trying to serve and, finally,
(3) Implement our segmentation by optimizing our products/services for that segment and communicating that we have made the choice to distinguish ourselves that way.

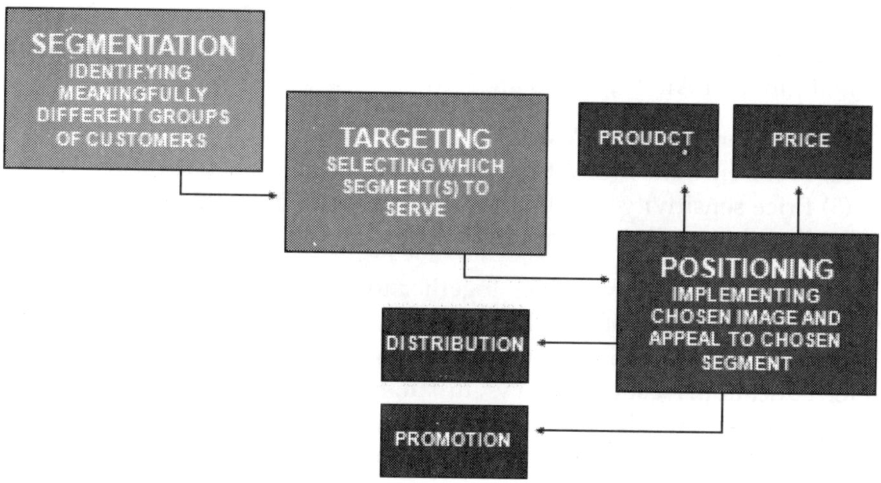

Fig. 7

Segmentation involves finding out what kinds of consumers with different needs exist. In the auto market, for example, some consumers demand speed and performance, while others are much more concerned about roominess and safety. In general, it holds true that "You can't be all things to all people," and experience has demonstrated that firms that specialize in meeting the needs of one group of consumers over another tend to be more profitable.

Generically, there are three approaches to marketing:

- ***Undifferentiated*** **strategy**, all consumers are treated as the same, with firms not making any specific efforts to satisfy particular groups. This may work when the product is a standard one where one competitor really can't offer much that another one can't. Usually, this is the case only for commodities.
- ***Concentrated*** **strategy**, one firm chooses to focus on one of several segments that exist while leaving other segments to competitors. For example, Southwest Airlines focuses on price sensitive consumers who will forego meals and assigned seating for low prices.
- ***Differentiated*** **strategy**, are followed by most of the airlines. They offer high priced tickets to those who are inflexible in that they cannot tell in advance when they need to fly and find it impractical to stay over a Saturday. These travelers—usually business travelers—pay high fares but can only fill the planes up partially. The same airlines then sell some of the remaining seats to more price sensitive customers who can buy two weeks in advance and stay over.

Note that segmentation calls for some tough choices. There may be a large number of variables that can be used to differentiate consumers of a given product category; yet, in practice, it becomes impossibly cumbersome to work with more than a few at a time. Thus, we need to determine which variables will be most useful in distinguishing different groups of consumers. We might thus decide, for example, that the variables that are most relevant in separating different kinds of Air Travellers are:

(1) Preference for FSA Vs LCC;
(2) Preference for round trip or one side trip;
(3) Price sensitivity—willingness to pay for brand names; and
(4) Regular vs. Occasional customers.

We now put these variables together to arrive at various combinations. Several different kinds of variables can be used for segmentation.

Demographic variables essentially refer to personal statistics such as income, gender, education, location (rural vs. urban, East vs. West), ethnicity, and family size. E.g. Facing flat sales of guns in the traditional male dominated market, a manufacturer came out with the Lady Remington, a more compact, handier gun more attractive to women.

Taking this a step farther, it is also possible to segment on *lifestyle* and *values*. Some consumers want to be seen as similar to others, while a different segment wants to stand apart from the crowd. Another basis for segmentation is behavior. Some consumers are "brand loyal"—i.e., they tend to stick with their preferred brands even when a competing one is on sale. Some consumers are "heavy" users while others are "light" users.

One can also segment on *benefits sought*, essentially bypassing demographic explanatory variables. Some consumers, for example, like scented soap (a segment likely to be attracted to brands such as Irish Spring), while others prefer the "clean" feeling of unscented soap (the "Ivory" segment). Some consumers use toothpaste primarily to promote oral health, while another segment is more interested in breath freshening. In the next step, we decide to target one or more segments. Our choice should generally depend on several factors.

First, how well are existing segments served by other Airline? It will be more difficult to appeal to a segment that is already well served than to one whose needs are not currently being served well.

Secondly, how large is the segment, and how can we expect it to grow? (Note that a downside to a large, rapidly growing segment is that it tends to attract competition).

Thirdly, do we have strengths as a company that will help us appeal particularly to one group of consumers?

Airlines like Kingfisher in India may already have an established reputation. Other like Jet airways. E.g McDonald's has a great reputation for fast, consistent quality, family friendly food, it would be difficult to convince consumers that McDonald's now offers gourmet food. Thus, McDonald's would probably be better off targeting families in search of consistent quality food in nice, clean restaurants.

Positioning involves implementing the marketing programs to establish a product or services image in the mind of the target customers. For example, Apple Computer has chosen to position itself as a maker of user-friendly computers. Thus, Apple has done a lot through its advertising to promote itself, through its unintimidating icons, as a computer for "non-geeks." The Visual C software programming language, in contrast, is aimed a "techies."

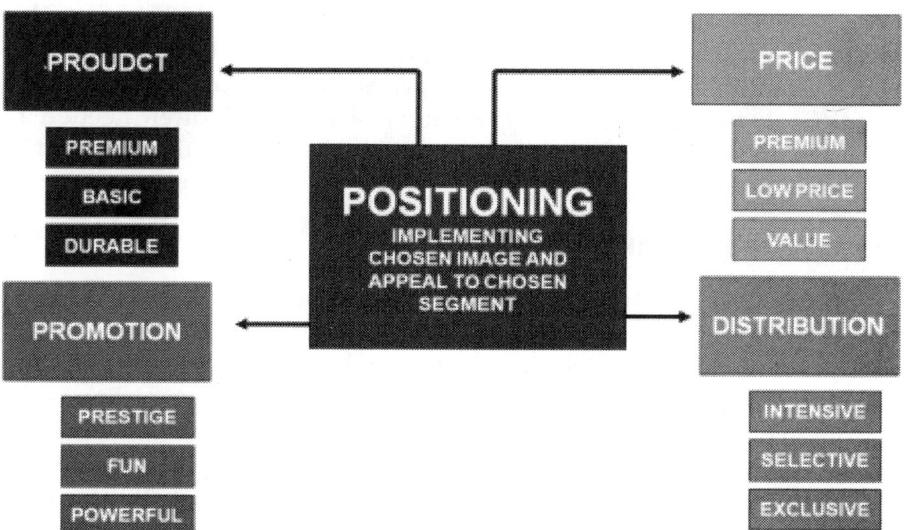

Fig. 8

Michael Treacy and Fred Wiersema suggested in their 1993 book *The Discipline of Market Leaders* that most successful firms fall into one of three categories:

- ***Operationally excellent firms,*** which maintain a strong competitive advantage by maintaining exceptional efficiency, thus enabling the firm to provide reliable service to the customer at a significantly lower cost than those of less well organized and well run competitors. The emphasis here is mostly on low cost, subject to reliable performance, and less value is put on customizing the offering for the specific customer. Wal-Mart is an example of this discipline. Elaborate logistical designs allow goods to be moved at the lowest cost, with extensive systems predicting when specific quantities of supplies will be needed.
- ***Customer intimate firms,*** which excel in serving the specific needs of the individual customer well. There is less emphasis on efficiency, which is sacrificed for providing more precisely what is wanted by the customer. Reliability is also stressed. Nordstrom's and IBM are examples of this discipline.
- ***Technologically excellent firms,*** which produce the most advanced products currently available with the latest technology, constantly maintaining leadership in innovation. These firms, because they work with costly technology that need constant refinement, cannot be as efficient as the operationally excellent firms and often cannot adapt their products as well to the needs of the individual customer. Intel is an example of this discipline.

Repositioning involves an attempt to change consumer perceptions of a brand, usually because the existing position that the brand holds has become less attractive. Sears, for example, attempted to reposition itself from a place that offered great sales but unattractive prices the rest of the time to a store that consistently offered "everyday low prices." Repositioning in practice is very difficult to accomplish. A great deal of money is often needed for advertising and other promotional efforts, and in many cases, the repositioning fails.

AIR PASSENGER MARKET

The objective of a firm's marketing policies should be to meet the needs of its customers, at a profit. We now have to deal with the problem that in one very real sense, this ideal objective is often unobtainable.

It is a truism to say that all customers are different. If an airline was to carry out market research into the requirements of its customers, the outcome would not be a uniform set of results. Rather, there would be a spectrum of needs, and it would be quite impossible for the carrier to meet all these needs exactly whilst at the same time retaining sound production economics.

The problem is a common one in all areas of marketing. For example, a car. company might set out with the reasonable-sounding objective of giving all its customers exactly the colour of car that they would like. This would mean, though, producing some cars in wildly eccentric colours in order to satisfy the more unusual requests, with the result of very high production costs. Instead, car companies usually produce cars in, say, eight or ten different colours. This gives them the benefit of much lower costs, but they have to accept that they will not be able to fully satisfy the requirements of all of their customers. Those with outlandish tastes will only be able to choose from cars which in no way give them the colour they are looking for. Even more conservative customers may find that a particular shade is too light or too dark.

The process of trading off customer requirements against production economics occurs in almost all industries notably so amongst airlines. It is called "market segmentation", and leads to the following definition of a "market segment":

A market segment is a group of customers who have sufficient in common that they form a viable basis for a product/price/promotion combination.

There are two possible mistakes which can be made when segmenting a market—those of under-segmentation and over-segmentation.

Under-segmentation occurs when customers are grouped into segments which are too large, and where there is actually a high degree of difference in the requirements of those included in the segment. A finer segmentation might allow at least some of these differences to be incorporated in product, price and promotion policies without an undue cost penalty being incurred. Over-segmentation is the situation where too many segments are isolated, with the result that they give insufficient indicators with regard to policy development.

The correct segmentation does, of course, depend on the question of the use that will be made of it. With product planning, almost all airlines are handicapped by the fact that only two or three classes of service currently exist on board aircraft. Therefore, a broad segmentation must be used for product planning purposes. In contrast, if the objective is to provide the basis for a database marketing campaign, a much finer segmentation can be employed.

Segmentation Variables

Segmentation of the air passenger market has traditionally been based on the use of three variables: the purpose of the passenger's journey, the length of their journey and their country or culture of origin. Each of these variable remains important in airline marketing today, and we will examine them in turn.

1. ***Purpose of Journey:*** Journey purpose has always been the fundamental segmentation variable in the air passenger market, with the essential division be1ng between business and leisure travel.

In using such a division, it should not be assumed that all air trips can be placed in one of these two categories. Some are completely outside them. For example, many airlines have significant markets which consist of pilgrims visiting Islam's holiest places in Saudi Arabia. Such trips cannot be viewed as either business or leisure—they constitute an entirely separate market segment. Or again, airlines often find that they derive business from the medical market where someone who falls ill finds that the treatment they need is not available locally. They therefore travel by air to a destination where medical facilities are better. Again, the medical market should be viewed as a separate market segment.

Despite the clear existence of exceptions, the distinction between business and leisure remains a valuable one in airline marketing and there is no doubt that a usefully high proportion of trips can placed in one of these two categories.

In looking at the journey purpose variable, worthwhile sub-segments can be isolated, in both the business and leisure categories. In business travel, a useful distinction is between corporate and independent business travellers. Corporate travellers are those who travel for a company, and who are able to put the price of their ticket and other business travel costs onto an expense account. They often adopt a rather cavalier approach to the costs of the services they buy, placing importance instead on high product standards. Independent business travellers, on the other hand, are those who are self-employed or who work for small companies. These people feel to a much greater degree that the price of an air ticket is coming out of their own pocket. They do, for example, still regard a high frequency of flights and good punctuality as essentials. They are, however, often prepared to make sacrifices in terms of product frills—for example, by travelling in the rear cabin on board the aircraft rather than choosing costly First or Business Class products, or by using one of the so-called "Cost Leader" airlines. There are now many signs that the size of the Independent sub-segment of business travel demand is increasing relative to the size of the Corporate sub-segment.

In the leisure segment of demand, again, two sub-segments can be isolated—those of Holiday and Visiting-Friends-and-Relatives (VFR) travel. When someone is travelling by air on holiday, they still have to pay for their meals and accommodation at their destination. This restricts the size of the market to those who have relatively high disposable incomes. With VFR travel, on the other hand, meals and accommodation are normally provided free-of-charge. This allows airlines to develop new markets most people with lower disposable incomes, especially in situations where recent population migrations have left strong residual ethnic links between two communities.

2. *Journey Length:* There are fundamental differences between the requirements of a short-haul traveller compared with someone who is flying a long-haul route. On short haul routes, the airport experience is an especially important one, whilst in-flight aspects such as seating comfort or food assume rather less significance. On long-haul routes, on the other hand, the in-flight experience is very important indeed in ensuring customer satisfaction.

An interesting debate is where the cut-off point between short-haul and long-haul services comes. No-one would presumably dispute that a flight of, say, forty-five minutes' duration should be regarded as short-haul and one of ten hours as long-haul. The difficult area is that of flights of, say, three or four hours. Here, for reasons of operational convenience most airlines continue to provide their short-haul product, despite the fact that passenger expectation is often for something substantially better. In particular, passengers will almost certainly respond unfavourably to being offered service in a single aisle aircraft with six abreast seating and a narrow seat pitch.

3. ***Origin of the Passenger:*** In the airline industry in recent years there has been considerable discussion of the concept of "global brands" and the possibility of truly global branding becoming a feature of marketing in the aviation business. At the same time, with many airlines grouping together in global alliances, attention has been has been focused on the supposed need for seamless service concepts whereby wherever anyone flies, anywhere in the world, on the traffic' system of the alliance, they should receive a comparable product.

Unfortunately, global branding and seamless service concepts in aviation come into conflict with the marked differences in customer requirements which occur between different cultures. For example, most people in north-west Europe or North America, would recognize a stereotype of the "business traveller" as being someone who is middle-aged, male and soberly dressed, carrying only a small amount of baggage. In contrast, in many third-world countries, "business travel" takes on a quite different meaning. It largely consists of traders who fly to a destination where consumer goods are available cheaply. These goods are then purchased and flown to the developing country where they are in short supply al1d can therefore be sold at a premium. In strong contrast to the extravagant product standards that might be expected by a European business traveller, in many developing countries such standards are irrelevant. Instead, overwhelmingly the most important customer requirement is that the airline should offer a high free baggage allowance.

Even within the confines of market segments derived from developed countries, significant market-by-market differences in customer requirements occur. For example, different races often vary significantly in terms of height and weight, with people from many Far Eastern cultures often smaller on average than their European or North American counterparts. They may therefore regard seating comfort as being a rather lower priority. Or again, questions of appropriate food-and-drink to be offered will vary from market-to-market. A suitable "breakfast" in France will be a different meal from what would be acceptable in the UK.

All-in-all, the question of culture or country of origin of the person who is travelling must be seen as a highly significant segmentation variable in aviation marketing.

BUSINESS TRAVEL MARKET

Given the segmentation of the air passenger market it was stated that "marketing is the management process responsible for identifying anticipating and satisfying customer requirements profitably". From this definition, it might be thought that our task is now a straightforward one. Having identified the main variables used to segment the market, we should now move on to discuss the requirements of customers in each of the main market segments. Unfortunately, there is a significant complication. Despite our definition of marketing encompassing the concept of satisfying customer needs it is rarely possible to immediately satisfy all possible customer requirements. The reason is that to do so would require a degree of spending that would prove uneconomic. Instead, airlines have to priorities needs so that what they are able to invest is focused on their customers most important requirements, on which their choice-of-airline decisions are most likely to depend. Customer needs, therefore do not just have to be identified, they have to be prioritized as well.

If this is the case, it raises the question of how both the identification and prioritization can take place. There are, of course, standard techniques of market research and analysis that airlines can use. Many carriers, for example, carry out in-flight surveys of their passengers. Often, such surveys include questions which are designed to ask passengers to list the factors they take into account in choosing their airlines. Unfortunately, in-flight surveys only allow carriers to sample the opinions of people who are flying with them already. They are potentially even more interested in the views of people who are at the moment choosing to fly with their competitors.

To remedy this problem, it is possible to engage firms of market research consultants and instruct them to carry out a survey of the whole of a market, rather than just amongst the airline's own customers. These surveys may be carried out by mail, by telephone or through individual or group interviews. Interview-based research at least should have the benefit of a better structure and more reliable answers, though at the penalty of a substantially increased cost. Even with such research, though, there are risks. In particular, respondents may give answers that they feel the questioner wants to hear, or which match up to their own, not necessarily accurate, view of their own importance. These latter issues often arise especially over questions as to who is responsible for the person's choice-of-airline decisions. There is a natural wish to give the impression that they are important enough to make this decision themselves, even if they are in practice bound by a company travel policy which allows them little or no flexibility.

An alternative way of understanding customer needs is increasingly open to airlines as the forces of deregulation and liberalization advance in the industry. It is one thing to ask people what their requirements are. It is often a more convincing policy to observe what they actually do when they are presented with a choice. Such situations often occur when new competitors arrive in a market, offering radically different service concepts from the pre-existing carriers that they are challenging. If these new competitors immediately achieve a substantial market share, it allows the analyst an opportunity to change and adjust views about the nature of market requirements. Many markets one of the major trends of the late 1990s was the rapid rise of airlines offering very low fares, and asking passengers to make carefully calculated sacrifices regarding frills in the product. In the USA, by far the most successful of these carriers has been Southwest Airlines. Recent estimates have suggested that upwards of 20% of US air travellers are now choosing one of the no-frills airlines, and that a significant proportion of these people are business travellers rather than the back-packers one might have expected to make such a choice. In turn, this has led to a reappraisal of the priorities of customers, especially in those markets with only a short flight time of an hour or less. Similar rethinking has been required in Europe as a result of the astonishing growth achieved by Ryan air and Easy jet.

Having made these qualifications, it is now necessary to set out some opinions as to the nature of customer needs, starting with the business travel market. We shall divide our discussion between the corporate and independent sub-segments of business travel demand, and between short and long haul routes. In turn, we shall begin with what the available evidence suggests are the high priority issues.

1. Timings and Frequency

In short-haul markets, frequency and timings are all important for the business traveller. Most business people find that their lives are extremely busy, and that their plans often change at short notice. If they do, an airline offering them a high frequency will have crucial advantage. Frequency will ensure that business travellers can fly out for a meeting shortly before it is due to begin and return to their offices or homes very soon after it has been completed. Because this is so, on almost all routes there will be a very strong correlation between the share of the frequency that an airline holds, and the share of the market it will obtain. Indeed, there is some evidence to suggest that this is an S-shaped relationship where the airline which dominates its competitors in terms of frequency will obtain an even higher share of the market than its frequency share would indicate.

Alongside the question of flight frequency, the timing of flights will also be a vital consideration. A high frequency of flights will be of no value if all the flights are concentrated at the weekend or during middle-of-the-day periods. It is essential that there should be extensive opportunities on short-haul routes for business travellers to make day-return trips. Flights will therefore need to be concentrated in the early morning and evening periods.

2. Punctuality

Punctuality of flights is of obvious, crucial importance to the business traveller, with flight delays meaning inconvenience, missed appointments and, perhaps, the loss of customers. No airline can hope to obtain a large share of the available business travel market if it is saddled with the handicap of a poor punctuality reputation.

3. Airport Location and Access

On short-haul routes, passengers will prefer service from a local, easily accessible airport, rather than from a more distant hub. This rule may apply even if the service from the local airport is with a "no frills" airline.

4. Seat Accessibility and Ticket Flexibility

"Seat accessibility" is a piece of aviation jargon which refers to the probability of a passenger being able to book a seat on a flight shortly before it is due to depart. It is a crucial product need for the business traveller. Some business travel is undertaken in response to a sudden crisis, which requires someone to travel on a "next flight out" basis. In other situations, a flight may be booked well in advance, but at the last minute a change of plan means that the booking must be cancelled and a new one made on an earlier or later flight. This requires that the ticket held by the passenger should be a flexible one, and that seats should be available near to flight departure time on the alternative service. Clearly, an airline can be giving a very high frequency on a route, but this frequency will be of no value to the business traveller if all the flights are fully booked days or weeks in advance.

A further aspect of ticket flexibility is that many business travellers expect the right to no-show for a flight, and then to be re-booked on a later one, without any penalty being charged. Of course, because of this, airlines have difficult decisions to make about the extent to which they will overbook flights to take account of the likely extent of no-shows.

5. Frequent Flyer Programme (FFP) Benefits

Today, almost all airline operate their own frequent flyer programme, or are partners in another carrier's programme. We shall be probing the question of the degree to which FFP benefits build market loyalty. It will be argued there that these benefits can be important in doing so, but that on short-haul routes their impact should not be exaggerated. For a short journey, the number of mileage points on offer will be quite small. It is true that the passenger will often happily take these by choosing the airline whose frequent flyer programme they are currently supporting. However, what is uncertain is the extent to which they will actually change their behavior and accept a less convenient option in terms of flight frequency, flight timings and departure airport in order to do so. The evidence is that on short-haul routes flights are chosen on the basis of an appropriate departure timing and the availability of a seat. If this is the case, then the offer of frequent flyer miles simply acts as a welcome bonus.

6. *Airport Service*

On a short flight, time spent at the airports at each end of the route may exceed the flight time. It is therefore not surprising that airport service should be a significant factor in choice-of-airline decisions. Business travellers will demand the opportunity to check in very late for a flight, by using a separate check-in desk to guard against the possibility of being delayed by a long line of less time-sensitive travellers. Today, they will expect expedited security and passport checks, and that a lounge should be available in which they can relax prior to a flight and make any last minute phone calls or send emails. Finally, they will expect a premium baggage service. For many, this will mean that they do not check in baggage at all, but instead are able to carry their baggage on board with them. This requires airlines to provide large overhead baggage bins on their aircraft. When a larger amount of baggage is being carried and business travellers have to check it in, they expect an opportunity to retrieve bags very quickly at the destination airport.

Airport service provides a good illustration of the differences between "apparent" and "true" needs. In all the factors mentioned above, the business traveller could make a good case for the service feature being as essential component of a product which will meet their air travel needs. For example, a late check-in will have a value in allowing them to maximise the time they spend in their office before leaving for an air trip. However, at the same time, the separate check-in desk also panders to true needs associated with pride and ego and the need for a recognition of status, something of great significance in terms of effective marketing to the business traveller.

7. *In-Flight Service*

On short-haul routes, the fact that flight times are short means that in-flight service often assumes a lower priority than frequency, punctuality and airport service in choice-of-airline decisions. Nonetheless, it can still be extremely important. in competitive markets airlines usually have little choice but to match the frequency of their rivals and to closely mimic their flight timings. Also, it is usually difficult or impossible to achieve a sustainable competitive advantage through airport service, at least in the large number of countries where airport terminal facilities are provided on a common user basis by airport operators. Because of these factors, the in-flight experience may be a crucial one for choice-of-airline decisions, even on routes where flight times are only three-quarters-of-an-hour or so. 10 terms of the factors which will be taken into account in evaluating the in-flight experience, seating comfort in terms of seat pitch and seat width will be significant. Also, even on a short flight a separate Business Class cabin may be appreciated. This will satisfy a need for a working environment away from crying children etc., where important documents, say, can be read before a business meeting. It does, though, once again pander to the true need for the recognition of status.

A final requirement in terms of in-flight service will be meals and drinks appropriate to the time of day. Here, it seems that breakfast, and an evening meal on after-business returning flights are especially welcome.

Having set down some of the fundamental requirements of the corporate business traveller on short-haul, point-to-point journeys, we can now use this basic model to probe customer requirements in related, but significantly different, situations.

Here, a first interesting case is to examine the requirements of the independent rather than the corporate, business traveller. The independent sub-segment of demand is growing relative to the corporate one. With independent business travellers, the fundamental needs remain exactly the same in terms of frequency, timings, safety, punctuality, seat accessibility and ticket flexibility. Price, though, assumes a greater significance than in the corporate market. As we discussed, independent business travellers feel that the ticket cost is coming out of their own pocket in the way that the corporate traveller does not, with only the fact that the ticket cost is tax-deductible lessening its impact. The independent traveller will therefore trade off cheaper ticket prices against product frills such as standards of seating comfort, free drinks, and in-flight meals. Interestingly, the willingness to do this makes the independent business travellers' set of requirements one which can be well-satisfied by the "Cost Leader" airlines.

A further difference between corporate and independent travellers comes in their attitude to frequent flyer points. For the corporate traveller, frequent flyer benefits are usually no more than an attractive perk of the job, providing opportunities for enjoyable free leisure flights. For the independent traveller, on the other hand, free flights are much more commonly used for business travel purposes and provide a welcome opportunity to reduce expenditure on air tickets. One would therefore expect a greater focus still on obtaining mileage points.

A next important area where the requirements of the business travller can differ is between the short-haul flights we have been considering and long-haul journeys. On long hauls, flight frequency and flight timings remain significant, but they take on a rather different meaning. On many long-haul routes, an adequate frequency is that an airline should give a daily flight. On denser routes, double daily flights may be appropriate, especially if they allow the airline to satisfy the need for both morning and evening arrivals at the destination. In few cases, though, will there be the need for the six or eight flights a day which may be required to provide adequate customer choice and to discourage entry by competitors on short routes.

On long-haul routes today, a significant consideration alongside frequency is often that there should be direct, non-stop flights available. As aircraft manufacturers have innovated with aircraft having longer and longer ranges, so it has become possible to fly a greater and greater number of the world's air routes on a non-stop basis. As airlines have, in turn, exploited this opportunity by introducing non-stop services, so passenger expectations have changed. Today, it is difficult or impossible for an airline operating a stopping service to compete for high-yielding traffic with one which flies a route non-stop.

As aircraft ranges have increased in recent years, so it has also been possible for aircraft manufacturers to introduce cost-effective, smaller long-haul aircraft. Planes such as the Boeing 767ER, 777, and Airbus A330 and A340 all come into this category. Such aircraft are allowing direct, non-stop services to be introduced on a secondary city to secondary city basis, a process which Boeing expects to accelerate when its new 250-seat aircraft—currently in its planning stages—is introduced. These services are removing from passengers the need to connect to hubs and are proving very attractive.

Another important difference between short and long-haul markets is in the attitudes to frequent flyer points. On a long-haul route, substantial numbers of points are at stake. Indeed, for many programmes, taking a long-haul flight with a particular airline, at least in First or Business Class, earns sufficient mileage for a short-haul flight on that airline's network to be taken free of charge. Because of this, there is a greater likelihood of a passenger on long-haul choosing the airlines whose FFP they are supporting, even if this means travelling earlier or later than they would ideally like.

As one would expect, there are differences in the attitudes towards airport and in-flight service on long-haul routes compared with short-haul. Seating comfort on board, a separate cabin to allow for sleep and work, meal quality and in-flight entertainment all figure prominently in the business traveller's long haul expectations. An especially telling point may be the attitude of different airlines' customer contact staff. On a long-haul flight, passengers will be exposed to uncaring attitudes for many hours, with the likelihood of lasting damage being done to the airline's reputation.

Airport service may, correspondingly, be of rather less importance. Long-haul passenger tend to check in earlier than those on short trips, presumably because, with lower frequencies, the penalty of missing a flight will be greater. The offer of a very late check-in time may therefore be less important. In contrast, though, lounge facilities will be of greater significance.

With the questions of seat accessibility and ticket flexibility, these are of lower importance on long-haul routes. A long-haul trip will often require at least three days out of someone's diary. Finding such a gap will normally take a great deal more pre-planning in comparison with a short-haul flight which can be carried out on a day-return basis. Therefore, the last-minute availability of a seat is of less importance on a long haul flight.

A last, interesting way in which the requirements of the business air traveller can be viewed concerns the needs of the connecting traveller. Some airlines make the mistake of assuming that everyone who flies on their short flights is a short-haul traveller. This is not so. Many of these passengers—upwards of 50% or more on very short routes—are connecting at hubs onto long-haul flights. They are therefore a long-haul passenger, on a short part of a long and tiring journey.

The requirements of the connecting passenger are, as one would expect, a mixture of those which prevail in the short-haul and long-haul point-to-point markets. The question of flight timings is an especially interesting one in this situation. The connecting passenger requires a high frequency of flights in exactly the same way as the point-to-point market does. The optimum flight timings, though, may be quite different. The point-to-point market has a requirement which peaks early and late in the business day. The connecting market, on the other hand, requires a spread of flights throughout the day, because long-haul flights depart from a hub at different times.

Punctuality assumes even greater importance for the connecting passenger. A delay of, say, an hour will certainly annoy the point-to-point traveller. It may not, though, destroy their entire itinerary. A delay of an hour, though, to a connecting passenger's flight into a hub may result in the long-haul flight being missed. This, in turn, may cause an actual delay of a day or more, on routes which are only served at a comparatively low frequency.

A further difficulty with the connecting passenger concerns the question of cabin comfort. That for the point-to-point short-haul traveller, cabin comfort was a relatively low priority, given that the person concerned will only be exposed to poor standards of comfort for a relatively short time. For connecting passengers, on the other hand, cabin comfort assumes great importance. This will be especially so on return flights when they may have spent many hours in a long-haul business class with very comfortable seating only to be faced, when exhausted, with completing their journey in a very cramped environment which airlines are basing on the needs of the point-to-point passengers.

To demonstrate that, for all airlines, the business traveller is a demanding customer. There is no easy or cheap way of meeting the business traveller's needs, with carriers heavily dependent on the better yields obtainable from the business travel market to cover what will, inevitably, be high production costs. Crucially, at the time of writing most airlines are finding these better yields to be inadequate to ensure reasonable profitability.

The Business Travel Market—Demographics and Psychographies

In market segmentation exercises, the word "Demographics" is used to describe the physical and tangible characteristics of the members of the segment. "Psychographics" is the term used to describe the intangible attitudes, preferences and, perhaps, prejudices of the members of the segment.

In terms of the demographics of the business travel market, the traditional stereotype of the business traveller of being male and middle-aged still holds true. In Europe for example, still over 80% of business travellers are men, whilst the average age of those who travel on business is 41. In some markets, this situation is unlikely to change radically. In Japan, for example, the part played by women in business is still a limited one, whilst the "jobs for life" principle still followed by many Japanese firms means that people continue to be business travellers up to the official age of retirement. In Europe and North America, though, radical change is beginning to occur. Women are becoming much more important in business travel, with forecasts suggesting that by the year 2010 perhaps 25-30% of all business travel will be undertaken by women. At the same time, many firms are attempting to down-size and to reduce their labour costs. The expedient to do so is often to offer incentives for early retirement. Where this is done, the age profile of the firm's employees will fall, with a corresponding effect on the average age of those who fly on business.

Another important demographic feature of the business travel market is that it is undertaken by relatively wealthy individuals, drawn from that small—often very small—proportion of a country's population where average income levels are high. The significance of this is that such people are fortunate to enjoy a lifestyle of comfort and affluence. They naturally expect the airline that they choose to reflect this.

A final, vital, demographic feature of business travel is that it is a highly concentrated market. As has been previously mentioned, in all countries, it is undertaken by only a small number of individuals, each of whom on average travels a great deal. In the UK, the average number of air trips made per year by a member of the business travel community is more than ten.

A number of consequences stem from this high trip frequency. Business travellers become experts, familiar with the standards offered by different airlines, and able—and willing—to make comparisons between them. They also become extremely attractive to airlines, because the carrier which can establish and maintain their loyalty over a lifetime of business travel (which may extend for twenty years or more) will gain a large amount of revenue as a result. Finally, the fact that these so-called Lifetime Values are so high justifies substantial investment in the establishment and maintenance of databases, and in a Relationship Marketing strategy designed to encourage and reward loyalty.

In terms of the psychographics of business travellers, two characteristics stand out. Business travellers tend to have strong opinions, and are often prepared to communicate these opinions loudly and frequently, especially when they wish to complain about a particular airline. Carriers should not be surprised by this. Over a long period of time, almost all airlines have tried to encourage people to fly with them using advertising approaches which make unqualified promises of servic.e excellence. If they do this, they should not be disappointed if people complain when the promises that have been made to them are not fulfilled.

A further important feature of the business traveller is that attitudes vary through time, with a pronounced life cycle effect often discernible. The young executive who is first promoted to a job which will require extensive international air travel will probably regard such travel as exciting, and will do all they can to ensure that as many trips as possible are undertaken. After a few years, though, attitudes can change dramatically. The person concerned realises that travel is not all it is maqe out to be, often consisting of long, tedious and boring journeys, repeated doses of jet lag, interrupted weekends, and often acute difficulties in maintaining social and personal relationships. From then onwards, instead of trying to find reasons why trips should take place, efforts may be focussed on avoiding at least some of these journeys. Of course, it is at this stage of the life cycle that the possibility of using video-conferencing and other forms of electronic communication to replace air travel will be at its most appealing.

As an overall summary of the characteristics of the business travel market it is true to say that many airlines have regarded the business traveller as being at the core of their marketing efforts. This is not surprising, bearing in mind the fact that yields per passenger-kilometre have generally been much higher than those obtainable from the leisure segment. It would be a mistake, though, to assume that high yield is the same thing as a high profit contribution. It is true that typically airlines obtain a high proportion of their revenue from business travellers. However, such travellers also account for a high proportion of airlines' costs. Besides the intrinsically high costs of meeting the product, in recent years the business travel market has become a bloodbath of costly competition. There have been successive rounds of innovation which have raised the product specification offered to the business traveller to higher and higher levels, without, sometimes, corresponding opportunities to raise fares in order to maintain profits.

At the same time as the costs of meeting needs and competing effectively in the business travel market have risen, so the proportion of air trips made up by business travel has progressively fallen due to the rapid growth of the leisure segment of demand. As has already been noted, though demand forecasting in air transport remains extremely difficult, all forecasters agree that this is a trend which will continue, with, if anything, the relative growth rates of business and leisure travel diverging even further as business growth slows and that of leisure accelerates. If this is the case it will lend further weight still to the vital conclusion that today no airline is likely to be successful if it ignores the leisure segment. As we shall see, ensuring profitable exploitation of leisure demand is equally challenging, but the nature of the challenge is different from that in business travel due to the strong contrasts in the characteristics of business and leisure demand.

LEISURE SEGMENT—DEMAND

The differences between business and leisure air travel begin with the demographics of leisure travel. Unlike the domination by men of business travel, leisure travel consists of an approximate balance between males and females. Indeed, with leisure travel by older people—say, those over 65—in many markets female travellers dominate because of their longer life expectancy. In terms of age profiles, the situation is also very different. Business travel tends to be concentrated in the middle-aged 35-55 age group.

Leisure travel, on the other hand, encompasses all ages. Children are important in leisure travel, whilst young adults, benefiting from reasonable incomes and few commitments, usually have an especially' high propensity to fly. A period of lower disposable income then often follows, due to the costs associated with family life. Once children have left home, though, disposable income often rises and may remain at high levels until quite late in life if pension arrangements are good enough.

Average personal incomes in leisure travel are often in strong contrast to those in the business travel market. The days when air travel was only enjoyed by wealthy members of a so-called "jet-set" are long gone. Today, rising disposable incomes and even more the falls in the real cost of air travel which have taken place have broadened the base of the leisure market enormously, taking it well beyond the relative few who make up the segment of business travel demand.

Besides differences in demographic characteristics, there are also substantial contrasts in leisure customer requirements.

In leisure air travel, the dominant requirement is for a cheap air fare, for obvious, but vitally important, reasons. Unlike in at least the corporate sub-segment of business travel demand, people are spending their own money, not their company's. Their spending is not tax deductible in the way that benefits someone who is an independent business air traveller. Often, too, leisure air travel is undertaken in a family group. If it is, the amount of cash payable will be multiplied several times over, making access to a low fare an even more important requirement. Finally, in the leisure market airlines suffer through being at the back of the queue in terms of people being willing to spend more. When a family travels on holiday a choice often has to be made between spending on a luxurious but expensive flight, or on a good quality hotel and meals in decent restaurants at the destination. Not surprisingly, the focus of spending tends to be on the destination, because people will only be on the aircraft for a few hours whereas they will be at their holiday destination for perhaps two weeks.

The overall effect of these factors tending towards price sensitivity is a clear one: the leisure air travel market is and always will be low-yielding. Revenue earned per passenger-kilometre is usually low, whilst decisive marketing advantage will often accrue to an airline able, through low costs, to charge and sustain fares lower than those of its rivals.

Despite the fact that yields tend to be low, it should not be assumed—as is often done that involvement in the leisure market will necessarily result in airlines losing money. The leisure market has a number of characteristics which allow efficient airlines to meet their customers' requirements much more cheaply than is possible in the business travel market, in ways which may allow the leisure market to be a substantial, and welcome, source of profits. Foremost amongst these characteristics is the fact that leisure travellers do not generally require frequent, on-demand service. This allows airlines to use relatively large aircraft to serve the leisure market, and gain the benefits of the lower seat-kilometer costs available from such aircraft. They can also operate at very high load factors—often in excess of 90%—because no last minute availability of a seat needs to be offered. This will minimize the difference between available and revenue seat-kilometer costs.

A further benefit of serving the leisure market is that its peaking patterns and timing needs are generally quite different from those which characterize business travel. It is true that leisure demand often shows pronounced seasonal peaking which increases the cost of serving it because of the need to provide costly peak-time resources which are poorly utilized at off-peak periods. This, though, is offset by the fact that flights for the leisure traveller can be spread throughout the day and often, the night as well because there is none of the marked peaking of demand during the early morning and after-business evening hours which characterizes the business market, at least on short-haul routes. The result is that airlines serving leisure routes can achieve very high annual aircraft utilizations. The so-called charter airlines in Europe are often able to achieve utilizations of 4,000-4,200 hours per year, in contrast to scheduled carriers carrying large numbers of business travellers which only usually reach 2,500-2,700 hours. Therefore their fixed costs of aircraft ownership or lease rentals are spread much more widely, with a correspondingly beneficial effect on unit costs.

A final, interesting, point-of-debate concerns the willingness of leisure passengers to sacrifice product features which, though desirable, can be traded off against the availability of cheaper fares. Some product features leisure travellers will clearly not sacrifice, safety being the clearest example. It is also suspected that reasonable standards of punctuality performance are essential, at least if people are to make repeat flights with a particular airline. Amongst the product areas where people will, apparently, accept sacrifices are seating comfort, airport service and catering.

With seating comfort, many airlines serving the leisure market find that their passengers will accept lower standards in both seat pitch and seat width. This allows many more seats to be placed in a given aircraft type. For example, in an Airbus A330-200 series aircraft, a typical schedule service seating configuration would be to equip the aircraft with 8-abreast seating at a 32- or 33-inch seat pitch. This allows just over 250 seats to be placed in the aircraft. A charter airline, on the other hand will use 9-abreast seating at a 28 or 29 inch seat pitch. This increases the number of seats to over 340, reducing seat-kilometer costs by more than 20%. (Concern over Deep Vein Thrombosis may reduce the ability of these airlines to use very low seat pitches in the future.)

In the area of airport standards, leisure passengers will often accept longer minimum check-in times. This allows carriers to process a flight using a smaller number of check-in desks.

With in-flight service of meals and drinks, a considerable number of "no frills" airlines now offer no complementary meal or drinks service at all. Many others give a free meal—sometimes of a lower, cheaper, standard than that obtainable on a scheduled flight, but charge for drinks, at least for alcoholic ones. This provides a useful cost saving, and also turns drinks service into a revenue, rather than a cost item.

Overall, the leisure segment of demand now constitutes the dominant one in the air transport industry today and we shall make further reference to it throughout the book.

AIRLINE MARKET SEGMENTATION

A market segment is an identifiable group within a market that seeks the same benefits or has the same needs.

Market segmentation is the *process* of identifying the distinct groups or segments of the market that might need different services or marketing mixes to satisfy them. By its very nature, market segmentation is a customer-orientated process that can be applied to almost any type of market.

Let's look at some examples of some groups of travelers—or *market segments—that* share characteristics and needs:

- Newly married couples who are on tight budgets, but who wish to visit a memorable and romantic destination
- People on a relatively low income that require cheap packages in order to afford to fly as leisure travellers
- Business people who require ticket flexibility and most convenient flights to their destination
- First-time travellers who require help with visa formalities.

While we have named only four segments here, there are many more. In the previous chapter, we looked in depth at one of Airmedia's business traveller segments. As we will see, there are at least 5 such segments in the business travel market.

This process, whereby more and more segments are identified, will not stop, meaning that airline marketers will need to be increasingly vigilant in order to succeed; as we have seen, the trend is towards treating customers more and more individually.

We are going to start by classifying major segments, using some real airline case study material.

Airline Segmentation Criteria

We have already listed and used the following criteria for defining Market Segments:

- **Value**: for example, some people place a higher value on convenient flights, while others feel price is more important
- **Motivation**: reason for travel, for example
- **Travel Pattern**: travel frequency and pattern can vary
- **Buying Pattern**: How is travel purchased and why?
- **Needs and wants**: What are their primary requirements? What unmet needs do travellers have? How price sensitive are they?
- **Satisfaction**: How committed are different travellers to the airline(s) they use? How likely are they to switch carriers?
- **Influence**: Are there particular individuals within a segment that are opinion-leaders? Do they. exert influence over the travel decisions of others?

Business Segments (Sponsored by a company)	Leisure Segments (self-sponsored)
1. Corporate Business Travellers 2. Individual Business Travellers 3. Meetings and Conventions 4. Incentive Groups 5. Ship Crews 6. Labour traffic	1. Group vacationers 2. Individual vacationers 3. Sports interest travellers 4. Adventure travellers 5. Cruise passengers 6. Eco-cultural travellers
Other Segments (sponsored by an organisation)	**Other Segments (self-sponsored)**
1. Government workers 2. Refugees (10M) 3. Non-governmental organisations (NGOs) 4. Teachers 5. Military	1. Students 2. Immigrants 3. Visiting Friends (VFR) 4. Religious travellers

Fig. 9

- **Demographics**: What age range do travellers come from, what sex, what social class? Where do they live?

There are several other important criteria we can now add. These include:

- Is there a very specific reason for a trip being made, for example a religious journey or a honeymoon?
- Who pays for the trip and who decides on which class of travel and airline to use?
- Does the trip involve a group of customers travelling together?

Based on all of these factors, Airlines have developed a "Master List" of Market Segments given on next page.

There are over 20 segments listed above. Each ot these can be further sub-divided to give a more detailed segmentation to be used by airline marketers.

This is particularly true of the first of the 6 business travel segments shown on the diagram—corporate business travellers. This large segment contains all the Business Travel generated by large organisations. 'This can range from senior executives travelling in First Class down to relatively junior employees in Economy Gob status is the main criterion used by these organisations to decide on the class of travel that different individuals can enjoy).

Here, Airlines have learnt a great deal through analysing the customer data that comes from their FFP databases. This information enables Airlines to develop and use additional criteria to refine their Market Segmentation approach, and in this case these new criteria relate directly to individual customer behaviour. Because this behaviour can be linked to individuals that

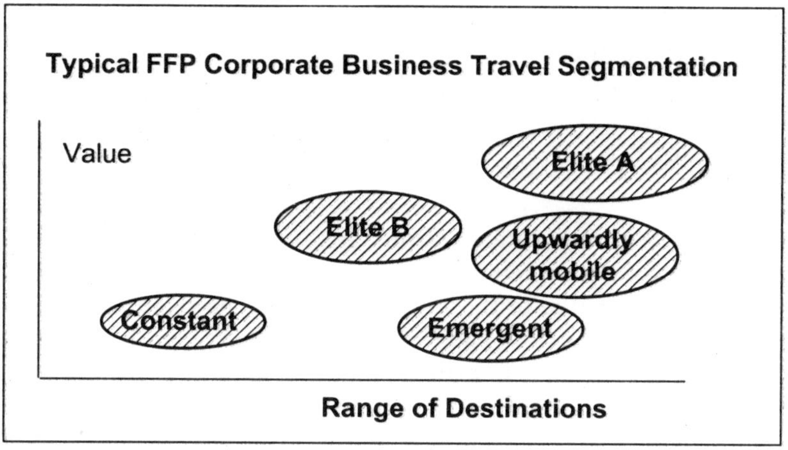

Fig. 10

the Airline can communicate with directly, it becomes possible to tailor the product offer to much more specific groups.

The chart on next page gives a typical picture of the new segments that Airlines with FFPs have discovered within the corporate business traveller area using these new behavioural criteria.

"Elite A" customers usually travel First or Business class, and have a wide repertoire of destinations. They will represent the most valuable segment in most markets, and will be very demanding in terms of its needs and wants. Quality is a key requirement, and these customers will often be in the Gold Tier of at least one FFP. They are quite often nationals of the market in which they reside. Whilst still being First or Business class users.

"Elite B" have a less frequent travel pattern, and visit a narrower range of destinations.

In the Air media Case Study used in the previous chapter, the group of Foreign Nationals travelling in First or Business class that was referred to are an example of the "Elite B" segment.

The "upwardly mobile" segment is important to identify because the customers in this group represent the "Elite customers of the future". One of the key benefits of having a FFP is that tracking individual travel patterns enables you to identify this group early and anticipate their rising value in your marketing strategy.

"Emergent" business travellers are those who are just moving into jobs where business travel is involved. They usually have lower status in the organisations that they work for, meaning that they tend to travel in Economy. Typically, airlines have tended to ignore this segment, and have focused exclusively on others. Given that most of the individuals in this segment are younger and may in time progress to the higher value segments listed above, you should question the wisdom of this approach.

The "constant" segment represents travellers that do not have a high frequency or a wide repertoire of destinations. Here are some examples:

- The head office manager of a large corporation that attends biannual review meetings of an overseas subsidiary company.
- A foreign diplomat that needs to return home every few months for briefings.
- A sales executive that visits the same overseas trade fair every year.

The action that can be taken from this more refined segmentation of corporate business travel is to ensure that your marketing strategy 'takes into account the different value of these segments, and the relative strengths and weaknesses of your airline in each customer group when compared to the competition. This enables you to make more informed marketing decisions, and explain the logic behind them within your own Airline.

The Need for Relevance

As we can see, market segments are not just limited to mite groups of individuals. For example, a segment can contain various organisations (like football clubs or household associations), specific business types (like high-tech companies or oil exploration firms), or public institutions (like hospitals or government ministries). The process of market segmentation can be applied to almost any type of market and can produce any number of new referents.

Multi-Criteria Segments

The more relevant criteria that can be applied to your segmentation process, the better. For example, adding the criteria of value and destinations visited to corporate business travel helps fine-tune the segments, as we have just seen.

More segments can be formed throughout a travel market on this basis. For example:

- Spouses of British executives living in Mumbai.
- Second-generation Vietnamese immigrants in Paris who have two or more children.
- Single male Gennan engineers age 25-30 working in Dusseldorf Financial controllers among the 100 largest banks in New York City.

One of the largest multi-criteria segments of travellers in the world, for example, is made up of single, female, Japanese office workers between the ages of 25-35 living in Osaka and Tokyo.

But please note the word "relevant", If your airline flies between Mumbai and London, spouses of British executives based in Mumbai could be an important segment to define. Of course, if your airline does not serve London, then this segment becomes irrelevant.

A further test of relevance is how large the segment is in the market(s) that you are responsible for. If this segment accounts for only 2% of the market, it is not going to be as relevant as it would be if it accounted for 52%.

The Benefits of Segmentation

As we can see, the process of market segmentation helps the airline marketer divide an otherwise large and generic marketplace into meaningful "slices" or segments that will make his or her job much easier. More specifically, segmentation gives the following key benefits:

Identification of Customer Needs

Segmentation improves your understanding of customers' needs and reasons for purchasing a particular product/service. As a result, it allows you to meet these all-important customer requirements. For example, corporate customers that require better ground services and FFP benefits.

Identification of New Opportunities

Segmentation allows you to discover business opportunities in markets that are not being adequately served by the competition. The World Cup sports traveller segment, for example, would be worthwhile if your airline flies to the next venue.

Discovery of New Trends

Segmentation helps airlines identify the various market trends in a rapidly changing market. For example, the emergence of the adventure-seeking segment in Tokyo has some very distinct requirements.

Marketing Resource Efficiency

Segmentation enables you to adopt a more systematic and cost-effective approach when planning present and future marketing programmes. For example, the development of a joint direct-mail program with a local travel agency and credit card company that targets the honeymoon segments.

Market Segmentation versus Target Segmentation

A concept that is often confused with the segmentation process is something called target segmentation. While market segmentation is the process by which the marketer analyses and divides the total market into smaller, more meaningful groups, *target segmentation* is the process by which marketers decide which segments to focus op. and develop.

The correct process, therefore, is to first segment the market and then decide on which segments to target afterwards.

Once your total market has been properly segmented, this approach of targeting particular segments within the total market has the following major benefits in your Marketing Strategy and Planning activity:

- **Focus**—it is impossible for an Airline to target all segments of the market equally and he successful at doing so
- **Identifying resource requirements**—by choosing from all the segments in your market, it will be easier to identify the resources required as different segments require different resources. For example most business travel segments will require better schedules, whereas some leisure segments will trade convenience for lower prices
- **Setting priorities**—to really make segmentation work, it is necessary to rank your target segments in order of importance.

SAS Airlines and Segmentation

In an interview with Thomas Havnegjerde, of SAS Airlines, he expresses the importance of segmentation in their marketing strategy.

"The most important aspect is to understand the customer in our markets, irrespective of whether or not they are SAS customers," says Thomas. "In order to see reality in measurable terms we are now putting together in-depth data about the market in the form of a customer segmentation model. By a segment we mean a number of people identified by several common requirements, who can be regarded as a customer group.

"With segmentation we map the market and decide which segments we want to fight for," says Thomas when asked how this model will help SAS.

The model is based on demographic considerations (such as age, education and income), habits/behaviour (travel frequency, manner of purchase; etc.) and situation (why people travel and where to). "Our base is comprised of interviews with, and the identification of, more than 1,000 business and leisure passengers in Scandinavia and the UK," says Thomas. "Consequently, these people have been contacted and asked more in-depth questions. Internal data, obtained from e.g. the Euro Bonus database and CPQ surveys, has provided further information."

In this interview, SAS shows how they are systematically going about Market Segmentation, and what criteria they are using to do this.

But the most important insight lies in the middle paragraph: "with segmentation, we map the market and decide which segments we want to fight for". In the first chapter of this book, we discussed how Marketing is a matter of "trade-offs", and here is another example of this being identified by Thomas Havnegjerde. What he is saying is that in the airline business, it is not possible to please "all of the people all of the time"!

This is why the decisions that you take on ranking target market segments is so important; make a bad decision and your Airline could lose significantly in the medium to long term. One very good example of this occurred in the second half of the 20th Century in Europe. Here, some very small charter airlines began to operate holiday flights between countries like the UK and Mediterranean destinations like Majorca. The major scheduled carriers regarded this new market segment of holiday travellers as irrelevant on the grounds that the traffic flows were very small, and probably would not last.

Within 20 years, charter flight were carrying millions of passengers within Europe, and had become so predominant on some "sunshine routes" that scheduled airlines had been forced to withdraw from them.

Another issue that you will notice from looking at the SAS Airlines strategy is that it clearly involves targeting more than one segment.

In practice, few Airlines decide to concentrate on just one segment. There are several reasons for this:

- One segment may not be enough to achieve economies of scale—for example, many carriers have found that they cannot expand their route network without targeting several segments.
- There may be "synergy" in serving several segments—for example by serving large leisure market segments, you may be able to increase frequency, providing a benefit that is valued by business travellers as well.
- There may be less risks involved in serving different segments—for example, a decline in growth in one segment may occur at the same time that another is growing fast, enabling you to compensate for this decline.

Despite this, a small number of airlines are now pursuing a "single segment" type of strategy, for example the low cost carriers in North America and Europe. In practice, even these Airlines are serving more than one segment, and some of them are already showing signs of recognising this by introducing new products and services that target specific customer groups.

Once you have prioritised the segments in your total market and picked the ones that are most important to you, the next step in the Marketing Strategy and Planning process is to conduct a "SWOT" analysis for each target market segment.

Ranking Market Segments

About 50 years ago, a group of experts in North America developed a brilliant way of looking at a company's portfolio of businesses called the "Boston matrix." Although this technique was actually applied to Airlines in general—or to Airline Market Segmentation in particular—the basic idea works well in our specific environment.

The key to ranking market segments consists of three variables:

1. The attraction of the segment.
2. Your Airline's performance in the segment.
3. The size and growth prospects of the segment.

The diagram below illustrate this concept:

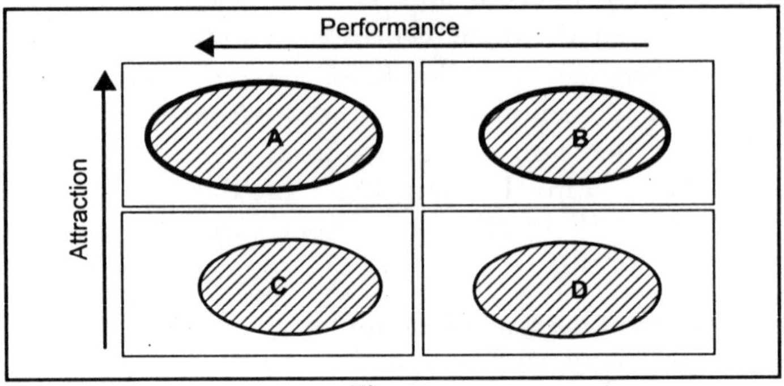

Fig. 11

Here, we have four segments. The larger size of Segment A denotes that it is the largest revenue producer, and the double lines around it are used to indicate that it is fast-growing in relation to the others. Let us imagine that this is "Elite 1" from our list of corporate business travel segments mentioned earlier in this chapter, and that our Airline's mission is to serve the business travel community. This customer group is very attractive to us, because the individuals within it travel frequently on business, and use First and Business class fares. Also, these segments are performing well here, meaning that this segment will be profitable. From all of this it is clear that Segment A ranks Number 1 in our Marketing Strategy and Planning. We must aim to maximise our share here, and in order to do so we need to assign it this priority.

Segment B is an "unknown quantity". Let us imagine that it is independent holiday travel. We don't have the products and services required to perform well in this relatively new market segment, but we know that:

- It is growing fast, having already become the second largest in terms of revenue.
- Operating margins in this segment are high.

For these reasons, we need to invest carefully in order to improve our performance in this market, and evaluate whether it continues to be very attractive to us or not. But this must be subordinate to the importance of Segment A, so Segment B is ranked second.

Segment C could be VFR travel. We are performing well here too, but this customer group is less attractive. It is relatively small, and the single circle around the segment on the diagram denotes lower growth. However, this segment is profitable because our performance is good. We could therefore give it Number 3 priority—we need to put enough marketing effort into the segment to maintain share, but no more.

Segment D could be group holiday travel. Perhaps there are large tour operators in this market that demand very low rates. Because our competitors are more prepared to discount to get some of this business, it is not an attractive segment for us to focus upon—so it is Priority 4, and only gets minimal, if any, attention.

As an excellent illustration of how this approach works in practice, just read the quotation from Thomas Havnegjerde of SAS Airlines on how this carrier uses segmentation:

SEGMENTATION—AIR FREIGHT MARKET

For many years, air freight was the "poor relation" of the passenger business. Freight income made up only a small proportion of airline revenues, and it was consequently starved of both resources and management attention. It was often seen as no more than a by-product operation, to fill belly-hold space in passenger aircraft that would be available anyway.

Such attitudes are no longer acceptable. Some airlines are now able to specialise in carrying nothing but air freight, and to be highly profitable in doing so. For many others, freight now accounts for a highly significant and increasing proportion of profits. With the exception of 2001—a poor year for air freight—average annual growth rates in the air freight business have exceeded those in the passenger markets by two or three percentage points. This is a trend which is likely to continue, making freight's contribution through time greater still.

At the same time as freight revenues have increased, competition in the air freight market has grown steadily, and it is becoming less and less likely that airlines treating freight purely as a by-product will be successful. Professional marketing is therefore a prime requirement and it is essential that we should give proper attention to the marketing of air freight, beginning with the question of the segmentation of the air freight market.

Segmentation Variables—Air Freight Market

Market segmentation is as important in the air freight market as it is on the passenger side of the business. Only if markets are properly segmented can airlines find a basis for their product, price and promotional policies.

Using the criterion of the reasons why air freight rather than cheaper transport should be employed, a clear first segment of air freight demand is that consisting of Emergency traffic. Emergency situations occur when goods have to be moved by the fastest possible mode of transport, with the costs of achieving a fast transit a secondary consideration. In turn, emergency situations may be divided into two types. An Operating Emergency occurs when a firm has to rectify an operational problem. For example, an oil company may find that one of its rigs has to increase production because of a breakdown. Every hour of lost production time will then have a substantial cost associated with it—a cost which can be minimised if air freight is used to ship the spare parts which are needed to enable production to resume.

Another example of this type of emergency is an ironic one. Deep-sea shipping companies are air freight's biggest competitor's on long-haul routes, yet these companies are major users of air freight. When a ship has to remain in port because spare parts are needed before a fault can be repaired, the shipping line operating it would be very foolish if it did not use air freight to move these parts. If it did not do so, the ship in question would be stranded in port for a longer period than would be necessary.

The second type of emergency situation is termed the Marketing Emergency. Such a situation occurs when a supplier is in danger of missing a deadline or one of its customers has expressed dissatisfaction with service levels. Then, again, air freight is the obvious choice, though the justification will be based on the maintenance of customer loyalty rather than cost reduction. In terms of customer requirements, the emergency segment has clear customer needs which airlines must satisfy if they are to compete in the market.

A first need is for the fastest possible door-to-door transit time. In order to able to offer this to the shipper 'an airline has first of all to give a high frequency flights. Emergency situation do not give advanced notice of when they will occur. Therefore, a carriers with a high frequency will give the shipper the best likelihood that a flight will be available within a short time after the need to ship the goods has arisen.

Frequency, though important, will not be enough on its own. It must be accompanied by a capacity management policy ensuring that space will be available to shippers who need to book emergency consignments shortly before a flight is due to depart. It is of no value to an emergency shipper if an airline has a high flight frequency, but all its cargo space is fully booked days or weeks before flights are due to leave. Of course, once a booking has been offered it is important that freight should be flown on the flight on which it is booked and that it should benefit from safe and reliable ground handling.

A very important customer requirement in the emergency traffic segment is that the selected airline should have the ability to track shipments at all times and be able to communicate accurate and timely information about the status of a consignment. It will also be important to provide a door-to-door collection and delivery service, so that the shipper feels that once a booking has been made, their troubles are over with someone taking responsibility for the entire transit.

The emergency traffic segment presents airlines with both problems and opportunities. The emergency segment of demand has always been, and remains, highly important to an airline's air freight business. It would be an un-ambitious airline, though, which sought to do no more than exploit the emergency market. This would confine air freight to a comparatively small role in the international logistics industry. To avoid this, it has been necessary to develop arguments as to why air freight should be the preferred option for the routine as well as the emergency shipper.

An area where it has been possible to do this constitutes the second major segment of air freight demand. It concerns traffic which is routine perishable in nature—routine as opposed to emergency, and perishable because the goods in question only remain saleable for a limited period of time.

Perishability in international logistics occurs for two reasons in particular. Physical Perishability describes situations where goods physically deteriorate.

Cut flowers and soft fruits are good examples of this. With them, the argument for using air freight is clear. Producers of, say, cut flowers can always attempt to sell them in local markets close to where they have been grown. If they do so, prices will be low due to market saturation. A more profitable option might be to send the flowers to distant markets where they will have scarcity value. Then, though, air freight will have to be used in order to ensure that the goods reach the market in a saleable condition.

Economic Perishability is the second type. It occurs not when goods are prone to deteriorate physically, but when the life cycle within which they remain saleable is a short one. Newspapers have been such a commodity. Other examples include fashion clothing, children's toys, and pop music tapes and CDs. These goods can be sold in large quantities and at good prices if they reach the market when demand for them is still rising rapidly. Air freight often provides the only realistic way of ensuring that this happens, at least in long-haul markets.

In terms of customer requirements, the routine perishable market differs in some respects from the emergency segment. At least for physically perishable goods, it may be possible to forecast further ahead when the need for shipment will occur. This is because many commodities which come into this category have a pronounced seasonal pattern to their production. In turn, though, this gives problems to airlines attempting to exploit the market. Flows of emergency shipments occur throughout the year, even though it will not be possible to forecast exactly when a particular emergency will occur. Perishable traffic, on the other hand, may only be offered seasonally. Airlines may therefore have surplus capacity at the off-season.

A further problem of perishable traffic is that it tends to result in routes having marked directional imbalances. As we have already noted, this is because an area noted for primary production of perishable foodstuffs may not be one which attracts significant in-bound flows of commodities suitable for air freighting.

Besides the problems associated with capacity being available at the right time and place, perishable freight often needs special handling. It may be fragile in nature, or need refrigeration, both of which forces up airlines' handling costs. It will certainly require airlines to achieve high standards of regularity and punctuality, and to ensure that freight should always be carried on the flight on which it is booked. There also needs to be a comprehensive monitoring and control service in place, to make sure that if a mistake is made it is discovered in time for it to be rectified.

The question of the importance of price to the routine perishable shipper is an interesting one. High service quality will clearly be necessary if goods are to reach the market in time and in the right condition. Airlines may thus reasonably hope that customers will be prepared to pay more if this is the only way to obtain the required service, and that the market will be a relatively high yielding one. In practice, this may be true, but only in the short term. The economics of exporting perishable goods by air are based on the premium price being obtained in the distant market being sufficient to cover the extra costs of air freight while still leaving a profit. The more air freight rates rise, the more such profits are threatened, leading to the possibility that the trade may have to be abandoned. Therefore, the lack of price-sensitivity in the routine perishable market should not be exaggerated.

Both the emergency and the routine perishable markets are important in the modem air freight industry. Despite this, though, by far the greater part of the goods which move in international logistics cannot be placed in either of these categories. They must therefore be described as being routine and non-perishable. The air freight industry must be able to demonstrate the value of its services for shippers of this type of freight. If it cannot do so, then the industry will never achieve its fun potential.

The industry's problem in developing this market is that shippers of routine, non-perishable freight often have an alternative. They can use a surface transport instead of air freight and they will normally pay a substantially lower freight rate if they do. The task of air freight marketing is to demonstrate that if air freight is used rather than apparently-cheaper surface transport, significant advantages will accrue, advantages which will often be sufficient to outweigh the freight rate differential. Isolating these advantages and communicating them effectively has proved to be a major challenge. The customer must be persuaded to compare all the costs associated with using surface transport with the benefits of employing air freight.

In three relevant areas, a direct comparison will be possible:

1. ***Air freight*** should bring important cash flow advantages. Most international trade is carried out on a credit basis. The consignor usually allows the consignee a period of time before they have to pay for goods that they have received. The credit period does not begin when the goods are dispatched but rather when the consignee takes delivery of them. If surface transport is used, the transit time on a long-haul route may be several weeks. During this time, the consignor will be incurring interest charges, because they will have invested money in producing the goods but will not have been paid for them. If, on the other hand, they dispatch the goods by air freight they should be received by the consignor in a matter of two or three days. If they are, cash flow will be several weeks faster and interest payments will be correspondingly reduced.
2. ***Packaging costs*** will generally be lower when air freight is employed. Air freight often allows less packaging to be used, 'due to its more favorable environment for carriage. Because of this, costs will be reduced both because of the lower cost of packaging materials, and because this cheaper packaging will result in a saving on freight costs due to each consignment having a lighter weight.
3. ***Insurance costs*** will usually show a substantial saving in favor of air freight—again, a reflection of air transport's superior environment for carriage, and the shorter times for which goods are at risk.

Defining the remaining advantages of air freight over slower surface transport is more difficult, because they depend on a comparison of different logistics philosophies.

If a manufacturing company wishes to minimize its transport costs it will, of course, use surface transport modes. Surface transport will therefore be used to bring raw materials to its production points and then to move finished products to customers. Though low transport costs will be the result of such a policy, significant adverse consequences will also ensue. With regard to the supply of raw materials and components to production points, it will be necessary to hold large stocks. This is because surface transport cannot generally provide the high frequency of deliveries which air freight can, and which allow supply to take place under so-called "Just-in-Time" (JIT) principles. With surface transport usage, stocks of components must be held in sufficient quantities to allow production to continue in the intervals between deliveries.

With delivery of finished products to customers, again the use of surface transport will require extra stock to be held. For many products, demand will rise from time-to-time, in a way which cannot be precisely forecast. For example, demand for some products is weather-related, so precise demand forecasts cannot be prepared for them more than a few days in advance. If demand for a particular product does rise, it is extremely important that firms should be able to keep their wholesalers and retailers supplied with stock to sell. If they fail to do so, they risk losing the loyalty of these marketing intermediaries.

Ensuring continuity of supply given random and un-forecast able fluctuations in demand requires companies to hold substantial amounts of so-called "safety stock". In order to distribute silt stock, again surface transport can be used, and direct transport costs will be minimized as a result. However, many other logistics costs will be increased substantially.

By way of illustration of this point, let us take the case of a European firm exporting electrical consumer goods to a distant market such as Australia. If surface transport is used by the exporting company, it will be necessary to invest in substantial local warehousing. This is because, with surface transport transit times of perhaps six to eight weeks, customers will not be prepared to wait for goods to be dispatched and sent once an order has been placed. Instead, they will expect their goods to be available within a few days of an order being placed. In the case of the Australian market, full coverage will probably require a warehouse in the East—perhaps in Sydney and one in Western Australia.

The consequences of the need to invest in local warehousing will be substantial and costly. As stated earlier, stock will have to be held which is not only sufficient to cover day-to-day demand. There must also be considerable safety stock to prevent the collapse of service levels should a random and un-forecastable increase in demand occur. This will mean investment in warehousing to hold the stock, and also in the capital costs of stockholding. For some items, there may be a risk too of deterioration or obsolescence, with falling demand meaning that the value of the stock falls while it is held.

Besides the cost of local warehousing, the need to invest in such warehousing results in a significant loss of marketing flexibility because it makes entering a new market a very slow process. Before the firm can begin selling in the new market, it will need to obtain warehousing capacity and ship out substantial quantities of stock so that adequate service levels can be offered to early customers. This will take time. As a result, when selling does finally begin, the market conditions which prompted the decision to enter may have changed. The initiative may then fail, with the result that the stock has to be withdrawn—a costly process in itself—and the new warehouses sold off.

The use of air freight avoids all of these problems. Instead of large amounts of field stockholding being necessary, local stocks can be reduced or eliminated. Most stock—especially safety stock—can be held at one central location—in the case we are looking at, in Europe. This means that aggregate amounts of safety stock can be reduced, because it becomes a reasonable proposition that demand fluctuations in the different market that the firm serves will tend to some extent to cancel one another out.

If local stockholding can be reduced or eliminated, marketing flexibility will also be greatly increased. Markets can be entered quickly when demand is strong. Should demand falter at a later stage, withdrawal from the market will be equally easy. Therefore, the company concerned can market its product on a world-wide basis, focusing attention always only on those countries where demand for the product is buoyant.

Though there can be no doubt about the power of the arguments relating to the use of air freight for routine non-perishable traffic, it is important that those concerned with the marketing of air freight should also understand the limitations of the concept.

Foremost amongst these is that the air freight solution can be portrayed as a high risk one. It is based on firms keeping field inventories to a minimum, and supplying customers from central stockholding points after orders have been placed. If something happens to prevent the warehouses at these central points from working effectively—a strike, for example—or if there are delays in transport from them due to such factors as industrial action or bad weather, service to customers will be immediately and seriously affected. Such problems are, of course, avoided to a degree if local inventories are held. It is therefore important that any logistics system based on low inventories and fast transportation should be a reliable one.

With the question of the use of air freight to minimize packaging and insurance costs, this argument only has weight if there are large differences between the environment for carriage available from surface and from air transport. These differences are steadily being reduced through time as surface operators adopt the principles of containerization and roll-on/roll off. These allow goods to be sealed and protected from the beginning of a journey to its end, with a much reduced risk of damage.

Overall, this chapter should have made clear that a sound understanding of the marketplace is an absolutely essential building-block in the successful application of marketing principles to the airline industry. Without this building-block in place, all other aspects of marketing become pointless. It is therefore impossible to exaggerate its importance.

Differences between the Air Passenger and Air Freight Markets

In order to do so it is first of all necessary to examine the principal differences between the air passenger and air freight markets. It is true to say that only the fact that aircraft are used to carry the demand coming forward links these two markets. In all other respects they are totally different.

A first area of contrast is that air freight travels only one way on a route. It is true that some passengers are emigrating. They therefore settle in the country they are flying to and do not return. A small number are unfortunate enough to die at their destination. However, almost all passengers who fly out on a route will also return on it. Therefore over a year most passenger markets end up approximately directionally balanced, even though there may be directional problems associated with particular seasonal traffic flows. On the freight side, a directional balance will be no more than a happy co-incidence. Directional imbalances will be most marked on routes to and from countries which are mainly primary producers. These countries, especially if they are relatively wealthy, such as Australia, may import many items which are suitable air freight commodities. However, a lower proportion of their exports will come into this category, consisting as they do largely of primary products. It is certainly possible to correct such a situation in the long-term by offering attractive low prices, in the weaker direction. Poor yields are, though, then being substituted for low load factors.

A further problem in air freight marketing is that freight is extremely heterogeneous. Passengers are homogenous in the sense that they each occupy a seat. Freight, on the other hand, varies in every possible way. Consignment sizes vary from small packages and letters weighing less than a kilo up to consignments of 30,000 kilos or more. Consignment density and "stow ability" will also vary. Some commodity types—books are a good example—are both dense and easy to stow. Others—for example bicycles—are of low density and have poor stowing characteristics. Unless airlines keep a very close check on their pricing policies, carrying such commodities can easily become unprofitable.

A final area of variation is in the handling and stowage conditions that different commodities require. For example, some are fragile and need especially careful handling. Others are of high value, such as banknotes. Therefore, special security arrangements will be needed. A further, and increasingly common requirement is for the refrigeration of physically perishable goods.

The most important difference between the air passenger and air freight businesses concerns the nature of the competition that airlines face in these different markets.

On the passenger side of their business, airlines are very fortunate that, on long-haul routes, almost all passengers who travel do so using air transport. With air freight, the situation is very different. Air transport faces intense competition from surface on all routes. This competition is especially difficult to meet because it is based on low prices. It is true that in some cases air and surface rates are comparable due to the different charging methods that are adopted with respect to consignment density.

Such situations are, though, rare. In almost all cases, air freight will be significantly more expensive than the surface transport alternative, if analysis is confined merely to a comparison of freight rates. These differentials can be extremely large, often reaching the level where air freight is ten times as expensive as surface transport.

The competitive situation makes the marketing of air freight an especial challenge. Airlines have to find and demonstrate arguments to justify the use of an apparently much more expensive mode of transport. These arguments form the basis for the segmentation of the air freight market.

CHAPTER 3

Airlines Strategic Analysis and Planning

We have now completed our coverage of the essential building blocks. In the application of marketing principles in the airline industry. No airline can hope to apply these principles successfully without the understanding of customer needs and the marketing environment. Once such understanding is in place, the next requirement is the challenging one of the formulation of a sound strategy.

In one sense, the news here is good in that in today's airline industry there is no single, unique strategy which must be followed if success is to be achieved. There is a range of possible strategies available. What is essential, though, is that one strategy must be selected from this range. It must then be implemented well, and continued on a long term basis. The aim of this chapter is to set out and discuss the types of possible strategy, and their advantages and disadvantages.

PLANS AND PLANNING

Plans are needed to clarify what kinds of strategic objectives an organization would like to achieve and how this is to be done. Such plans must consider the amount of resources available. One critical resource is capital. Microsoft keeps a great deal of cash on hand to be able to "jump" on opportunities that come about. Small startup software firms, on the other hand, may have limited cash on hand. This means that they may have to forego what would have been a good investment because they do not have the cash to invest and cannot find a way to raise the capital. Other resources that affect what a firm may be able to achieve include factors such as:

- *Trademarks/brand names*: It would be very difficult to compete against Coke and Pepsi in the cola market.
- *Patents*: It would be difficult to compete against Intel and AMD in the microprocessor market since both these firms have a number of patents that it is difficult to get around.

- *People*: Even with all of Microsoft's money available, it could not immediately hire the people needed to manufacture computer chips.
- *Distribution*: Stores have space for only a fraction of the products they are offered, so they must turn many away. A firm that does not have an established relationship with stores will be at a disadvantage in trying to introduce a new product.

Plans are subject to the choices and policies that the organization has made. Some firms have goals of social responsibility, for example. Some firms are willing to take a greater risk, which may result in a very large payoff but also involve the risk of a large loss, than others. Strategic marketing is best seen as an *ongoing and never-ending process*. Typically:

- The organization will identify the *objectives* it wishes to achieve. This could involve profitability directly, but often profitability is a long term goal that may require some intermediate steps. The firm may seek to increase market share, achieve distribution in more outlets, have sales grow by a certain percentage, or have consumers evaluate the product more favorably. Some organizations have objectives that are not focused on monetary profit—e.g., promoting literacy or preventing breast cancer.
- An analysis is made, taking into consideration issues such as *organizational resources, competitors, the competitors' strengths, different types of customers, changes in the market*, or *the impact of new technology*.
- Based on this analysis, a plan is made based on *tradeoffs between the advantages and disadvantages* of different options available.
- This strategy is then carried out. The firm may design new products, revamp its advertising strategy, invest in getting more stores to carry the product, or decide to focus on a new customer segment.
- After implementation, the results or outcome are evaluated. If results are not as desired, a change may have to be made to the strategy. Even if results are satisfactory, the firm still needs to monitor the environment for changes.

Levels of planning and strategies. Plans for a firm can be made at several different levels. At the *corporate* level, the management considers the objectives of the *firm as a whole*. For example, Microsoft may want seek to grow by providing high quality software, hardware, and services to consumers. To achieve this goal, the firm may be willing to invest aggressively.

Plans can also be made at the *business unit* level. For example, although Microsoft is best known for its operating systems and applications software, the firm also provides Internet access and makes video games. Different managers will have responsibilities for different areas, and goals may best be made by those closest to the business area being considered. It is also more practical to hold managers accountable for performance if the plan is being made at a more specific level. Boeing has both commercial aircraft and defense divisions. Each is run by different managers, although there is some overlap in technology between the two. Therefore, plans are needed both at the corporate and at the business levels.

Occasionally, plans will be made at the *functional* level, to allow managers to specialize and to increase managerial accountability. Marketing, for example, may be charged with increasing awareness of Microsoft game consoles to 55% of the U.S. population or to increase the number of units of Microsoft Office sold. Finance may be charged with raising a given amount of capital at a given cost. Manufacturing may be charged with decreasing production costs by 5%.

The firm needs to identify the business it is in. Here, a *balance* must be made so that the firm's *scope is not defined too narrowly or too broadly*. A firm may define its goal very narrowly and then miss opportunities in the market place. For example, if Dell were to define itself only as a computer company, it might miss an opportunity to branch into PDAs or Internet service. Thus, they might instead define themselves as a provider of "information solutions." A company should not define itself too broadly, however, since this may result in loss of focus. For example, a manufacturer of baking soda should probably not see itself as a manufacturer of all types of chemicals. Sometimes, companies can define themselves in terms of a customer need. For example, 3M sees itself as being in the business of making products whose surfaces are bonded together. This accounts for both Post-It notes and computer disks.

A firm's mission should generally include a discussion of the *customers served* (e.g., Wal-Mart and Nordstrom's serve different groups), the kind of technology involved, and the markets served.

Several issues are involved in selecting target customers. We will consider these in more detail within the context of segmentation, but for now, the firm needs to consider issues such as:

- The *size* of various market segments;
- How well these segments are being *served by existing firms;*
- *Changes* in the market—e.g., growth of segments or change in technology;

How the firm should be *positioned*, or seen by customers. For example, Wal-Mart positions itself as providing value in retailing, while Nordstrom's defines itself more in terms of high levels of customer service.

The Boston Consulting Group (BCG) matrix provides a firm an opportunity to assess how well its business units work together. Each business unit is evaluated in terms of two factors: market share and the growth prospects in the market. Generally, the larger a firm's share, the stronger its position, and the greater the growth in a market, the better future possibilities.

UNDERSTANDING THE MODEL

Market Share and Market Growth

To understand the Boston Matrix you need to understand how market share and market growth interrelate.

Market share is the percentage of the total market that is being serviced by your company, measured either in revenue terms or unit volume terms. The higher your market share, the higher proportion of the market you control.

The Boston Matrix assumes that if you enjoy a high market share you will normally be making money (this assumption is based on the idea that you will have been in the market long enough to have learned how to be profitable, and will be enjoying scale economies that give you an advantage).

The question it asks is, "Should you be investing your resources into that product line just because it is making you money?" The answer is, "not necessarily."

This is where market growth comes into play. Market growth is used as a measure of a market's attractiveness. Markets experiencing high growth are ones where the total market share available is expanding, and there's plenty of opportunity for everyone to make money.

By contrast, competition in low growth markets is often bitter, and while you might have high market share now, what will the situation look like in a few months or a few years? This makes low growth markets less attractive.

The Matrix Itself

The Boston Matrix categorizes opportunities into four groups, shown on axes of Market Growth and Market Share:

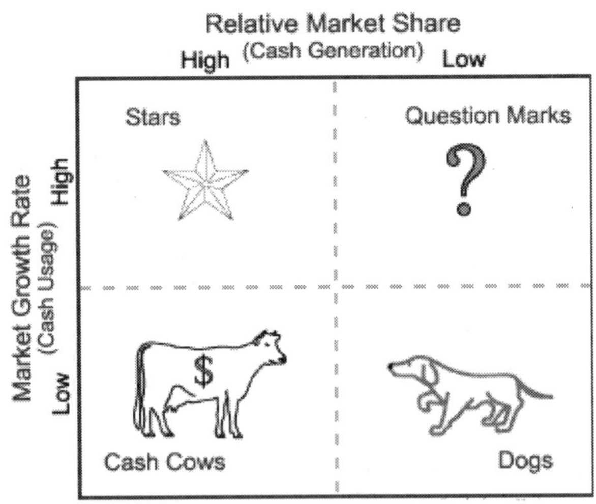

Fig. 12

Four Combinations Emerge

- **Stars: High Market Share/High Market Growth**: Here you're well-established, and growth is exciting. These are fantastic opportunities, and you should work hard to realize them. A *star* represents a business unit that has a high share in a growing market. For example, Motorola has a large share in the rapidly growing market for cellular phones.

- **Question Marks (Problem Child): Low Market Share/High Market Growth**: These are the opportunities no one knows what to do with. They aren't generating much revenue right now because you don't have a large market share. But, they are in high growth markets so the potential to make money is there. Question Marks might become Stars and eventual Cash Cows, but they could just as easily absorb effort with little return. These opportunities need serious thought as to whether increased investment is warranted. A *question mark* results when a unit has a small share in a rapidly growing market. The firm's position, then, is not as strong as it would have been had its market share been greater, but there is an opportunity to grow. For example, Hewlett-Packard has a small share of the digital camera market, but this is a very rapidly growing market.
- **Cash Cows: High Market Share/Low Market Growth**: Here, you're well-established, so it's easy to get attention and exploit new opportunities. However it's only worth expending a certain amount of effort, because the market isn't growing and your opportunities are limited. A *cash cow* results when a firm has a large share in a market that is not growing, and may even be shrinking. Brother has a large share of the typewriter market.
- **Dogs: Low Market Share/Low Market Growth**: In these areas, your market presence is weak, so it's going to take a lot of hard work to get noticed. Also, you won't enjoy the scale economies of the larger players, so it's going to be difficult to make a profit. A *dog* results when a business unit has a small share in a market that is not growing. This is generally a somewhat unattractive situation, although dogs can still be profitable in the short run. For example, Smith Corona how has a small share of the typewriter market.

How to Use the Tool

Step One: Plot your opportunities in terms of their relative market presence, and market growth on the blank matrix provided on the worksheet.

Step Two: Classify them into one of the four categories. If a product seems to fall right on one of the lines, take a real hard look at the situation and rely on past performance to help you decide which side you will place it.

Tip: Be careful about these lines – there's nothing magical about them or their position. There may be very little real difference between a "Problem Child" with a market share of 49%, and a "Star" with a market share of 51%. It's also not necessarily true that the line should run through the 50% position. As ever, use your common sense.

Step Three: Determine what you will do with each product/product line. There are typically four different strategies to apply:

- *Build Market Share:* Make further investments (for example, to maintain Star status, or turn a Question Mark into a Star)

- *Hold:* Maintain the status quo (do nothing)
- *Harvest:* Reduce the investment (enjoy positive cash flow and maximize profits from a Star or Cash Cow)
- *Divest:* For example, get rid of the Dogs, and use the capital to invest in Stars and some Question Marks.

Tip 1: *From a personal perspective, you can evaluate the opportunities open to you by substituting the dimension of "Market Share" with one of "Professional Skills". Plot the options open to you on the personal version of the BCG Matrix, and take action appropriately.*

Tip 2: *A similar (and equally powerful) tool is the Action Priority Matrix, which helps you pick projects which legitimately give you the quickest and highest value returns. By using the BCG Matrix and Action Priority Matrix together, you get the best of both worlds.*

Key Points

The Boston Matrix is an effective tool for quickly assessing the options open to you, both on a corporate and personal basis.

With its easily understood classification into "Dogs", "Cash Cows", "Question Marks" and "Stars", it helps you quickly and simply screen the opportunities open to you, and helps you think about how you can make the most of them.

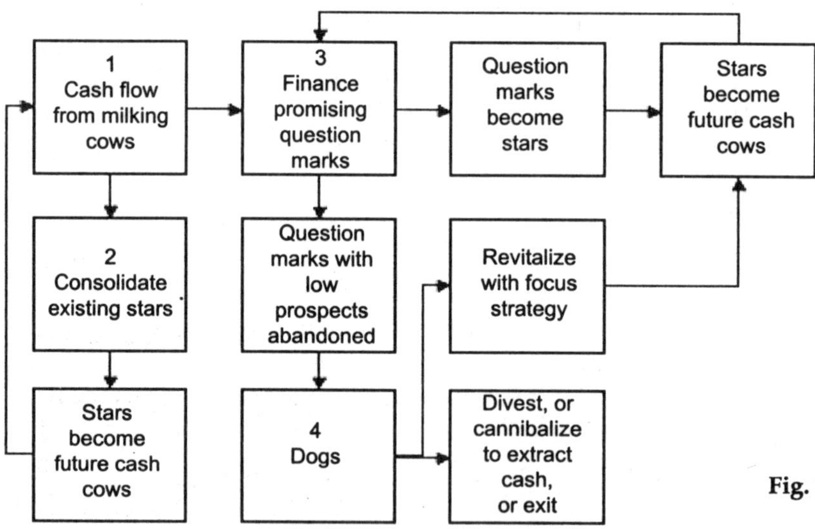

Fig. 13

Firms are usually best of with a portfolio that has a balance of firms in each category. The cash cows tend to generate cash but require little future investment. On the other hand, stars generate some cash, but even more cash is needed to invest in the future—for research and development, marketing campaigns, and building new manufacturing facilities. Therefore, a firm may take excess cash from the cash cow and divert it to the star. For example, Brother could "harvest" its profits from typewriters and invest this in the unit making color laser printers, which will need the cash to grow. If a firm has cash cows that generate a lot of cash, this may be used to try to improve the market share of a question mark. A firm that has a number of promising stars in its portfolio may be in serious trouble if it does not have any cash cows to support it. If it is about to run out of cash—regardless of how profitable it is—is becomes vulnerable as a takeover target from a firm that has the cash to continue running it.

Portfolio Analysis—GE Matrix

The **business portfolio** is the collection of businesses and products that make up the company. The best business portfolio is one that fits the company's strengths and helps exploit the most attractive opportunities.

The company must:

(1) Analyses its current business portfolio and decide which businesses should receive more or less investment, and
(2) Develop growth strategies for adding new products and businesses to the portfolio, whilst at the same time deciding when products and businesses should no longer be retained.

The two best-known portfolio planning methods are the Boston Consulting Group Portfolio Matrix and the McKinsey/General Electric Matrix. In both methods, the first step is to identify the various Strategic Business Units ("SBU's") in a company portfolio. An SBU is a unit of the company that has a separate mission and objectives and that can be planned independently from the other businesses. An SBU can be a company division, a product line or even individual brands—it all depends on how the company is organised.

In consulting engagements with General Electric in the 1970's, McKinsey & Company developed a nine-cell portfolio matrix as a tool for screening GE's large portfolio of strategic business units (SBU). This business screen became known as the **GE/McKinsey Matrix** and is shown below:

The GE / McKinsey matrix is similar to the BCG growth-share matrix in that it maps strategic business units on a grid of the industry and the SBU's position in the industry. The GE matrix however, attempts to improve upon the BCG matrix in the following two ways:

- The GE matrix generalizes the axes as "Industry Attractiveness" and "Business Unit Strength" whereas the BCG matrix uses the market growth rate as a proxy for industry attractiveness and relative *market share* as a proxy for the strength of the business unit.
- The GE matrix has nine cells vs. four cells in the BCG matrix.

Industry attractiveness and business unit strength are calculated by first identifying criteria for each, determining the value of each parameter in the criteria, and multiplying that value by a weighting factor. The result is a quantitative measure of industry attractiveness and the business unit's relative performance in that industry.

GE / McKinsey Matrix

	Business Unit Strength		
	High	Medium	Low
High			
Medium			
Low			

Fig. 14

Industry Attractiveness

The vertical axis of the GE/McKinsey matrix is industry attractiveness, which is determined by factors such as the following:

- Market growth rate
- Market size
- Demand variability
- Industry profitability
- Industry rivalry
- Global opportunities
- Macroenvironmental factors (PEST)

Each factor is assigned a weighting that is appropriate for the industry. The industry attractiveness then is calculated as follows:

$$\text{Industry attractiveness} = \text{factor value}_1 \times \text{factor weighting}_1 + \text{factor value}_2 \times \text{factor weighting}_2 + \text{factor value}_N \times \text{factor weighting}_N$$

Business Unit Strength

The horizontal axis of the GE / McKinsey matrix is the strength of the business unit. Some factors that can be used to determine business unit strength include:

- Market share
- Growth in market share
- Brand equity
- Distribution channel access
- Production capacity
- Profit margins relative to competitors

The business unit strength index can be calculated by multiplying the estimated value of each factor by the factor's weighting, as done for industry attractiveness.

Plotting the Information

Each business unit can be portrayed as a circle plotted on the matrix, with the information conveyed as follows:

- Market size is represented by the size of the circle.
- Market share is shown by using the circle as a pie chart.
- The expected future position of the circle is portrayed by means of an arrow.

The following is an example of such a representation:

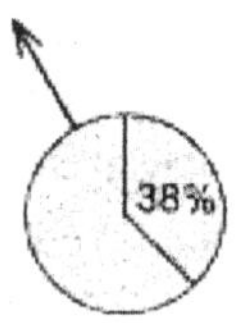

The shading of the above circle indicates a 38% market share for the strategic business unit. The arrow in the upward left direction indicates that the business unit is projected to gain strength relative to competitors, and that the business unit is in an industry that is projected to become more attractive. The tip of the arrow indicates the future position of the center point of the circle.

Strategic Implications

Resource allocation recommendations can be made to grow, hold, or harvest a strategic business unit based on its position on the matrix as follows:

- **Grow** strong business units in attractive industries, average business units in attractive industries, and strong business units in average industries.
- **Hold** average businesses in average industries, strong businesses in weak industries, and weak business in attractive industries.
- **Harvest** weak business units in unattractive industries, average business units in unattractive industries, and weak business units in average industries.

There are strategy variations within these three groups. For example, within the harvest group the firm would be inclined to quickly divest itself of a weak business in an unattractive industry, whereas it might perform a phased harvest of an average business unit in the same industry.

While the GE business screen represents an improvement over the more simple BCG growth-share matrix, it still presents a somewhat limited view by not considering interactions among the business units and by neglecting to address the *core competencies* leading to value creation. Rather than serving as the primary tool for resource allocation, portfolio matrices are better suited to displaying a quick synopsis of the strategic business units.

SWOT Analysis

SWOT is an abbreviation for **Strengths, Weaknesses, Opportunities and Threats** is used to help the firm identify effective strategies. SWOT analysis is an important tool for auditing the overall strategic position of a business and its environment.

Once key strategic issues have been identified, they feed into business objectives, particularly marketing objectives. SWOT analysis can be used in conjunction with other tools for audit and analysis, such as PEST analysis and Porter's Five-Forces analysis. It is also a very popular tool with business and marketing students because it is quick and easy to learn.

Successful firms such as Microsoft have certain strengths. Microsoft, for example, has a great deal of technology, a huge staff of very talented engineers, a great deal of experience in designing software, a very large market share, a well respected brand name, and a great deal of cash. Microsoft also has some weaknesses, however: The game console and MSN units are currently running at a loss, and MSN has been unable to achieve desired levels of growth. Firms may face opportunities in the current market. Microsoft, for example, may have the opportunity to take advantage of its brand name to enter into the hardware market. Microsoft may also become a trusted source of consumer services. Microsoft currently faces several threats, including the weak economy. Because fewer new computers are bough during a recession, fewer operating systems and software packages.

Rather than merely listing strengths, weaknesses, opportunities, and threats, a SWOT analysis should suggest how the firm may use its strengths and opportunities to overcome weaknesses and threats. Decisions should also be made as to how resources should be allocated. For example, Microsoft could either decide to put more resources into MSN or to abandon this unit entirely. Microsoft has a great deal of cash ready to spend, so the option to put resources toward MSN is available. Microsoft will also need to see how threats can be addressed. The firm can earn political good will by engaging in charitable acts, which it has money available to fund. For example, Microsoft has donated software and computers to schools. It can forego temporary profits by reducing prices temporarily to increase demand, or can "hold out" by maintaining current prices while not selling as many units.

The Key Distinction—Internal and External Issues

Strengths and weaknesses are Internal factors. For example, a strength could be your specialist marketing expertise. A weakness could be the lack of a new product.

Opportunities and threats are external factors. For example, an opportunity could be a developing distribution channel such as the Internet, or changing consumer lifestyles that potentially increase demand for a company's products. A threat could be a new competitor in an important existing market or a technological change that makes existing products potentially obsolete. It is worth pointing out that SWOT analysis can be very subjective, two people rarely come-up with the same version of a SWOT analysis even when given the same information about the same business and its environment. Accordingly, SWOT analysis is best used as a guide and not a prescription. Adding and weighting criteria to each factor increases the validity of the analysis.

Areas to Consider

Some of the key areas to consider when identifying and evaluating Strengths, Weaknesses, Opportunities and Threats are listed in the example SWOT analysis below:

	Positive	Negative
Internal factors	*Positive* • Strengths • Technological skills • Leading Brands • Distribution channels • Customer Loyalty/Relationship • Production quality • Scale • Management	*Weaknesses* • Absence of Important skills • Weak brands • Poor success to distribution • Low customer retention • Unreliable product/service • Sub-scale • Management
External factors	*Opportunities* • Changing customer tastes • Liberalisation of geographic markets • Technological advances • Changes in government policies • Lower personal taxes • Change in population age-structure • New Distribution channels	*Threats* • Changing customer tastes • Closing of geographic markets • Technological advances • Changes in government policies • Tax increases • Change in population age-structure • New Distribution channels

Fig. 15

Criteria for effective marketing plans. Marketing plans should meet several criteria:

- The plan must be specific enough so that it can be implemented and communicated to people in the firm. "Improving profitability" is usually too vague, but increasing net profits by 5%, increasing market share by 10%, gaining distribution in 2,000 more stores, and reducing manufacturing costs by 2% are all specific.

- The plan must be measurable so that one can see if it has been achieved. The above plans involve specific numbers.
- The goal must be achievable or realistic. Plans that are unrealistic may result in poor use of resources or lowered morale within the firm.
- The goals must be consistent. For example, a firm cannot ordinarily simultaneously plan improve product features, increase profits, and reduce prices.

To develop strategies that take into account the SWOT profile, a matrix of these factors can be constructed. The SWOT matrix (also known as a **TOWS Matrix**) is shown below:

SWOT / TOWS Matrix

	Strengths	**Weaknesses**
Opportunities	S-O strategies	W-O strategies
Threats	S-T strategies	W-T strategies

Fig. 16

- **S-O strategies** pursue opportunities that are a good fit to the company's strengths.
- **W-O strategies** overcome weaknesses to pursue opportunities.
- **S-T strategies** identify ways that the firm can use its strengths to reduce its vulnerability to external threats.
- **W-T strategies** establish a defensive plan to prevent the firm's weaknesses from making it highly susceptible to external threats.

Applying SWOT Analysis in airline business

Many airline marketers find this exercise a difficult one to accomplish satisfactorily. What it involves is a very careful consideration of your Strengths, Weaknesses, Opportunities and Threats in each major target market segment.

Start at the top left of the chart by considering your Strengths. Let us use the "Elite 1" segment of Business Travel as an example. This is a segment of frequent business travellers from corporations that fly First and Business class. Strengths in this market could include:

- Current performance: a strong market share and high approval

ratings from customers are two indicators of the high performance of a market leader in this segment
- Competitive products: better schedules on the routes served and superior in-flight service are examples of this, but remember that you must be objective to do this exercise properly. Why are the schedules' better for this target market segment, and how is in-flight service superior?
- Effective marketing: excellent customer communications using the Frequent Flyer Programme database could be a strength here, but only if you are really better in this area than the competition.

Weaknesses could include:

- Lack of some key routes needed to offer a complete network to these customers who we know travel extensively. Notice that this is a weakness that is very applicable to this target market segment because of its need for a wide range of destinations.
- Recent punctuality problems. As we saw with the Air media case study in the last chapter, frequent business travellers will be the first to get to know about this type of problem, and it is one that greatly affects their airline selection decisions.
- Shortages of skilled sales staff needed to manage relationships with the major companies and other organisations that generate this travel.

This last weakness is included in this example to underline the importance of being thorough. Marketing people in airlines tend to focus purely on "product issues" when they do a "SWOT"—schedules, aircraft types, seat pitch, catering standards and the like. This is not good enough. In the example above, the shortage of skilled sales staff is crucial; without them, how is the airline concerned going to do its best to minimise the impact of punctuality problems on its share of this particular target market segment?

Next, move on to consider Opportunities and Threats. These will all come from the future competitive situation and market environment that an Airline faces, and any major changes to its own resourcing. Possible Opportunities could include:

- A continuing trend of underlying growth in the market segment.
- The emergence of new segments of travellers. Honeymooning couples from Korea, or female adventure travellers from Germany, for example.
- New aircraft that will improve punctuality and comfort, enabling a higher quality of service to be offered.
- Economic growth and an increase in consumer buying power.

If appropriate, we could also add other opportunities such as new route licenses that can be obtained, or the possibility to form partnerships with other airlines to offer a wider network.

Threats might be as follows:

- A period of international economic instability, that may reduce travel demand and lead to downgrading from First and Business class
- Increased competitor activity, particularly through recruiting customers from this segment into FFPs
- A growing trend to use e-commerce and video-conferencing as a substitute for business travel.

As you will see from the above, many of the elements of this "Model SWOT" are taken from the Air media case study in the previous chapter, showing you how specific items of information from the Market Audit become invaluable for this analysis work. In the case study, we saw that Air media:

- Lacks at least one key route
- Has punctuality problems
- Is operating in a fast growing business travel market
- May suffer from a temporary downturn in the international economic climate
- Is replacing old aircraft with a modem fleet
- Has found out that ground service improvements have a high priority among customers in this target segment

Below a summary of the completed SWOT using all this information:

Strengths	**Weaknesses**
Market leader based on share and approval Superior schedules and service Effective FFP	Lack of some key routes Recent punctuality poor Shortage of account management staff
Continued total market growth New fleet=better reliability and comfort Be a leader in better ground service	Temporary economic downturn FFP competition More use of substitutes
Opportunities	**Threats**

Fig. 17

What you see is a little bit like a **"Marketer's Balance Sheet"**, with assets on the left-hand side and liabilities on the right. The current state of your marketing assets and liabilities is contained under Strengths and Weaknesses; future changes are indicated under Opportunities and Threats.

Please spend a few moments thinking about how you might use this in the next two steps of the Marketing Process—setting Objectives and creating Strategy.

Porter's "Five Forces" and their Application to the Airline Industry

Michael Porter described a concept that has become known as the "five forces model". This concept involves a relationship between competitors within an industry, potential competitors, suppliers, buyers and alternative solutions to the problem being addressed. We used the five-forces model as a basic structure and built on it with concepts from the works of many other authors.

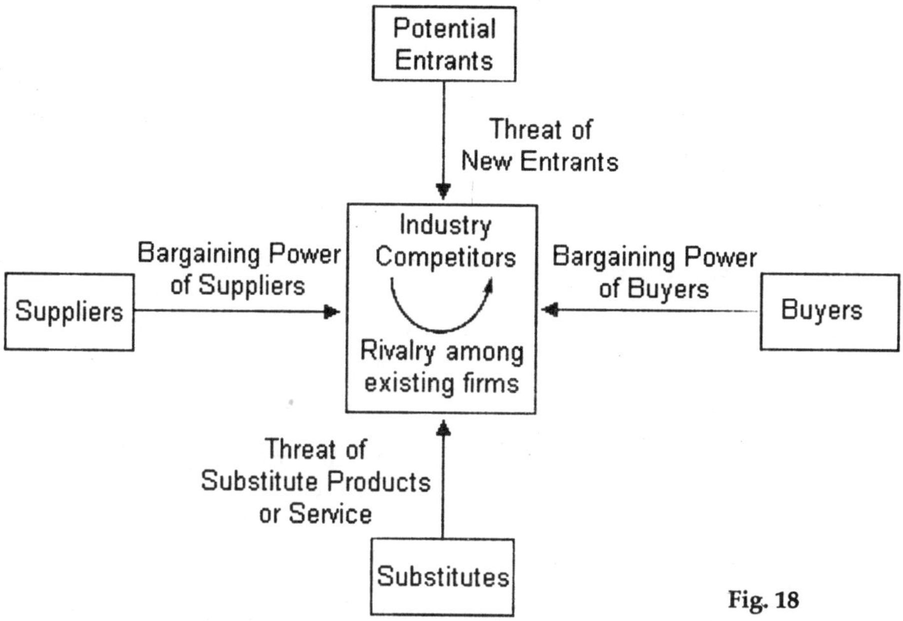

Fig. 18

Understanding the nature of each of these forces gives organizations the necessary insights to enable them to formulate the appropriate strategies to be successful in their market (Thurlby, 1998).

Force 1: The Degree of Rivalry

The intensity of rivalry, which is the most obvious of the five forces in an industry, helps determine the extent to which the value created by an industry will be dissipated through head-to-head competition. The most valuable contribution of Porter's "five forces" framework in this issue may be its suggestion that rivalry, while important, is only one of several forces that determine industry attractiveness.

- This force is located at the centre of the diagram;
- Is most likely to be high in those industries where there is a threat of substitute products; and existing power of suppliers and buyers in the market.

Porter argues that, in many industries, often little of the true competition and the drive for change comes from long-established firms. These long established firms often resemble one another in terms of the strengths which they have, and in their problems and weaknesses. They therefore can only identify benefits from aggressive competition at the n their activities. In the air transport industry, the policies of the long-establish of Europe illustrate this point only too well, especially in their markets. As we saw in the last chapter, there are now no regulator which preclude intense competition between them. Since April airlines of the European Union have competed in a Single A vital where there have been only the very loosest controls over net and fares. Yet, one would hardly know this in those situations old-established airlines have faced one another in he competition. They have mostly flown similar aircraft (usually d the Airbus A320 family), and placed in them identical or nee seating configurations. Frequencies and timings have been with few airlines prepared to allow their competitors advantage. The on-board products have been comparable.

Force 2: The Threat of Entry

Both potential and existing competitors influence average industry profitability. The threat of new entrants is usually based on the market entry barriers. They can take diverse forms and are used to prevent an influx of firms into an industry whenever profits, adjusted for the cost of capital, rise above zero. In contrast, entry barriers exist whenever it is difficult or not economically feasible for an outsider to replicate the incumbents' position (Porter, 1980b; Sanderson, 1998) The most common forms of entry barriers, except intrinsic physical or legal obstacles, are as follows:

- Economies of scale: for example, benefits associated with bulk purchasing;
- Cost of entry: for example, investment into technology;
- Distribution channels: for example, ease of access for competitors;
- Cost advantages not related to the size of the company: for example, contacts and expertise;
- Government legislations: for example, introduction of new laws might weaken company's competitive position;
- Differentiation: for example, certain brand that cannot be copied (The Champagne)

The second of the forces which may disturb the competitive equilibrium amongst the existing players is that of new entry. In some industries, new entry is difficult or impossible. In others, it is commonplace. In the modern aviation industry, the latter is very much the case, especially in short-haul, point-to-point markets. This is because of the many possible so-called "Barriers to Entry", most have become low or are now non-existent. A first possible barrier to entry may result from regulatory limitations. There are still regulatory barriers to entry in many international markets, and airlines are constrained in their market entry policies by out-of-date and anachronistic limitations on ownership and control. However, it is now the case that many of the world's largest domestic markets, such as those of the United States and the European Union, now operate without any significant entry controls, apart from those applying to so-called Cabotage Rights.

In others cases, *resources* may act as a Barrier-to-Entry. If vital resources are unavailable or very costly, entry will clearly be constrained. In the aviation industry, airport slots provide a classic resource barrier to entry. As long as airport slots continue to be awarded under the Grandfather Rights principle, it will be very difficult for new entrants to gain access to attractively-timed slots at congested hub airports. Significant though slot constraints already are, with a likely worsening of them in the future, radical strategies are possible which find a way round them.

In particular, Europe's vibrant low-fares scene, has largely grown free of airport slot constraints because of the willingness of the airlines to use uncontested airports, sometimes located a considerable distance from the cities they are designed to serve.

Slot constraints may provide some comfort to existing airlines in Europe today, but they can derive little more from the remaining possible resource constraints to entry. Especially during downturns, such as the one become experienced in the industry at the time or writing, resources to underpin entry are actually remarkably cheap and plentiful.

This is certainly the case with the question of the aircraft fleet that will be needed by a new entrant airline. In a recessionary period, aircraft manufacturers will be prepared to strike very attractive deals for the white-tailed aircraft which result from order cancellations. Also, there will be large numbers of parked aircraft—many of them owned by leasing companies—where the owners will offer extremely low lease rates in order to get their idle aircraft flying once again.

Staff resources—especially of pilots and mechanics—will also be important. Again, in a recessionary period many trained people will unfortunately lose their jobs, and may well be prepared to take new ones at relatively low salaries and wages in order to obtain employment.

As a final, and, at first sight, odd feature of resource constraints on entry in the aviation industry, it will always be possible for a new entrant to buy the support services, such as maintenance and ground handling that it needs. Many airlines have built subsidiary businesses offering such services and they will be prepared to sell these to a new entrant, even if the new entrant's business plan involves competing with them. They will reason that if they do not meet the need, this will not stop the new entrant. Instead, the required services will be bought elsewhere, denying the first airline some useful revenue.

Several more issues need to be covered in assessing the nature of barriers to entry in the airline business. Some industries are characterised by marked *Economies of Scale*, where lower unit costs can be obtained by large scale producers. Many heavy industries such as steel, chemicals and car-making are like this. In them, existing firms are likely to be protected against entry because they will have been able to achieve a scale of production which is unlikely to be available to a new entrant.

In the airline business, there are some aspects where existing players are protected against new entry by scale economies. In particular, hubbing operations where short-haul passengers are collected together in order to feed long-haul services are increased in their effectiveness by being undertaken at a substantial scale. It is hard for small new entrants to break in. In point-to-point markets, however, no such protection for incumbents exists. Economies of scale in areas like pilot training and maintenance quickly run out with increasing size, and are counterbalanced by the bureaucracy and poor staff morale often characteristic of the organisations. In some industries, incumbents have a lot of protection against new entrants because of so-called *Learning Curve* effects. In these industries mature firms achieve lower costs than new entrants because the intricacies of the production process mean that substantial experience is required before optimum cost levels can be achieved.

Airlines, on the other hand, seem to show opposite effect, with the concept of *Start-up Economics* a well-established one. Airlines often achieve their lowest costs of operation during the fir five years of their existence. Later on, costs tend to rise as more sit ascend seniority scales towards higher rates of pay and bureaucracy am declining staff morale start to impact on cost levels.

The existence or stall up cost advantages does of course, make the task facing a new airline" significantly easier one. One final issue with regard to entry into the airline industry is difficult to analyse, but very important. Over the last twenty years, the list airlines which have entered the industry and then left it again through bankruptcy is a depressingly long one. All the evidence one could possible) require is there to illustrate the point that investing in and setting up a new airline is, at best, highly speculative, with an overwhelming likelihood 01 failure. From this, one might assume that new entry into the aviation industry would largely be a thing of the past, especially given the depressed state of the industry in the early years of the new century. Nothing could be further from the truth, with the pressure of entry seemingly as strong, or stronger, than ever. One explanation for this apparent contradiction is that aviation is seen as a glamorous and exciting industry by many, and that the dream to set up and own one's own airline is a continuing one for those with large egos and deep pockets. Industries with dirty, unpleasant processes at their heart do not have the same appeal, despite the fact that profits and returns on capital may be much better within them. The English expression, "where there's muck there's brass" is a telling one. As an overall conclusion to the question of entry, incumbent airlines must prepare themselves for a continuing challenge from new entrants, especially in their short-haul, point-to-point markets.

Force 3: The Threat of Substitutes

The threat that substitute products pose to an industry's profitability depends on the relative price-to-performance ratios of the different types of products or services to which customers can turn to satisfy the same basic need.

The threat of substitution is also affected by switching costs – that is, the costs in areas such as retraining, retooling and redesigning that are incurred when a customer switches to a different type of product or service. It also involves:

- Product-for-product substitution (email for mail, fax); is based on the substitution of need;
- Generic substitution (Video suppliers compete with travel companies);
- Substitution that relates to something that people can do without (cigarettes, alcohol).

Porter argues that disturbance to the competitive equilibrium of long-established firms can come from two possible sources, these being that of Substitution. Substitution occurs when firm: industry find a new and better way of meeting the same customer are being targeted by the existing players. There are a number of substitution issues affecting air! present time. Of these, potentially the most serious is the electronic methods of communication on the market for business. Video-conferencing, teleconference email all have the potential to mean that business of international travelers will and still satisfy their needs for effective communication. At writing, there are worrying signs that this is exactly what is h; effect which is likely to increase still further during future down Surface transport, especially by rail, also raises important issues. Unlike airlines, railways can provide city centre to travel, and have been shown to severely impact on the market once these city-centre to city-centre journey times can down below three hours.

The air freight industry is also being affected by Substitution issues. Email is substantially reducing the market for the movement of urgent documents by air. Also, newspapers do not provide the lucrative air freight commodity they once did. They still lose their value completely soon after they have been published. The problem is, though, that today media publishers are increasingly reaching their readers through the Internet, or by setting up satellite printing stations which enable newspapers to be printed simultaneously in a large number of different markets. They therefore no longer have to make use of air freight.

Force 4: Buyer Power

Buyer power is one of the two horizontal forces that influence the appropriation of the value created by an industry (refer to the diagram). The most important determinants of buyer power are the size and the concentration of customers. Other factors are the extent to which the buyers are informed and the concentration or differentiation of the competitors. Kippenberger (1998) states that it is often useful to distinguish potential buyer power from the buyer's willingness or incentive to use that power, willingness that derives mainly from the "risk of failure" associated with a product's use.

- This force is relatively high where there a few, large players in the market, as it is the case with retailers an grocery stores;
- Present where there is a large number of undifferentiated, small suppliers, such as small farming businesses supplying large grocery companies;
- Low cost of switching between suppliers, such as from one fleet supplier of trucks to another.

Porter argues that the power of their customers will be a crucial determinant of profitability for the firms in any industry. In turn, customer power will be related to two variables: the number of customers a firm h, and the existence—or otherwise—of so-called *Switching Costs*.

In principle, the point about the number of customers is an obvious one, If a firm has many customers and some of these defect to f competition, there will still be a large number of customers remaining. On the other hand, the firm has only two or three customers, the loss of 0 of them will result in a third or more of its business being lost. In such situation, customers will have extreme amounts of bargaining power. They will be able to cut deals on terms which are extremely attractive to the! holding down the profits of the companies from which they are buying.

Despite the unambiguous nature of this point, a series of indus1 trends during the 1990s suggested that airlines were ignoring it. They allowed the size of their customer base to decline steadily, with serious consequences for their profitability.

This decline resulted from at least three factors. Firstly, as we ha seen, there was an increase in the extent to which firms in business travellers were prepared to use their bargaining power to conclude corporate deals which a degree of loyalty was traded for substantial price discounts, TJ changed the nature of the business travel market. Instead of the airline *customers* being the business travellers who actually flew, they w(increasingly negotiating with a relatively small number of finance a purchasing people who had been given the responsibility of negotiating corporate deals.

The structure of the travel agency industry also changed 'during 1 1990s, In many countries, life became harder for the smaller, independent agent. Instead, an increasing share of the market was held by large multinational, agency chains, who achieved substantial power as a result their ability—often exaggerated, but still significant—to switch passenger between airlines according the commissions they were being paid.

Such a trend did not arise by accident. Many airlines adopted a pool of paying so-called over-ride commissions to agents according to volume of business delivered to them. In the short term, such a pool gained them the greatest amount of revenue. It did, though, give import advantages to large travel agents who could meet their revenue targets over-rides, These agents were in turn able to use their higher commission to fund market share battles against their smaller rivals, further cement their domination.

In the last ten years have seen a revolution in the distribution channels used by airlines. The Internet has become a very important channel, and from the issues raised in this section, it is easy to see why. The Internet allows carriers to begin the process of broadening their customer base once again, and to make better contact with the true sources of their revenue. They are therefore able to address the problems of escalating commission costs and falling yields, which were a clear consequence of the mistaken polices of the 1990s.

A final question with the size of the airline customer base is in some senses the most worrying of all. Porter warns that if one, or a small number of the firm's customers become too big, they may take the view that it would be more cost -efficient to take on the resources to do the job themselves. If they do, a firm may lose all of the large amount of business currently being obtained from a singly source. Worse still, the former customer may decide that there is actually money to be made in the new area of activity. If it does, it will not only cease to supply business to the firm in question, but will actively begin to compete with the firm for its remaining customers.

In the aviation industry, a common situation where a customer turns into a competitor occurs when a tour operator grows bigger and bigger, giving larger amounts of business to existing charter airlines. Often, a point arrives where it will make sense for the tour operator to buy its own aircraft, in order to set up an airline to carry its own passengers and perhaps also the competition in the open market for other airlines' passengers as well. The tax benefits associated with aircraft ownership can be an added incentive to do this, given that tour operators ordinarily do not have significant capital assets to use to offset against their tax liabilities.

The subject of so-called *Integrated Carriers* is also an interesting one with regard to the question of customers becoming competitors. In summary, they are freight companies specialising in the movement of relatively small, urgent, packages. When they begin service on a new route, it is normal for them to offer substantial amounts of business to existing combination airlines. This helps them to grow their traffic. Unfortunately for the combination airlines, once they have done so, it has been common practice for them to then put on their own specialist freighter aircraft.

The question of *Switching Costs* is an equally difficult one. In s industries, there are very substantial costs associated with switching 1 one supplier to another. Airline fleet planning illustrated this point well. An airline only using, for example, Boeing aircraft will have bui] a large investment in Boeing spare parts, Boeing-orientated t1 simulators, and in the training of its staff to be familiar with Bo products. There will therefore be a strong financial incentive to continue buy from Boeing. If Airbus is to break the stranglehold of Boeing at an airline, they will have to offer very large discounts on the purchase I of their aircraft, in order to effectively pay themselves for the switch costs of moving away from Boeing. They will probably have to offer n other incentives as well, such as large amounts of free pilot training.

The problem for airlines is that they do not have the Switching protection which assist aircraft manufacturers in retaining their customer base. An airline may be getting a worthwhile amount of business fn major customer as a result of having a corporate deal with them. It will be a simple task, though, for another carrier to come along and offer customer a more attractive level of discount, with the result that corporate deal with the first airline is cancelled and transferred in second. This will easy, because little capital investment or trainer required to work with one airline rather than another.

Force 5: Supplier Power

Supplier power is a mirror image of the buyer power. As a result, the analysis of supplier power typically focuses first on the relative size and concentration of suppliers relative to industry participants and second on the degree of differentiation in the inputs supplied. The ability to charge customers different prices in line with differences in the value created for each of those buyers usually indicates that the market is characterized by high supplier power and at the same time by low buyer power (Porter, 1998). Bargaining power of suppliers exists in the following situations:

- Where the switching costs are high (switching from one Internet provider to another);
- High power of brands (McDonalds, British Airways, Tesco);
- Possibility of forward integration of suppliers (Brewers buying bars);
- Fragmentation of customers (not in clusters) with a limited bargaining power (Gas/Petrol stations in remote places).

Most obviously, suppliers of air traffic control and airport services may have it, with many airlines having no choice but to pay whatever ATC and airport charges are levied on them. It is most noticeable that at the time of writing airline profits have been severely affected in a major industry downturn, but the pain of this is not being evenly distributed across the industry. Many airports are continuing to show strong financial returns, reflecting the monopoly power that many of them have. Sometimes, airlines' fleet planning can be affected by powerful supplier issues. The Boeing 747 was introduced into airline service in 1970, and was unchallenged by any other aircraft for the next 25 years. If a carrier's requirement was a long-range aircraft with 400+ seats, the 747 was the only option available to them. Not surprisingly, the aircraft became a very profitable project for Boeing. In the future, a similar situation may develop with the 555 seat Airbus A380, where it is now clear that there will be no Boeing competitor when deliveries of this aircraft begin in 2006.

Perhaps the best, and most controversial, example of powerful suppliers in the aviation industry has concerned the so-called *Global Distribution Systems* (GDSs).

Since their inception in the late 1980s, the GDSs have provided the switching technology which allows travel agents to make reservations with hundreds of different airlines, hotels, car rental companies and tour operators through a single computer keyboard.

Unlike airlines, the GDS business is one of immense scale economies. The capital costs of entering the business are very high, but running costs are low. Large firms can therefore spread their capital costs over greater volumes of output and achieve lower unit costs. As a result, there are only four significant players in the global GDS industry—the US based SABRE and World span, and European-originating Galileo and Amadeus. All were first set up by airlines or consortia of airlines, though in recent years their ownership has become more diverse.

Besides strongly concentrated patterns of ownership, the GDS industry also shows a trend towards the establishment of geographical monopolies. For example, a high proportion of travel agents in the UK use Galileo. An equally high proportion in France and Germany are Amadeus customers.

The GDS companies do not, of course, provide their services free.

When they were first proposed, the plan was that the costs associated with them would be shared equally between travel agents and airlines. Travel agents would pay substantial rent to the company which supplied them with a GDS service, reflecting the fact that the GDS allowed them to substantially increase the productivity of their staff.

It has not worked out this way. Because of the economies of s involved, the GDS companies have seen it as a major business objective, increase their market share in order to boost transaction volume. They done so by engaging in aggressive pricing, so aggressive in many cases travel agents have been given a GDS service free-of-charge if they switch from one firm to another.

The result of such a policy has been that the costs of GDS are disproportionately on airlines, with the current level of booking fee the, paying being between $4 and $4.50 per passenger.

Not surprisingly, such a situation has been regarded as unsatisfactory by many airlines, particularly by those which have benefited by having a shareholding in a GDS.

Some carriers, the UK firm Easy jet, have from the beginning adopted a radical policy direct selling, completely by-passing the travel agency distribution system Besides avoiding commission payments, this policy has also allowed airline to save on GDS booking fees. This has been something of, importance to a low fares airline given that booking fees are levied on booking made and thus potentially make up a disproportionate amount cost for such an airline.

For traditional carriers, the travel agency system has overwhelm been their main channel of distribution, with 85-90% of their booking coming from this source. They have not, therefore, been able to refund pay GDS booking fees. Had they done so, the GDS firms would have removed the schedules and fares information of the recall airlines from their database, with the result that almost all the booking they might have received from travel agents would have been Therefore, in Porter terms, the GDS companies were monopoly supplier (vital resources, and it should have come as no surprise that during) 1990s they were highly profitable.

"Disintermediation"

Sometimes, in the application of the Five Forces model, situations where relationships between firms change radically. This is espe4 likely when a particular player or group of players is not adding sufficient value to justify the prices that they are charging. An attempt may then be made to by-pass them, in a process which Porter describes a *Disintermediation*. Two examples, one actual and one potential, illustrate this process in the aviation industry. Returning to the example of the Gm firms given above, the recent rapid growth in the use of the Internet as a distribution channel reflects a clear attempt by airlines to disinter media the GDS companies, one which has already saved them substantial amount in terms of booking fees.

Another interesting case comes from the freight side of the industry. In recent years, a number of companies have grown up which have specialized in providing so-called *wet-leasing* services for large freighter aircraft—(mainly the Boeing 747F). The American firm Atlas air is the most notable of these. By using their services, an airline can offer its customers main deck freight capacity, without the costly overheads of owning and operating freighter aircraft themselves. In particular, they can save money because Atlas air crew salaries are generally very much lower than the often stratospheric rates of pay given to 747 crews by traditional airlines.

The potential problem of such policies is, though, very clear, in that the airlines using wet-leased freighters are adding very little value. Mostly, they are taking pre-loaded Unit Load Devices (ULDs) from air freight forwarders, and loading these onto the wet-leased freighters. Sooner or later, the freight forwarders may decide that it will be more profitable for them to wet-lease the freighters themselves, and employ local handling agents to perform the simple task of dealing with the pre-loaded units. When they do, this will be a classic case of *Disintermediation*.

Overall, Porter's Five Forces model provides a valuable backcloth against which to view airline strategic decision making. Any airline strategy, if it is to be successful, must deal with a complex interplay of often conflicting forces.

Generic Strategies

Generic strategies were used initially in the early 1980s, and seem to be even more popular today. They outline the three main strategic options open to organization that wish to achieve a sustainable competitive advantage. Each of the three options are considered within the context of two aspects of the competitive environment:

Sources of competitive advantage—*are the products differentiated in any way, or are they the lowest cost producer in an industry?* Competitive scope of the market—*does the company target a wide market, or does it focus on a very narrow, niche market?*

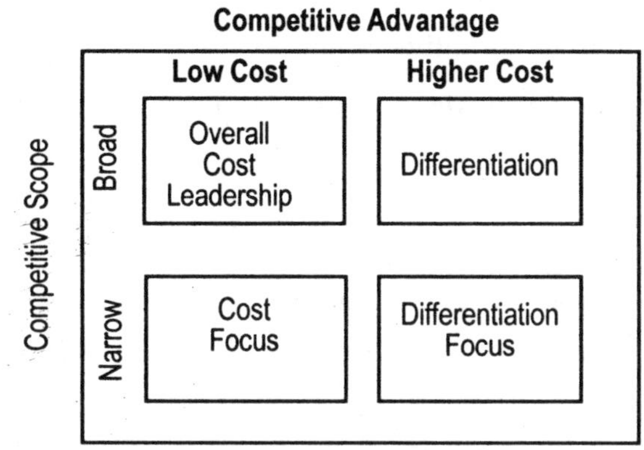

Porter's Generic Strategies

Adapted from Michael B. Porter, The Competitive Advantage of Nations (New York: The Free Press, 1980), p. 39.

Fig. 19

The generic strategies are: *1. Cost leadership, 2. Differentiation, and 3. Focused.*

1. COST LEADERSHIP STRATEGIES

The low cost leader in any market gains competitive advantage from being able to many to produce at the lowest cost. Factories are built and maintained; labour is recruited and trained to deliver the lowest possible costs of production. 'cost advantage' is the focus. Costs are shaved off every element of the value chain. Products tend to be 'no frills.' However, low cost does not always lead to low price. Producers could price at competitive parity, exploiting the benefits of a bigger margin than competitors. Some organizations, such as Toyota, are very good not only at producing high quality autos at a low price, but have the brand and marketing skills to use a premium pricing policy.

This strategy emphasizes efficiency. By producing high volumes of standardized products, the firm hopes to take advantage of economies of scale and experience curve effects. The product is often a basic no-frills product that is produced at a relatively low cost and made available to a very large customer base. Maintaining this strategy requires a continuous search for cost reductions in all aspects of the business. The associated distribution strategy is to obtain the most extensive distribution possible. Promotional strategy often involves trying to make a virtue out of low cost product features.

To be successful, this strategy usually requires a considerable market share advantage or preferential access to raw materials, components, labour, or some other important input. Without one or more of these advantages, the strategy can easily be mimicked by competitors. Successful implementation also benefits from:

1. Process engineering skills.

2. Products designed for ease of manufacture.
3. Sustained access to inexpensive capital.
4. Close supervision of labour.
5. Tight cost control.
6. Incentives based on quantitative targets.

Examples include low-cost airlines such as Easy Jet and Southwest Airlines, and supermarkets such as Big bazaar.

A firm pursuing a cost-leadership strategy attempts to gain a competitive advantage primarily by reducing its economic costs below its competitors.

If cost-leadership strategies can be implemented by numerous firms in an industry, or if no firms face a cost disadvantage in imitating a cost-leadership strategy, then being a cost leader does not generate a sustained competitive advantage for a firm. The ability of a valuable cost-leadership competitive strategy to generate a sustained competitive advantage depends on that strategy being rare and costly to imitate.

Sources of Cost Advantage

Economies of Scale

One of the most cited sources of cost advantage for a firm is its SIZE. There is a relationship between firm size measured in terms of volume of production—and costs—measured in terms of average costs per unit of production. The optimal volume of production is reached when the average costs per unit of production is minimum.

Sources of economies of scale:

1. **Volume of production and specialized machines**: A company with a high level of production, it is able to purchase and use specialized manufacturing tools that cannot be kept in operation in small companies.
2. **Volume of production and cost of plant and equipment**: A high volume of production may allow a firm to build larger manufacturing operations. Large-volume firms will be able to build lower per unit cost manufacturing operations and will have lower average costs of production.
3. **Volume of production and employees specialization**: High volumes of production are also associated with high levels of employee specialization. Adam Smith first observed that cost advantages may be associated with the division of labour.
4. **Volume of production and overhead costs**: A firm with high volumes of production can spread its overheads costs (accounting, control, R&D,) over more units.

Diseconomies of Scale

Sources of diseconomies of scale:

1. **Physical limits to efficient size**: There are physical limitations to the size of some manufacturing processes.
2. **Managerial diseconomies**: As a firm increases in size, it often increases in complexity, and the ability of managers to control and operate it efficiently becomes limited.
3. **Worker motivation:** A third source of diseconomies of scale depends on the relationship between firm size, employee specialization and employee motivation. One of the advantages of high volumes of production is that it allows workers to specialize in smaller and more narrowly defined production tasks. However, researches suggest that these types of specialized jobs can be de-motivating for employees and can affect productivity and quality. Solutions have been experienced: participation schemes, quality circles, etc
4. **Distance to markets and suppliers:** A source of diseconomies of scale can be the distance between a large manufacturing facility and the place where the goods are sold, or the places where essential raw materials are purchased (large transportation costs).

The Learning Curve

The learning-curve model attempts to relate the volume of production and coats over time. Economies of scale focuses on the relationship between the volume of production at a given point in time and average unit costs. The learning-curve focuses on the relationship between the cumulative volume of production and average unit costs.

- **Differential Low-Cost Access to Factors of Production**
  Differential low-cost access to factors of production may create cost differences among firms producing similar products in an industry. Factors of production are any inputs used by a firm in conducting its business activities. They include labour (human resources), capital, land, raw materials, knowledge)
- **Technological Advantages Independent of Scale**
  A possible source of cost advantage—not depending on economies of scale—may be the different technologies that firms employ to manage their business. Technologies include not only technological hardware of companies but also technological software of firms (quality of relations among labour and management, an organization's culture, the quality of managerial controls). All these characteristics of a firm have an impact on a firm's economic costs.
- **Policy Choices**
  In general firms that attempt to implement a cost-leadership strategy will choose to produce relatively simple standardized products that

sell for relatively low prices compared to the products and prices of firms pursuing other business or corporate strategies.

When does a low-cost producer strategy work best?

- When price competition among rival sellers is a dominant competitive force
- When the industry's product is a standard, commodity-type item readily available from a variety of sellers
- When there are not many ways to achieve product differentiation that have value to the buyer
- When most buyers use the product in the same ways and have much the same needs/requirements
- When buyers incur low switching costs in changing from one seller to another and are prone to shop for the best price
- When buyers are large and have significant bargaining power

The competitive strengths of a low-cost producer strategy

- A low-cost leader is in the strongest position to set the floor on market price (competitive strategy principle)
- A low-cost producer strategy provides attractive defenses against competitive forces: rival competitors, buyers, suppliers, potential entrants, substitutes)

Cost leadership and the Five Forces Model

Threat of Entry: If an incumbent firm is a cost leader, the new entrants may have to invest heavily to reduce their costs prior to entry. Often, new entrants will enter using another business strategy (differentiation, alliance) rather than attempting to compete on costs.

Threat of Rivalry: This threat is reduced through two choices of pricing strategies.

1. The cost-leader can set its price equal to the price of higher-cost competitors. By doing this, it reduces the chance that competitors will imitate the low-cost firm. However, keeping prices equal to a competitor's prices does sacrifice market share and sales volume. At this competitive price, the cost-leader firm earns an above-normal profit.
2. The low-cost firm can price its goods or services below the prices of its high-cost rivals. The lower price of the low-cost firm will attract numerous customers and increase its market share and sales volume but the cost is a lower profit earned. This strategy sends a signal to competitors that lower costs are possible. Such a signal may motivate competitors to try to reduce theirs costs.

Threat of Substitutes: Cost-leader firm has the ability to keep its products or services attractive relative to substitutes.

Threat of Suppliers: Suppliers can become a Threat to a firm by charging higher prices for the goods or services they supply or by reducing the quality of those goods or services. However, when a supplier sells to a cost leader, that firm has greater flexibility in absorbing higher-cost suppliers than does a high-cost firm. Higher supply costs may destroy any above-normal profits for high-cost firms but still allow a cost-leader firm to earn an above-normal profit.

Threat of Buyers: Cost leadership can also reduce the threat of buyers. Powerful buyers are a threat to firms when they insist on low prices or higher quality and service from their suppliers. Lower prices threaten firm revenues. Higher quality can increase a firm's costs. Cost leaders can have their revenues reduced by buyer threats and still earn normal or above-normal profits. These firms can also absorb the greater costs of increased quality or service and may still have a cost advantage over their competition.

Competitive advantage through cost leadership

Cost leadership is valuable if:

- Buyers do not value differentiation very much
- Buyers are price-sensitive
- Competitors will not immediately match lower prices (do game theoretic analysis)

Competitive advantage through cost leadership is sustainable if:

- there are no changes in consumer tastes, technology and exogenous prices/costs
- the activities taken to achieve low costs are rare and costly to imitate

Organizing for sustained cost advantage

A firm that has a cost advantage that is rare and costly to imitate has significant potential for earning above-normal returns.

Organizational attributes for firms implementing cost leadership strategies:

- Firms generally have few layers in their reporting structure. Corporate staff in these firms are kept small. These firms do not vertically integrate into a wide range of business functions. Most operating decisions are delegate to unit (or plants) managers who have fully profit-and-loss responsibilities for their operations.
- Sustained capital investment and access to capital.
- Process engineering skills.
- Product designed for ease in manufacturing.
- Tight cost control systems: frequent and detailed control reports and

close supervision of labour, raw material, inventory, distribution, and other cots.

- Reward for cost reduction and incentives based on meeting strict quantitative targets and increasing or maintaining quality.
- A cost leadership philosophy.

Cost control tools

- Full costing method.
- Direct Costing Method (Uniform System of Accounts for Hospitality Industry).
- Activity Based Costing (ABC): costs per activity. This creates an entirely new approach to costing. This also leads to activity management.

Risks of cost leadership

- Technological change that nullifies past investment or learning
- Low cost learning by industry newcomers
- Inability to see required product or market change
- Inflation in costs

Cost Leadership in the Airline Industry

The concept of Cost Leadership strategies is by no means new in the airline industry. In 1973, a new carrier, Southwest Airlines, was set up (after a series of drawn out legal battles instigated by incumbent carriers), to serve the intra-state Texan market in the USA. The airline became profitable in 1975, and, remarkably, has stayed profitable ever since. It has remained in the black even during the recessionary periods of 1991-94 and from 2000 until the time of writing, when the losses made by almost all the other airlines in the USA have been very large indeed.

It has been the period since the middle 1990s that has seen the rapid spread of the use of Cost Leadership strategies around the world. We now have two large, and rapidly growing airlines employing it in Europe, Ryan air and Easy jet, as well as many smaller new entrants. A new airline, Jet blue Airways, has appeared in the USA, and has made a very successful and profitable beginning. This has been no mean feat considering the sea of red ink which is currently engulfing the US airline industry. Other examples of new entrant Cost Leader players around the world include West jet in Canada, Virgin Blue in Australia, Gol in Brazil and Air Asia, a domestic and regional carrier in Malaysia.

Besides these existing players, a high proportion of the start-up proposals being put forward at the moment currently include Cost Leadership elements in them.

It is instructive to ask the question why recent times have seen this explosion in the use of Cost Leadership strategies, when the success of the pioneer, Southwest, had been obvious for many years.

Regulatory liberalisation is one obvious explanation. The agreement for the setting up of the Single Aviation Market of the European Union in 1993 has given opportunities for new entry which never existed before. Liberalisation of various domestic markets—notably those of Canada and Australia—has also been helpful in allowing start-up entrepreneurs to fulfill their ambitions. It is notable that those markets which have so far seen the least development of Cost Leadership—for example South East Asia—are also still amongst the most regulated.

The arrival of the Internet as a channel for airline distribution has also been highly significant. Until the middle 1990s, distribution was both a challenging and costly for airlines, which were mostly forced to rely on one channel of distribution, that provided by the travel agency industry.

The Internet has changed this situation beyond all recognition. For carriers that have been prepared to break with the past and simplify their fares and reservations procedures, the Internet has provided a route to speedy and cost-effective distribution.

The changing nature of the business air travel market provides a final and interesting explanation for the growth of Cost Leadership strategies. Up until the middle 1990s, airlines were greatly favoured by the fact that business travellers generally paid high prices for expensive, but prestigious travel in Business Class on board airlines which dedicated a great deal of effort to meeting a range of needs centered around prestige and status.

Some of them are still prepared to do this, but a number of changes have now taken place. In recent years have seen an increase in the importance of the so-called "Independent" business traveller. These are people who work for themselves or for small firms, and who feel that the price of an air ticket comes out of their own pocket. Even in the corporate travel market, business travellers are being forced to become more price-sensitive by the corporate purchasing of business travel, whereby companies trade lower fares for loyalty. Even travel agents now join in the quest for lower fares as they seek to prove their ability to get value-far-money, in order to retain their increasingly demanding corporate clients.

Whatever the explanation, the interest being shown around the world in Cost Leadership strategies now makes this the most important strategic development in the industry in recent years.

Fundamentals of the Business Model

The business principles that underlie Cost Leadership need hold no terrors for the analyst. They are now very well understood, and remarkably straight forward.

Underlying all these principles is one fundamental philosophy—that of *simplicity*. Some of the world's most successful and profitable businesses have taken processes which from the point-of-view of the user were complicated and simplified them.

Outside of the aviation industry, computing provides a good example. Thirty years ago, the use of computers was restricted to a relatively small and highly trained group. Today, computers are used by almost everyone, because software firms such as Microsoft have taken all the mystique and difficulties away. The result has been a remarkable virtuous circle. Growing demand for PCs and laptops has lead to very large economies of scale in production, which have in turn allowed for further price reductions. *Coming to the airline business, the example* of *so-called* Integrate Traditional airlines were only interested in relatively easy job of moving shipments from airport to airport. This left the shipper to make arrangements for collection and delivery, documentation and customs clearance. The result was that large organisations, air freight forwarder grew up to handle air freight shipments, because lay people could not undertake the task themselves. Over the years, forwarders have cost airlines immense sums in commissions and in the consequences of reduced market control.

The situation today for the non-expert who has a small package needing air transportation is very different. Integrated carriers—for example, DHL, FedEx, UPS and TNT—all offer a collection and delivery service. They have simplified documentation so that non-expert people can easily complete it, and arrange customs clearance. For added peace of mind, they also have a comprehensive tracking and tracing service available over the Internet.

The result has been exactly as one would expect. The market for small, urgent packages—the so-called "Express" market—is the fastest growing part of the air freight market. The growth, though, is not benefiting the traditional airlines with the complicated demands which they place on the customer. Rather, the market share of the Integrators is steadily increasing, allowing them to further reduce their prices as they benefit from the substantial economies of scale inherent in small package operations.

If we turn now to the strategies of traditional airlines on the passenger side, the importance of simplicity or, rather, the lack of it becomes clearer still. This is best illustrated in the area of pricing policy. To the passenger, the question "what will the fare be?" for a given journey on a given day, seems to be completely straightforward, but airlines have been incapable of giving a straightforward answer. Often, fifty or more fares are available on a given route. Which one the passenger will actually be able to use will depend on their ability to satisfy a range of conditions around such things as advanced booking, length of stay and cancellation/rebooking opportunities.

The consequences of such complexities are severe. They make the training of new reservations and ticketing personnel a costly and time-consuming process. Even more so, the point-of-sale task becomes a slow and complex one.

Overall, achieving and sustaining simplicity in business processes is absolutely fundamental requirement for a successful Cost Leadership strategy. Bearing this point in mind, let us now explore the basic feature of the strategy:

1. Low Fleet Costs

Most successful Cost Leader airlines today; pursuing a so-called "fleet commonality" policy, having only one type aircraft in the fleet. In turn, for most, this one type is the various members of the Boeing 737 family. Whatever this aircraft may now lack (at Ie according to Airbus) in passenger appeal and the use of the lat, technology, it has rugged and proven reliability as its greatest asset. That are exactly the qualities needed by a Cost Leader airline, and Southwest Airlines (with a fleet now consisting of more that 360 737s) a Ryan air illustrate very well a commonality policy with 737s. By sticking to one type of aircraft, they are gaining substantial economies in such an as pilot training and maintenance.

Jet blue Airways at the moment is alone amongst the main 0 Leaders, in that it follows a fleet commonality policy, but around the A3 family aircraft rather than 737s. Easy jet began as a 737 operator, but 2002 signed a very large deal for the acquisition of A319s, a small version of the A320. One must assume that the deal offered by Airbus so attractive that it led the airline's management to conclude that acquisition costs would outweigh the costs associated with a mixed fleet.

2. Low Landing Fees

Leadership was for a firm to establish and sustain a cost and through the pricing advantage over all its rivals. In order to do so, it must address to "big ticket" cost items, those which will have a substantial impact on costs.

Table presents cost data for British Midland Airways, a short-hi airline providing a conventional service on UK domestic and regional routes. The cost information is broken down on a departmental cost bas It shows that landing fees and passenger embarkation charges are a ma; cost item, accounting for nearly 10% of costs. Any airline which substantially reduce them will have taken a very successful first step towards a sustainable Cost Leadership position.

Southwest Airlines illustrates the principle well. Throughout its history the airline has pursued a policy of seeking out unused airports, even if these are old, sometimes dilapidated and unfashionable. At its home base, Dallas, it uses Dallas/Love Field airport, rather than the much larger DFW. At Chicago, it flies to Midway, rather than O'Hare, whilst in the New York region the relatively remote airport of Islip, on Long Island, is used rather than the congested and expensive Kennedy, Newark or LaGuardia.

In Europe, Ryan air pursues such a policy in an even more exaggerated fashion. Indeed, the airline has stated that in its route expansion policy, the existence of an under utilized airport, even if it is a long way from the city it purports to serve, is the most fundamental requirement.

Table 1: British Midland—Cost Structure: Financial Year 2000/01

	Cost Category	*Per cent*
1.	Depreciation and Rental	18.2
2.	Handling Costs, Parking Fees & Station Costs	11.1
3.	General & Administrative	10.1
4.	Landing Fees, Passenger Embarkation Charges	8.8
5.	Flight Crew Costs	8.0
6.	Maintenance & Overhaul	7.7
7.	Aircraft Fuel & Oil	7.1
8.	Commission	6.0
9.	Passenger Services	5.2
10.	Cabin Crew Costs	4.7
11.	Navigation & En Route Charges	4.1
12.	Reservations	3.2
13.	Advertising & Promotion	2.2
14.	Sales	1.5
15.	Specific Cargo Costs	1.0
16.	Insurance	0.8
17.	Other Operating Costs	100.0%

Source: CAA.

The benefits of using underutilized airports are enormous. The airline gains from very low landing fees, as airport operators reason that they are better off having substantial numbers of passengers (who will, provide commercial income for the airport from such activities parking and shopping) rather than none at all. It will also be able to rapidly, free of the slot-availability constraints that bedevil congested Interestingly, at the present time, not all Cost Leader airline sticking to the "pure" form of the model with respect to airport. In strong contrast to Southwest, the new entrant Jet blue Airways h itself at Kennedy Airport In New York. Easy jet is making use congested European airports—notably Gatwick, Schiphol and CDG airports at Paris.

3. *Short Turnarounds/High Aircraft Utilisation*

Once uncontested have been selected, the Cost Leader airline is well on the way to a its next requirement, that of short turnarounds and high aircraft but Southwest Airlines has always scheduled turnarounds of 20-25 minute contrast to the 50 minutes to one hour which the industry has trade used. This greatly helps the airline in its aim of achieving 10 because it allows additional rotations to be operated each day.

Of course, short turnarounds are not the only requirements turnarounds must be engineered so that they can be achieved constantly. Otherwise an unacceptable punctuality penalty will result. Most Cost Leader airlines do not use air bridges at airport.

The fact that this leaves their passengers unprotected in wet or cold. The benefit of this is that it allows both the front and rear aircraft are used, speeding passenger enplaning and deplaning. Controversial Cost Leader airlines do not pre-allocate seats. This leads to the "Cattle Truck Handling" as passengers rush for the seats. It means, though, that passengers are likely to be at the gate at the boarding time, and that they encouraged to sit down by the cabin crew in any available seat are on the aircraft.

4. Limited On-board Service

The data presented in Table is instructive, in that it shows that a short-haul airline, British Midland, spends 5.8% of its costs on "Passenger Services" the meals and drinks given away free to passengers.

It might at first sight be assumed that Passenger Service costs would only be high for long-haul airlines, where passengers need to be offered generous hospitality because of the length of time they are on board the aircraft. This is not so. Traditional short-haul airlines (especially in Europe) have given passengers a complementary drinks and meal service, even on flights with a duration of only an hour or so. The costs of doing so can then only be spread over a small number of passenger miles, and therefore have a disproportionate impact on unit costs.

Cost Leader airlines have a choice to make with respect to on-board catering. Some have chosen to be completely "no-frills". This allows cheaper aircraft acquisition costs due to the absence of galley space, speeds aircraft cleaning and allows extra seating. Others—in fact, today, most of them—do offer a meals-and-drinks service, but charge relatively high prices to what are captive customers. Passenger service then becomes a worthwhile source of revenue rather than a cost item.

5. Point-to-Point Only

One of the most important, but most overlooked, reasons explaining the recent success of the Cost Leader model is that airlines using it have concentrated on point-to-point traffic, eliminating what has hitherto been an unacceptable level of cross-subsidy from point-to-point to connecting passengers.

Any airline offering a transfer and connections product at a hub will incur substantial additional costs. Passengers checking in for a connecting flight will expect to be given a boarding pass not only for their first sector, into the hub, but also for their onward flight. Providing such a service will involve the airline in significant investment in communications. Passengers will also assume that they can check-in their baggage at their point-of-origin, and reclaim it only at their final destination. All interim baggage handling will be taken care of by the airline, at a substantial cost. Once they reach their hub airport, they will expect to wait for their onward flight in a comfortable and well-appointed lounge.

Important though these costs are, the provision of a connecting product will have still wider—and greater—cost implications. Implicit in the idea of hubbing is that flights will be co-ordinated in banks, so that connections can be made in the shortest possible time. These banks require a peak availability of resources, resources which will be poorly utilised as soon as the peak is over.

The costs of a connections product would be a severe problem in themselves. The problem is made worse, though, by the low yields often obtainable from transfer traffic. A passenger making a connection will generally have a worthwhile choice available to them, because they will be able to travel via the hubs of a range of different airlines. Carriers know this, and will try to entice the passenger to choose their hub rather than that of a rival. Yields are therefore generally poor in the market of transfer traffic.

In the past, traditional airlines have been able to compensate for these low yields by charging disproportionately high prices to people travelling on a point-to-point basis, to whom the hub serves as a local airport. The result has been that it has commonly been cheaper to fly from a point behind the hub, into the hub and then beyond, than it has been to travel on a point-to-point basis. Such absurd and discriminatory pricing practices have led to so-called Cross-Border Ticketing, an "abuse" which airlines have repeatedly tried and failed to eliminate.

Cost Leader airlines have removed all the costs and revenue dilution associated with a transfer product by concentrating exclusively on point-to-point traffic. It is, of course, possible to transfer form one flight to another on these airlines, though the fact that the emphasis is placed on high aircraft utilisation rather than the scheduling of banks of flights makes connecting opportunities less likely. Nothing is done, though, to assist the connecting passenger. When they reach their transfer airport, they will heave to reclaim their own bag, and take it to the check-in desk for their onward flight themselves. No luxurious lounges are, of course, provided. With fares and yields, there is no dilution, because the airlines follow a "sum-of sector fares" pricing principle, rather than the complex "pro-rating" procedures.

6. Simple Fares Cost

Leader airlines follow significantly different pricing practices from traditional airlines in other ways as well. As we saw earlier in this section, the disciplines of Revenue Management have led airlines in the direction of greater pricing complexity, with often fifty or more fares being on offer on a particular route, most of them having different, and confusing, conditions associated with them.

Cost Leader airlines do make use of Revenue Management techniques, but generally with one crucial difference compared to traditional airlines. When someone looks at the website of one of these airlines, at the time they do so there is only one fare on offer for the flight in which they are interested. They are therefore faced with a clear "take it or leave it" choice. The fare on offer will certainly vary through time, being generally low well in advance of flight departure and rising as the departure day nears. The, fact that there is only ever one fare available at a particular time makes the whole reservations procedure a very simple one, and, as we move onto now, allows the Internet to be the cornerstone of distribution.

7. Low Distribution Costs

We will see there that the 1990s saw a rapid and unacceptable increase in the distribution costs of traditional airlines. This was due to the overwhelming domination of one channel of distribution that provided by the travel agency industry. This near-monopoly caused a rapid increase in the commissions being paid to travel agents, as well as seeing airlines very vulnerable to the pricing practices of the Global Distribution Systems. Any airline seeking a Cost Leadership position must address the question of distribution costs. If it can eliminate travel agents' commissions, a major step will have been taken towards the establishment and maintenance of a cost advantage, especially when it is born in mind that by the end of the 1990s it was common to find that 12-14% of a traditional airline's costs were made up of commissions.

In some sense, the elimination of GDS booking fees has been even more important for Cost Leader airlines. The GDS companies have always charged on a flat rate basis, currently about $4.50 per booking made. This is a reasonable policy given the structure of their costs, but it means that booking fees fall disproportionately on low fares carriers. $4.50 on a Business Class return fare of $3000 is an irrelevance. The same booking fee on a $50 fare most certainly is not.

The answer to the distribution problem for Cost Leader airlines has, of course, been to use the Internet. In this regard, the UK airline Easy jet has been the pioneer. From its foundation in 1995, Easy jet has paid no commission to any travel agent, and, because of this, no booking fees to any GDS company. The cost savings it has achieved as a result have been Immense.

Easy jet has been followed by the airlines set up before it—Southwest and Ryan air—which have progressively eliminated the use of travel agents, and now have almost as high a proportion of their seats sold direct as Easy jet. Later entrants into the market have almost totally relied on Internet-based direct sales.

8. Non-Refundable Tickets

In the past, most airlines have had a policy of making their more expensive tickets fully refundable. This makes them very much more attractive, especially for the business traveller whose exact schedule cannot be predicted very far in advance. It means, though, that these airlines have always had a significant no-show problem, which they have resolved, to a degree, by overbooking.

All the Cost Leader airlines have a policy of allowing no refunds. Bookings can be changed, in return for a substantial fee (in the UK, generally £25 plus any difference between the fare already paid and the current fare available on the flight to which the booking is to be transferred) but no money is ever refunded. This allows the airlines a better and more certain cash flow, which in turn brings useful savings in interest costs.

Current Issues—Cost Leader Airlines

We have now looked at the different policies which airlines in the Cost Leader sector pursue. They illustrate perfectly Porter's principles of Cost Leadership set out successful players have to establish and sustain a cost, and through that, pricing advantage over their rivals. They must also correctly identify what their customers will, and will not give up to gain access to cheap prices. Cost Leader airlines have discovered that their customers will give up, amongst other things, service from their ideal airport, complementary meals and drinks, seat selection, the opportunity to buy a ticket through a travel agent and ticket refunds.

The consequences of such policies, if correctly applied, are remarkable. Cost Leader airlines seem to be the ones which have found a way round the chronic airline industry problem of cyclicality. The business model of Differentiation in the airline industry has generally allowed carriers to make reasonable returns in the buoyant upswing periods of the trade cycle. It has left them hopelessly exposed, though, in slow-down and recessionary times when large parts of the high yielding Business Class market—on which these airlines depend has evaporated.

The Cost Leadership position, though, addresses such issues through what appears to be a remarkable virtuous circle. Low costs allow for profitable lower prices, which in turn substantially increase the size of the market. In times when the economy is strong, this market growth comes from new passengers being brought into the market, who would not otherwise have flown. In times of slowdown or recession, Cost Leader airlines also appear to gain as people who are still anxious to fly trade down from the full service airlines as they seek lower prices.

A controversy currently affecting the Cost Leader sector is the question of the importance of customer service standards. The Cost Leader pioneer, Southwest, is a remarkable airline in that despite the fact that it is now a very large and mature carrier, it has retained a high degree of popularity with its passengers. The Department of Transportation in the USA collects, and publishes, data about passenger complaints, with the Major carriers being compared on the basis of the numbers of complaints received per 100,000 passengers carried. Southwest has been the airline with the lowest number of complaints for more than ten years, despite its "no frills" service. The secret seems to be that the airline makes a limited promise but keeps it consistently. It has also made great play on a warm and friendly style of service, and a solid approach to customer service if things go wrong.

Amongst the other Cost Leader players, a different approach is apparent. Ryan air in particular, if media reports are to be believed, takes the view that customer service is unimportant. Providing fares are cheap enough, people will mostly keep coming back. Those who desert the airline after experiencing a severe service failure will soon be replaced by new people brought into the market by the airline's extraordinarily low prices.

It will be interesting to see which of these philosophies turns out to be the correct one in the long term.

Another major issue in Cost Leadership at the moment concerns the best way for a Cost Leader airline to be set up. Today, the successful Cost Leader players are all independent, in that they have been put together entrepreneurially, without links with any pre-existing airline. Given the profits that they have enjoyed in recent years, and the threat that they pose to longer-established airlines, it is not at all surprising that these "Legacy" airlines have adopted the philosophy that, "If you can't beat them, join them". A common way for a Cost Leader airline to be set up has been as a subsidiary of a full service carrier.

So far, little success has attended these efforts. During the 1990s, three of the US majors, United, Delta and US Airways set up low fares subsidiaries, using the branding of Shuttle-by-United, Delta Express and Metro air respectively. Within 4 years, each of these airlines had been closed down. In 1995, British Airways set up a Cost Leader subsidiary called Go. Presumably, the airline did not regard this carrier as a success, because it was eventually sold off (to its management, who then sold it to Easy jet), at what seems now to have been a very low price.

At the time of writing, there is renewed interest in the idea of full-service airlines setting up low fares subsidiaries in order to try to compete with independent Cost Leader players. For example, Air Canada has set up two subsidiaries, using the sub-branding of Tango and Zip, to compete, presumably, with the very successful and rapidly-growing West jet. Delta Airlines has amlOunced a second attempt to enter the Cost Leader business with a new subsidiary branded Song. In Europe, British Midland has set up BMI Baby, and Lufthansa has a shareholding in German wings, a new player in the German domestic market. SAS has announced a candinavian no-frills airline under the Snowflake branding.

Some of these new initiatives may be successful, but it is impossible to be optimistic. The essence of Cost Leadership is that firms are able to establish and *sustain* a cost advantage over their rivals. With low fares subsidiaries of full service (and highly unionised) airlines, concessions may be given in a time of crisis which allow a lower cost base to be established. However, once things begin to improve, it often becomes a major objective of union negotiators to ensure that wages, salaries and conditions of employment at the subsidiary start to move nearer to those which prevail in the mainline operation. The cost advantages are then progressively eroded. Also, the setting up of a low fares subsidiary involves significant branding problems. When someone experiences no-frills service on a low-cost subsidiary it may colour their view of what will happen on their next flight with the full-service parent. Finally, low fares subsidiaries will perhaps allow an airline to compete more successfully with Cost Leader players which are challenging its dominance. Another, less desirable effect is that the subsidiary may take traffic away from its parent, and lead to criticism of the parent's relatively high prices.

The Future—Cost Leader Airlines

The question of the future of the Cost Leader sector is one of the most fascinating in the airline industry at the moment. In answering it, it is first of all clear that Cost Leadership positions are much easier to establish and sustain in short-haul and regional markets than on long-haul. This is because many of the cost advantages we have been discussing as resulting from the Cost Leadership model are most marked there.

The use of underutilized airports to lower landing fees and increase aircraft utilisation is a case in point. Landing fees are obviously a much higher proportion of operating costs in short-haul markets, whilst on long haul, all airlines can achieve similar, high, aircraft utilisations. Shorter turnarounds do not allow extra rotations to be fitted into the flying day. A no-frills approach is a problem on long-haul, where a meals and drinks service will be regarded as more important by passengers spending many hours on an aircraft.

Also a point-to-point only approach is less possible, with few long-haul markets having sufficient density on their own to be viable without hubbing. Finally, GDS booking fees, being charged on a flat-rate basis, are obviously less of a burden for the long-haul airline. One could argue that the long-haul services mounted by many of Europe's charter airlines in recent years amount to Cost Leadership in long haul markets. However, in establishing and sustaining a cost advantage, these airlines have relied on low seat pitches commonly 28 inches.

Such a policy certainly has a dramatic effect on seat-kilometer costs, allowing 25% or more extra seats to be put on an aircraft compared with the more traditional pitches of 32 or 33 inches. However, we may now be getting to the stage where such a lack of seating comfort is becoming an unacceptable sacrifice which people will not make. Sitting in such uncomfortable seating for many hours is not the same as it would be, for example, on a two-hour flight to the Mediterranean. Also, growing concern about Deep Vein Thrombosis means that airlines may leave themselves open to legal action if they continue to restrict seat pitches to such low levels.

A further question for the future of the Cost Leader sector concerns safety standards. Safety is, of course, an absolutely fundamental concern for all airlines, but it has to especially be so for Cost Leader players. When tickets are extremely cheap, passengers must be wondering, perhaps subconsciously, as to why prices are so low. Do they reflect the fact that comers are being cut on safety?

Whilst the Cost Leader sector continues to enjoy a good safety record, for example, southwest has never had a fatal accident in more than thirty years of flying—its growth will continue unabated. However, the experience of an airline called ValuJet in 1996 was a salutary one. At the time, it was a successful and rapidly growing new entrant into the Cost Leader sector, but suffered a tragic fatal accident when one of its aircraft crashed in the Florida Everglades with a large loss of life. It never recovered, and was shortly afterwards taken over in a near-bankrupt condition.

At the time of writing, the major issue concerning the future of the Cost Leader sector concerns its explosive growth, and the large number of new entrants that are appearing.

Of course, the fact that the market is growing quickly would in any case be likely to induce a great deal of entry. However, there are particular effects at work at the moment, which are exacerbating "normal" Life Cycle effects. As we have seen, resources are extremely cheap, with leased aircraft plentifully available at remarkably low lease rentals. Also, in the short-haul markets where cost leaders operate there are few of the economies of scale which (through hubbing) to some degree protect existing players on long-haul. In long-haul, there are often still regulatory barriers to entry which protect long-established airlines against the threat of entry.

These things are important, but perhaps the biggest factor explaining the current explosion of entry into the Cost Leader sector at the moment, is that entrepreneurs are being drawn to it. It seems to be the one business model which offers the possibility of profitability, in an industry otherwise characterised by a sea of red ink.

The effect of all these factors is remarkable, and frightening. At the time of writing (summer 2003), many markets, notably so the UK, Germany and Scandinavia, are seeing a frenetic pace of growth by existing Cost Leader airlines, and the setting up of large numbers of independent newcomers. At the same time, as we have just seen, many threatened incumbent airlines are introducing their own Cost Leader brands.

The result of all these developments will be to make the Cost Leader sector a very volatile and unstable one over the next few years. It is true that the airlines in it will continue to be able to generate large amounts of new traffic, but it seems inevitable that there will still be significant problems of overcapacity. As a result, some of the high profits which are currently being made will disappear, and less well-managed firms will be forced to leave the industry. Those that remain, and succeed, will be those that apply Porter's Cost Leadership model in its purest form. They will establish and sustain a clear cost advantage over their rivals.

The other issues concerning the future of the Cost Leader sector are mainly European, and stem from a looming set of possible regulatory problems.

To achieve and sustain their success, Cost Leader airlines need very attractive deals from airport operators. To a remarkable degree, they have succeeded in obtaining these deals. Sometimes, though, the deals have been given to them by loss-making airports which are owned by local and regional governments and subsidised by them. This therefore raises the questions as to whether or not the airlines, by an indirect routing, are receiving "illegal" State Aid. Ryan air has been accused of doing so in its deal with Charleroi Airport in the south of Belgium, which is currently under investigation by the European Commission.

It appears that Ryan air may win the argument. They have claimed that the Charleroi offer is not preferential and discriminatory in their favour, and is in principle available to any airline. Also, it represents actions which an economic market investor from the private sector would also take, given the loss that the airport was incurring before, and the very substantial amounts of commercial revenue which Ryan air's large passenger volumes allow the airport to earn. Nonetheless, it is a development which should be watched carefully, because large numbers of small airports are still state-owned in Europe, and their freedom of action in offering deals to Cost Leader airlines will be severely affected by an unfavorable outcome.

Another possible regulatory problem concerns the developing argument about Passenger Rights. During the autumn of 2002, a vigorous debate took place in the European Parliament about the need for airlines to compensate the victims of airline service failures in particular those who have experienced cancelled or delayed flights. Such compensation schemes would be in addition to those which already apply to a passenger experiencing denied boarding as a result of flight overbooking.

Not surprisingly, Cost Leader airlines have mounted a strong lobby against such proposals. They have argued, with reason that a person paying a very low price should hot be entitled to the same compensation as someone using an expensive ticket, which they would be under the scheme as it is currently proposed. However, at the time of writing it appears that such lobbying may not be successful.

A final regulatory issue concerns environmental taxation. In some senses, the Cost Leader sector is becoming a victim of it own success, in that it has produced often remarkable levels of traffic growth. This has in turn brought concerns to a head about the environmental impact of air transport, with the argument being put forward that the growth is only occurring because air passengers are not made to pay for the full environmental impact of aviation. If they are required to do so, through some form of additional taxation being imposed, it would certainly slow growth in the Cost Leader sector, especially if, as seems likely, it was imposed on a flat rate basis rather than as a percentage of the fare.

Overall, it is impossible to exaggerate the impact of the Cost Leader revolution on the air transport industry. Over the next few years, its implications will become ever more apparent in the markets where its effects have already been felt. It will also spread to hitherto unaffected markets.

Low Cost Carrier (LCC) Model

A low-cost carrier or low-cost airline (also known as a *no-frills, discount* or *budget* carrier or airline) is an airline that offers generally low fares in exchange for eliminating many traditional passenger services. The concept originated in the United States before spreading to Europe in the early 1990s and subsequently to much of the rest of the world.

The term originated within the airline industry referring to airlines with a lower operating cost structure than their competitors. While the term is often applied to any carrier with low ticket prices and limited services, regardless of their operating models, low-cost carriers should not be confused with regional airlines that operate short flights without service, or with full-service airlines offering some reduced fares.

Typical low-cost carrier business model practices include:

- a single passenger class
- a single type of aeroplane (commonly the Airbus A319 or Boeing 737), reducing training and servicing costs
- a minimum set of optional equipment on the aeroplane, often excluding conveniences such as ACARS, further reducing costs of acquisition and maintenance
- a simple fare scheme, such as charging one-way tickets half that of round-trips (typically fares increase as the plane fills up, which rewards early reservations)
- unreserved seating (encouraging passengers to board early and quickly)
- flying to cheaper, less congested secondary airports and flying early in the morning or late in the evening to avoid air traffic delays and take advantage of lower landing fees
- fast turnaround times (allowing maximum use of aircraft)
- simplified routes, emphasizing point-to-point transit instead of transfers at hubs (again enhancing aircraft use and eliminating disruption due to delayed passengers or luggage missing connecting flights)
- encourage the use of direct flights. Luggage is not automatically transferred from one flight to another, even if both flights are with the same company
- generation of ancillary revenue from a variety of activities, such as a la carte features and commission-based products
- emphasis on direct sales of tickets, especially over the Internet (avoiding fees and commissions paid to travel agents and computer reservations systems)
- employees working in multiple roles, for instance flight attendants also cleaning the aircraft or working as gate agents (limiting personnel costs)
- a disinclination to handle Special Service passengers, for instance by placing a higher age limit on unaccompanied minors than full service carriers
- aggressive fuel hedging programs.

Not every low-cost carrier implements all of the above points. For example, some try to differentiate themselves with allocated seating, while others operate more than one aircraft type, still others will have relatively high operating costs but lower fares.

The price policy of the low cost carriers is usually very dynamic, with discounts and tickets in promotion. Even if the advertised price may be very low, sometimes it does not include charges and taxes.

As the number of low-cost carriers has grown, these airlines have begun to compete with one another in addition to the traditional carriers. In the US, airlines have responded by introducing variations to the model. and JetBlue Airways advertise satellite television. Advertiser-supported Skybus Airlines launched from Columbus in 2007, but ceased operations in April, 2008. In Europe, the emphasis has remained on reducing costs and no-frills service. In 2004, Ryanair announced proposals to eliminate reclining seats, window blinds, seat headrest covers, and seat pockets from its aircraft.

The budget airlines frequently offer flights at low prices – often flights are advertised as free (plus applicable taxes, fees and charges.) Perhaps as many (or as few) as ten percent of the seats on any flight are offered at the lowest price, and are the first to sell. The prices steadily rise thereafter to a point where they can be comparable or more expensive than a flight on a full-service carrier.

India's Budget Airlines

Low Cost Carrier are mushrooming in India and the customer is becoming the king. Tighten your seat belts as the scream of engines rises to a crescendo and the nose lifts up. Boom! The Indian budget airline industry is taking to the skies. Wallet-friendly aviation players are cropping up, much to the delight of the Indian budget air traveller. Enjoy your journey, but sorry, snacks won't be part of the menu.

It took some time for the budget airline industry to catch on in India. The concept originated in the west and was quickly picked up in the East Asian countries. Richard Branson of Virgin Airlines was the front runner in Britain, while Qantas took the major chunk of the Australian budget skies. In the post-WTC days of aerial terror, seat occupancies in established carriers crashed, leaving them to operate on losses. That was the time when the wallet-friendly carriers took off and still operated with profit margins. The non-frillers were characterized by few on-board services, elimination of catering and assistance services and little inflight glitz. Basically, a barebones mode of aerial transport from Point A to Point B. As Captain G.R. Gopinath, MD, Air Deccan unabashedly claims, "We are the Udipi hotel in airline industry."

Air Deccan can claim credit for bringing the budget airline concept to the Indian skies. Started last year, the Bangalore-based company is a subsidiary of Deccan Aviation, which operates chartered air services, mainly with helicopters. Air Deccan unleashed cut-throat competition in the aviation scene with fares mostly equalling similar train fares. In response, leading domestic airlines like Indian Airlines, Jet Air and Sahara Airlines slashed rates and unveiled Advanced Purchase schemes (Apex) to take on the new challenger. Competition, as always, brought the best to the customer. "Our mission is to keep our fares low and keep lowering them with time," says Air Deccan's

Gopinath. Air Deccan is initially planning to tap the budget air traveler to and from metros to non-metros.

But competition was not far behind. Barely a year after Air Deccan took to the skies comes news of Vijay Mallya's Kingfisher Airline. In June this year, Mallya announced his plans to take to the skies with his own Indian no-friller. The flamboyant chairman of the multi-crore UB group is not known to do things half-way. And Mallya will be flying on the wings of the well-established Kingfisher brand. Bangalore's King of Good Times, a trained pilot himself, went the whole hog with plans for a 16-strong Airbus A-320 fleet to run its operations. (Four have been ordered from Airbus, with options to buy eight more, and operating another four on lease basis.)

"It is always good to welcome a new customer to the Airbus family, and we derive great satisfaction in being its partner in delivering comfort and value to passengers," says Airbus President and CEO Noël Forgeard. Kingfisher is investing Rs. 150 crore to kick off operations. Expect a dazzling show. Mallya's birds will be taking to the skies in early 2005.

Here's a sneak preview: Kingfisher Airlines, Mallya says, will not be a run-of-the mill Indian budget airline. Expect a value-added designer no-friller. Kingfisher Airlines will be emphasizing on spunky, well-done interiors and trained airhostesses. Each A-320 will carry 180 passengers. Borrowing from the Kingfisher beer tagline of "The King of Good Times", Mallya is pushing the theme of "Fly The Good Times" for his unborn baby. Kingfisher is planning to capture the Indian budget airline market with the twin engines of 'special flying experience' and 'value for money'. Contests like `Kingfisher flying face of the month' are on cards.

The Kingfisher air hostesses will be selected through a nationwide contest. Expect designer staff uniforms. The Kingfisher "Funliners" will have in-flight silent auctions for lifestyle products and sales of packaged food and beverages. Mallya is sure to leverage on the Kingfisher brand of exuberant, youthful and fast-paced image. The man behind the Kingfisher swimsuit calendar can be expected to put up a stiff challenge to Air Deccan and other low-cost aspirants. To begin with, Kingfisher Airline has roped in model Katrina Kaif to endorse the airline. We hope you get it. Don't expect an Udipi hotel from Mallya. Await the smart fast food joint.

Vijay Mallya already has a company called UB Air, which is a non-scheduled airline. He will be probably moving the civil aviation authorities to convert this licence to one for a scheduled airline. Kingfisher Airline charges are expected to be higher than Air Deccan's, but substantially less than those of the big players.

Even as the budget carrier battle hots up, the airline biggies are not sitting idle. Country's flag carrier Air-India recently announced its move to set up a subsidiary called Air India Express, which will be an international low-cost airline. Air India Express will be taking to skies in March 2005. There will be a fleet of 14 Boeing 737-800s, which will be taken on dry lease in three phases. These aircraft will have 181 Economy Class seats in single class configuration.

The new airline will operate 63 flights per week when six aircraft are inducted on dry lease at the time of the launch. With the induction of four more aircraft, effective winter 2005, Air India Express will operate 38 additional flights, and add another 26 flights in the third phase effective April 2006, when four more aircraft will join the fleet. Thus, within a year of operations, Air-India Express will operate a total of 127 flights with 14 aircraft to destinations in the Gulf and South-east Asia.

All Air India Express flights in the first phase, operated on Quick Turn Around (QTA) basis, will cover three online points in Kerala, Delhi-UAE/Oman and Chennai-Singapore/Kuala Lumpur. In the second phase, Air India Express will operate daily flights on Chennai-Dubai, twice-daily flights on Delhi-Dubai and Chennai-Singapore sectors. In the third phase, flights will be operated between Kerala, Mumbai and Doha/Bahrain; between Kerala, Mumbai, Chennai and Kuwait; and between Kolkata/Guwahati and Bangkok.

Meanwhile, Australian carrier Qantas Airways is planning to include Indian cities among many others for its low-cost airline to be launched in November this year. The as-yet-unnamed airline will be operated from Singapore, says Qantas Airways manager (India and South Asia) Khursheed Lam. The inclusion of Indian cities for Qantas low-cost low-cost airline is subject to bilateral seat sharing agreement and code-sharing, according to Ms Lam.

Bilateral discussions over seats and code-sharing between the two countries are likely to be held next week. "We have a flexible approach as far as flights, destinations in India and code sharing are concerned," Qantas Airways, head of sales and distribution, Rob Gurney said. The planned Qantas budget airline is a move to participate in the booming intra-Asia travel mart. The no-frill airline is set to commence with four A320 aircraft in November out of the eight A320 aircraft, for which lease agreements have been signed. The airline has plans to build a fleet of more than 20 aircrafts over the next three years.

The ambitious plans notwithstanding, the history of private sector aviation in India is not very heartening. Ratan Tata is still sore that the Air India nationalisation left the Tata group high and dry. Tata's late attempts to bid in the botched Air India privatization process came a cropper. Air India divestment plan itself was abandoned. Earlier, Indian private airline operators like NEPC Airlines and East West Airlines disappeared without a trace. Every few weeks, leading private carrier Jet Airways is faced without questions about its funding and promoters. It was Arun Shourie himself who said when he was divestment minister that he doesn't know if Jet Air is an Indian or a foreign firm!

Meanwhile, another low-cost Indian carrier is reportedly facing problems in starting up. The Bangalore-based Air One Feeder Airline, was supposed to start its flights with two Embraers from Brazil. The delay in Embraer delivery has forced AirOne Feeder to postpone its launch twice already. AirOne is now expected to take off only in early 2005. The company is looking at leasing two new Embraers with 50-seat capacity. The Embraer brand is not generally used in India. AirOne is believed to be targeting non-metro routes to corner its share of the market.

As the catfight hots up, expect fur to fly. Air Deccan says its aim to keep reducing fares further and further. More carriers, both Indian and foreign are expected to come up. Airline industry experts believe that there is space for at least five domestic low-cost airlines in India. Meanwhile, expect the big daddies of domestic aviation to match up with cost-cutting and aggressive Apex schemes. The battle for budget skies has just begun.

Challenges Faced by LCC

Low cost carrier growth

As low cost carriers look to evolve their business models and differentiate their services to travelers, their margins are suffering from the rapid growth. As they move up market to fill the void left by big network carriers, they must implement scalable environments to address growing complexities. Business infrastructure must broaden to sustain growth, which could allow for international routes, more outsourcing and code sharing. The risk is that low-cost carriers could start to feel the same high-costs pressures that made their network competitors so vulnerable. During this period of growth, low-cost carriers will find that scalability will not remain linear, and they will, at some point, face a costly system migration.

Increased capital spend for core operations

Thanks to this rapid growth, low cost carriers are currently ordering more new planes than the traditional network carriers. But this increased capital spends leads to reduced cash levels and liquidity, which may lead to an increased need to outsource some operations.

Certain, non-core functions can take resources and focus away from a company's core strategic goals.

Public awareness and market branding

Large network carriers have lowered their fares to compete with low cost carriers. As pricing transparency increases, low cost carriers need to continue and even increase their public awareness and customer loyalty by shifting from traditional to online distribution to improve their service and optimize revenues.

High fuel costs

With oil prices currently hovering near twenty-year highs, and increases projected to continue through 2005 and beyond, low cost carriers are feeling the pressures of lower yields cutting into their margins. Fuel Hedging, winglets and tankering are options that all airlines are pursuing.

Business pressures

As the business landscape in the travel industry continues to change, low cost carriers will most likely experience financial limitations now and well into the future. Collaborations with strategic partners could lead to joint venture opportunities and leveraged business environments.

Security Issues

Recently enforced government regulations have created operational inefficiencies and higher costs for low cost carriers. How can carriers follow these mandated regulations and still attain their goals of high customer service and lean operations? For example, many of today's travelers may soon be lucky enough to participate in a unique travel program. After an initial screening and registration, these travelers are issued a card embedded with radio frequency identification (RFID) technology, and cleared to enjoy shorter waiting times, preferred baggage handling, and access to select waiting areas – thanks to the use of RFID, real-time location system (RTLS) and Biometrics. Biometric solutions are being used today in airports as an effective tool for authentication and access control. When used in conjunction with key cards and RFID chips, these technologies can not only safeguard airports, but also simplify the entire travel experience for travelers worldwide.

Effective use of emerging technology/infrastructure

As transportation enters a new era, technology must move ahead and become more efficient to enable simple processes, cost controls, labour reductions and flexibility. Technology must also provide a platform for improved customer services. Low cost carriers can better connect with their customers through mobility devices and "edge" technologies. Companies want to reduce dependency and spend on legacy system maintenance costs so that they may redirect their IT spend to prepare for the future. This goal is especially true for low cost carriers, where maintenance costs are quickly approaching 85 percent, thus driving down the ability to invest in customer focused or competitive advantage activities.

Commercial off-the-shelf COTS applications, leveraged opportunities, near-shore/flexible operating models, kiosks, and Microsoft. NET technology are just of few of the enablers for low cost carrier technology.

2. DIFFERENTIATION STRATEGIES

Differentiated goods and services satisfy the needs of customers through a sustainable competitive advantage. This allows companies to desensitize prices and focus on value that generates a comparatively higher price and a better margin. The benefits of differentiation require producers to segment markets in order to target goods and services at specific segments, generating a higher than average price. For example, British Airways differentiates its service.

The differentiating organization will incur additional costs in creating their competitive advantage. These costs must be offset by the increase in revenue generated by sales. Costs must be recovered. There is also the chance that any differentiation could be copied by competitors. Therefore there is always an incentive to innovated and continuously improve. Differentiation involves creating a product that is perceived as unique.

The unique features or benefits should provide superior value for the customer if this strategy is to be successful. Because customers see the product as unrivaled and unequaled, the price elasticity of demand tends to be reduced and customers tend to be more brand loyal. This can provide considerable insulation from competition. However there are usually additional costs associated with the differentiating product features and this could require a premium pricing strategy. To maintain this strategy the firm should have:

1. strong research and development skills
2. strong product engineering skills
3. strong creativity skills
4. good cooperation with distribution channels
5. strong marketing skills
6. incentives based on subjective measures
7. be able to communicate the importance of the differentiating product characteristics
8. stress continuous improvement and innovation
9. attract highly skilled, creative people

"Differentiation" in the Airline Industry

Large numbers of airlines—mainly those which are long-established—in today's airline industry do not seek out a Cost Leadership position for their mainline activity (though, as we have seen, increasing numbers of them are forming Cost Leader subsidiaries). Instead, their argument is that they provide a value-for-money solution to a wide range of customer requirements, exploiting the synergies which become available to a firm producing a range of different products under the same umbrella.

At the time of writing, many airlines in the Differentiation sector are suffering chronic and, in some cases, perhaps unsustainable, losses. This is especially so amongst the airlines of the United States, and to a lesser extent, Europe. Indeed, in many cases, the term "Legacy Airline" is a good description of these carriers, as they seem to be dinosaurs finding life difficult or impossible in a fast-changing world.

This dire situation has, though, only arisen relatively recently. Whilst financial returns in the Differentiation sector have never been good, the period from about 1996 until 1999 was as prosperous a time as many of them had enjoyed in their entire history. Indeed, at the time it did seem that a business model was becoming established which would allow, at long last, a good and consistent return for shareholders. We need, firstly, to define this model, and then to come onto the difficult and painful question as to why, in a comparatively short time, it appears to have been disastrously undermined.

In order to be successful in the Differentiation sector it has always been necessary for airlines to be innovative. Indeed it is not co-incidence that two of the most successful airlines in this sector, Emirates and Singapore Airlines, are also the airlines with a strong reputation for innovation. Both are launching customers for the Airbus A380 large aircraft project, and both have consistently aimed to be at the forefront of new developments in such areas as cabin comfort, in-flight service and in-flight entertainment.

Of course, over time, almost all innovations are capable of being matched by competitors and most of them are. However, Emirates and Singapore Airlines illustrate the concept of so-called "First Mover Advantage", in that they have continued to reap the benefits of innovation even after matching by competitors has taken place. It seems that consumers continue to think well of a pioneer that took the risks and made the investment in an innovation which improves their lot.

Despite the importance of a product which matches the state-of-the-art, the standards of personal service which are offered assume even more significance for a Differentiation airline. The business traveller of crucial importance to differentiation players consists of a relatively small number of people, many of whom travel frequently over a long period of time. They get to know the airlines that give them a warm and caring welcome and those which do not. Naturally, they prefer to travel, all other things being equal, with carriers which treat them well.

Personal service standards assume an even greater importance because they can provide a sustainable competitive advantage. An airline may find that its standards of seating comfort, for example, have fallen behind those available on it rivals. If it does, it is then a straightforward, albeit costly, task to order, and install the new seats which will correct the anomaly. Things are not so straightforward if it has customer-contact staff who are ill-disciplined, poorly motivated and incompetent. Correcting such a state of affairs may take concerted action on many fronts over a long period of time. During this time, the airline will be losing out to its rivals if these competitors do not have the same problems.

Brand building forms another, vital, part of the business model for successful Differentiation in the airline industry. For the moment, though, it is worthwhile to note that for many airlines, their problem is that they have become commoditized. Passengers tend to feel that all airlines are the same and that there are no strong reasons for choosing one rather than another. A small number of airlines do, though, managed to rise above such generalizations, and to achieve valuable status as a brand. The British carrier Virgin Atlantic is an example, as are the aforementioned Emirates and Singapore Airlines.

A further aspect of the traditional business model for Differentiation carriers is that they need to be well-represented in each of the major market segments, those of business travel, leisure travel and air freight.

Such a policy will bring with it the major disadvantage that the airline will be setting itself a complex management task, in which contradictions and compromises will be a major feature. However, the synergies available to the multi-product airline will often more than compensate. A presence in the business travel market will give an airline access to the highest yields, whilst the leisure market is the one which is producing the highest growth rates. Also, almost by definition, the business and leisure markets have complementary demand patterns, as when business travellers aren't travelling because it is a holiday season, there will be a peak in leisure travel.

The synergies available from a strong presence in the air freight market are perhaps even greater. Belly-hold space in passenger aircraft will be cheaply available, and will also allow freight customers to benefit from the frequency essentially provided for passengers. Air freight will help airlines' cash flow during the times when passenger demand is affected by wars or a terrorism threat. Also, there is some evidence that air freight helps airlines respond to the challenges of the trade cycle, in that it tends to be affected by a recession earlier, but to come out of it sooner, than the passenger side of the business.

Points about the importance of innovation, customer service, brand building and a synergistic presence in all the major market segments have always been true and remain so today. The other major issue with regard to the business model for Differentiation airlines is much more controversial.

During the 1990s a fashion grew up in the airline industry that "Big is Beautiful"—that only airlines with a wide—preferably a global—network had any real hope of survival in a rapidly changing world.

It is easy to see why such ideas should have arisen. In principle, an airline with a wide network is better insulated against risk, in that it is unlikely that traffic will turn down across the whole of a global network at exactly the same time. Too many carriers in practice have their success or failure linked to the fortunes of a single, or at least a small number, of markets.

A large route network also, by definition, allows airlines to offer a greater number of "on-line" rather than "transfer" connections. An on-line connection is one where the passenger uses the same airline both for the flight into a hub and for the one beyond. In the transfer case, two different airlines are used.

All surveys of passenger preferences show that on-line connections are preferred to transfer ones. People are more confident that they will get the boarding passes for both sectors when they first check in, removing the need for a visit to the Transfer Desk when they arrive at the hub airport. They feel there is a greater likelihood of the baggage handling system working, and their bag arriving at their final destination at the same time as they do. They may hope that the gates for their two flights will be closer together, avoiding the need for a long walk and, perhaps, an inter-terminal transfer. Finally, they may be more confident that they will actually make the connection, with greater efforts being made to help them if their inbound flight is late.

Where an airline is too small to have a large number of on-line connections, it has to fall back on the expedient of code-sharing. This is where it lends its code to other airlines, or borrows theirs, so that connections appear as on-line in the Global Distribution System displays when they are nothing of the sort. Here, though, the downside may be one of customer alienation if passengers end up flying on airlines they would specifically prefer to avoid.

A final reason why big came to be regarded as beautiful in the airline industry, was because of the introduction of Frequent Flyer Programmes. In principle, the FFP of a large airline is more attractive than that of a small carrier. Points can be earned more quickly, in that there is a greater probability that an airline will have a service to all the destinations to which a passenger will need to travel. Once they have been earned, redemption opportunities for free flights will be greater, in that a wider range of destinations will be available.

Given this range of factors, it was no surprise that the second half of the 1990s saw a trend towards consolidation, as a fashion for wide networks gripped the industry. However, there were strict limits as to how far such a trend could develop. In any "normal" industry, the quest for size would have meant entering new markets and significant amounts of merger and takeover activity. These trends—though they arose—were very muted in air transport because of the ownership and control rules which Airlines attempted to grow where they could, but ownership and control issues meant that such organic growth was limited to the domestic markets of the countries in which they were based, and largely to international routes to and from these countries. Merger and takeover activity certainly did take place, but purely with national boundaries. Still, very few examples exist in the airline industry of true cross-border merger and takeover activity.

The United States market was the one where growth and consolidation of the industry was able to proceed furthest, due to the size of the market and the permissive attitude towards mergers and takeovers adopted by successive administrations in Washington. By the middle 1990s, the industry had consolidated to the point where it was overwhelmingly dominated by five mega-carriers—American, United, Delta, Northwest and US Airways.

The US experience does not lead to a confident view that consolidation is the way to financial success for the world's "Differentiation" airlines. During the 1990s, each of the Big Five became a hotbed of militant trade unionism, with unions finding fertile ground on which to work amongst labour groups who felt isolated and threatened. Freed of the fear of a strong competitive response by the fact that each of the big airlines held strong, hub-based, geographical monopolies, each airline progressively gave way to demands for large increases in wages and salaries. The result was that by the end of the decade, wages and salaries had risen to unsustainable levels. This left the airlines extremely vulnerable to the business downturn which then began to affect them. Once it did, the airlines showed themselves slow to respond, their sheer size leading to bureaucracy and inertia.

Outside of the United States, the quest for greater size has been just as strong but has been incapable of fulfillment. One attempt was made in 2000 to grow by a policy of cross-border takeover, when British Airways proposed a takeover of the Dutch airline KLM. This, though, merely illustrated the inflexibility inherent in the anachronistic regulatory system, because the proposal had to be abandoned in the face of threats (from the United States in particular) that KLM would have to forfeit its international traffic rights if it became British controlled.

As airlines sought the benefits of size through the 1990s and found that they were unable to obtain them through the "normal" processes of organic growth and merger and takeover, they progressively fell back on another expedient, that of alliance.

"Differentiation" Airlines—The Future

The Concept of the "Legacy Airline"

We saw that, during the second half of the 1990s, whilst profitability was still inadequate, these airlines were generally doing as well as they had ever done. Good returns were being earned by the industry's traditionally stronger airlines such as American, Delta and British Airways, whilst even some of the weaker players (such as the Belgian carrier Sabena) moved into the black after years of losses. Only a few short years later, the picture could not be more different. The losses amongst the once-strong airlines of the USA have been staggering, whilst in Europe airline profitability is generally very weak. Some airlines have been unable to survive, notably so Swissair and the aforementioned Sabena. Many more may not do so unless things improve. Only in south east Asia did the traditional business model still seem to be working well, for such airlines as Singapore Airlines and Cathay Pacific. They were being joined by some of the carriers of mainland China where strong traffic growth was assisting them in joining the small elite of Differentiation airlines which were still achieving profits. Now, the SARS epidemic has ended even this favourable trend.

In looking for any explanation for this rapid and catastrophic turnaround in airline financial fortunes, the managements of the airlines concerned would no doubt like us to look to factors wholly outside their control.

To some extent, we are right to do so. The terrorist attacks on New York of September 11 2001 dented the confidence of travellers, notably US travellers. This confidence has yet to return. The subsequent "War on Terrorism" and the allied attack on Iraq has worsened the problems of depressed demand, as passengers fear reprisal attacks on civil aviation. In turn, the need for increased security checks at airports have added to the hassles associated with air travel, making the discretionary traveller who does not have to make a particular trip much more likely to stay at home. For the business traveller who chooses not to fly, they can now, of course, continue their business much more easily than before because of advances in electronic forms of communication.

External factors associated with wars and terrorism are a part, but by no means the whole, explanation for the current woes of the Differentiation airlines. They would also want us to use as an excuse the economic slowdown which began in the United States in 2000, and subsequently spread to other markets.

Airlines are never likely to find things as easy in a recession as they do in prosperous times, but we should be wary of giving too much credence to arguments that the economic slowdown is an "external" factor about which airlines can do nothing. During the boom years of the 1990s, many airlines pursued aggressive expansion programmes, despite the fact that the evidence of history that the world economic boom then in progress was overdue for a correction. Even more unforgivably, they often based their expansion plans on a concentration on "Premium Traffic"—that in First and Business Class cabins. It is schoolboy economics to say that this was a mistake, because all the evidence one could possibly require is there to say that this is the type of traffic most severely affected by the onset of recession. British Airways is one airline at which the criticism can be levelled that its strategy involved an extremely risky concentration. on the premium end of the market.

Of course, as we have seen, at the same time as Differentiation airlines have struggled in a recession-hit market, Cost Leader airlines have seen little effect on their growth and profitability. This is because their business model has shown itself to be far more resilient in the face of the ups and downs of the trade cycle.

Aside from "Terrorism" and "Trade Cycle" issues, Differentiation airlines have been affected by fundamental changes in customer needs and market segmentation. The rapid rise in the importance of the "Independent" business traveller, who regards the price of the ticket as being much more important than their corporate counterpart, has been one factor in this, depressing yields significantly. The rapid increase in the amount of business travel sold on the basis of corporate dealing has had a similar effect. It is not convincing, though, for airlines to argue that they have been the innocent victims of these trends. It is certainly possible to argue that successful airlines are always likely to be those which anticipate change and are ready when it occurs. Unsuccessful carriers are often those which wait for change to happen and then make a belated response to it. In many ways, the problems being endured by many traditional Differentiation airlines at the present time illustrate exactly the latter failing.

Other criticisms of these airlines are in a sense even more damning. Table presents data giving average salaries for selected work groups at a number of European airlines. By any standards, some of the numbers are excessive, 'find reflect the fact that, as we have seen, airlines had little incentive to control their costs when regulatory protection meant that they had nothing to fear from the potential threat of lower cost new entrants. Nor can such high rewards be said to reflect what people might be entitled to expect from working for highly profitable and successful businesses. For example, TAP Air Portugal, one of the highest paying of all the airlines in the table 2, last declared a profit in 1973.

Table 2: Staff Costs 1999 (Average Annual Remuneration, US$)

	Airline	*Pilots and Co-pilots*	*Cabin Attendants*
1.	Air Portugal	$144,570	$44,215
2.	British Airways	$121,153	$30,815
3.	British Midland	$ 94,995	$28,721
4.	Iberia	$188,091	$59,340
5.	Lufthansa	$141,646	.$50,017
6.	SAS	$129,445	$58,441
7.	Virgin Atlantic	$ 85,048	$18,810

Source: ICAO.

Of course, high wages and salaries need not indicate high unit costs, if they are offset by extremely high productivity. Southwest Airlines has always prided itself on not being a sweatshop. All the work groups at Southwest are rewarded at market rates, or at levels which are even somewhat above the average. Its remarkable ability to maintain low unit costs, even now when it is a very large and mature airline, reflects the fact that its labour productivity is very high.

The same conclusion cannot be reached for most traditional airlines. For example, the rules governing pilots' hours as set by the various regulatory bodies are complex, but in summary allow pilots to work a total of 900 duty hours in a year. Many European airlines have agreements with their pilots which require them to work only two-thirds or even a half of the permitted maximum. Not surprisingly, Ryanair has made it a condition of the jobs offered to pilots that they will be rewarded at market rates, but that they should expect to work the full number of hours which the regulators allow.

Besides having a cost base which is no longer sustainable in today's difficult market conditions, there are two other aspects of the traditional business model of Differentiation which renders it under threat, especially in short-haul markets.

We have already referred to the way in which Cost Leader airlines concentrate on point-to-point traffic, avoiding the extra costs and revenue dilution associated with connections and transfers. The whole of the traditional business model of Differentiation has been based on transfer traffic and hubbing. Fares have been kept extremely high for point-to-point passengers who have few choices available to them. Much lower prices have been offered to connecting passengers to encourage them to use the airline's hub, rather than the hubbing possibilities offered by other carriers.

There is an economic defence to be offered for such a pricing policy. Rubbing passengers, even though they are low yielding, contribute to the spreading of overheads and allow for frequencies to be increased over a wider route network. They also permit larger aircraft to be used, which may allow the passenger to benefit from the lower seat-mile costs associated with bigger planes. The model is, though, entirely dependent on high fares being paid by point-to-point passengers if overall costs are to be covered. In that sense, it can be argued that it is based on cross-subsidy from point-to-point to connecting passengers.

Today, this aspect of the business model of traditional airlines is no longer working. As we have seen, the Cost Leader players specialise exclusively in point-to-point traffic, and do not contain this element of cross-subsidy. They are taking away a significant proportion of the point-to-point traffic of rival airlines, meaning that, overall, the business model for short-haul routes is no longer offering the prospect of profitability.

A final set of criticisms can be made of airline revenue management policies. It can be stated that a sound revenue management policy will have many components. One aspect will be to vary prices according to people's willingness and ability to pay.

Traditional airlines have taken such a policy too far. On short-haul routes prices have been kept extremely high for those people who have needed a flexible ticket. Much lower fares have been made available, but on a strictly controlled basis whereby those using them have had to comply with tight conditions regarding (sometimes) an advanced booking requirement, length-of-stay rules and restrictions on cancellation and re-booking. The result has been that those using flexible tickets have paid prices which to the airlines charging them have been extremely high yielding.

The fact that they were was long regarded by revenue management professionals as a triumph. People who had to travel, often at short notice were paying prices which reflected their very low price elasticity. Unfortunately, it is now clear that these policies were having another, less desirable effect. They were responsible for a strong feeling of resentment against the airlines whose pricing policies were actually reflecting the fact that those using high priced tickets had no choice. All traditional airlines were using the same pricing policy, and regulation was preventing the entry of new airlines into the market.

Today, the situation is very different, with the explosion of entry of Cost Leader airlines. In turn, this entry has shown up what could be described as the "water behind the dam" effect of airline revenue management policies. Those who paid very high fares before were not "willing" to pay them as the jargon of revenue management would suggest—rather they were "forced" to pay them by the lack of choice. Now that a choice is available, many have taken a particular pleasure in voting with their feet and transferring to Cost Leader airlines, partly to punish those whom they believe exploited them. Overall, one can say that the attitude of consumers to air fares has changed for all time. Cheap point-to-point fares are now regarded as the norm, and high prices as exceptional and unacceptable.

Overall, we are forced to a depressing conclusion about the business model of Differentiation in the airline industry. Only a short time ago, this model was earning reasonable returns for the better-managed airlines. Today, it is failing to do so. Wars and terrorism fears are depressing demand, with no likelihood of any worthwhile improvement in the situation facing the industry—in fact it may worsen. The business model has been shown to be incompatible with the ups and downs of the trade cycle, with airlines hoping against hope for an early resumption of strong economic growth to rescue them. Market segmentation and customer needs are changing. lowering yields and giving opportunity to the rapidly developing competitors from the Cost Leader sector. The business model of the airlines has been shown to be built on the sand, being based on the charging of unacceptably high prices to supposedly "captive" business travellers, and on cross-subsidy from point-to-point to connecting passengers.

Such a litany of problems would be very serious indeed for airlines trying to navigate their way through difficult times with fully competitive cost structures. Unfortunately indeed, long-established airlines often have a high cost legacy built up during times of state-ownership and the absence of price competition or, in the case of US airlines in particular, during a time of strong union militancy in a then—buoyant market.

Over the last year or so. a new term has come into common usage to describe many of these carriers—"Legacy Airlines". It is an appropriate one. They are attempting to navigate extremely difficult waters with a set of problems left over from a time when circumstances in the industry were very different. They have competition from newer airlines that have had the priceless advantage of setting out in today's competitive market conditions, and therefore have no legacy from the past to deal with. The question we now have to turn to is, where do they go from here?

"Legacy Airlines"—Strategic Options

For these airlines, it should be emphasised that their situation is by no means hopeless. They carry with them some very valuable strengths today, and have worthwhile opportunities which will open up for them in the future. For example, the very fact that they are long-established means that they have Grandfather Rights on airport slots which stretch back many years. They will retain these rights into the future, unless the industry radically changes the methods used for slot allocation, something which, at the time of writing, appears unlikely. Also, and despite the criticisms of hubbing made in the previous section, their hubs do give them opportunities to gather in traffic from a wide geographical area, and provide a worthwhile fortress against new entrants. As we have seen, their frequent flyer programmes are valuable, and pose a difficult competitive issue for smaller newcomers.

Perhaps of greatest value to these airlines is that they still have a defendable position in long-haul markets. As we have seen, it is much harder for Cost Leader approaches to succeed on long-haul routes, because of the difficulties such airlines have in establishing and sustaining a substantial cost advantage.

Finally, the very fact that "Legacy" airlines are long-established allows them to make the branding claim that they are "proven". A carrier with an unblemished safety record stretching back for many years is likely to be able to persuade the nervous traveller to choose them rather than a new entrant, whose safety promise needs largely to be taken on trust. Unfortunately, for British and American airlines, the fact that they may have a proven safety record may not be enough to stave off the perception that they are a possible target for terrorist attack, following on from the Second Gulf War of 2003.

Despite these strengths, the Legacy airlines have to change their strategies. Unless they do so, they will simply die. In some cases, their death will be almost immediate. With the better managed carriers it will be much slower—a lingering "Death of a Thousand Cuts". The question is, what strategic options are open to them? Fortunately, there are a number. No single option provides all the answers. Carriers will have to select the best parts of each one in order to define an overall strategy.

A first option might be described as a "Retreat to Core" strategy. As we have seen, the Legacy carriers still have a defendable position in long haul markets. Also, despite the radical nature of the developments which have taken place on short-haul, they have not affected every passenger. There is still a hard core of business people who will pay high prices for a flexible ticket and a seat in a comfortable Business Class, even on short journeys. Is it possible to retreat to this core of high-yielding and hopefully profitable business?

Strategies of retrenchment are notoriously difficult to implement in the airline industry. They require, to begin with, a complete re planning of the fleet around smaller aircraft. Those high yielding passengers who constitute the supposed core will normally be business travellers, who will in turn be extremely frequency-sensitive. Airlines will also need to maintain frequency to ensure that there are sufficient numbers of connecting passengers feeding into their long-haul services. Fortunately, there are now suitable aircraft available. The smaller versions of the B737 and Airbus A320 families are well-proven, if less than optimal, aircraft. Embraer is now introducing its 170 and 190 families of new aircraft with around 100 seats.

Although these aircraft have good operating economics, inevitably their seat-mile costs are quite high, especially given the very generous salaries normally paid to pilots by Legacy carriers. These salaries are, of course, especially punitive when spread over only the hundred seats or so of a small aircraft.

This aspect of "Retreat to Core" strategy is one aspect of a more general problem. Such a retreat will involve cutting back on the scale of an airline's activity. The reduction in revenue will be immediate. Far more problematic will be the carrier's ability to reduce overhead costs at the same rate, or, hopefully faster, than revenue declines. Achieving this in the airline industry is notoriously difficult. A far more likely situation is that the decline in overhead will be less than the decline in revenue. Each passenger who remains will then, through the fares that they pay, have to cover a greater proportion of overhead if overall profitability is to be achieved. Given the long term trend in the industry for yields to decline rather than rise, it is unlikely that they will.

The other major problem of "Retreat to Core" strategies is that they can leave market opportunities open to competitors. The situation in the UK aviation industry illustrates this problem well. Many short-haul destinations are served from both Heathrow and Gatwick Airports. Generally, profitability is much better on the routes from Heathrow. If an airline is making money by serving a destination from Heathrow, whilst incurring losses on the equivalent route from Gatwick, the solution appears to be obvious. By cutting out the Gatwick service, the profitable core can be identified and overall profitability achieved. Unfortunately, in practice, the situation may not be so simple. Giving up a route may involve the relinquishing of airport slots which under the "Grandfather Rights" rules, can then be awarded to another airline on an "in perpetuity" basis. This airline may then use the slot to sharpen its attack on the rival which gave it up in the first place. This may involve beginning service on the specific route abandoned by the first airline. If the challenger has lower costs and more attractive fares than its competition, traffic may be taken from the "core" route, turning it from profit into loss. making.

The second strategic option is a very clear one, If "Legacy" airlines find that their position in short-haul markets is being undermined by "Cost Leader" players, it seems the most obvious of initiatives for them to fight back by setting up Cost Leader subsidiaries of their own. The jury is still out on the question as to whether this is a sound strategy or not. So far, the results produced by it have been, at best, mixed. Those airlines which have recently decided to use it will no doubt argue that lessons have been learned, and that we should now be talking about "second generation" Cost Leader subsidiaries which will achieve much better results. This may apply to Delta's "Song", SAS's "Snowflake" and Air Canada's "Tango" and "Zip". The early signs are not hopeful, though. In the case of both Delta and Air Canada, the airlines' respective pilots unions have refused to agree to lower salaries for their members working in the supposedly "low cost" subsidiaries. These subsidiaries will therefore be fighting their highly efficient Cost Leader rivals with one arm tied behind their backs.

It is interesting to note that some airlines have examined and rejected the idea of a Cost Leader subsidiary. Aer Lingus has never set up such an airline, despite being the first European airline to face competition from a Cost Leader player (Ryanair is based in Dublin), and to face it in a particularly severe form. As we have seen, British Airways set up a Cost Leader subsidiary called Go, but sold it in 2001. Ifthe public statements of the Chief Executive are to be believed, they have no plans to re-enter the sector.

All Legacy airlines, whether they set up a Cost Leader subsidiary or not, will have to follow the third strategic option. They will have to do all they can to reduce their cost base. If they can reduce the often enormous disparity between their costs and those of the newer Cost Leader airlines, they will be in a position to lower their fares themselves. They may also be able to regain some of the passengers who may be unhappy at the sacrifices the Cost Leaders require them to make to gain access to their cheap prices.

Some of these cost reductions can be achieved relatively painlessly. All airlines are undoubtedly leaning on their suppliers and demanding concessions from them. In a recession-hit industry, these suppliers have little choice but to agree, especially if airlines pursue tough policies to reduce the number of their suppliers so that they are able to exercise the maximum amount of buying power over them. Commission costs and GDS booking fees are coming down everywhere as airlines rely on such initiatives as electronic ticketing and selling over the Internet. A growing self-service culture is being encouraged through useful developments as self-service check-in. Finally, some successful attempts are being made to cuts out some of the complexities which Legacy airlines have traditionally built into their business model. This should in turn allow for lower costs as a result of a reduction in overhead expenses.

Important though such initiatives are, they do not address the key question. As always, it will be those airlines which successfully deal with the perennial Legacy airline problem of labour costs which will be the best places to deal with what is bound to be very rough weather in the future.

Labour costs are vital to Legacy airlines because they are the biggest single input cost item for them. Commonly, 30% or more of their costs are made up by wages, salaries and benefits. Addressing labour costs will therefore have the greatest single impact on unit costs. Unfortunately, in doing so, airlines are faced with the fact that their unions are generally in a very powerful bargaining position. The list of work groups who can paralyse an airline through strike action is a very long one. As service businesses, carriers have no opportunity to build up inventory with customers in advance of a strike. Once it begins, the effect of a strike on cash flow will be immediate. In the case of one work group, pilots airlines have to deal with people who are articulate and intelligent and with a long record of militancy at many carriers. Finally, in the view of this writer at least, airlines have worsened what would in any case be a difficult labour relations environment by their continuing belief that big is better. Too often, people working in large airlines feel isolated and threatened, providing fertile ground for trade union militancy.

In some cases, carriers have resorted to extreme measures to bring down their labour costs. The US Chapter 11 bankruptcy code allows a firm to receive, for a period of time, court protection from its creditors. Several airlines have used their time in Chapter 11 to radically change their labour contracts, emerging from bankruptcy with a much lower cost base. USAirways did this in 2002/3. Air Canada is using the Canadian equivalent at the present time. Others have used the possibility of bankruptcy as a threat. American Airlines in March 2003 obtained significant concessions from its normally militant unions by suggesting that a bankruptcy filing would take place if these concessions were not granted.

More generally, it often proves possible for airlines to lower labour costs in a time of crisis. The threat of bankruptcy, or at least of large job losses, will usually be enough to focus minds. The problem, of course, is that demands will be made for the old conditions of service to be re-instated once happier times arrive. In the meantime, customer standards will slip, if the workforce becomes punch-drunk and demoralised.

A further possibility for addressing labour cost issues is to make a proportion of the rewards available depend on company performance through stock options and profit-sharing schemes. Such methods have been used by some of the new entrant Cost Leader airlines, where profits have been good and share prices rising. They are of no relevance, though, to Legacy airlines where share prices have fallen to very low levels and profits are non-existent. In any case, the whole question of employee shareholdings in the airline industry has been discredited by the experiment we have already referred to at United Airlines. Here the fact that the employees owned the majority of the shares of the company did not turn out to be a recipe for harmonious labour relations—much the reverse. The experiment was finally abandoned in March 2003.

Overall, we can say that if there was an easy, miracle solution to the problem of labour costs and labour productivity at the Legacy airlines, it would have been found by now. Moving forward on the labour cost front is though vitally important, and inaction is not an option. Progress will depend on the correct policies being pursued in a wide range of areas. This author believes that the most important factor will be inspiring, sympathetic and considerate leadership, by a leadership team which convincingly demonstrates that it does not have its own snout in the trough whilst asking others to make sacrifices.

If costs *can* be brought down, and the reductions maintained on a permanent basis, exciting new opportunities will appear. It is clear that from the consumer viewpoint, flying with these airlines does have its drawbacks. People may have to use an inconvenient airport, accept a "no frills" on board product or be denied a seat-selection service. Most importantly, some of the Cost Leader airlines appear to be taking a gamble on questions of customer service. If things go according to plan—and they usually do—passengers benefit from remarkably cheap fares. If things go wrong, though, the passenger experience may be very different. The European press and media regularly carry horror stories about the problems experienced by passengers whose flight is badly delayed or whose bags are lost. Once such a severe service failure has been experienced, is a passenger's view of Cost Leader airlines changed for all time, and will they become willing to pay more to fly on an airline which does give appropriate attention to customer service? If they do, full service airlines can be expected to benefit from the gradual build-up of a so-called "Army of the Disaffected", or those who feel that they have been let down by the Cost Leader sector.

It would be wrong to exaggerate the importance of this trend. There will be no return to the days of extremely high airfares. Sound standards of customer service may, though, allow the Differentiation airlines to hold prices a small amount above those of the lowest pricing Cost Leaders. For those that can reduce their costs down to these levels, a return to profitability for their short-haul services may still be possible.

A strategic option followed by many Differentiation airlines is to subcontract some of their short haul feeder services to airlines with a more appropriate cost structure. As we have seen, service on thinner routes often presents traditional airlines with particular problems. Pilots unions have generally successfully made the case that pilot salaries should be higher for flying bigger aircraft. They do not usually accept the corollary that if an airline introduces smaller planes, salaries should fall. The result it that carriers often end up flying regional jets on the basis of high pilot salaries, making profitability on thin routes impossible.

The answer to this problem is to ensure that the thinner routes are flown by regional airlines with better cost structure, using code-sharing and franchising relationships. Though such expedients raise questions about brand integrity, the policy has generally turned out to be a sound one. The large airline gains the benefit of feed onto its long-haul routes without the costs of trying to do the job itself. The smaller carrier also benefits through such aspects as membership of the major carrier's frequent flyer programme.

During the 1990s, a trend grew up for the majors to buy up regional airlines, to bring them under their direct control. American Airlines with its American Eagle subsidiary is a case in point, as is the British Airways Citi express subsidiary.

Despite the usefulness of franchising, up until now there has been a limit on the extent to which it can be employed. Strong resistance has been encountered from pilots unions, who interpret it—often correctly—as being a device to reduce the number of highly paid pilot jobs, as regional subsidiaries or franchise partners take over an increasing proportion of short-haul flying. The result has been their insistence on "Scope Clauses" which limit the number of small regional jets that can be flown to a fixed, small percentage of the aircraft in use by the mainline airline. The present, disastrous, state of airline finances gives opportunities for these clauses to be renegotiated along more flexible lines.

A last strategic option open to threatened Legacy airlines might be described as "Jugular Marketing". If the position of a long-established airline comes under attack from new entrants, it may respond aggressively. Fares may be cut to the levels of the newcomers, or even below them. Capacity may also be added so that there is a glut of seats in the market. Such a policy will be designed to drive the new entrants out of the market, and also to send a clear message to others to keep away.

Such tactics now have to be employed with caution. It will depend on the particular legal jurisdiction under which the airline is operating, but they may well be interpreted by the courts as representing an "Abuse of a Dominant Position." None-the-less, the dividing line between what is an abuse and what is a legitimate (and, from the consumer viewpoint, desirable) response to a competitive challenge will always be a fine one.

This has been a difficult section of the book, and it will be a relief in the next one to reach happier ground. The facts, though, cannot be avoided. The undermining of the position of many once strong Differentiation airlines has been the major strategic trend in the industry over the past five years. The best managed of these carriers certainly do have a future, but they must expect to radically reform their ways of doing business.

3. FOCUSED STRATEGIES

The focus strategy is also known as a 'niche' strategy. Where an organization can afford neither a wide scope cost leadership nor a wide scope differentiation strategy, a niche strategy could be more suitable. Here an organization focuses effort and resources on a narrow, defined segment of a market. Competitive advantage is generated specifically for the niche. A niche strategy is often used by smaller firms. A company could use either a cost focus or a differentiation focus.

With a cost focus a firm aims at being the lowest cost producer in that niche or segment. With a differentiation focus a firm creates competitive advantage through differentiation within the niche or segment. There are potentially problems with the niche approach. Small, specialist niches could disappear in the long term. Cost focus is unachievable with an industry depending upon economies of scale e.g. telecommunications.

In this strategy the firm concentrates on a select few target markets. It is hoped that by focusing your marketing efforts on one or two narrow market segments and tailoring your marketing mix to these specialized markets, you can better meet the needs of that target market. The firm typically looks to gain a competitive advantage through effectiveness rather than efficiency. It is most suitable for relatively small firms but can be used by any company. As a focus strategy it may be used to select targets that are less vulnerable to substitutes or where a competition is weakest to earn above-average return on investments.

Types of Focussing in the Airline Industry

We looked at the two-by-two diagram of generic strategies developed by Michael Porter to describe different business strategies. Using the diagram, he suggests that there are two possible focussing positions. They both involve the same principles by giving up all benefits of synergies by concentrating on one single activity. Sustainable Competitive Advantage can then be found through the expertise built up in one area. Where focussing works successfully, this expertise will be so great that the firm will be able to use it to hold off the competitive challenge of the Differentiation players, who often will base their pursuit of competitive advantage on the synergies available to the multi-product firm.

Earlier, Porter proposes that successful focussing can come about in two ways. Some focussing firms achieve a defendable position by adding a great deal of value, which allows them to cover high production costs and still sustain profitability. Others use their expertise to achieve very low costs. The airline industry illustrates both of these positions.

"Value Added" Focussing

The best examples of "Value Added" focussing in the airline industry come with "Integrated Carriers" such a FedEx and UPS. Both these firms are now long-established, and both have modified their basic business strategies in recent years to reflect changing market conditions. They have, though, always had a strong emphasis on a single activity—the provision of guaranteed next-day delivery services for shippers who need to send small, urgent packages.

Such a service cannot be provided cheaply. Indeed, capital investment needs are enormous. Integrators need to invest in very large fleets of freighter aircraft. They generally cannot rely on the services of existing airlines, which, on short-haul routes at least mainly provide capacity in the daytime, in passenger aircraft belly-holds. They also must construct and run costly sortation centres at their hubs, centres which are capable of dealing with millions of packages in a short two to three hour window in the middle of the night. Huge investment will be needed in the surface transport vehicles which they will need in order to offer the collection and delivery part of their service. They will also be involved in heavy spending on information technology in order to provide the tracking and tracing options which their customers expect.

Such large capital requirements provide a formidable barrier to entry. It now looks likely that UPS and FedEx will be the leading players in the duopoly which has always been likely to be the mature structure of the integrated operations industry. It is possible, though, for those that make the investment to cover their costs and achieve profitability because of the uniqueness of their product and the substantial amount of value that they add. Prior to the arrival of the integrators, the shipper of a small urgent package was required to solve most of their problems themselves. Traditional airlines were only interested in the undemanding task of moving goods on an airport-to-airport basis. Collection and delivery had to be arranged by the shipper, normally using the services of an air freight forwarder. In addition, it was rarely possible to achieve the late afternoon collection, early next morning delivery ideal because, as we have seen, combination airlines relying on belly-hold capacity had most of their freight space available in the daytime. Little was available at the dead of night, as it would need to be if true overnight delivery was to be available.

Another value-adding focussing proposition has been tried frequently in the airline industry, but appears to offer a much poorer chance of sustainable profits. This proposition is based on the idea of focussing exclusively on meeting the needs of the business air traveller.

At first sight, the strategy appears to be a promising one. Market surveys amongst higher status business travellers show that they expect such things as high standards of seating comfort and in-flight service from the airlines they choose. Sometimes, though, an additional factor emerges. Business travellers often say that they dislike flying with those on vacation, who may be noisy and disruptive. They say that they would prefer their own airline, where their needs and status can be properly recognised.

Given such apparently fertile ground, there has been a regular supply of start-up airlines focussing purely on the market of high status business travellers. MGM Grand Air was a United States example—it ceased trading in 1995. From 1995 until it closed in 1998, Fairlines was a European equivalent, flying all First Class services from its Paris base. At the time of writing, there are start-up proposals being actively promoted in both the UK and Germany for airlines which will fly B767 aircraft in an all Business Class configuration.

Despite its popularity with start-up entrepreneurs, no business travel focussed airline has yet stood the test of time, because the concept is based on a misunderstanding of the priority of need of the business traveller. Business people certainly appreciate high standards of in-flight service and the benefits in terms of status and exclusivity which having their own airline can give them. Their most important needs, though, are more mundane. They must have a high frequency of conveniently-timed flights over a broad *route* network. They also appreciate the personal gains available to them (using their employer's money) of a frequent flyer programme. All these needs can be better met by Differentiation airlines, exploiting the synergies available from carrying both business and leisure travellers. Indeed, one of the great problems of business traveller focussed airlines is the question of what they do with their aircraft during holiday periods and over the weekend when the business market falls away.

There is one possible way in which a business traveller Focus may work and that is under the umbrella of a full-service airline. In many senses, the Concorde flights of Air France and British Airways were exactly this, being focussed on the tiny "tip of the pyramid" market. Both airlines continued with them for a long period, so one must assume that a profit was made, though "profit" has a doubtful meaning when the airlines received the aircraft free of charge from their respective governments. At the time of writing, though, Concorde services appear to be under a cloud as a result of the age of the aircraft and the severe impact which economic slowdown in both the USA and Europe has had on demand. Plans have been announced to withdraw them in the autumn of 2003.

An experiment has recently been mounted by the German carrier Lufthansa which may have interesting possibilities. Both Boeing and Airbus offer corporate jet versions of their narrow-bodied aircraft, Boeing with its 737 and Airbus with the A319. In essence, because corporate jets do not need large amounts of belly-hold space to be available for passenger's baggage, the manufacturers have used some of the belly-holds of their aircraft to install the extra fuel tanks necessary to give corporate customers the long ranges which they expect.

During 2002, Lufthansa entered into an arrangement with the Swiss based corporate jet operator Privatair that Privatair should provide corporate jet services on three routes between Germany and the USA, with the aircraft configurated with 48 all Business Class seats. The services are branded by Lufthansa and sold through the Lufthansa marketing system. Users are given privilege and exclusivity, but have all the back-up in tens of frequency and network of Lufthansa's "normal" services. They are also able to gain points in the Lufthansa "Miles and More" frequent flyer programme.

A final example of *Value Added* focussing in today's airline industry marks the policies being pursued by many smaller airlines from tourism receiving countries. Airlines such as Air Mauritius and Air Seychelles could be said to be engaging in a form of "Geographical" focussing. They cannot set out to conquer the world, but they can claim to know the particular country 'where they are based better than anyone else. Someone on holiday choosing them might. feel that their vacation was beginning sooner than would be the case on, say, British Airways or Lufthansa where the flight to their holiday destination would be just like any other.

"Low Cost" Focussing

The airline industry does show one good example of firms which use their focussing expertise to achieve very low costs, rather than to add value. Europe has a long tradition of aviation activity by "charter" airlines. Originally, these airlines developed because of a gap in the regulatory blanket enveloping European carriers, whereby charter carriers were given much more freedom than scheduled airlines, providing they kept to the so-called "Inclusive Tour" principle. This meant that they could not retail seats direct to the public. Instead, they were limited to a wholesaling role, wholesaling seats to tour operators.

The tour operators would then add in the accommodation and other elements to make up a packaged holiday, and undertake the retailing of these holidays.Today, these regulatory limitations have been completely removed (at least with the European Union) but the business model they gave rise to has proved resilient. European charter airlines developed a way of working which saw them focus on one single activity i.e the wholesaling of blocks of seats to tour operators. In order to attract the business of these tour operators, they had to achieve one thing above all others i.e low seat-mile costs. Such costs have been achieved in a number of ways.

The airlines have used relatively large aircraft, because their customers are not frequency sensitive. It increasingly looks as if the Airbus A330 will be the standard aircraft used by Europe's charter airlines. Seat pitches have been kept low, commonly at only 28 or 29 inches. Aircraft utilisations have been pushed to remarkably high levels of 4200-4300 hours per year, spreading ownership and lease-rental costs. Achieving such figures has been especially challenging because the market has a clear winter off-peak period. During the summer peak, aircraft are often flown throughout the night as well as the day, reflecting the fact that a proportion of package holiday customers are prepared to use "dead-of-night" departures providing that fares are low enough.

Also, and in advance of the "Cost Leader" revolution which is now affecting them so much, charter airlines kept with the idea that the provision of food and drink on board the aircraft need not be on a complementary basis. Instead, it could be a source of revenue. Today, the situation facing Europe's charter airlines is a very challenging one. The industry has mostly consolidated into two huge, vertically integrated firms under the leadership of the German-based TVI and CN Tourist groups. This has made life hard for smaller independents. Also, customer needs have changed radically. Many people do not now require rigid package holidays containing the three elements of airline seat, accommodation and surface transfers.

They certainly will not if they have their own accommodation with a villa or a timeshare, but generally now people are more experienced and adventurous, and are often prepared to put together their own holidays using the Internet. In many ways, the newer Cost Leader airlines are better suited to these trends than the rigid model of traditional charter airlines, and the charter carriers have had to respond.

Some have set up their own Cost Leader subsidiaries e.g. My Travel Lite and Lloyd Express, whilst almost all of them have now set up web-sites to enable at least a proportion of their capacity to be retailed direct to the public. In doing so, they have one crucial advantage over the scheduled airlines. Because competition amongst the charter carriers has been intense for a long time, these airlines generally do have the low operating costs necessary for them to compete. If they can maintain these, the charter airlines of Europe do have a sound future, even if their business model will have to be substantially modified.

"Lost-in-the-Middle"

Porter's Competitive Advantage model has one more concept we need to consider in the context of today's aviation industry—that of the "Lost-in-the-Middle" firm. Porter argues that there are firms that do not fit into any of the boxes. Their costs are too high for them to pursue Cost Leadership and there is too little about them which is distinctive for true Differentiation to be achieved. They are also too broadly-based in their activities to gain the benefits of expertise through Focussing. Sadly, the airline industry today has an almost endless list of firms to which this description could be applied. As we have seen, the structure of the industry has always been distorted by ownership and control issues, with the result that there are many more airlines in the world today than would be the case if market forces had been allowed to prevail. If ownership and control rules are changed in the future, which is now looking increasingly likely, many of them will not survive, especially if rules about State Aid for struggling airlines are more rigidly enforced.

Recent Developments

Michael Treacy and Fred Wiersma (1993) have modified Porter's three strategies to describe three basic "value disciplines" that can create customer value and provide a competitive advantage. ***They are operational excellence, product innovation, and customer intimacy.***

Airline Business and Marketing Strategies—Common Mistakes

We have now almost completed our survey of the strategic options open to carriers in today's airline industry. Unfortunately, the world's smoothest diplomat could not argue that the industry presents a picture of strategic success. Periods of severe loss-making have occurred regularly throughout the industry's history and, as we have seen, at the time of writing these losses are at a catastrophic level for many airlines. Bankruptcy has been a common feature, whilst a large number of carriers would not have survived without substantial government handouts.

When an airline fails, it is of course, a tragedy for those affected. A bankruptcy does, however, give an opportunity for lessons to be learned. The problem with the airlines is that they rarely are. Each airline failure does, of course, reflect some unique circumstances, special to a particular case. What is so depressing, though, is that the same issues, mistakes and problems seem to arise time and again. In this last section of the chapter, we review some of these common mistakes made by failed airlines.

Objectives

The writing of classical economists suggests that firms should be viewed as rational entities, lead by entrepreneurial managers whose objective is profit maximisation. In the airline business, such a theoretical position is often far from the true one. Airlines are set up and run for many reasons, which often make the achieving of satisfactory profits impossible. Sometimes, these objectives may be imposed from the outside. Equally, they may reflect the failings of the firm's Directors.

This situation presents itself most clearly in the case of many state-owned airlines. Almost all governments which still own airlines presumably expect that the carrier should be run to make a profit, to ensure that it is not a burden on the taxpayer. The problem is that either explicitly or implicitly, it is set a series of objectives which make profitability difficult or impossible. Amongst these is the need to maintain services on unprofitable routes for social or political reasons, or to assist economic development of backward regions. Also, airlines may be required to keep domestic air fares artificially low, due to the desire to control inflation, or to maintain unnecessary high levels of staffing because the government wishes to minimise unemployment. Even worse, though not strictly related to the question of objectives, governments often seek to interfere with airline management appointments, with senior management jobs being given to political supporters who have few qualifications to fill these demanding positions. A final, but sadly common problem in the developing world is that government employees and supporters travel a great deal on the national airline, but the government does not then pay the bill for this transportation. Ironically, many state-controlled airlines in developing countries are owed millions of dollars by the governments that own them.

The question of conflicting objectives is most obvious in the case of state-owned airlines, but as an issue it is not confined to them. Many private airlines are in practice operating to a mixed and confusing set of objectives.

Some privately-owned carriers are ego-trips for their owners. This is because aviation is a high profile activity where it is normal to achieve easily a great deal of media coverage. It is remarkable in the airline industry how many small airlines have grandiose names playing on the themes of an "intercontinental" or "world" presence. It is also noticeable that these airlines are often based in impressive head office described as a "global headquarters" building. A further indication of an airline being driven forward by its owner's ego is that the owner then ensures that their name is incorporated in the name of the airline and that it is painted on the side of each aircraft in large letters. Ego-driven airlines are rarely successful because they tend to grow based on the owner's desire for more publicity and a still higher profile rather than on opportunities for profit.

A further problem with some airlines is that they are essentially hobbies for those that set them up. Besides being a business, aviation also provides a fascinating hobby for many people. It is one thing to pursue this hobby by plane-spotting. It is quite another to take it to the extent of setting up an airline. Hobby-based carriers only tend to survive if the owner is extremely rich and prepared to lose a great deal of money.

A final, difficult objective for an airline to pursue in practice is that of being a vehicle for revenge. There have been a number of cases where someone who has been fired from one airline sets up a rival carrier designed to allow them to get even with the people who dismissed them. Again, emotion rather than economics will be the driving force behind decision-making and success will be very difficult to achieve.

All-in-all, the "'foundation for a successful airline must be that the carrier must be profit-based in terms of the objectives it is pursuing.

Diversification vs Specialisation

Successful airlines are often those which strike a very difficult balance between over-diversifying and over-specialising.

Over-diversification can take on a number of different forms. In the past, some airlines have diversified into travel-related businesses such as hotel and car rental. At first sight, this appears to be a sound move by allowing carriers to trade on the synergies resulting from being a "one stop shop" for the business traveller. It has, though, mostly turned out to be a mistake. It has resulted in a dilution of the top management attention being given to the demanding task of running the airline, and has provided competition for financial resources. More seriously still, it has meant diversification into industries which have exactly the same cyclical problems as the airline business. If airline seats are unoccupied in a downturn, hotel rooms will also be vacant and cars unrented, because suppliers are relying on the same person for each of these activities.

If there is an argument for an airline to pursue a diversification policy into other industries (which is doubtful), a stronger case could be made that they should concentrate on counter-cyclical activities which are likely to remain resilient in a downturn.

Another aspect of over-diversification occurs when an airline tries to cover too broad a route network with too few aircraft. If each route in a network is only served at a low frequency, a great deal of opportunity will still be available for competitors to invade the firm's markets. Southwest Airlines now has a fleet of more than 360 aircraft, but it still only serves 58 cities in its route network. It has always had a clear policy to build frequency as quickly as possible on a new route, to cement its control of the market. "Do the job properly. or not at all" is a sound maxim.

Despite these arguments, over specialisation can be an equal problem. It occurs when an airline bets its future on success in a single market. For example, in the past, some airlines (notably so the now forgotten UK carrier British Caledonian) have tried to build a route network concentrated on serving oil-producing regions. Such a policy will work well when the oil price is high, but will fail disastrously during times of oversupply and low oil prices.

Pace of Expansion

A difficult issue with regard to successful strategies is that of the appropriate rate of growth which the airline should aim to achieve. It will be hard to ensure success without growth, for two reasons. Firstly, as they mature, airlines tend to find that their costs rise. This is mainly because many groups within the airline are paid according to salary scales which mean that their pay increases each year that they remain on the payroll. Growth means that new members can be recruited at relatively low salary scales. Secondly, unless an airline grows it will not be taking advantage of new market opportunities as they become available. Besides a possible loss of profit, there is a risk that these opportunities will be taken up by competitors who will use them to further build the strength of their competitive challenge.

In the airline industry there is another, peculiar factor ensuring that growth opportunities need to be taken, reflecting the way in which airport slots are allocated. If an airport still has slots available, there is strong pressure on an airline to grow and use them because, once they have been obtained, they will be kept forever under the in-perpetuity principle which underlies slot awards.

Growth rates can, though, easily become over-ambitious. If a carrier attempts to grow too quickly, it will run the risk of becoming dependent on borrowed rather then equity capital. In turn, this may mean exposure to exchange rate and interest rate fluctuations. Also, over-rapid growth may mean that an airline falls apart operationally. Airlines are very complex interacting systems where all aspects of the system much be functioning well together. If one component is not, then the whole is at risk. At the extreme, this may manifest itself in a poor safety record and the disastrous consequences of a fatal accident. Less severe, but still serious problems might, for example, be that potential customers are unable to make bookings because of a shortage of reservations capacity. Of all the airlines that fail, a proportion does so because they do not grow fast enough. European Cost Leader airlines which, at the time writing are attempting to grow at rates exceeding 30% a year.

Competitive Response

Successful airlines tend to be those that manage their competitive strategies well, and unsuccessful ones those that fail to do so. This is especially a problem for new, small carriers. When a small, start-up airline first begins to fly, it poses a difficult problem for its larger, more powerful rivals. These carriers may launch a vigorous competitive response, and make life very hard for the newcomer. If they do though, they will be spending a great deal of money to deal with what is a minor threat to them.

In particular if larger airlines respond with aggressive pricing, they will certainly be competing with a smaller rival. What they will also be doing, though, is offering discounted fares to the many customers who would have flown with them anyway. Because of this, they may be reluctant to respond strongly at first to any challenge. They may also fear that, if they do, they will be exposed to court action over allegations of anti-competitive behaviour. Because of these factors, a small new airline may often find that its early days of flying are marked by considerable success.

On the basis of this, plans are then formulated for rapid expansion. These plans are usually helped by aircraft manufacturers being willing to offer large numbers of aeroplanes at low prices, and by suppliers of finance being quite happy to accept risk based on the asset value of these aircraft, or to lease aircraft on flexible terms. Unfortunately, once the expansion has began the new airline changes from an irritant to a significant threat to its more powerful rivals. It must then anticipate a strong competitive response, a response which will be especially serious if it coincides with a cyclical downturn as the industry enters a recession. As we have seen, the aviation industry never seems to have a shortage of start-up entrepreneurs, wanting to set up airlines.

Even severe recessions do not dampen this enthusiasm—indeed they may increase it due to the cheaply available resources which are on offer at such times. All the evidence of history, though, says that most of these airlines will fail, many after a very short time. Since the liberalisation trend began with US domestic deregulation in 1978, the proportion of failures has exceeded 90%. Many have ended up doing so because they underestimated the response of threatened competitors.

"Control"

The "Dotcom" excesses of the period from 1998 to 2000 have many lessons for airlines. Too often, the entrepreneurs who set up dotcom businesses were seduced by the lifestyle that sudden wealth made possible, ' and lost sight of the fact that any business needs to meet a worthwhile set is of customer needs and to charge profitable prices. Airlines have just as much to fear. Some have failed because vast sums have been spent on building an extremely expensive head office building and on funding the lifestyles of the Directors and Senior Managers.

Over-optimism/Fall Back Position

No-one who chooses to work in the aviation industry should be under any illusion. It will be a roller-coaster ride. Periods of relative prosperity will alternate with times of real difficulty, with recessions and now wars and the threat of terrorism providing tremendous challenges.

'In such an industry, the most fatal business plan of all will be one which is based on the principle, "if everything keeps going my way, I'll be fine". Business plans have to be resilient to deal with sudden increases in uncontrollable costs such as the price of fuel. They have to address the likelihood that demand and yield will from time-to-time fall away badly as a recession bites or a destabilizing war or terrorism incident affects the industry. They especially have to deal with the likelihood that a whole set of unfavorable circumstances may arrive at the same time, as they often do.

In order to be able to do so, they need to have a fall-back position, the components of which will include a number of expedients. They may, for example take a proportion of their aircraft on relatively costly short-term operating leases, allowing for a return to the lesser if trouble strikes. Also, a proportion of support services could be bought in on a sub-contracted basis, allowing contracts with suppliers to be renegotiated in a down-turn.

This chapter on Airline Strategies has inevitably been long and involved. The whole subject, though, is of vital importance. No airline can hope to implement successful marketing policies unless these are underpinned by a sound strategy.

STRATEGIC ALLIANCE

A **Strategic Alliance** is a formal relationship formed between two or more parties to pursue a set of agreed upon goals or to meet a critical business need while remaining independent organizations.

Partners may provide the strategic alliance with resources such as products, distribution channels, manufacturing capability, project funding, capital equipment, knowledge, expertise, or intellectual property. The alliance is a *cooperation* or *collaboration* which aims for a *synergy* where each partner hopes that the benefits from the alliance will be greater than those from individual efforts. The alliance often involves *technology transfer* (access to knowledge and expertise), *economic specialization*, shared expenses and shared risk.

Benefits of Strategic Alliances

Strategic alliances often bring partners the following benefits:

1. Access to their partner's *distribution channels* and international market presence.
2. Access to their partner's products, technology, and intellectual property.
3. Access to partner's capital.
4. New markets for their products and services or new products for their customers.
5. Increased brand awareness through partner's channels.
6. Reduced product development time and faster-to-market products.
7. Reduced R&D costs and risks.
8. Rapidly achieve scale, critical mass and momentum (Economies of Scale—bigger is better).
9. Establish technological standards for the industry and early products that meet the standards.
10. By-product utilization.
11. Management skills.

Types of Strategic Alliances

Various terms have been used to describe forms of strategic partnering. These include 'international coalitions' (Porter and Fuller, 1986), 'strategic networks' (Jarillo, 1988) and, most commonly, 'strategic alliances'. Definitions are equally varied. An alliance may be seen as the 'joining of forces and resources, for a specified or indefinite period, to achieve a common objective'.

Strategic alliances may be intra-industry (e.g. U.S. car manufacturers developing electric car technology) or inter-industry (e.g. GlaxoSmithKline with Matsushita, Canon, Fuji and Apple). They can range from handshake to merger, from licensing to equity joint venture.

Contractual

1. Licensing
2. Cross-licensing
3. Supplier relations
4. Collaboration
5. R&D Consortia
6. Industry Cluster
7. Innovation Network
8. Franchising
9. Management Contract
10. Turnkey project
11. Virtual Company

Equity

1. Joint venture
2. Joint R&D
3. Mergers and acquisitions
4. Purchase of equity share
5. Equity swap

Stages of Alliance formations

A typical strategic alliance formation process involves these steps:

- **Strategy Development**: Strategy development involves studying the alliance's feasibility, objectives and rationale, focusing on the major issues and challenges and development of resource strategies for production, technology, and people. It requires aligning alliance objectives with the overall corporate strategy.
- **Partner Assessment**: Partner assessment involves analyzing a potential partner's strengths and weaknesses, creating strategies for accommodating all partners' management styles, preparing appropriate partner selection criteria, understanding a partner's motives for joining the alliance and addressing resource capability gaps that may exist for a partner.
- **Contract Negotiation**: Contract negotiations involves determining whether all parties have realistic objectives, forming high caliber negotiating teams, defining each partner's contributions and rewards as well as protect any proprietary information, addressing termination clauses, penalties for poor performance, and highlighting the degree to which arbitration procedures are clearly stated and understood.
- **Alliance Operation**: Alliance operations involves addressing senior management's commitment, finding the caliber of resources devoted to the alliance, linking of budgets and resources with strategic priorities, measuring and rewarding alliance performance, and assessing the performance and results of the alliance.
- **Alliance Termination**: Alliance termination involves winding down the alliance, for instance when its objectives have been met or cannot be met, or when a partner adjusts priorities or re-allocated resources elsewhere.

Risks of Strategic Alliance

Strategic alliances can lead to competition rather than cooperation, to loss of competitive knowledge, to conflicts resulting from incompatible cultures and objectives, and to reduced management control (Chan and Heide, 1993). A study of almost 900 joint ventures found that less than half were mutually agreed to have been successful by all parties (Harrigan, 1986; Dacin et al, 1997 Spekman et al, 1996).

An alliance can fail for many reasons (Vyas et. al 1993; Duysters et al, 1999)

- failure to understand and adapt to a new style of management
- failure to learn and understand cultural differences between the organisations
- lack of commitment to succeed
- strategic goal divergence
- insufficient trust
- operational and geographical overlap
- unrealistic expectations

The Five Factors of a Strategic Alliance

As companies gain experience in building alliances, they often find their portfolios ballooning with partnerships. While these partnerships may contribute value to the firm, not all alliances are in fact strategic to an organization. This is a critical point, since, as this article will explain, those alliances that are truly strategic must be identified clearly and managed differently than more conventional business relationships. Due to the levels of organizational commitment and investment required, not all partner relationships can be given the same degree of attention as truly strategic alliances. The impact of mismanaging a strategic alliance or permitting it to fall apart can materially impact the firm's ability to achieve its core business objectives.

The five criteria of a "strategic" alliance. What is it that makes an alliance truly strategic to a particular company? Is it possible for an alliance to be strategic to only one of the parties in a relationship? Many alliances default to some form of revenue generation—which is certainly important—but revenue alone may not be truly strategic to the objectives of the business. There are five general criteria that differentiate strategic alliances from conventional alliances. An alliance meeting any one of these criteria is strategic and should be managed accordingly.

1. Critical to the success of a core business goal or objective.
2. Critical to the development or maintenance of a core competency or other source of competitive advantage.
3. Blocks a competitive threat.
4. Creates or maintains strategic choices for the firm.
5. Mitigates a significant risk to the business.

The essential issue when developing a strategic alliance is to understand which of these criteria the other party views as strategic. If either partner misunderstands the other's expectation of the alliance, it is likely to fall apart. For example, if one partner believes the other is looking for revenue generation to achieve a core business goal, when in reality the objective is to keep a strategic option open, the alliance is not likely to survive. Examining each of the five strategic criteria in depth provides insight into how the strategic value of alliances can be leveraged.

1. Critical to a Business Objective

While the most common type of alliance generates revenue through a joint go-to-market approach, not every alliance that produces revenue is strategic. For example, consider the impact on revenue objectives if the relationship were terminated? Clearly, a truly strategic relationship would have a great bearing on the prospects for achieving revenue growth targets. In addition to a single strategic alliance, related groupings of alliances—networks or constellations—may also be critical to a business objective. Sun Microsystems has established a group of integrator alliances that function as an effective marketing channel and drive significant revenues for the company each quarter. (See article, *Constellation Strategy*, elsewhere in issue of IBJ Online). This category also includes alliances with high potential, such as alliances that have large but unrealized revenue opportunity. Consider the impact of new industry standards that make it possible for products from different manufacturers to work together. This can unlock customer value and boost the revenue potential of new, technology-based products. From writable DVD formats to next-generation wireless technologies, technical standards are democratically determined in consortiums of interested industry participants. With product development racing in parallel, the first mover's advantage can be substantial, and hence alliance development and lobbying within an industry become paramount to financial success. Cost reduction may also be a core business objective of the alliance, particularly among supply-side partners. By investing together in new processes, technologies and standards, alliance partners can obtain substantial cost savings in their internal operations. Again, however, a cost-saving alliance is not truly strategic unless it has an underlying business objective, such as "to achieve an industry-leading cost structure."

2. Competitive Advantage and Core Competency

Another way in which an alliance can prove to be strategic is to play a key role in developing or protecting a firm's competitive advantage or core competency. Learning alliances are the most common form of competitive/ competency strategic alliances. An organization's need to build incremental skills in an area of importance is often accelerated with the help of an experienced partner. In some cases, the learning objective of the relationship is openly agreed between the partners; however, this is not always the case. Learning alliances work best when:

1. The objectives are openly shared.
2. There is little chance of future competition (such as when the partners are in adjacent industries).

3. The cultures of the organizations are similar enough to enable process and methods to be leveraged.
4. The governance structure of the alliances is established to promote learning at the executive, managerial and operational levels.

3. Blocking a Competitive Threat

An alliance can be strategic even when it falls short of establishing a competitive advantage. Consider the case of an alliance that blocks a competitive threat. It is strategic to bring competitive parity to a secondary segment of a market in which the firm competes, when the *absence* of parity creates a competitive disadvantage in the related primary segments of that market. For example, competing in the high and medium price range of a market with a premium product may leave the firm vulnerable to a low-priced entry. If the firm's manufacturing processes do not permit the creation of a low-priced product entry, a strategic alliance with a volume partner in an adjacent market can successfully block the competitive threat. Another example of strategic alliances that block competitive threats are the airline alliances that permit route-sharing among carriers. The two primary determinants of customer flight selection are routing and cost. Therefore, the adoption of route-sharing alliances by the airlines blocks the competitive threat of preferential routing in the specific markets in which the airline chooses to compete. In essence, strategic alliances within the airline industry ensure competitive parity with respect to routing and force other factors such as on-time departures and customer service to become the bases for competitive differentiation.

4. Future Strategic Options

From a longer-term perspective, an alliance that is not fundamental to achieving a business objective today could become critical in the future. For example, in 1984, a U.S. consumer products company needed to expand distribution beyond the Midwestern states. Faced with the prospect of European competition at some point in the future, the firm made a strategic decision to invest in an alliance with a distribution and support services company that had incremental distribution capacity in the U.S. and a similar presence in Europe, rather than invest in expanding its own local distribution capabilities. With the option to expand into European distribution at any point, the firm could work to sew up the U.S. market before expanding too quickly internationally.

5. Risk Mitigation

When an alliance is driven by intent to mitigate significant risk to an underlying business objective, the nature of the risk and its potential impact on the underlying business objective are the key determinants of whether or not it is truly strategic. Dual sourcing strategies for critical production components or processes are excellent examples of how risk mitigation can become the context for supply-side strategic alliances.

As process manufacturing companies advance the yield of their operations, suppliers often collaborate with the manufacturer to ensure their new products fit within its new operations. The benefits of such an alliance are cost savings to the manufacturer and accelerated product development for the supplier. In situations where the supplier's product is critical to the manufacturer's operation, it may be necessary for the manufacturer to have strategic alliances with two competing suppliers in order to mitigate such risks as unilateral cost increases or degradation in quality of service. Joint ventures and minority equity investments among relationship commitments, joint ventures and equity investments are closest to the strategic end of the spectrum. However, investing a large sum of money in a partner does not automatically make the relationship strategic.

One needs only to survey the wreckage of the dot-com era for proof of failed minority equity investments in alliances. It may be economically sound to invest $1 million in a distribution relationship that is projected to return $1.5 million in incremental sales the following year. This would not necessarily be strategic to a firm with $800 million in annual sales, unless the alliance also served an alternate purpose that met one of the five strategic criteria. For example, if the achievement of a core business objective, such as access to a new market, were enabled by the investment, then it would be strategic to the firm. Management How, then, should strategic alliances be managed differently than traditional alliances? There are countless lists of reasons why alliances fail.

However, aside from ensuring "sound strategic alignment" between the partners, most determinants of failure are less than strategic in nature. Lack of executive sponsorship is often a source of alliance failure with strategic alliances, the key to effective executive sponsorship is visibility and accountability. Since failed alliances can directly impact a business in a meaningful way, or even have adverse implications for the executive's own financial bonus or prestige, he has a strong incentive to consider the strategic alliance as important as his other primary responsibilities. Metrics determine just how the alliance and accountable executives are kept on track. While clear metrics are required of any alliance, shared metrics between the partners are absolutely critical to the success of a strategic alliance.

Shared metrics bring immediate alignment of focus between the parties, and when executive sponsors are held accountable for the shared metrics, the two firms become aligned as one. Poor alliance governance structures are another common source of alliance failure. Strategic alliances are best served by formalized governance structures with clear mandates that are directly linked to the shared metrics underpinning the partnership. At Hewlett-Packard we often create strategic alliance executive committees using an "N by N" mapping of key HP executives to their counterparts at the alliance partner. The number ("N") and position of the executives participating in the review meetings are usually on a quarterly basis which is tailored to the specifics of each strategic alliance.

The attending executives represent the business unit(s) and core functions that are critical to execution of the strategic alliance. Regular meetings of executives from the partner companies continue the relationship building that begins while formulating and negotiating the terms of the strategic alliance. Trust is perhaps the foundation of a strategic alliance and these relationships are the building blocks for establishing trust amongst the individuals who represent the two parties in the strategic alliance. The real reason that most alliances fail is the constant change in the business environment. Trust allows the parties in a strategic alliance to have the difficult discussions that will transform the alliance over time and give it longevity. When corporate strategies change as a result of a changing business environment, the assumptions upon which the strategic alliance was originally based also change.

What was once a strategic investment may no longer remain strategic without modification to the terms of the alliance. In the most extreme cases, the trust built between the two companies enables the adaptability—even renegotiation of the financial terms—to accommodate changes in market or other conditions that impact one of the partners. Strategic alliance organizations are feeling increased pressure. As critical personnel become stretched and financial resources become scarce, strategic alliance organizations must allocate their resources in the most efficient manner possible so that truly strategic alliances can support and accelerate the strategy of the business.

The five strategic criteria outlined in this article are primary determinants of the strategic value of an alliance. Using these criteria to identify genuine strategic alliances in the portfolio today and as a guide for developing future strategic alliances are the first steps to improving the impact of an alliance organization. The management principles, also described above, are the next steps towards improving the effectiveness of the strategic alliances themselves.

AIRLINES ALLIANCES

It has been pointed out earlier that US airlines found the US market place too crowded to fight the competition. Doganis (1994) observed that in 1989 the six largest US carriers generated 84% of US domestic passenger kilometres, as per year 2000 data, the top 6 airlines in US in terms of RPKs, have a share of over 72% of the total US RPKs. Europeans took a cue from the US experience and found that the size was necessary not to get the economies of scale, but to attain economies of scope with deeper and wider reach in the market.

To achieve the desired economies of scope, alliances were a handy solution as the cross-border alliances or mergers had the potential for generating traffic feed between an airline and its partner. European airlines threatened by the US moves to garner large shares of the transatlantic air passenger market decided to enter into marketing alliances. However, these marriages of convenience proved to be short-lived and less beneficial to the partners. The alliances between United Airlines and British Airways and that between Air France and Lufthansa were such examples (Doganis, 1994).

In order to achieve desired economies of scale, European carriers came up with a three-pronged approach (Doganis, 1994 and 2001). The first step of this approach was to make sure that the airlines had a dominant position in its home market. This was done through purchasing the smaller airlines in the market (e.g., KLM buying into shares of Netherlines and a charter carrier, Transavia) or by increasing the shares through launch of new airlines that cater to a different market segment. As in the case of British Airways which merged its wholly owned subsidiaries, British Regional Airlines and Brymon Airways in March 2002 to British Airways Citi Express. Its 2001 acquisition of British Regional airlines group further strengthened its position in the UK domestic market.

The *second* step was to gain foothold in other major European markets. The major constituents of the European market are the UK, Germany and France. SAS did this by purchasing shares of British Midland's parent company in 1988. British Airways acquired majority stakes in Deutsche BA in Germany. It also bought equity in Air Russia. As discussed above, recently the launch of British Airways Citi Express also made it garner a larger share in the European pie. It has now increased its share in the European air passenger market.

The *third* strategic option was to establish a global presence through marketing alliances with other non-European airlines or making share purchases in them. The point was to enter the markets that were under-represented by the incumbent airline. Obviously, the market choice for the European carriers was the American market and the Asia-Pacific market as they are the largest markets outside the European Common market for air passenger traffic. With this aim British Airways purchased stakes within 2 months in Qantas in 1992 and in US Air in 1993.

These purchases made some room for British Airways in the Pacific and the US market. de Wit (1996) makes similar observation when he identifies that European airlines are restructuring their networks to increase their competitiveness. The airlines in Europe are entering into alliances of all sorts by way of equity purchase, code share agreements, block-space arrangements, wet leases, franchising agreements and joint ventures. Transnational alliances as in case of SAS and Swissair, BA-Deutsche BA, TAT and Maersk Air, KLM and Air UK were also observed. These alliances were expected to lead to network economies and the reinforcement of home base, thereby ensuring increased feed and formation of fortress 'Euro' hubs, similar to those in US. Sabena, SAS, KLM and Lufthansa have reportedly developed such hubs at their respective home bases.

KLM, Lufthansa, Swissair (now Swiss) and SAS, all followed similar three pronged strategies during late 1980s and the 1990s. BA, however, was the first to develop a clear plan of taking 3 steps to gain the market. It continuously increased its stake in various airlines. BA bought 40% share in Brymon Airways in 1987 and subsequently purchased it outright in 1993. Its moves of taking over of British Celadonian in late 1987; 1992 acquisition of principal European and domestic scheduled routes of Dan Air which eventually helped it to strengthen its hold on Gatwick Airport; 1993 franchisee arrangements with Maersk Air and City Flyer Express further solidified its position in the market. The only other significant UK airline was British Midland. When low cost carriers like Easy Jet and Ryan air started out in 1995, BA set up Go, a low cost no frills airline, in 1998.

In the second part of the strategy, BA and a consortium of German banks, acquired 49% stakes in Delta Air (a domestic German airline) in 1992. In 1997, it acquired the remaining 51% stake as well. In 1993, it bought 49.9 % of TAT, France's largest independent domestic airline. As the industry gains maturity over years, airlines all over have been constantly revising their strategies for growth and encountering competition. This has been driven by one particular need, survival. Ironically, prosperity in this glamorous industry is secondary.

These strategies cover cost cutting measures, better management and most importantly, strategic alliances with other airlines. These alliances are guided by the bilateral air services agreement system. In many cases code-sharing agreements have been made to maintain or expand coverage. This international code sharing has become a part of bilateral negotiations. Such code-share alliances have served many purposes for the airlines operating in the domain. They do not need to own and operate aircraft in a particular region to earn revenues. Also, this has shielded the airlines from unprofitable operations that would have resulted from their operations if undertaken all alone. Alliances also create marketing advantage for the partners.

Alliance is a catchall expression that airlines have adopted for various strategies they have adopted to expand their services (Yergin et al., 2000). These range from cooperation on activities like ticketing and baggage handling or reciprocal participation in frequent-flyer programmes to integration that includes code-sharing, revenue sharing for the use of network *(pro-rate agreement)*, joint ground service, joint telephone call centres, joint marketing, sharing aircraft and now, even aircraft purchases. The customers have also shown preference for airlines with larger networks to minimize their own cost of travel, get better services and to take advantage of better frequent flyer programmes. In addition the alliances offer better access and passage at congested airports, which is an attraction to both consumers and airlines alike. The benefits of economies of scale are self-evident that flow in as a result of such activity. The overall aim of the alliances is to create a win-win situation for all the alliance partners. In other words, their ultimate aim is to enhance partner airlines' competitive positions and to achieve higher profits for all the partners in the alliance. The first international alliance took place between Air Florida and British Island in 1986. This was of code sharing nature. Since then there has been a frenzy of alliances in the industry.

Rationality for Alliances

It has been pointed out above that the enhanced US competitiveness due to deregulation made it necessary for the other big players in the market to look for alternatives, which could shield them from the onslaught of US airlines at their home turfs/dominant markets.

There may be several reasons as pointed out in the strategic management literature. Oum, Park and Zhang (2000, pp. 4-5) have observed that there is no universally accepted definition of strategic alliance. For the airline industry they define the term as "... a long term partnership of two or more firms who attempt to enhance competitive advantages collectively vis-à-vis their competitors by sharing scarce resources including brand assets and market access capability, enhancing service quality, and thereby, improving profitability." They have then extended it to practical application as, "In practical terms, a strategic alliance is one involving strategic commitment by top management to link up a substantial part of their respective route networks as well as collaborating on some key areas of airline business."

Several authors have pointed out various reasons for formation of strategic alliances in the airline industry. Burton and Hanlon (1994) opine that alliances are central to formulation of business strategy. Further, they argue that in airline industry there are no *a priori* reasons for consolidation through alliances. The airlines enter into alliances to gain economies of scale and more importantly, that of scope. Youssef (1992, as quoted in Youssef and Hansen, 1994) has put forth two theories that try to explain the reason for alliances to take place. The first theory is related to attaining the technical efficiencies of lower production costs/better service characteristics available to larger aïrlines in comparison to smaller airlines. The alliances allow the partners to consolidate facilities like maintenance bases. Also, each airline then has increased geographical reach and the network increases. This increase in network coverage has the benefit of improved quality and quantity of service (with assumptions about passenger acceptability) that are fallout of either better schedule coordination or perception by the passengers. Secondly, with increase in network there will be enhanced benefits of frequent flyer programs that may be offered to the passengers. Thus, there will be more attractions for passengers to fly a particular airline and the airlines are immensely benefited as they have increased coverage without increasing their individual route systems. This may then lead to lower unit production costs and economies of network density result.

The second explanation for the formation of strategic alliances is their possible use to limit competition in the markets. As there exist several restrictions on market and route entry, capacity and pricing in domestic and international aviation markets, strategic alliances enable formation of virtual monopolies in markets between the hubs of alliance partners. This can limit the competition through monopolization in the hubs. In addition, there will be disincentive for any other airline to expand through internal expansion.

Clearly, the biggest motivation for airlines to enter into alliances is to expand market feed. Some airlines that are dominant in their home markets have entered into an alliance with an international airline to provide feed to their airlines. The agreement between Jet Airways (an airline operating in the Indian domestic market) and KLM is one such example. Then, there are other reasons like the governments seeking better management practices in the airlines by improving performance and economic returns. The two authors then summarize the requirements for partners for entering into alliances into 3 categories with their example of SAS and Swissair alliance.

Convergence—Similar images of carriers in quality of service, safety and technical competence.

Competitiveness—The incumbents need to be competitive in their own markets that can then yield to increased competitiveness for all in the joint schemes.

Complementarily—In terms of routes served so that there are more routes than before that could be served. This will provide the necessary scope economies.

Besides the alliances come in handy to overcome restrictive entry policies as enforced by some countries. Airline industry is clearly an example of such restricted policies. It is highly paradoxical that though this has perhaps the greatest role in quick spread of globalization, there are several restrictions around the world that have held it back from becoming fully global by itself. Similar views are expressed by Staniland (1998) quoting KLM chairman who himself had expressed alliances as being a reasoned response to the antiquated regulatory system and facilitators for providing indirect access to restricted markets.

Further, they cite the risk sharing advantages of the alliances and the advantages accruing due to convergence of technology and products across the industries. Lastly, when the resources of one player are scarce, pooling of resources may provide the necessary global scales in branding as well. Such common branding then contributes to increased mind space and increased market share. (Alpert and Kamins (1995) argue that consumers have a favourable perception and attitude towards pioneer brands.)

Then, Oum et al. (2001), focus on the airline industry and identify the following as the most common and most important reasons to form strategic alliances:

(a) **Reach of Seamless Service Networks**: A connection of networks gives the consumers a large choice of destinations to choose from and plan better, connections are eased out and there are increased benefits of Frequent Flyer Programs (they have a broader range of benefits to offer) and lesser possibilities of lost baggage. Also, the alliances' network comes in handy when operations are to be made in highly competitive, unprofitable and price sensitive market conditions (e.g. pooling in of resources by two airlines to coordinate to overcome otherwise unprofitable routes). By connecting the networks, partners are able to expand their routes beyond their country territories. Also, there are several restrictions on foreign ownership and fifth, seventh and eighth freedom rights are generally not available. Even if some carriers manage to get the requisite legal permissions, the costs associated of time, risk and capitalact as virtual barriers (potential facilitators) to direct entry by foreign airlines in other markets (for forming strategic alliances).

(b) **Enhanced Traffic Feed**: With linkage of the airline networks the carriers can increase their load factors with the increased feed. Also, flight frequency can be increased without increasing the size of the fleet.

(c) **Cost Reduction**: The partners in the alliance can have the benefits of attaining the economies of scale (through joint operations of air and ground services) and scope (through increased reach and efficient connections) and increased traffic density (through network expansion and additional traffic feed).

(d) **Service Quality Improvement**: Ease of online connections, frequency and schedule convenience has been marked as the dimensions of an airline's service quality. By entering into alliances, the schedules can be better-coordinated and waiting time for passengers reduced. Further, the increase in itinerary choices is another benefit that an alliance can offer to passengers.

(e) **Marketing Advantages**: The frequent flyer programs are pooled in an alliance and the passengers thus have a wider choice as well as more chances to accrue points to use later. Then there are many display benefits of Computerized Reservation System for airlines entering into strategic alliances. The visibility on the CRS is increased manifold as all the partners in the alliance show the flight to the same destination as their own. Consequently, the chances that a traveller will fly a particular airline are increased manifold. (Also observed in Burton and Hanlon, 1994.) Increased market share and cooperative pricing that is possible is another reason that airlines enter into strategic alliances. There have been concerns raised over time about the anti-competitive effects of the alliances, there have been exemptions like KLM Northwest alliance, which received anti-trust immunity. This is reportedly one of the reasons that Netherlands became the first country to sign an Open Skies pact with the US. As Doganis (1994) has also observed that the larger airlines offer the FFP members more opportunities to collect and use points. They may also act as a potential entry barrier for small start-ups. In addition, they provide access to information on passenger characteristics and needs and also direct marketing access to large number of frequent travellers. The data as provided in the same paper suggests that there is high non-redemption rate that offsets the potential huge costs that the airlines may have to incur in flying passengers for "free".

Another reason to enter into alliance has been put forward by de Wit (1996), where he finds alliances a convenient way to form a multiple hub structure. This multiple hub structure will give the alliance an edge over any other airline that wishes to operate in Europe. A pan European alliance or an alliance dominant in Europe will be an attractive partner that will be sought to become one of the members of a global alliance. This is also one of the identified pre-requisites of a potential partner willing to join a global network (Oum, Taylor and Zhang, 1993).

Classifying Alliances

There is no consensus on classification of alliances in airline industry. There exist several ways in which alliances are classified. One preferred way is to categorize them into 3 categories depending on the extent of co-ordination:

(1) Simple route by route alliance (interline),
(2) Broad commercial alliance,
(3) Equity alliance.

(A) **Interline Alliance**: The Interline Alliance is simplest of them all. It involves low level of co-ordination on few routes. Potential areas of co-ordination include ground handling, joint use of ground facilities, code sharing and joint operations, block space sale, and co-ordination of flight schedules for directly related flights.

(B) **Broad Commercial Alliance**: The Broad Commercial Airline Alliance extends the areas of co-ordination to joint development of systems and joint marketing activities. It is wider for it may comprise of code sharing and sharing frequent flyer programmes. This may also include transfer of traffic at hub airport to other airline. An example is the One World Alliance that was founded on February 1, 1999. The founder members of the Alliance are American Airlines, British Airways, Cathay Pacific and Qantas. Later, in September 1999, Finnair and Iberia joined in the alliance. This expanded further with the inclusion of Aer Lingus (June 2000) and LAN Chile (June 2000). This alliance has assets of nearly 2000 aircraft with more than 300 still on order. It is spread in more than 130 countries across more than 550 destinations, employs nearly 260,000 people. This is an example of how the alliances can be useful to customers for they can offer the benefits that are way beyond the reach of individual airlines.

(C) **Equity Alliance**: In Equity Alliance, as the name suggests, there may be equity swap among the partners. Thus, the partners generally co-operate in all areas of joint activities. It may involve code sharing on a large number of routes so that all the partners gain the leverage from the strategic alliance they have entered into. The alliance between American Airlines and Canadian Airlines International of 1994 is an example of this kind of alliance. AA invested US$190 million in equity and voting shares of CAI. This is most durable type of alliance, but the proportion of such type has declined and the carriers mostly enter into commercial alliance.

It should be borne in mind that alliances are just another milestone in this very bumpy ride of the aviation industry. They are in no way the end of the journey because international air transport is a dynamic industry. Changes may occur in any area of alliance. There are cases where the alliances continue for years and on the other end, alliances break away in a few weeks' time.

Another view of the airline alliances is to see them in the light of alliances between airlines. The inter-airline alliance arrangements are complex. They can be broadly divided into two categories (Doganis, 2001):

(i) Strategic Alliances
(ii) Commercial (Marketing) Alliances

Strategic Alliances: When the partners co-mingle their assets in order to pursue a single or joint set of business objectives. These co-mingled assets may be terminal facilities, maintenance bases, aircraft, staff, traffic rights or capital resources. This is extended to two or more airlines offering a common brand and a uniform service standard. The franchisee partner may be much smaller than the other, however the fact, that they share a common objective of leveraging the alliance to increase their profits, makes the alliance strategic.

Marketing (Commercial) Alliances: They are different from strategic alliances as the partners stay independent of each other and each partner pursues his own objectives. Thus, many code-sharing agreements, joint frequent flyer programmes and some block space arrangements are essentially marketing alliances. Literature suggests another classification of alliances on the basis of GEOGRAPHIC SCOPE. This again can be done in two ways:

(i) **Regional Alliances:** These alliances are on a wider scale. They can further be of two kinds. The *first* is a commercial agreement covering many routes, though usually from a particular geographical region or a country. Such agreements, generally, involve, code-shared flights, joint marketing and sales, some capacity coordination, use of each other's business lounges and so on. (Example, 1999 alliance of Malaysian Airlines and Thai Airways covering code sharing on several routes with in their countries. Similar alliance existed between SIA, Air New Zealand and Ansett. This alliance covered routes between South East Asia and Australasia as well as some routes within Australia. Also, the alliances between Swissair and Austrian or Lufthansa and SAS would also fall under the category of regional alliances.)

The *second* kind of regional alliance is a franchise agreement between a larger carrier and a smaller regional or feeder operator carrier. The regional operator adopts the livery, brand and service standards of the franchiser and normally only carries the regional operator's flight code. (In 1999, British Airways had nine franchise partners, seven of them being in UK and one each in Denmark and South Africa. Together they added 74 destinations to BA's network.

(ii) **Global Alliances:** These have global scope and are the most significant strategic alliances in terms of network expansion. The prime purpose here is to achieve all the marketing benefits of scope and cost economies from any synergies through linking two or more large airlines operating in geographically distinct (ideally continents) markets. Global alliances normally involve code sharing on a large number of routes. They may, however, extend to include schedule co-ordination, joint sales offices, ground handling, combined frequent flyer programmes, joint maintenance activities as well as some equity stake transfer. The individual members may have a large number of route specific and a small number of regional alliances. Burton and Hanlon (1994) provide yet another categorization. They argue that alliances can be categorized on the basis of extent of cooperation, motive and scope of co-operation. When the alliances are graded along extent of cooperation, the resulting strategic alliance is horizontal (pooling for cooperative scheduling and joint marketing), vertical (customer services like car rentals, travel agents) or external ('diversification' alliance, e.g. alliance between AT&T and Delta to handle computing requirements not related to reservations).

The motives behind forming the alliance may be technical or market related. Alliances that allow the airlines to leverage their maintenance facilities for mutual use fall in such category. In 1968, KLM, SAS, Swissair and the former UTA got together to form KSSU. This was found with the objective of economizing on aircraft maintenance. This is also handy in shifting the base from a high cost base to a low cost base. Besides, code share agreements, frequent flyer programs and block-space arrangements are all covered under the marketing motives. Another important area where both motives are evident together is the development of sophisticated computer reservation systems. These systems are very important as marketing tool and are very costly to build. The pooling in of resources by various airlines is definitely of help.

The third area is on the lines of scope of cooperation and largely relates to inter-firm governance. There are instances when there is informal understanding amongst the boards and there is no managerial control exchange. In other instances, there is change and the directors of both the partners are represented on the board of the allying airlines. There is the extra element of managerial control exchange brought in it, and obviously, the stakes are higher. Thus, huge investments of BA in purchasing equity in other airlines shows a more definitive commitment towards better performance and a serious interest in long-term collaboration.

The alliances can also be viewed along a spectrum (Doganis, 2001). The spectrum starts from a very straightforward marketing alliance (as in interlining agreement or a joint frequent flyer program; example is Jet Airways (India) and KLM alliance). These agreements move towards strategic alliances as the overlap in the use of assets and integration of businesses increases. Mergers occupy the other end of the spectrum, which is called as the ultimate strategic alliance. However, it is important to note that share purchases or mutual swaps do not necessarily indicate a strategic alliance if the partners continue to pursue their own objectives. Such arrangement can best be called commercial agreement that is concerned with joint operations with the underlying purpose being cost reduction and market increase, rather achieve a common goal with common philosophy of business.

Here it is useful to note once again that though the aviation industry is a great enabler in the process of globalization, it itself has been subject to severe restrictions all over the globe and cannot yet be said to be a global industry (Yergin et al., 2000; Staniland, 1998). Nonetheless, the airlines all over find it increasingly necessary to become a part of a major alliance at the global level. Some of the benefits of a global alliance have already been highlighted earlier. The impact of global alliances can be gauged from the fact that there are 4 major global alliance networks viz.; Star Alliance, One World Alliance, Sky Team Alliance and the Wings alliance, which is smallest of the 4. These four alliances accounted for about 57 percent of the world's passenger km in 1998 (Doganis, 2001, p. 71) and carried over 70 percent of the scheduled international traffic in 1999 (Yergin et al., 2000 p. 47).

Table 3

Name of Alliance	*No. of Partners*	*Countries Served*	*Revenue (Approx.) (US$)*	*Fleet size*	*Passengers served*
Star	15	124	67.5 billion	2,058	292 million
One World	8	135	51 billion	1,983	230 million
Sky Team	6	114	50 billion	1,224	228 million
Wings	3	100	25 billion	899	114 million

These figures are for the latest financial year available with the sources.
Sources: Company literature, Air Transport World – World Airlines Report, 2002.

Advantages of Alliances

Yergin et al. (2000) have found that global alliance formation is most apparent change to the public eye in the last 5-7 years. The initiative to rationalize their operations, build more effective marketing coverage and offer more seamless, hassle-free transportation than competitors in the face of tight regulatory environment overlooking the industry.

The airlines benefit from the economies of scale and scope (Burton and Hanlon, 1994; Doganis, 1994, 2001; Oum et al., 2000). Most of the benefits that arise out of airline alliances have also been the reasons for entering into alliances. Still to recapitulate, airline alliances bring in the benefits of shared costs thus leading to lower costs per unit for the allying partners. Then there are economies of scope that arise out of increased reach and enhanced feed brought in by network partners. The marketing alliances that allow use of brand name, livery, uniform, brand image (Burton and Hanlon, 1994), blocked space arrangements that guarantee availability of seats and revenues and the benefits of code sharing all on a global scale are easiest promised only by strategic alliances. It would be very difficult for an airline to build a global network on its own because of the prevailing regulations and restrictions in the globalization of the greatest enabler of globalization. In a report released by the US Department of Transportation in October 2000, the alliances between Northwest-KLM, United-Lufthansa, and between Delta, Austrian, Sabena, Swissair were studied to get empirical evidence on the benefits that were made available to consumers in the transatlantic market. It was found that these alliances coupled with the Open Skies initiative resulted in decline in average fares in the period 1996-99. It was concluded that airlines can offer improved, more marketable services and that they are the principal driving force behind transatlantic price reductions and traffic gains. The traffic gains were not simply diversion from others, but largely due to addition of new traffic. Also, it was evident that geographic expansion taking place resulted in growth of traffic and as the improved services were provided to more passengers in more markets, the competitive overlap too increased with expansion. The alliances between the carriers under observation also revealed that there was development of new European hubs consequent to increase in traffic levels in beyond Europe markets. There were significant increases in the traffic levels and price decreases between smaller cities of Europe and not so well developed hubs (like Portland, Oregon) of USA. For instance, the fare levels for smaller European destinations declined by 33 percent in the period 1995-99, while the traffic increased by huge 138 percent in the same period. The report finally concluded that international airline alliances have improved services in historically underserved regions of the world, and as a result, have stimulated additional demand for air transportation in those markets.

Gudmundsson (1999) has pointed out the benefits of alliances to be code-sharing, amalgamation of frequent flyer programs, increased traffic feed (economies of scope and density come into play to the benefit of the airlines), schedule coordination leading to enhanced 'perceived' seamlessness, elimination of duplication of certain tasks (such as offices), easier access to congested airport gates, technical cooperation, access to established system of travel agents' and finally, the halo effect that stems from the tendency of travel agents to book a well known domestic brand.

While studying the international alliance between SAS and the erstwhile Swissair, Youssef and Hansen (1994) concluded that the alliance increased both the quantity and quality of the partners' connecting services. Also the cost savings resulting in from the alliance were expected to lower fares in the market to the extent competition existed in a particular. Thus the fare reductions were at best expected to be in line with market conditions rather across the board reduction that will benefit the passengers at large.

The international marketing alliances that take place between the airlines offered two additional advantages. One, they enabled the airlines to expand their existing markets through extra traffic generated by the feed to and from the airline partner; and two, new markets were developed that were previously inaccessible to them (Doganis, 2001). Lufthansa had claimed in 1997 that its marketing alliances with United, SAS, Thai, South African and VARIG were producing benefits of DM 250-270 million a year. Clearly after the much broader and larger Star Alliance was formed the potential will have gone even higher. The international airline alliances have also proved beneficial to the underserved regions like Africa wherein the alliance partners could increase services due to better market penetration. This is evident from data that yields to Africa, Middle East and Far East have decreased by 32, 29 and 35 percent respectively over a period spanning from 1992 to 1999 (USDOT, 2000). This has stimulated additional demand for air transportation in such markets. The alliances and the cooperation results in lower fares in interline markets. The competition loss in the inter-hub market tends to effect a raise in fares in that particular market. Also, the rise in traffic in the interline market offsets the increase in fares in the inter-hub market (Brueckner, 2001). From 1997 data, the fare charged by alliance partners for a representative trip in a behind the gateway market is 18 percent lower than fare charged by 2 non-allied carriers. It also reveals that there are lower fares in the behind the gateway markets and higher fares in the gateway to gateway markets. Also, the benefits arising out of a multitude of behind the gateway market might actually offset the harms caused by the increase in gateway-to-gateway markets. The total outcome is therefore, expected to be positive (Brueckner and Whalen, 2001).

A study on the business travel decision-making revealed that corporates were increasingly looking forward to global alliances to sign contracts that will allow access to lower/cheaper rates of travel to companies for their employees. As many as 47 percent companies studied felt that alliance groups resulted in cheaper travel and 75 percent of the travel managers believed that their companies would sign a global deal with an alliance group in next 5 years. In that study, the major benefits were seen as the more attractive FFPs, seamless travel experience and service enhancements that result from the alliance (Mason, 2002).

The reduction in IATA's authority on deciding fares over a period of time, fares are now mostly set through a process of strategic interaction. This process results in elimination of "double marginalization". Consequently, fares are lowered (Brueckner, 2001). An important observation is that the anti-trust immunity has to be maintained. There are views in the literature that domestic airline alliances, like that of Delta and United Airlines in the US, induce international benefits for the airlines. The cost and benefits of the alliance in the domestic market are almost the same (Clougherty, 2000). It is the gain through improved performance in the international market that is the guiding factor. Going back to the Delta and United Airlines' alliance, the Delta lacks extensive international routes that United has. The new international routes gained through the alliance will ably support the extensive domestic coverage of Delta. Clougherty (2000) argues that when international markets are characterized by Cournot competition, domestic airline concentration improves international performance of a national airline industry. This is achieved on the supply-side through improved scale economies and reduced competition in the domestic market. These economies of scale come through:

(a) extensive and enhanced use of hub and spoke network, and
(b) lower competition that helps the airlines reap density economies in that market segment. As a natural consequence, better domestic coverage means that there are more passengers available to the network (alliance) to feed international flights.

On the demand-side, there is product differentiation resulting from enhanced Frequent Flyer Programmes, marketing, visibility and other service amenities. Thus, while the number of competitors in the international market remains constant, the allying airlines increase efficiency. Clougherty (2000) finds that the US domestic airline industry stands to gain approximately $350 million in additional producer surplus due to alliances in domestic market. Additionally, 4 million passengers may be fed in to the international flights of various US operators. Also, home nation international consumers likely face more competitive international markets with lower fares. Thus providing for the equivalence between the gains and the costs of the domestic alliance, the international gains resulting from these alliances as discussed above, likely, improves national welfare.

Oum et al. (2000) found that strategic alliances have significant effects on productivity, pricing and profitability of alliance partners. They also found that formation of alliances had a positive effect on the value of partner firms. In their study of 58 international alliances over 1989-98 period, they found that share value of firms participating in the alliance has increased and such increase was similar irrespective of the size of the firm. In addition, the alliances with a broad scope of strategic cooperation create more value than alliances with a narrow scope of tactical cooperation. Furthermore, when a strategic alliance with a broad scope of cooperation is combined with equity investment, the value creation effect of the alliance is further strengthened.

There are concerns that infrastructure constraints by way of availability of slots at the airports located at the major cities/ hubs. In such cases, alliances between airlines can provide much needed slots for landing or take off. The alliances have the potential to provide the allying partner easier access to certain desired slots (held by other partner) that are otherwise unavailable or are too costly to be bought. This was an important issue in BA/ AA/ Iberia alliance as identified by Gudmundsson (1999) and also Flôres Jr. (1996). Further, alliances are a way out to bypass the costly airport charges that need to be paid for every landing and take-off. The alliance partner's flights could be used to ferry in the passengers at a higher load factor (i.e. the number of flights remaining the same, more passengers are carried to and from the airport), thus reducing the costs for the airlines.

There is a caution however, to the alliances. It should not be taken for granted that all alliances will be beneficial. Vander Kraats (2000) observes that extent of benefits of the alliance depends on geographic scope of agreement, degree of operational and marketing integration between partners and revenue sharing agreement. He further suggests that true economic advantage can be gained only through making a single entity unifying all business aspects. This suggests increased concentration and the consumer welfare is likely to be jeopardized.

Disadvantages of Alliances

Borenstein (1992) found that with deregulation setting in the US domestic airline industry there was fall in prices in long distance routes while the short distance routes had little or negative change as prices increased in some markets. He also understood that TACOs (Travel Agent Commission Override) play an important role in increasing the feed to the carrier and also results in increased market power of the airline. Also, the horizontal mergers between direct competitors (a result of some strategic alliances, also discussed by Burton and Hanlon, 1994) were found to have negative effect on the welfare of the passengers in the short-run. Whatever production efficiency the mergers may have permitted was reflected not in the prices but in the increased market power. The long run effects could not be estimated because of possible extinction without such mergers of some of the firms in the study. It has also been reported that as the alliances increase there is increased concentration in the industry (Borenstein, 1992; Brueckner and Whalen, 2000; Cooper, 2001).

Furthermore, the code sharing holds the potential to be a mask for anti-competitive arrangements between competitors to allocate markets, limit capacity, raise fares or push the rivals out of the markets (Vander Kraats, 2000).

There are instances when previously there were 2 carriers operating on a route. However, after the alliance was formed there was just one player on the route. E.g., Swissair purchased 49.5% of Sabena and services between Switzerland and Belgium were rationalized. Effectively, routes where there was duopoly earlier, now were monopolies. Competition was eliminated, capacity growth could be constrained and fares could be kept high. In their study, Brueckner and Whalen (2000) have also concluded that absence of an anticompetitive alliance effect must be viewed as a tentative conclusion. They could not establish if an alliance between two previously competitive carriers would result in an increase of fares. In an analysis of a strategic global alliance (between the Northwest Airlines and the Continental) by the US General Accounting Office (as quoted in Hemphill, 2000) it was found that there was acute potential for reduction in competition in one-stop market because many such routes were served by alliances joining the same alliance.

Transport Research Board (TRB) of the National Research Council of the US in its report issued in 1999 recommended a number of suggestions to safeguard and further competition in the US airline industry. This report showed concerns that code sharing and other collaborative arrangements among large US airlines would result in considerable consolidation among current and potential rivals. Additionally, global alliances between airlines of the US and that of other countries could, reportedly, be harmful in the long run by reducing competition in primary international routes and making it harder for non-aligned carriers to compete domestically as well as internationally.

Oum et al. (1993) argued that there would be global networks that would provide service to most of the large and medium sized cities around the world, particularly in North America, Europe and Asia. They also expected that there would be consolidation as witnessed in US, US-Canada and Europe and that major chunk of the world air passenger market will lie with 5-6 alliances. Today, with 4 major global alliance groupings (Star, Wings, One World, KLM/ NW) ruling over 70 percent of international air travel (Yergin et al., 2000), the authors' prognosis has come true. Doganis (1994) also studied the liberalization of the European airlines also concluded that there will be concentration in the industry and it will become increasingly oligopolistic in character following mergers and alliances that themselves will be the results of deregulation of the European market. Burton and Hanlon (1994) also found that there would be an increased market power that will be available to larger players (who are members of large alliances). The anticompetitive effects of market power were likely to be most marked for short haul markets. Also, there was a potential threat that the old-horizontal pooling arrangements will return. The competition was likely to reduce if there was no new entry in the markets.

In their study of SAS and Swissair alliance, Youssef and Hansen (1994) put that alliances had the potential to stop competition that could otherwise have occurred from airlines that sought to increase their market share through internal expansion. All this was in addition to direct reduction of competition through monopolization effect that alliances brought along.

The alliance in question resulted in an increased concentration in the markets where they had competed earlier and the fares in nonstop markets between alliance partner hubs have increased more than in other nonstop markets in the same region. This, too, was mediated by concentration. Though the cost savings from the alliance were expected to bring down the fares, the increased market power was expected to nullify the effect. As noted earlier, while commenting on market power and mergers, Kim and Singal (1993) pointed that loss of one competitor increases fares by approximately 10% on average. Also it was hypothesized that with increase in market concentration the potential to exercise market power is greater. It was also found that on routes where the merging firms had neither common hubs nor overlapping service there was exercise of increased power.

In cases, where merger involved a financially distressed airline, there was steep increase in fare levels. The consumer was thus worse off. Stavins (2000) while testing for price discrimination in competitive markets found that though there was a decrease in price discrimination with market concentration and the discounts were lesser on routes with higher market concentration. Gudmundsson (1999) also noted that there was enhanced market presence through code sharing. This was a strategic advantage derived from the alliance and had a potentially negative impact on consumer interests.

Brueckner and Whalen (1998) also found that alliances increased fares in gateway-to-gateway markets and that they were beneficial only in behind the gateway markets. The negative effects in such markets could be offset only by intervention by regulatory authorities. In addition the domestic alliances had the potential of exercising greater anti-competitive effects than the international alliances and it needs to be checked. Brueckner and Spiller (2000), however, could not gather enough evidence of an anticompetitive effect in gateway-to-gateway markets. Though they found that there would be an increase of 5 percent in case of an alliance, this was found statistically insignificant. Flôres Jr. (1998) has pointed out that alliances were essentially a tool used by main players in the industry to enlarge their market share. The innate desire was to gain total market control within the prevailing regulatory framework. In other words, their main utility was to gain or protect market share rather use them for cost saving or efficiency improvement purposes.

Flôres finds it difficult to define the global pressures on the airline alliances except for negative characterization in the sense that they are all kinds of agreements that are less than a standard, autonomous joint venture. He also opined that the alliances are transitionary in nature and as such, are doomed. There will be bigger carriers emerging from each group of alliances. This further strengthens the opinion that there will be increasing concentration in the airline industry that will further increase the market power of the players in the industry which can then be exploited against consumer benefits. Various reports have indicated that the mergers (another form of strategic alliances, broadly speaking) in the airline industry, especially in the US have resulted in formation of a cartel. A handful of major firms are dominating the market and they rarely compete with each other. The formation of fortress hubs is being used as effective entry barrier and the advantages of hub and spoke networks are not passed on to the consumers (Cooper, 2001).

Further, the US Department of Transportation has identified 15 airports where market share of dominant firm exceeded the monopoly limits of 70%. The industry was found to be in the moderately concentrated market with an Index (HHI) of 1400.(HHI 1000-1800 => moderately concentrated; 1800+=> Highly concentrated). With another two mergers allowed—United/US and American/TWA and Delta/NW or Delta/Continental—HHI levels shall cross 2200 mark.

Cooper (2001) also contemplates that in reality, market power is abused and the theoretical benefits of the alliances are actually never passed on to the consumers. Also, there should be actual competition on the routes rather have potential competition as the beneficial effects of potential competition are much smaller compared to those of actual competition.

Hub concentration measures of 1995 (GAO study) resulted in 22.1% increase in the prices. Morrison and Winston (1995) have found that hubbing; frequent flyer and CRS manipulation activities together could affect the prices to the extent of 22.7%. These together with fare restrictions could result in 46% effect on the prices. In a DOT (US) study, low cost carrier entry or exit at all hubs could affect the prices by 35%. This is even more significant at the concentrated hubs, where it touches the level of 40%.

Bryer (1990) also upholds Cooper's view that it is difficult to estimate the number of potential competitors and thus the downward effect on prices cannot be ascertained. Further, he concludes that there is a need for a strong antitrust policy to maintain competitive market structures which otherwise stand under threat. News reports on mergers in airline industry have vociferously demanded that regulatory authorities should intervene and stop the drive towards monopolization and predatory pricing. (Barry, 2001; Lochhead, 1998)

SURVIVAL OF ALLIANCES

There have been several news items speaking of strategic alliances as short-term marriages that hardly stand pressures of time. In a BCG report of 1995, it was pointed out that Intercontinental alliances had a higher failure rate. About 67% of the alliances formed in 1991/92 fell by 1995. These failures had been in all the categories, whether Non-Equity (Agreements or JVs) or Equity Alliances.

Flôres (1998) has also argued that the alliances are heading towards doom and that in the future there will be no alliance but a few major airlines that will rule over the market. This makes it all the more necessary to look at the longevity of the alliances. There were various factors pointed out from the case study of alliances in the air passenger transport industry. Aviation Economist (1993) documented reasons for failure as:

- Too broad setting of objectives/Incongruent objectives – It is realized later on that very few practically possible opportunities exist.
- Asymmetry of partners, in the size, for example.
- Asymmetry of benefits versus expectations.
- Differing product/service standards (this was also pointed out in Mason, 2002, as this has potential of creating dissatisfaction among the consumers travelling on different partners).
- Lack of Exclusivity.
- Lack of management structures to make the alliances successful.

It also outlined design parameters and key issues for creating a successful alliance.

The key design parameters include:

- Symmetry of partners by way of relative power, control over assets
- Familiarity with partner as to have no hidden agenda, cultural and management style mix
- Term/horizon for the alliance
- Equitable terms of sharing.

BCG outlined a model (Avmark Aviation Economist, 1993, p 22) which reveals that alliances are an iterative process and they move on from setting of Objectives (with mutual understanding) Design and Implementation (laying down appropriate structures and systems) for the Reassessment and Redesign of Relationship which then in turn leads to resetting or relooking at the objectives of the alliance.

Doganis (2001) has suggested a 3-phase model for alliance building in Fig. 20 below.

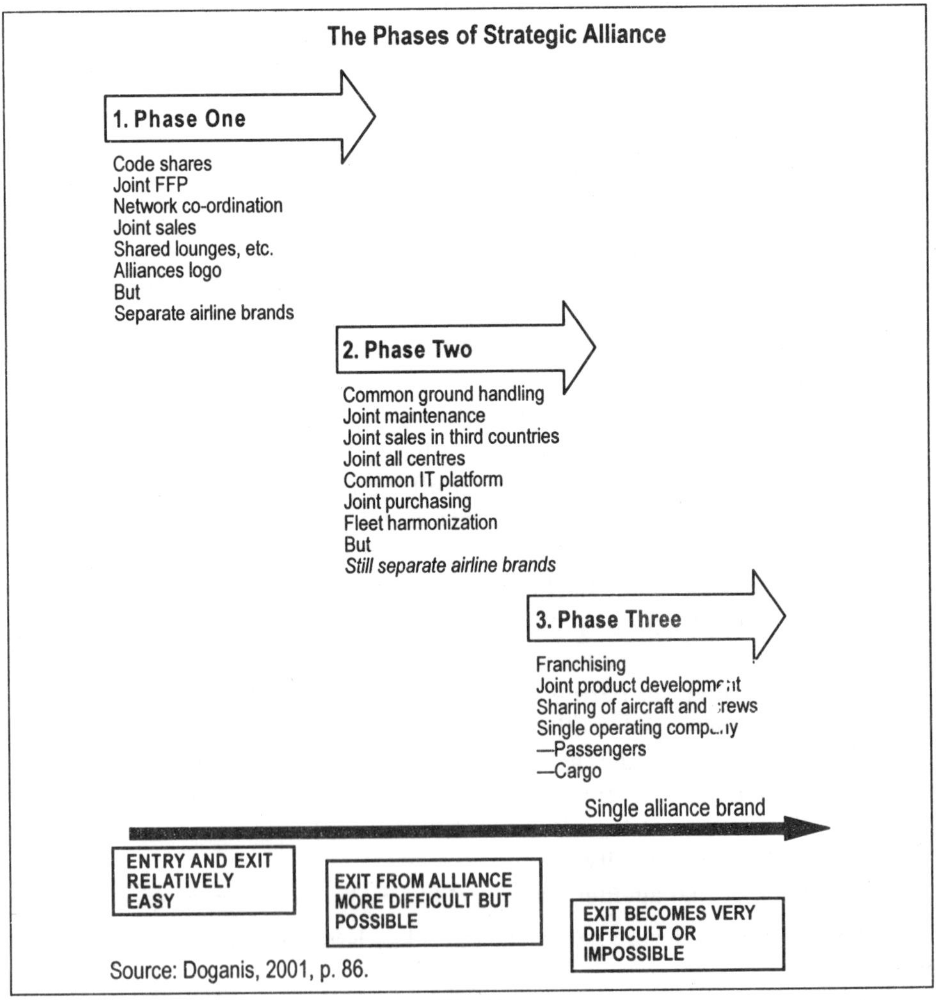

Fig. 20

The first phase concentrates chiefly on revenue gains. These alliances have to be of commercial nature. In other words, there is easy entry into and exit from the alliance.

Phase two involves continuing and reinforcing cooperation extended in Phase one, thus bringing in operational gains to the alliance partners. This phase is likely to involve separate agreements in one or more specific areas where joint operations can reduce costs, as in ground handling or maintenance. These two phases, however, do not necessarily cement the alliance.

Cementing of the alliance takes place in the third phase when partners commingle their assets and start using them jointly. There is joint product development and creation of joint companies to manage different aspects of operations. The partners are expected to move from having separate brand identities to emphasising and even adopting a single alliance brand. The exit from the alliance is very difficult. It is notable that though there are large global alliances in the world skies, most of the alliances have not moved beyond the first phase. The revenue focus of the partners makes the alliance highly vulnerable to sudden exit of the alliance partners. Delta walking out of the Atlantic Excellence alliance in June 1999 is an example of this. It is also necessary to understand that this approach of cementing the partnership has to follow all the phases. KLM and Alitailia alliance is a case in point. The partners were too eager to move to phase 3 without understanding the necessities of going through phase 2. The alliance collapsed in May 2000.

The Key Success Factors in making the alliances can therefore be:

- Set up concrete, realistic and specific goals.
- Due diligence to be carried out by both partners.
- A clear horizon and understanding of future direction of the alliance is necessary.
- Cost/benefit analysis has to be carried out and there should be a move to create a sense of mutual dependence.
- Appropriate resources to be allocated to the alliance.
- Communication amongst the partners should continue and success measured from time to time.
- Lastly, the alliances should be done away with when the partners feel that the issues to them are no longer valid.

There is no doubt that air passenger transport has grown globally since deregulation. With deregulation there was a move towards economising operations and attaining economies of scale. The air transportation evolved from point-to-point, to, hub and spokes, to, network formation amongst various hub and spokes networks. These networks essentially involved strategic alliances of various forms. This led to increase in passenger welfare in the form of lower fares and various programmes to enhance perceived customer value. This, in turn, gave rise to strategic alliances of various kinds and scope amongst the industry incumbents. There can be several parameters on which the alliances could be classified and literature shows that there is no consensus on the parameters.

Further while discussing the advantages and disadvantages of strategic alliances it is observed that though the alliances were initially for the purpose of airline welfare through cost reductions, the industry is gradually concentrating into a few hands. It was observed that the phenomenon is evident at some US airports (reported by Cooper, 2001). Globally, with 4 major alliances holding more than half the market, it clearly is getting concentrated.

The fallout of this is clear. Firstly, smaller airlines (like that of Air India, Indian Airlines) are likely to grow only as traffic feeders to bigger alliance partners due to operating economies. Secondly, as it emerges, there is concentration happening in the industry. This concentration may lead to cartel formation among airlines and the benefits to consumer may actually get reduced and the basic premise of airline deregulation stands negated.

CHAPTER 4

Airline Marketing Mix

Marketing is certainly one of the most important activities in any company and the airlines are no different. Approximately one-half of a major or any, national carrier's employees are engaged in the marketing process.

Reservations personnel, ticket and customer service agents, baggage handlers, flight attendants, food service representatives, passenger and cargo sales representatives, and pricing and market research analysts are involved in marketing the company's product-air transportation.

Marketing is that broad area of business activity that directs the flow of services provided by the carrier to the customer in order to satisfy customers' needs and wants and to achieve company objectives. Marketing is more than selling: it involves a number of business activities, including forecasting, market research and analysis, product research and development, price setting, and promotion, including advertising. Marketing also involves the finance activities such as credit and collection that are associated with ticket sales. Marketing is customer oriented. Creating products and services that fulfill the needs of existing customers and attract new customers is the primary goal. Determining who the customers are or could be and what their needs are is part of the process. Marketing must also assist in achieving the company's objectives: an acceptable return on investment, a reasonable level of profits, and an adequate market share.

Why is marketing so important? Without marketing and sales, there would be no airlines. Marketing is the stimulus that encourages innovation, research, and investment. A carrier can have the latest equipment and the most efficient human and capital resources available, but unless somebody is there to sell the output produced, it is all for naught.

The carriers' marketing history prior to World War II was considerably different from what goes on today. In the early years, emphasis was placed on the carriage of mail, not passengers. There was more profit in carrying mail, and besides, the mail didn't complain if it arrived late or was too hot or too cold. Furthermore, people still had a love affair with railroads and automobiles.

Market demand for air travel was just sufficient to absorb the available capacity. This era was the production-oriented period in airline marketing history a time when services were so scarce that customers accepted whatever was available.

After the war, airline executives knew much more about how to operate their companies than they knew about how the product they produced—air transportation-should be sold. This was natural in an industry In which the public would have confidence, an industry that after the war was confronted with selling soothing relatively new, and an industry that basically had to improve its product entirely out of capital, not out of earnings. Furthermore, while many' of the newly hired airline personnel in the postwar period brought technical skills acquired in the military, nobody really had any experience in marketing the product.

For hundreds of years, people had traveled by land and water. The airlines the postwar period had to offer a higher-quality product than consumers demanded at the time. Probably no other product ever offered to the public had to be so perfect, so safe, so convenient, so passenger oriented, and so liable as did air transportation before public acceptance could be expected. As the carriers' capacity increased, many companies assumed much more active roles in convincing consumers to purchase the new services offered. At this point, it could be said that the airlines entered their sales-oriented period. More often than not, this approach produced services that reflected the operations and selling talents of the company, and only secondarily the needs of the flying public. It was basically a shotgun approach to marketing, convincing people to fly rather. than drive or take the railroad. The airlines' success cannot be disputed in light of the tremendous growth during the two decades following the war, combined with the demise of passenger rail service in the United States. By the late 1960s, market demand had outstripped available capacity, and so the wide-bodies were developed to alleviate this problem.

Unfortunately, the airlines have been plagued with excess capacity ever since the introduction of the wide-bodies in the early 1970s. Since that time, many carriers have focused on the marketing concept, which stresses shaping services to meet consumer needs rather than molding consumer needs to fit the available services. This concept has played an important part in the emergence of the consumer-oriented period in the airline business, with its many tests and new-product surveys designed to discover what consumers really want. We have moved from the shotgun approach of marketing air transportation to the target market approach-that is, identifying the specific groups of customers to whom the company wishes to appeal with its services. Once this is determined, the next step involves the selection of the appropriate blend of marketing activities, the kind and amount of activities necessary to reach the target market. Let's take a look at these marketing activities, which many analysts refer to as the *marketing mix.*

THE MARKETING MIX

Customer-focused marketing involves a set of activities that are directed at satisfying the needs and wants of the customer. In all industries, when taken together, these activities have become known as the Marketing Mix, and have been divided d into four well-known categories called "the Four P's": Product, Price, Promotion and Place.

The Classical Marketing Mix

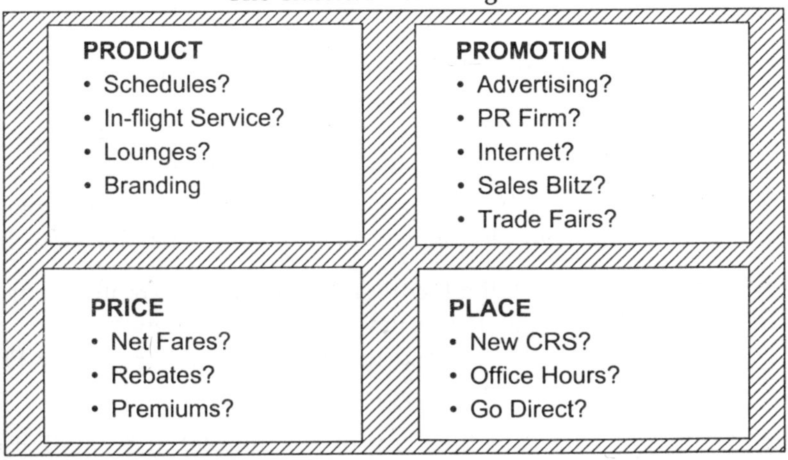

Fig. 21

Product

A product or service is defined as a "bundle of attributes" that satisfies a customer's needs. In the airline industry, these attributes include which destinations to fly to, schedules, the classes of service onboard, check-in facilities, and relatively minor issues like the selection of wines offered to passengers travelling in a particular cabin. Airlines normally offer a range of products, each of which has its own particular bundle of attributes like these.

Many airlines today have "Product Managers" or "Brand Managers" who are responsible for one or more products. For example, there may be a Product Manager that is responsible for the "Economy Class product". This person will:

- Develop the "Product Specification" for the Economy Class product, a document describing exactly what the product includes in every detail.
- Establish and monitor delivery standards to measure "product integrity".
- Use customer feedback and competitive information to make decisions on how to improve the Economy Class product.

Price

Decisions relating to a product's price are extremely important because it is the only "P" that brings in revenue for the airline. Strictly defined, price is simply the amount of money that an airline charges for each of its products or services. Some examples of pricing decisions are:

- Charging a "premium" for a higher quality of service.
- Offering "off peak discounts" to stimulate demand during the low season.
- Offering "introductory prices" to help launch a new route.

Promotion

Activities relating to the promotion of an airline's products or services involve simply communicating to the intended customer that his or her needs will be satisfied by the services offered. As we will learn later on, marketers have available to them a sub-mix of promotional tools that includes advertising, direct mail, the Internet, public relations and personal selling to achieve this communication. Some examples of an airline's promotional decisions include:

- How can we reach the Japanese expatriate market in Amman?
- How will we promote our new schedules to New York?
- How often should we send mailings to members of our Frequent Flyer Program?

Due to the growing consumer use of the Internet and email, a shift is taking place in promotional methodology. Whereas marketers have traditionally focused on mass-marketing mediums like television and newspaper, the emphasis is now on micro-marketing that takes a narrower—and more cost effective—approach to customer identification and retention. Unlike television advertising that might reach two million viewers, micro-marketing tactics like e-mail promotions might reach 1,000 readers with highly personalized messages.

Place

Also known as distribution, place is the marketing activity by which products and services are made available to the consumer to purchase and consume. It therefore includes everything from the airline's global reservations system to the travel agent's local counter!

Of the "Four P's", "place" or distribution has been rather neglected by the airline industry in the past. Some industry experts have even taken the view that the travel trade 'only grew to reach its current size because airlines were too busy expanding their capacity and developing their reservations systems to pay attention to the actual process of handling customer enquiries and selling tickets.

There is no doubt that any such neglect in the past is unlikely to be repeated in the future. Technological changes are creating new opportunities for airlines to achieve major savings by using the Internet as a "distribution channel" for achieving direct sales at low costs. Meanwhile, large corporate accounts are demanding that travel agents' commission, which has traditionally been the "cost of distribution", be replaced by handling fees that are based on performance.

Airline marketers therefore face many challenges here, such as:

- How can the various distribution channels be best used *to* deliver business?
- Where will investments in improved technology produce the best return?
- How can relationships with the travel trade be developed *to* ensure best customer service as well as mutual profitability?

AIRLINE PRODUCT PLANNING

To the average consumer, a product is simply a physical item with certain Uses and a Particular appearance. In terms of the marketing mix, It is much than this. A product purchased by consumers encompasses functional psychological, and aesthetic features as we as convenience, reliability and so forth. All of these characteristics are simply called the *product.*

The airline product is not a physical item at all, but services that consumer find useful. Safety, on-time reliability, convenience in terms of airport proximity or seat availability, frequency a departures, in- flight cabin services ground services including ticketing and baggage handling, aircraft type and even the carrier's image are part of the airline product. This definition is consistent with the airline marketing concept, which stresses the importance of services that satisfy certain consumer needs.

Quite frequently, airline marketing analysts discuss the *product differentiation* that exists in the industry. If we consider the output of an airline to be a seat departure, some analysts will argue that we are basically dealing with an undifferentiated or standardized product. A seat departure on United is the same as one on Delta or American. *Or* is it? A seat departure from Chicago to New York at 11:30 A.M. and including meal service is not the same as a seat departure at 1:00 P.M. with no meal service. Thus, the product is differentiated. There is some truth to both arguments. If three carriers are serving the same market, all using the same aircraft and providing basically the same cabin service, on what basis do they compete? Generally, the answer can be found in the frequency of service. The carrier with the most frequent service at times consumers wish to fly will generally capture the largest market share. Consequently, each carrier attempts to schedule more flights than its competitors around the popular early-morning and late-afternoon hours' to capture the biggest share of the market. Unfortunately, too much capacity in terms of seat availability will reduce load factors to a point at which no one can earn a reasonable profit. As a result, there is a trade-off between meeting consumer' needs in terms of seat availability and meeting the company's objectives, including a reasonable return. In marketing the airline product, certain unique characteristics must be recognized:

1. The product (service) cannot be kept in inventory to match fluctuations in demand. The revenue lost as a result of an unfilled seat when the aircraft departs is lost forever.
2. The service is usually personalized. Two people who take the same flight might come away with completely different opinions about the service, depending on their individual experiences.
3. There is no such thing as replacement of a bad product, as is the case in the sale of other products.
4. It is difficult to check the quality of the service before the final sale. There is no showroom to visit to test the product before purchase.
5. Delivery of the product cannot always be guaranteed, due to mechanic problems or the unpredictability of the weather.
6. The service can be produced only in patches, as opposed to individual units.

These characteristics have prompted the airlines in today's extremely competitive environment to intensify their efforts in two areas: (1) offering better qualitative and quantitative service to passengers, and (2) enhancing their image. *Qualitative service* includes such things as courtesy and efficiency in contacts with passengers. *Quantitative service* primarily includes such subtle additions as wider variety of on-board magazines and entertainment and greater seat-pitch angle. Enhancing the company image is most evident in recent advertising campaigns in which the general theme projects an airline team ready to serve any and all customer needs.

Once an airline has its strategy in place, attention needs to shift to the translation of this strategy into the product design process. This chapter looks at the theory of product analysis in marketing and discusses the ways in which it can be applied to marketing in today's airline industry.

What is the "Product"?

At first sight, it might be thought that applying theoretical product principles to the airline industry is inappropriate. These principles have mainly been developed for industries dealing with tangible consumer products. The airline industry's "product" is, of course, an intangible one which is instantly perishable and cannot be stored.

This is an argument which can be rejected. The airline industry's product may be intangible and many-faceted. It is still capable of providing—or failing to provide—customer satisfaction. It is also the case that many of the analytical models developed for analysing products in fast moving consumer goods industries can also be used in the air transport industry. They do, though, have to be used in an analogous way, to take account of the intangible nature of the airline product.

In this chapter we shall begin by looking at questions of product innovation and product management using the theoretical principles that can be derived from the concept of the Product Life Cycle.

The Theory of Product Analysis and its Application to the Airline Industry

The Product Life Cycle

In all areas of marketing, the processes of product development, product innovation and product management need to be continuous and never-ending. The reasons for this are derived from the model in Figure.

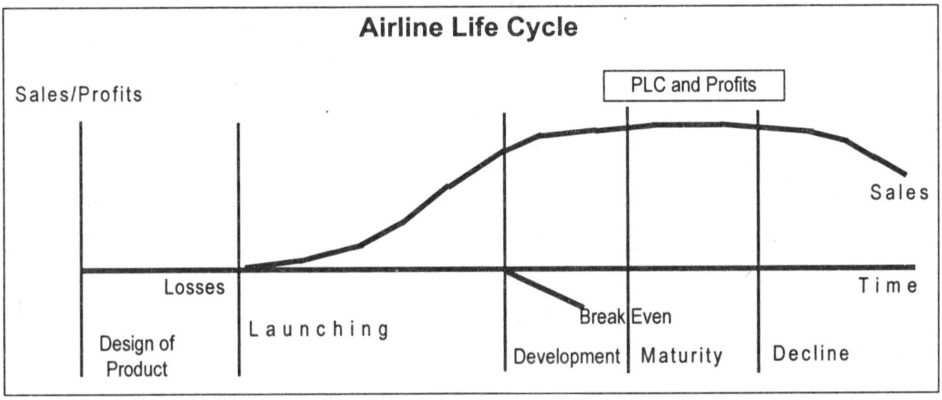

Fig. 22

When a new product is introduced into the market, it is inevitable that it will first be faced with the so-called Introductory stage of the Product Life Cycle. The product is new, so there will not have been time for advertising and promotional work to come to fruition. Also, the product will not benefit from so-called "Imitative Buying", because few people will know about it, and fewer still will be using it.

The Introductory stage will be a crucial stage in the life of a product. Some pass through it and go on to be successes. A far greater number do not Instead, sales are disappointing and the product has to be withdrawn from the market after a short time. Somewhere between 60% and 80% of new products eventually come into this category.

Sadly, the aerospace industry illustrates well some of the risks involved in product innovation. For example, the Concorde was completely unsuccessful in achieving commercial sales and had to be withdrawn production as a marketing disaster. The only aircraft operated commercially have been those given to Air France and British Airways under the most favourable terms. A more recent case has been the Advanced Turbo-Prop of British Aerospace. This aircraft, a 64 seat propeller-driven aircraft was abandoned after fewer than 40 had been produced. Even renaming it the Jetstream 61 failed to change its fortunes.

The Saab 2000 aircraft had a similarly short and disappointing life cycle, again being withdrawn after very few had been sold. At the time of writing, there appears to be a risk that the Boeing 717 and Airbus A318 will go the same way.

Airline marketing also illustrates the perils of innovation. Many airlines have the experience of launching a new route amidst great optimism, only to find that the financial results are so disappointing that they have to give up after only a short time. Some have made an innovation in the in-flight product, only to find that this is unpopular with passengers and has to be quickly withdrawn. An example of this came in 1990 when Lufthansa up-graded product standards in the rear cabin of its aircraft in Europe, and re-named the whole of this cabin "Business Class". It was a change which was unacceptable to those passengers who had paid higher fares and who felt that they were entitled to greater recognition. Innovation can also be risky in terms of selling or distribution concepts. For example, in the late 1980s British Airways invested in a new chain of up-market travel shops in Britain's high streets using the branding of "Four Comers Travel". Again the concept had only a short life. It was soon discontinued, with, presumably, substantial losses having to be written off.

There is now substantial literature in the theory of marketing about product innovation. This has largely been derived from the work of the US marketing professor, E.M. Rogers. Using Roger's principles, it is possible to suggest that new products must show at least the following characteristics if they are to be long-term successes:

1. ***Relative Advantage*** Clearly, new products must be substantially better value-for-money than those they are replacing, in order for consumers to accept the risks of using them
2. ***Compatibility*** An innovation is unlikely to be successful if it is a very radical departure from the existing ways in which business is done in the market sector in question.
3. ***Complexity*** Some innovations fail because they are perceived as being extremely difficult to use, requiring purchasers to invest a great deal of time and effort in becoming familiar with them
4. ***Divisibility*** It is often easier to persuade consumers to take a series of short' steps, rather than one very large and risky one. Each small step can then be portrayed as a trial, the successful completion of which allows confidence to be built.
5. ***Communicability*** Customers are unlikely to be persuaded to buy a product if the benefits this product will bring cannot be communicated to them persuasively.

If these features illustrate some of the requirements of successful product innovation in air transport marketing, it is equally instructive to look at some of the common mistakes that lead to product failure. Products will fail if the size of the market for them has been over-estimated through inadequate or non-existent market research. They will also fail if the product cannot be delivered on time, or does not perform well even when it is. Mistakes can also be made in pricing policy, with the product either being offered at a price which is too high relative to the benefits it will bring, or too low (in the case of so-called

"Status Goods") to give the necessary aura of exclusivity. Finally, promotional or distribution policies may be poorly thought out. For example, advertising campaigns may offend rather than excite potential customers, or the incentives which are given to distribution channel intermediaries may not be enough to encourage them to push the product strongly.

All in all, product innovation represents an extremely challenging part of the product management process, with the range of possible mistakes explaining easily why so many products fail to get beyond even the Introductory stage of their life cycle.

Let us now make the assumption that a new product *does* get beyond this stage, and enters the so-called Growth phase of the Cycle. Here, sales of the product accelerate markedly as advertising and promotional work comes to fruition, and the product benefits from imitative buying as consumers see it being bought and used by others.

Clearly, the onset of the Growth phase is good news for the innovating firm. Cash will begin to flow in, allowing the original research, development and promotional costs invested in the product to be recovered. Also, production volumes can be increased allowing access to the economies of scale and learning curve effects which will permit lower unit production costs.

The Growth phase does, though, hint at some of the problems which will have to be addressed at the later, much more challenging, stages of the cycle. During the early part of it, there will be the task of ensuring that production rates are increased to meet the rapidly-rising volume of demand. If they cannot be, there is a risk that a major marketing opportunity will be lost if potential customers are not prepared to wait in order to take delivery. Later in the Growth phase, there will almost certainly be the first worrying signs of a classic problem of product management: the firm's competitors will see the success of the innovation, and will begin the research and development of their own rival products. In a sense, they will not have to carry out their own market research or demand forecasting exercise. The innovating finn will have done this for them.

The leading finn will hope that the Growth phase will go on for as long as possible. It cannot, though, continue forever. Eventually, the Maturity stage of the Product Life Cycle will arrive. Here, firstly, the growth in the size of the total market for the product begins to slow. Most of the people who can be persuaded to buy the product have already done so. The market therefore begins to progressively change from one of growth to one of replacement. Replacement sales are rarely enough to maintain, let alone expand, the volume of demand.

The other change of the Maturity phase is more serious still. By this time, rival finns will have had time to complete the research and development of their own, competing products. These will be introduced into the market, probably in rapid succession. Worse still, these finns will have had the benefit of being able to study the product of the innovator. They will have been able to isolate its weaknesses and, almost certainly, to develop a product which will leapfrog the standards set by the innovating finn.

The Maturity phase of the Cycle is a very challenging one. By this stage, the market is no longer growing rapidly. It is also becoming saturated with competition. Strong product management skills will be needed if the success established during the Growth phase is to be continued in Maturity.

In responding to the challenges of Maturity, the situation is by no means hopeless. By this stage, the original costs of developing and introducing the product will have been recovered. It will therefore be possible to make profits at lower prices. Also, the finn should be getting the maximum benefits from production scale economies and from the Learning Curve effects which make production more efficient. Again, these factors will increase financial flexibility. The task in managing mature products is to use this flexibility in the most telling way.

The keys to doing so lie in the "4Ps" of marketing discussed under the heading of the Marketing Mix. A first possible response to invest money in the product itself. This can be used to improve its specification so that it catches up with and preferably overtakes the value-for-money on offer from the products which have arrived in the market later. It can also be used to modify the product so that it can be used to exploit other, hopefully less saturated, markets.

Alongside investment in the product, discounted prices can be offered as a possible way of ensuring that growth in the total market resumes, or that a greater share of the existing market is obtained. Also, increased investment in advertising and promotion can be sanctioned with the same two purposes in mind. Finally, greater incentives can be offered to firms in the distribution channel through higher commissions or greater mark-ups.

If the right balance of these measures are correctly applied, there is no reason why the success of a product established during a Growth phase cannot be continued for a considerable time once the onset of Maturity has begun. For many products, though, such success cannot be prolonged indefinitely. They will eventually reach the Decline phase of the Life Cycle. This is where market growth comes to an end, and the product is overwhelmed by newer rivals, Once Decline sets in, there is no choice but to abandon the product and take the resources devoted to it and use them for more rewarding purposes.

The inevitability for many products of a Decline phase poses another challenge in product management. If a firm wishes to continue in business and expand, it will be making a grave mistake if it leaves investment in research and development of new products until the Decline phase of its existing products sets in. If it does, the result will be a disastrous period of poor sales and loss of reputation. Instead development and innovation of new products must take place whilst existing' products are still doing well.

The Product Life Cycle is well-illustrated by applications which can be found both in the aerospace industry, and, by analogy, in airline marketing as well.

In aerospace, the perfect illustration of successful product management comes with the world's biggest-selling commercial aircraft, the Boeing 737. The 737 family has a long history—the first 737s were introduced in 1967—yet the aircraft continued to sell well through the 199Os and into the new century. It did so because, at all stages of its Life Cycle, Boeing has managed the product skilfully.

It is now often forgotten, but when the first 737s were delivered in the late 1960s, there were no signs at all of the enormous success that the aircraft has become. Early sales were slow, and the initial aircraft—now designated 737-100s—performed poorly. Such was the scale of the early disappointments that, when it faced a financial crisis in 1972, Boeing came very near to withdrawing the aircraft and stopping production. Thus the 737 was very close to being one of the many product innovations that fail to get beyond the Introductory stage of their life cycle.

Boeing did not do so, though. Instead, an improved version of the aircraft, the 737-200 was put on the market. This entered a very clear Growth phase in the 1970s, achieving more than 1000 sales during the decade.

By the early 1980s it became clear that the success enjoyed by the 737-200 could not continue indefinitely. The aircraft was not especially fuel efficient at a time when fuel prices were very high. It was also noisy, when environmental resistance to aircraft noise was increasing and the first signs were appearing that excessively-noisy aircraft would be banned. Finally, the early 1980s saw Boeing's increasingly-confident European rival Airbus Industries planning what has become the highly-successful A320 family.

The B737 was clearly reaching the Maturity stage of its Product Life Cycle. The reaction of the company was a very positive one. Instead of ceasing production as they might have done, Boeing invested further by introducing three new versions of the aircraft, the -300, -400 and -500 series. These featured a fuselage stretch (in the case of the -300 and 400. The 737-500 was the same size as the -200), a more up-to-date cockpit and quieter, more fuel-efficient engines. These new models revitalised the product, to the extent that more than 2000 aircraft were sold between the beginning of the 1980s and the early 1990s.

By 1994, the 737 was again under threat as the Airbus A320 family expanded and became better established. Then, though, Boeing launched further developments in the form of the -600, -700, -800 and -900 737's. These aircraft have again sold well, confirming the 737 as by far the most successful aircraft family ever in terms of the number of units sold. Boeing is currently proposing extending the family still further with another stretch of the aircraft.

A second, equally convincing, illustration of Product Life Cycle concepts in the aviation industry can be found in the history of Frequent Flyer Programmes. FFPs are a major issue in airline marketing today.

The first programme, the A Advantage programme, was introduced by American Airlines in 1981. It was, of course, perfectly possible that this would turn out to be an unsuccessful idea, unpopular with customers and abandoned quickly. It did not, though. The programme passed quickly through the

Introductory stage of its Product Life Cycle and entered a rapid Growth phase. Soon, the programme had millions of members and was having a significant impact on choice-of-airline decisions in the US domestic market.

Once this had happened, it was certain that American would not be left alone to enjoy its success. The very extent of this success meant that its rivals had no choice but to follow. They did so, first in the US domestic market and then, progressively, internationally as well. At the time of writing, FFPs are at the Maturity stage of their Life Cycle. Almost all airlines are participating in FFPs either by running their own programme or by forming partnership and franchising agreements with those who do.

Also, most of the programmes are now similar in terms of the benefits they offer—a clear sign of the commoditization one would expect at Maturity.

There are now signs that FFPs may be reaching a Decline phase of their Life Cycle. The programmes are becoming increasingly unpopular with corporate travel purchasers, who argue that they tempt irresponsible employees to take unnecessary journeys to accumulate extra mileage or to protect their programme status. FFPs also make it more difficult to implement changes in corporate travel policy due to "Switching Cost" effects. Many corporate travel managers are now insisting that FFP points are awarded to the company, or are not given at all. Instead, they require increased levels of corporate discounting. All these factors may, in some cases, make FFPs less important in airline marketing in the future then they are today. Also, airlines are now moving to neutralise their effects. The growing links between the different FFPs in airline alliances mean that in some cases passengers can obtain mileage points in the programme of their choice, irrespective of the airline they actually fly with. This is, in reality, an admission by the airlines concerned that the effect of FFPs on market share is increasingly a neutral one, but one which comes at a high cost.

A third, and especially fascinating, illustration of the application of the Product Life Cycle comes with the marketing of leisure air travel and of vacation resorts. It requires an understanding of a further aspect of Life Cycle theory.

Fleet and Schedules-Related Product Features

We have already spent considerable time looking at the product from the point of view of the customer. We will focus more on the supply side of the product, by examining the product decisions that airlines must take. ill doing so, they fact a dilemma. They presumably wish to offer a product which is as attractive as possible to the customer. However, an attractive product will often be an expensive one to produce. Therefore, decisions must often be based on a complex tradeoff between product quality and production costs.

In making this tradeoff, the overriding factor to be taken into account will be the business strategy of the airline concerned. Optimum decision-making for an airline in a Cost Leadership position will be quite different from one aiming at multi-product Differentiation.

Cabin Configuration and Classes of Service

The principle of trading off product quality against production costs is well-illustrated by this first area of decision-making.

An airline seeking the lowest costs of operation will configure its aircraft in a single class, and will place as many seats as possible in leach plane. Safety considerations will give an absolute limit. These will reflect both the structural capabilities of the aircraft and the need to meet standards for emergency evacuations. The other question will be that of passenger comfort. There seems to be an acceptance in the industry that a seat pitch of 28 inches is the minimum which passengers will accept. Even with modem, lightweight seats this represents a poor standard of comfort, and most airlines do not go as far as this extreme. 29 inch or 30 inch seat pitches are usually given, even by airlines focusing on the European leisure air travel market where low production costs have been a traditional pre-occupation.

Decisions about basic seating comfort standards have a very significant impact on unit cost levels. For example, leisure-orientated airlines will usually place 235 seats into their most commonly-used aircraft, the Boeing 757. This results from a mix of seats at 28 and 29 inch seat pitches. Raising the seat pitch to 33 inches—typically used by scheduled airlines reduces the number of seats that can be placed in the same aircraft to around 180. Thus a decision about cabin comfort can affect unit costs by 30%.

An airline whose marketing strategy is based on targeting both the business and leisure traveller, cannot rely on a cabin configuration aimed at producing the lowest operating costs. Instead, they must develop a multi-product philosophy, one of the manifestations of which is the need to have different classes of service on board their aircraft. The cost implications of doing so are substantial, and are becoming greater all the time.

The problem is that as they search for competitive advantage, many airlines are making the cabin configuration of their first and business classes more and more attractive. They are doing so by using new and costly seats, and also by giving more and more space to each passenger. This in turn is forcing their rivals to match or exceed their product specification. The result is what at the moment appears to be a never. ending and fruitless search for competitive advantage. One airline may establish such an advantage, but this does not turn out to be sustainable. The very fact that customers like its new cabin configuration forces its rivals to respond with something equally or even more appealing in order to protect their market share. The end result of a round of competitive innovation in seating comfort standards is that market shares remain the same, but all the airlines which have taken part in it have significantly higher costs. The history of First Class and Business Class cabin configurations illustrates this point well. Today, a competitive Long-Haul First Class cabin will have seats which fold down into horizontal beds. In order to accommodate this, a seat pitch of around 70 inches will be needed. In Business Class, a competitive seat pitch is now around 55 inches, an increase from the

38 or 40 inches typical of only ten years ago. At the time of writing, there is a growing trend to extend the flat -bed principle to Business as well as First Class. It will be hard, though, to get a return on this investment because of the effect that the current business slowdown is having on the Business Class market.

In some cases, airlines have opted competition over cabin service. In particular, many carriers have withdrawn from the First Class market entirely and have instead put their faith in a much-enhanced Business Class product. Air Canada, Aer Lingus, KLM and Northwest are all examples of airlines which have made this decision. They risk losing some of their highest-yielding business, but have much greater freedom of action. In particular, they can improve their Business Class so that it is fully competitive with the highest standards, without the concern that by doing so, they will be competing with their own First Class market. Airlines that stay with First Class often find that by improving their Business Class to keep up with market trends, they succeed in persuading some of their own First Class passengers that it is no longer worthwhile for them to pay the First Class premium.

On short-haul routes, questions of cabin configuration and classes of service are rather different. On there routes, almost all airlines outside of the USA have given up First Class, on the grounds that it has become harder and harder to persuade passengers to pay the higher fares for sectors of only an hour or so. In Europe Swissair and Lufthansa were the last airlines to withdraw First Class, doing so in 1993. Instead, short-haul flights now are usually based on a two class cabin, divided between Business and Economy seating.

Until very recently, airlines that had such a cabin configuration based it on a uniform standard of seating comfort throughout the aircraft. Seat pitches were the same throughout at 32 or 33 inches, as was the number of seats abreast. On Boeing and Airbus single aisle aircraft such as the 737, 757 and A320, this meant six-abreast seating with three seats either side of the aisle. (McDonnell-Douglas aircraft such as the MD-80, being slightly narrower have been used at 5-abreast. This is also the same with the Boeing 717.) The division between Business Class and Economy Class was made by using a flexible cabin divider which could be moved up and down the aircraft according to the relative demand for Business and Economy seats.

Such a philosophy gave the airlines the benefit of valuable operational flexibility, but it was probably only sustainable in the tightly-regulated market that then prevailed. The problem it gave was that seating comfort standards were very poor in Business Class, particularly for those people who on busy flights had to sit in the middle seat of three. Business passengers generally came to feel that not enough was being done to recognize the fact that they had paid very much higher fares—often four or five times as high—as those who sat in the rear cabin.

The solution which has been adopted recently is to install convertible seats. These seats are expensive and also rather heavier than standard seats. They do, though, allow a row of six-abreast seating to be converted into one of five-abreast very quickly, during an aircraft turnaround period. This is an expensive option because, besides the capital costs of the seats, it also means that there were seats are available for sale on busy peak-time flights. It is probably an inevitable move though, given the changing competitive scene in the industry.

The other current controversy with cabin configuration and classes of service is a similar one, but it applies to airlines' long haul rather than short haul routes. When three classes were adopted as the standard configuration on there routes, the principles appeared clear. First Class would accommodate passengers prepared to pay high fares for extravagant standards of comfort. Business class would be for all other passengers who paid full, flexible fares. The Economy cabin would offer only a low product specification for passengers paying discount and promotional fares.

As time has passed, these principles have become blurred. Business Class product specifications have risen steadily, and, in an attempt to permit carriers a return on their money, the fares that allow passengers to sit in Business Class have been very substantially increased. In turn, market demand has often meant that lower flexible fares have been introduced. These fares permit passengers to travel without restrictions. They only allow seating in the Economy Cabin, though.

The problem is that despite the fact that Flexible Economy Fares are lower than Business Class Fares, they are still very high in comparison with restricted discount fares. They again mean that a passenger who has paid a relatively high fare can end up sitting next to someone who has paid very much less.

The answer to this problem may be for a four-class aircraft, with the Economy cabin sub-divided so that a section of the aircraft is available exclusively for those people paying the higher economy fares. British Airways has introduced this idea with its World Traveller Plus cabin. More may do so when the new large Airbus A380 is introduced from 2006 onwards.

Network, Frequencies and Timings

The planning of an airline's schedule is again one where compromise between product quality and cost will be needed. There will also be many practical constraints which may mean that the carrier's freedom of action to meet the requirements of its customers will be significantly affected.

For business travellers, a broad network of direct flights is central to their product requirements. These are the features which will give them the flexibility they need. It will not be easy, though, to decide on exactly what should and should not be offered.

In terms of the practical constraints, route entry decisions can still sometimes be limited by government regulation of market access. On international routes, it may still be necessary for an airline to gain designation by the. home government under the terms of the relevant Air Services Agreement. Even if such designation is obtained, decisions about capacities and frequencies may also be constrained by regulatory factors. Many Air Services Agreements are still written in a way which is designed to ensure that airlines do not compete on capacity, with equal amounts provided by airlines from each country.

Airport slot availability is an increasing number of cases a constraint on route entry and scheduling. At the moment, the industry bases slot allocation at congested airports on the "Grandfather Rights" principle. Opportunities to land and take off at particular times are retained by established airlines on a permanent basis, from one season to the next. This can mean that there will be significant difficulties for a new airline wishing to begin services at a congested airport where all the attractively-timed slots will be in the possession of incumbent airlines. Even if slots can be obtained to allow services to begin, they may be at unsuitable times. It may also be difficult to get sufficient slots to allow the frequencies of established airlines to be matched.

Environmental factors may be another practical constraint. Many airports now impose restrictions on the amount of night flying they allow, and some ban it altogether. Whilst many airlines try to avoid "dead-of-night" arrivals and departures because of their unpopularity with passengers and difficulties with airport access, night flying is still a way for leisure-orientated airlines to boost aircraft utilisation and lower their unit costs.

In terms of current controversies regarding network and schedules planning, airlines are having to make a number of difficult decisions, many of which involve the familiar tradeoff between costs and product quality. On long haul routes, a very clear passenger preference has emerged in recent years. Passengers prefer non-stop flying to flights involving intermediate stops. To meet this requirement, aircraft manufacturers have responded by producing families of aircraft with longer and longer ranges, and the opportunities provided by such planes have been taken up enthusiastically by airlines. Many markets have now been transformed in terms of the ways in which airlines serve them. For example, almost all services between Southeast Asia and Europe, and Southeast Asia to the West Coast of the USA are now non-stop, and any airline which attempted to serve them with an intermediate stop would find itself at a severe competitive disadvantage. The industry's appetite for longer range non-stop services still appears to be insatiable. At the time of writing Airbus is introducing a variant of its A340 family—the A340-500—which will be able to fly non-stop over routes requiring 16-17 hours of flying time. Boeing is working on a comparable long-range variant of its 777 family. In principle, non-stop flying helps airlines to achieve low operating costs, but only up to a point. Non-stop flights allow for higher aircraft utilisation and of course the landing fees and turnaround costs associated with the intermediate stop are avoided. The very long ranges now being proposed, though, will on balance be a higher cost option for the airlines that decide to offer them to their customers. Very large quantities of fuel will have to be carried early in a flight for use later on, in turn raising aircraft weight and fuel burn. Also extra crews will have to be carried to permit proper rest periods. This will raise costs and take up seating capacity.

The other main area of controversy involves debate over the related issues of hub-and-spoke networks and so-called "market fragmentation".

Many airlines have based their strategic response to the competitive challenges of deregulation on the hub-and-spoke principle. The idea is a simple one. The airline selects and airport with a good geographical location relative to major traffic flows. Its flights in-and-out of this airport are then coordinated in carefully-timed "banks", so that passengers can transfer from an in-bound flight from their origin to an outbound flight to their destination.

Passengers benefit substantially from networks based on the hub-and. spoke principle. On each of the spokes, frequencies can be much higher because the airline is carrying the traffic heading to the end destination from all the origin points, rather than just passengers in one city-pair market. Also, it should be possible for larger aircraft to be used, giving access to lower seat-mile costs. This may in turn result in lower fares.

From the airline's point-of-view, hub-and-spoke concepts allow them to exploit a far larger number of origin-and-destination markets than they could do with a route network based on the point-to-point principle. It also protects them from competitive attack. The dominance they achieve at the hub airport and the higher frequencies achievable on each of the spokes both help in this regard.

Despite these advantages, the role of hub-and-spoke networks is becoming increasingly controversial. It is now clear that they are unpopular with passengers because of the delays and congestion associated with changing flights at the hub. They are also extremely resource. intensive. Because of the need to group flights together in coordinated banks, at some stages of the day a hub airport will be the scene of frenetic activity. At others, it will be almost deserted, and costly resources in terms of staff and equipment will be idle.

It is instructive to note that one of the most successful carriers of recent years, Southwest Airlines, is not a hub and-spoke operator. Instead, it uses a network based clearly on line-haul, point-to-point principles. This means that the airline has to use a relatively small aircraft, the Boeing 737. It does, though, achieve low unit costs through the intensive utilisation of resources. It also appears to be a remarkably popular airline with passengers.

The viability of hub-and-spoke networks is now being affected by another factor. Increasingly, aircraft manufacturers are producing smaller jet aircraft with reasonable operating costs. One of the main markets for these is airlines seeking to attack their rival's hubs with a so-called "hub overflying" strategy. The regional jets produced by Bombardier and Embraer are current examples of these aircraft.

On long-haul routes, similar trends can now be seen, though they are usually referred to as the trends towards market fragmentation rather than hub overflying.

During the 1970s and 1980s, a passenger wishing to fly from, say, a smaller city in Europe to one in the USA often had a difficult and tiring journey. They had to fly from their home city to a European hub and from there to a gateway hub in the USA. There, they had to pass through immigration checks, reclaim their bags and clear customs as it was their point-of entry into the USA. Their journey was only completed when they finally took their connecting flight domestically in the USA.

Again, this system brought advantages to both the airlines and their passengers. It allowed Boeing 747 aircraft to be used between the two hub airports, with a daily or better then daily frequency. As a large aircraft with low seat-mile costs, the 747 in turn allowed airlines to offer lower fares than might otherwise have been the case.

During the 1980s, though, a revolution in airline fleet planning began to take place. Controversially, the rules governing over-water flying with twin-engined aircraft were progressively relaxed, a relaxation which allowed airlines to choose a more-or-less optimum flight path for all their trans-Atlantic flights whether they were using two, three or four engined jets. The Boeing Company in particular responded by producing longer range versions of its 767 aircraft, and by investing in a new twin engined family, the 777. Airbus produced a competitor to the 777, the slightly smaller A330, although interestingly it stayed with the four-engined principle for its A340 family.

All these developments mean that airlines have access to a series of aircraft which are smaller than the 747 but which have attractive seat-kilometre operating costs. This, when combined with the substantial growth which has taken place in the market, has permitted an increasing number of direct non-stop services to be introduced, services which link two secondary cities on either side of the Atlantic. In turn, these allow more passengers to fly point-to-point, without the tiresome hub interchanges referred to earlier.

Of the different airlines flying the Atlantic, the one that has exploited the situation most fully is undoubtedly American Airlines. Despite having more than 20% of its activity in the international, rather than the US domestic market, American does not have any Boeing 747s in its fleet. Instead it focuses exclusively on the use of smaller aircraft on its long-haul services.

The controversy about aircraft downsizing on long haul routes continues. As has been noted, Airbus is now developing a new large aircraft, the A380. The initial version of this aircraft will have around 550 seats in a mixed-class configuration. It will certainly be stretched, though, and later versions may have 800 or even 1000 seats.

Alongside the Airbus proposal, Boeing had proposed building stretched and up-dated versions of the 747, to raise the 747s seating capacity to around 550. It is now clear, though, that this aircraft will not be built.

The Boeing argument for giving up the idea of a stretched 747 was an interesting one. Both Boeing and Airbus agreed that the crucial market for new large jets is that from AsiaJPacific markets to Europe and, especially to North America. Many of the airports in the region will suffer from runway congestion in the future. The disagreement between Boeing and Airbus is regarding the extent to which the fragmentation trends which have affected Atlantic routes will spread to AsiaJPacific markets. Boeing stated that it had come to accept that such a spread was inevitable, and that this would significantly undermine the demand for large aircraft, at least in the short and medium term. Airbus, seeking every opportunity to undermine Boeing's dominant position with the 747, argued that if fragmentation did occur to some extent, it would not eliminate the urgent need for a larger aircraft with, in their case, the technological edge available from an all-new design. It remains to be seen who will be right.

Punctuality

Planning to ensure high standards of punctuality is a central product issue for all airlines. It is true that some of the punctuality problems being experienced by airlines at the present time reflect outside factors such as airport and air traffic control congestion. Still, many trade-offs exist where airlines that are prepared to spend more may fare significantly better than those which opt for the lowest possible costs of operation. In turn, these carriers will have an important advantage in securing long-term customer loyalty.

An important first area for these tradeoffs is in airline fleet planning. Generally, an airline will obtain the best punctuality performance if it operates new aircraft of proven technology. This means that an airline seeking the best possible punctuality performance should avoid being a launching customer for a new aircraft containing significant amounts of new technology. An especially difficult situation is when both the airframe and systems and the aircraft engines are entirely new. It will, though, lose opportunities to take advantage of the attractive discounts manufacturers always offer to launching customers.

The airline should also have a policy of replacing aircraft with new planes after a few years. Some airlines—Singapore Airlines is an example—do so, and appear to gain significant punctuality benefits from it. This is because aircraft despatch reliability tends to decline with the age of an aircraft once a certain threshold has been passed.

A further punctuality-related decision is whether or not an airline should invest in the automatic landing capability which will enable its aircraft to operate in conditions of poor visibility. Heavy costs will be associated with such a decision. Besides the capital costs of buying the equipment and maintaining it, flight crew training costs will also be significantly raised both in initial training and also because of the regular opportunities which must be given for crews to practise their blind landing skills. As a further difficulty, it is an investment which for many airlines will be poorly utilized. Few airports in the world have a problem with low vioibility for more than ten or fifteen days per year, meaning that for almost all the time, a blind landing capability will not be needed.

Despite all these problems, investment in automatic landing is now a necessity for many airlines. Customers are now realising that fog need not delay an aircraft unduly, and competition is forcing more and more carriers to make the required investment.

Maintenance is another area where trade-offs between cost levels and punctuality performance will need to be made. An airline seeking to achieve the best possible punctuality record will need a substantial line maintenance capability, to ensure that technical problems can be corrected as soon as they arise. Also, a considerable investment in spares will be required, for the same reason.

It is in the area of schedules planning where the most significant trade-offs have to be made if an airline is to achieve a good punctuality performance. A carrier aiming at the lowest possible cost of operation will develop a schedule which will give a high annual utilization of each aircraft in the fleet. Such a policy will lower costs because it will result in the fixed costs of aircraft ownership or lease rentals being spread over the greatest quantity of output. Very high aircraft utilization will, though, often bring significant product penalties. It will result in some customers having to accept inconvenient departure and arrival times, because high utilization will require aircraft to be kept flying continuously except for essential maintenance and turnaround periods. Even more significantly, a policy of high aircraft utilization will almost certainly bring problems with punctuality. This is because once an airline experiences an initial delay, there will be no slack in the schedule to allow the delay to be made up. Thus, if an aircraft is delayed early in the day—perhaps for reasons outside the airline's control such as air traffic difficulties—all the remaining flights it is due to operate during the day will also be late.

Similar considerations apply to the question of the time which an airline allows in its timetable for a flight to be completed. A punctual departure is, of course, reassuring for passengers. However, it is a punctual arrival which matters to them even more, especially if they are trying to make a connection. If an airline allows a generous time in its schedule for the completion of flight, a punctual arrival is much more likely. It will also mean that a flight will arrive punctually even if it runs into stronger than expected headwinds. A slack schedule will, though, bring a cost penalty if it reduces the number of aircraft rotations that can be flown in a day.

Customer Service-Related Product Features

Point-of-Sale Service

Point-of-sale service is the term used to describe service offered to the customer at the point where they are actually making a booking. It is an area where revolutionary changes have come about over the last five years.

Point-of-sale service has always been difficult for airlines because of the large number and wide variety of sales outlets they have used. In the past, some airline customers have wished to deal with them direct. The traditional methods to allow this have been downtown ticket offices, airport ticket desks and call centres. In addition, airlines have had to make themselves accessible to travel agents, with over 80% of bookings traditionally being obtained through agents. A final source of business has been from other airlines on an interline basis.

Though the nature of interline relationships is now changing, it is still the case that a passenger wishing to book a multi-sector journey using several different airlines can do so by contacting only the first carrier (assuming that they are proposing to use a relatively expensive flexible ticket). This airline will then contact the others to make the necessary bookings.

Given this range of outlets, the point-of-sale task would always have been difficult for airlines. There can be little doubt, though, that by their own policy decisions traditional airlines made it a great deal worse. In particular, by adopting very complex fare structures and reservations procedures, they increased point-of-sale transaction times and also ensured that the systems could only be accessed by trained experts. In turn, this further increased the proportion of bookings coming through the travel agency system and raising commission costs.

To try to address the problem, the response of many airlines was to invest large sums in the development of so-called Global Distribution Systems such as AIlladeus and Sabre. Though to some degree these arrested the rise in processing costs by improving staff productivity, they have proved costly and controversial. They were also to a large extent addressing the symptoms of the problem rather than the problem itself.

It has taken the Cost Leader revolution we referred to in the last chapter as well as the growth of widely-available Internet access, to radically change the situation. As we have seen, by making fares and reservation's procedures very simple, these airlines have been able to move to a "self-service" approach, with a high proportion of their bookings being made on-line by passengers themselves. This has resulted in very large cost savings in terms of commissions and administration, and is a policy which many traditional airlines are now belatedly following.

Reservations and Overbooking

For most air travellers, a prebooked reservation they can rely on remains an integral part of the product that they expect from airlines, and today the availability of cheap computing power means that most of the technical problems of providing them have been resolved.

There is still one air transport product where a reservation is not offered. This is with the pure form of the so-called Shuttle concept. Pioneered by Eastern Airlines in the USA in 1961, the idea of the Shuttle is that passengers do not need to book in advance. Instead, the airline guarantees to fly all those who report for a flight. They can do so by keeping back-up aircraft and crews, which are called into action if the number of passengers checking in for a flight exceeds the capacity of the aircraft allocated to it.

The Shuttle concept brings a number of theoretical advantages. Passengers are saved the trouble of making reservations, and airlines the cost of. recording them. Also, most Shuttle passengers pay at the airport. The business therefore comes direct to airlines with a useful saving in commission costs and some cash-flow benefits. It also helps to cement market control.

Shuttle concepts continue to be used in the USA, with, for example, US Airways still flying Shuttle flights between New York, Washington and Boston. The concept is in decline, though, in other markets. It requires a very large commitment of resources of aircraft and crew. These only achieve poor utilization because of the rarity with which back-up aircraft will be needed outside of the peak periods. Also, airport slot constraints are becoming more and more severe. In order to protect their so-called "Grandfather Rights" on the slots they have been allocated, airlines need to use them on a minimum of 80% of occasions during a given traffic season. There can be no certainty that they will do so if these slots are allocated to Shuttle back-up flights. Finally, through the advent of very capable Revenue Management systems (dealt with in the next chapter), carriers are now much more successful at selling seats on off-peak flights at low. but still profitable, prices. It is therefore often a worthwhile option to fly a route with an aircraft which will cater for all the peak time full-fare demand. Though this aircraft will then be too big for the level of such demand at off-peak periods, lower fares and careful capacity management can be used to produce worthwhile returns even on these flights. This may well be a cheaper and more profitable option than flying all services with a relatively small plane and augmenting peak-time capacity with a costly back-up aircraft.

An illustration of changing attitudes towards Shuttle services came in the UK domestic market in 1997. British Airways had flown domestic trunk services from Heathrow using the Shuttle principle since 1975. In 1997, though, the guarantee of a seat for all those reporting for a particular flight was discontinued, with all passengers expected to make a reservation. At the same time, the making of reservations was made easier by the adoption of "ticketless travel",

If reservations are to be required in almost all cases, airlines still have to address another difficult problem: many passengers do not turn up and use the reservation they have made. The proportion of occasions where this is so varies from market to market, but it is quite common to find 10% of bookings coming into the "no-show" category. There are many reasons for this. Some passengers fully intend to get to the airport to check in for their flight but are prevented from doing so. They constitute *accidental* no-shows. Last minute illness or death will be an obvious reason for accidental no-showing. Other reasons will include traffic delays on the way to the airport and the passenger having a late in-bound connecting flight.

Not all no-shows are accidental, however. Many are *deliberate*. For example, business travellers who are uncertain about the time at which their meetings will end may book seats on several flights with different airlines. They will then have a convenient return flight whatever the actual finishing time. Another problem may occur when an unscrupulous passenger is holding a Standby ticket for a particular flight. They have an incentive to phone the airline a number of times making false bookings using fictitious names. The result will be no-shows, meaning that the Standby passenger will be accommodated.

Given such a significant no-show problem, it might be argued that airlines are themselves creating the problem by an over-generous attitude to those who book but fail to check-in for a flight. All service industries face the same problem as airlines, that their output is instantly perishable and cannot be stored. Some—cinemas are a good example—require customers to pay at the time of booking and no refunds are given if they fail to show up for the actual performance. They will only deal with customers who have credit cards. Credit card details are taken by the airline when a reservation is made and the card is automatically debited. This gives the carrier a guaranteed income and removes the necessity to overbook. Other, less radical airlines are increasingly making some of their lower fares non-refundable.

Despite the attraction of this idea, it is not a practical one for airlines in all circumstances. In particular, business travellers often regard the right to no-show as an important part of the flexibility they are buying when using a very expensive fare. If one carrier unilaterally made such fares non-refundable in the event of a no-show it would lose significant market share to its rivals.

If a degree of no-showing is inevitable, airlines have a strong incentive to overbook, and, perhaps perversely, their passengers will also benefit as a result of such a policy. By overbooking, load factors can be increased, which will in turn allow fares to be lower. Also, overbooking permits more passengers to travel on the flight of their choice. If an airline did not overbook it would only accept reservations up to the number of seats on an aircraft. All other requests for bookings would be refused. However, if, as would be very likely, there were no-shows, the flight would take off with some of the seats unoccupied. Ironically, there would then be passengers using later and presumably less convenient flights who could in fact have taken the flight of their choice. cost of recording them. Also, most Shuttle passengers pay at the airport. The Business therefore comes direct to airlines with a useful saving in commission costs and some cash-flow benefits. It also helps to cement market control.

Shuttle concepts continue to be used in the USA, with, for example, US Airways still flying Shuttle flights between New York, Washington and Boston. The concept is in decline, though, in other markets. It requires a very large commitment of resources of aircraft and crew. These only achieve poor utilization because of the rarity with which back-up aircraft will be needed outside of the peak periods. Also, airport slot constraints are becoming more and more severe. In order to protect their so-called "Grandfather Rights" on the slots they have been allocated, airlines need to use them on a minimum of 80% of occasions during a given traffic season. There can be no certainty that they will do so if these slots are allocated to Shuttle back-up flights. Finally, through the advent of very capable Revenue Management systems (dealt with in the next chapter), carriers are now much more successful at selling seats on off-peak flights at low, but still profitable, prices. It is therefore often a worthwhile option to fly a route with an aircraft which will cater for all the peak time full-fare demand. Though this aircraft will then be too big for the level of such demand at off-peak periods, lower fares and careful capacity management can be used to produce worthwhile returns even on these flights. This may well be a cheaper and more profitable option than flying all services with a relatively small plane and augmenting peak-time capacity with a costly back-up aircraft.

An illustration of changing attitudes towards Shuttle services came in the UK domestic market in 1997. British Airways had flown domestic trunk services from Heathrow using the Shuttle principle since 1975. In 1997, though, the guarantee of a seat for all those reporting for a particular flight was discontinued, with all passengers expected to make a reservation. At the same time, the making of reservations was made easier by the adoption of "ticketless travel."

If reservations are to be required in almost all cases, airlines still have to address another difficult problem: many passengers do not turn up and use the reservation they have made. The proportion of occasions where this is so varies from market to market, but it is quite common to find 10% of bookings coming into the "no-show" category. There are many reasons for this. Some passengers fully intend to get to the airport to check in for their flight but are prevented from doing so. They constitute *accidental* no-shows. Last minute illness or death will be an obvious reason for accidental no-showing. Other reasons will include traffic delays on the way to the airport and the passenger having a late in-bound connecting flight.

Not all no-shows are accidental, however. Many are *deliberate*. For example, business travellers who are uncertain about the time at which their meetings will end may book seats on several flights with different airlines. They will then have a convenient return flight whatever the actual finishing time. Another problem may occur when an unscrupulous passenger is holding a Standby ticket for a particular flight. They have an incentive to phone the airline a number of times making false bookings using fictitious names. The result will be no-shows, meaning that the Standby passenger will be accommodated.

Given such a significant no-show problem, it might be argued that airlines are themselves creating the problem by an over-generous attitude to those who book but fail to check-in for a flight. All service industries face the same problem as airlines, that their output is instantly perishable and cannot be stored. Some—cinemas are a good example—require customers to pay at the time of booking and no refunds are given if they fail to show up for the actual performance. They will only deal with customers who have credit cards. Credit card details are taken by the airline when a reservation is made and the card is automatically debited. This gives the carrier a guaranteed income and removes the necessity to overbook. Other, less radical airlines are increasingly making some of their lower fares non-refundable.

Despite the attraction of this idea, it is not a practical one for airlines in all circumstances. In particular, business travellers often regard the right to no-show as an important part of the flexibility they are buying when using a very expensive fare. If one carrier unilaterally made such fares non-refundable in the event of a no-show it would lose significant market share to its rivals.

If a degree of no-showing is inevitable, airlines have a strong incentive to overbook, and, perhaps perversely, their passengers will also benefit as a result of such a policy. By overbooking, load factors can be increased, which will in turn allow fares to be lower. Also, overbooking permits more passengers to travel on the flight of their choice. If an airline did not overbook it would only accept reservations up to the number of seats on an aircraft. All other requests for bookings would be refused. However, if, as would be very likely, there were no-shows, the flight would take off with some of the seats unoccupied. Ironically, there would then be passengers using later and presumably less convenient flights who could in fact have taken the flight of their choice.

There are thus clear advantages which will accrue to the customer if an artline practises overbooking which will be lost if it does not. Despite this, overbooking remains unpopular. Of course, an airline should use historical records to help fix the amount by which each flight should be overbooked, If a conservative estimate is made, on almost all occasions there will be no problem. The number of no-show passengers will exceed the amount of overbooking and all passengers will get on the flight. However, no matter what degree of care is exercised, there will be occasions—hopefully rare—when difficulties arise. Then, the random element present in patterns of no-showing means that the number of passengers reporting for a flight exceeds the capacity of the aircraft being used for it. Some passengers will therefore be "bumped".

In the past, airline approaches to this problem were totally unsatisfactory. Too often, the passengers selected for bumping were the last ones to check in. This was expedient, in the sense that these passengers would not have baggage already loaded into the aircraft lower holds, which would otherwise have to be retrieved for security reasons. However, these late-arriving passengers would often be business travellers. They would therefore be commercially important to the airline. Also, as business travellers it would often be vital that they should get the flight on which they are booked, because they will have meetings to attend, or onward connections to make.

Today, the best airlines are more sophisticated at handling bumping situations. Their aim is to identify, and to compensate, the passengers who are prepared to accept a delay. These are clearly unlikely to include business travellers. If such a passenger is, for example, flying to negotiate an important contract, no amount of compensation will be sufficient to make up for the fact that they miss their meeting. Many leisure travellers, though, will find the offer of compensation an attractive one. It may not matter to them a great deal whether they reach their destination today or tomorrow, especially if they receive a cash payment in compensation, Airlines should therefore seek volunteers for off-loading on those flights where they expect to have problems. In doing so, they can provide a valuable protection for their commercial reputation.

Airport Service

As in all other areas of product design, airline decisions about the level of airport service they offer to their customers will be a reflection of their overall business strategy. Low-fare airlines will find airport service a major area where they can achieve economies to ensure that their low fares will be profitable. They often use uncongested airports, which may sometimes impose inconvenience on passengers by being far from the cities they are designed to serve. They may insist on longer check-in times to enable a smaller number of check-in desks to be used. No special lounges will be provided, resulting in a significant cost saving. Finally, the boarding process will be a simple one on a "first come, first served" basis with no pre-allocation of seats.

For airlines aiming to penetrate the market of frequent business travellers the task could not be more different. Major efforts have been made in recent years to establish airport service as a significant area of product differentiation. Some carriers now provide limousine services to pick up premium-fare passengers at their home or office to bring them to the airport—Virgin Atlantic, Continental and Emirates are examples. Once there, kerbside check-in facilities may be on offer to remove the necessity of carrying heavy baggage into the terminal. If they do come into the terminal to check-in, a separate, uncongested desk will be provided. There may then be provision for a preferential channel for moving through passport and security formalities, before the passenger is invited to use what will generally be an extremely luxurious lounge with hospitality and business facilities available free of charge. At the arrival airport, business travellers can now expect preferential baggage service with their bags arriving on the baggage carousel first. There may also be an arrivals lounge allowing them to freshen up before going to their meeting.

All these advances in airport service do not come cheaply. They involve investment in extra staff and equipment, and in rental payments to the airport operator in respect of lounge space and extra check-in desks. It is essential therefore that airlines are able to raise their fares to pay for them or increase their share of the business travel market as a result of better airport service. It may be harder to sustain higher fares in a recessionary period, whilst increases in market share may only be transient if rival airlines also offer enhanced airport service.

In-Flight Service

There are, though, a number of additional aspects which will affect the nature of passengers' in-flight experience. One of these areas is the question of an airline's fleet planning policies. Naturally, all aircraft manufacturers argue that selecting their aircraft will in turn allow airlines to give their customers a superior in-flight product.

For example, Airbus claim that their A320 family is better than the B737 because it has a wider fuselage cross-section, allowing for wider seats and wider aisles. Equally, though, Boeing argues that its B767 is superior to the

Airbus A300 and A330 because it is designed for 7-abreast rather than 8-abreast seating in the. Economy cabin. For smaller aircraft, manufacturers of regional jets might argue that these aircraft bring significant benefits compared with turbo-props, at least over longer routes because they give a smoother flight, usually at higher altitudes.

There are, of course, many costs associated with in-flight service. However; despite what they spend on items such as food, drink and in-flight entertainment, airlines find that overwhelmingly the main costs are those associated with cabin staffing in terms of the salaries paid, the allowances given and the costs of hotel accommodation. The usual linking between the correct policy and airlines' overall business strategy applies.

For low-fare airlines, there might appear to be a temptation to dispense with cabin staff altogether. Because these airlines are generally "no-frills", the cabin service task is in any case a limited one. Such an option is not, though, a possibility. The primary function of cabin staff is that of ensuring safety on board, and regulatory bodies insist that a minimum number of qualified cabin staff are carried. The rules are rather complicated, but in essence they mean that there must be one cabin attendant per 50 passengers up to 200, and one per 25 passengers over 200. A "no-frills" airline will, though, work with the minimum legal number of cabin staff as will a typical charter airline.

Scheduled carriers will generally have a greater number of cabin staff than the minimum, to ensure more attentive cabin service for First and Business Class travellers. Some airlines, especially from the Far East, will greatly exceed the minimum number. For example, a typical European or North American airline will budget for 14 or 15 cabin staff on a B747. Carriers such as Thai International use 22 on this same aircraft.

Controlling Product Quality

Quality control is an essential part of the product design phase of marketing for any airline. Without it, the carrier cannot know which parts of its product are weak, and where improvements are needed.

Many aspects of the airline product can be quantified. For example, with point-of-sale service, modem telephone equipment can provide statistics on the proportion of calls answered within a given time period. Many airlines aim to achieve a standard that 80% of calls should be answered within 20 seconds. It can also give information about the calls that are lost at busy times, in the sense that callers become tired of waiting for someone to help them and abandon the call. An appropriate target for a full-service airline is that no more than 2% of calls should be lost.

Baggage service—or the lack of it—can also be quantified. The proportion of bags which are mishandled and fail to arrive at the destination at the same time as their owners is one useful statistic. Also, baggage delivery times can be monitored by recording the time taken for the first bag and the last bag to reach the baggage delivery carousel.

Punctuality and regularity performance should also be studied carefully. The proportion of flights departing and arriving within prescribed limits of the scheduled time is a fundamental measure, with on-time to within 5 minutes a suitable standard for short-haul routes, and on-time to within 15 minutes for long haul routes. In terms of regularity (the proportion of flights advertised in the timetable which are actually operated), the standard should, of course, be near to 100%.

Monitoring of customer compliments and complaints should also be undertaken. All airlines receive fraudulent or unjustified complaints. Although these require vigilance, the number of them should be relatively constant. Therefore, comparing the number of customer compliments with the number of complaints will provide a first quality control statistic. Airlines should also investigate the nature of the complaints they receive. If these focus to an increasing degree on only a small number of product components, this will be a strong indicator of the areas where management attention is needed.

The use of inflight and airport surveys as ways of collecting information about customer requirements. They can also form part of a quality control programme. An in-flight survey will have the advantage that passengers are actually experiencing the product at the time they fill in their questionnaire. If they are questioned at the airport of arrival their memories of the flight will still be fresh. In either case, asking passengers their opinions can have a valuable customer relations function, of convincing them that the airline is interested in continuous product improvement.

A further area of quality control work is one which should never be ignored—the opinions of the airline's own customer contact and sales staff. These people will regularly come into contact with customers and will have to listen to their complaints. Their reports can provide an accurate barometer of the airline's performance.

The Air Freight Product

Airlines with an interest in penetrating the air freight market need to spend a great deal of time in detailed planning of the freight product. There are, of course, many differences between the air passenger and air cargo businesses. The basic principles of product planning are, though, exactly the same. Successful airlines will Ix those that identify correctly their customer's requirements and then make the difficult tradeoff between product quality and costs.

Air Freight Capacity

With questions of air freight capacity, the advantages from the customer's point-of-view of an airline investing in pure freighter aircraft. These will allow capacity to be provided on the routings that the freight customer wants, at times which suit their demand pattern. They also offer a greater certainty that goods will actually be flown on the flight on which they are booked.

If it is decided that the provision of freighters will be worthwhile, a decision will have to be made about the type of aircraft to be selected. In deciding this, airlines will need to bring in some of the same considerations they will employ when selecting a passenger aircraft. For example, they will need information on the payload/range capabilities of the different aircraft types in comparison with their route networks and traffic flows. They will need data on capital and ownership costs, fuel consumption, field-length performance and available operating costs. In addition, though, there are two pieces of data which are unique to freight operations and which can be crucial in plane choice. First, *cabin door size* and *cabin cross-section* of the main deck of the aircraft will decide what size of consignment can be accommodated. All narrow-bodied jet freighters (such as the freight version of the Boeing 757) can only accept consignments of up to 86 inches in height through their cargo doors. They cannot, therefore. accept the 8 feet by 8 feet rectangular cross-section of International Standards Organization (ISO) standard-sized containers. Of the wide. bodied aircraft, the freighter version of the MD-II cannot accommodate two of these containers side-by-side in the main deck. The B747F is unique amongst civil aircraft in being able to do so at the moment, though the A380F will also be able to do so.

The second important performance measure for a freighter aircraft is its *design density*. Freighters do not only have a weight-limited payload. They also have a fixed volumetric capacity. If an aircraft only has a small volume relative to its maximum payload it will often become volumetric ally full before its maximum payload is reached. Older narrow-bodied jets such as the B707 and DC-8 all had significant design density problems because of their inadequate cabin volumes. The Boeing 747 has a design density approximately 40% below that of the 707. This aircraft, though, has a very large payload/range potential so in practice it can only be used on the busiest long-haul services.

The airline specialising in the air freight market will have to decide which types of freighter aircraft it is to employ. Total market airlines aiming to penetrate both the air passenger and air freight markets must decide whether or not they will use freighters at all. They need not do so. It is part of the synergy available to the total market airline that in providing passenger service it also produces lower-hold freight space. With narrow-bodied planes such as the B757, lower-hold capacity is not especially useful because these aircraft have belly-holds which are awkwardly-shaped and comparatively small. They can therefore carry only a small amount of freight, even when operating a flight where the passenger and baggage load is limited. The freight they do carry also poses time-consuming problems of loading and unloading. Wide-bodied aircraft, though, are much more capable. The B747 can carry 25 tones or more of containerized and palletized cargo in its lower hold. Other wide-bodies such as the A330, A340 and MD-II have a freight capability of 12 tonnes or more, depending on the passenger payload and the fuel needed for a given sector.

Given that it will have large amounts of freight capacity available in its passenger aircraft a total market airline operating wide-bodied planes can consider relying exclusively on lower-hold space. It will still be able to offer a good flight frequency, and it will not have to bear the heavy costs of operating a freighter fleet. Indeed, in the past an investment in narrow-bodied freighters has rarely been a successful one for such airlines.

Despite the attractions of not employing freighters, it is unlikely to be a viable option for an airline with a serious interest in the air freight market. To many customers, an exclusive reliance on belly-hold capacity will significantly reduce the quality of the product. For example, a shipper of hazardous cargoes needs freighter service because industry safety rules forbid the carriage of many types of hazardous goods in the lower holds of passenger aircraft. Also, freighter capacity is very important to the shipper of large consignments. The main deck of the B747F, the largest freighter aircraft currently in common use, can accommodate shipments of over 100 inches in height.

A further problem with a freight product based only on belly-hold capacity is that it fails to take into account shipper's requirements for space. Air freight peaks strongly at night, following production during the working day, and at the end of the working week. There is a pronounced trough in demand on Sundays and Mondays. Some belly-hold capacity will therefore be provided at times of the day or the week when little freight is moving. At other times, though, there may be a chronic shortage of capacity.

In the longer term, a policy of relying purely on belly-holds may be untenable for another reason. It ties the amount of freight space offered to passenger demand. Generally, air freight demand is growing more quickly then that for passengers, in itself leading to a progressive shortage of belly-hold freight capacity. Also, passenger demand growth is generally faster in the leisure rather than the business travel segment. Leisure-orientated flights tend to be on routes to holiday resorts where the quantities of air freight moving may be relatively small.

A final factor jeopardising a belly-holds only policy may be that in the longer-term, aircraft developments may mean that less space will be available for freight. The Airbus A380 will be a double-decked aircraft in terms of its passenger cabins, in order to keep its overall dimensions within those necessary for airport compatibility. This will mean that a large increase in the passenger carrying capabilities of the aircraft, without corresponding growth in belly-hold space. Consequently, a greater proportion of the belly-hold capacity will be taken up with passengers' bags, and less will be available for freight.

Overall, airlines with a major interest in building their presence in the air freight market will have to operate a fleet of freighters. They may operate these aircraft themselves, or wet-lease them from specialists such as the US fmn Atlasair. If they choose to operate the aircraft themselves, an attractive option may be to use conversions of obsolete passenger aircraft, rather than buy new and very expensive specialist freighters from the manufacturers. This will especially be the case if the passenger aircraft are comparatively new but have become obsolescent because of a lack of range. With freighters, shorter ranges are less of a problem because the aircraft can simply land and take on more fuel.

With questions of air freight capacity, there is an interim solution possible, with the use of so-called "Combi" and "Quick-Change" aircraft. A Combi is an aircraft where the main deck can be divided between passengers and freight with a moveable bulkhead to separate the two. A Quick-Change (QC) aircraft is one which can be converted from a passenger to freight aircraft quickly—generally in less than an hour. This is because the seats can be removed in a short time as they are placed on pallets.

Both Combis and QCs are more expensive and heavier than equivalent passenger aircraft because they need a large cargo door and a strengthened floor. Theoretically, though, both can bring significant benefits. Combis allow routes to be opened up where there is insufficient passenger demand to allow a service to begin at a marketable frequency. They also allow the airline to enter the large-shipment market without the risks associated with investing in pure freighters. QC aircraft can be valuable in short-haul operations. Here, passengers do not generally wish to travel at night, so aircraft have to be left on the ground then, with a—significant penalty in annual utilization resulting. Converting the aircraft into a freighter will allow for extra, night-time flights to be operated.

Despite these advantages, Combi flying is in decline at the moment whilst the QC concept has never achieved the popularity for which the aircraft manufacturers must have hoped. Combis have generally been unpopular with passengers, resulting as they do in a smaller-sized passenger cabin. Recent years have also seen the introduction of new fire suppression rules which have resulted in increases in both capital costs and aircraft weight. These in turn have challenged the economics of Combis.

With QC aircraft, these have generally been opposed by the passenger departments of airlines. Using an aircraft as a night-time freighter may mean that there will delays to early morning passenger flights if technical problems have occurred overnight. Also, in the past QC aircraft have suffered from the way in which the nightly conversions damage the aircraft interior. Lufthansa is one of the few airlines still making use of the QC concept.

Besides questions of freight capacity, an airline hoping to penetrate the air freight market will have to make decisions about the ground handling systems to be employed, and the investment to be made in information technology.

In the late 1960s and early 1970s a number of airlines installed sophisticated on-airport automated freight handling systems. These were intended to allow them to lower their ground handling costs and to improve the service they offered to their customers. This early move to highly automated cargo handling was not successful, though, largely due to the unreliability and inflexibility of the systems.

During the later 1970s, many airlines discontinued automated on-airport handling and returned to labour-intensive concepts. By this time, the advent of wide-bodied aircraft meant that more and more freight was loaded into aircraft in containerized or palletized form. As this trend developed, airlines found at least a short-term answer to their handling problems by offering concessionary rates to those air freight forwarders who were prepared to take the unit load devices (ULDs), load them and present them to the airlines in a ready-for-carriage form. This process, operating under the so-called Bulk Unitization Programme, rescued airlines from otherwise intractable problems of on-airport cargo handling. It did, though greatly increase the number of expensive unit load devices which they needed to purchase. The Programme also raised the bargaining power of air freight forwarders relative to the airlines. It is therefore significant that during the 1980s and 1990s large integrated carriers such as FedEx, UPS and DHL developed. These carriers adopted a policy of substantial investment in airport handling facilities, and largely chose to by-pass the forwarding industry. It is also the case that some airlines—British Airways and Air France are good examples—have now invested again in automated on-airport handling, despite having their fingers badly burnt in the. industry's first move in this direction. They are relying on the fact that the state-of-the-art in cargo handling has advanced considerably since then.

The design of the freight product is an interesting aspect of airline marketing. The total market airline can use the synergies available from the belly-hold space in its passenger aircraft. It can therefore offer flight frequency and cheaply available capacity as its main advantages. The pure freight airline, on the other hand, can supply capacity which will meet the needs of the freight customer without any requirement for compromise. It is these advantages that are becoming increasingly important.

AIRLINE PRICING PLANNING

Once a rather docile element in the marketing mix because of its control by the Civil Aeronautics Board, price has become one of the most volatile areas today. In fact, since deregulation, pricing has become the major competitive variable. This is not surprising in an industry with relatively few companies, each aware of the other's pricing policies and having to match the competition or lose market share. Because of its importance in the marketing process, pricing is discussed in detail here. Basically, two general factors-demand and supply-determine the level of prices in any market. *Demand factors* are the intensities and loyalties hat customers bring: how willing and able they are to pay for air transportation. *Supply factors* involve the quantity of seats that a carrier places in a particular market. The major component of supply is the total cost of producing a marketing the seats that are made available. Thus, we will consider two major factors that determine price levels: demand, and production an marketing costs.

Demand. The quantity of tickets purchased by customers in a particular market will largely depended on the price. Few customers would be willing or able to pay $1,000 for a flight from Miami to San Francisco, regardless of the service provided. Yet if this flight were priced at $100, the number of tickets that could be sold would probably far exceed the number of seats available.

As the price of an item falls, the quantity of that item purchased by customers normally rises. We can readily see the importance of price in determining the quantity demanded, but there are other factors in or determinants of market demand included are the preferences of passengers for one airline over another because of some real or perceived difference; the number of passengers in particular market; the financial status and income levels of passengers; the Prices of competitors and related travel expenses; and passengers' expectations regarding future prices.

Production and Marketing Costs. Production and marketing costs also have a bearing on the prices an airline sets. The cost per seat-mile flown must be covered by the price of the ticket. Included in an airline's total cost of operation are its direct operating costs-fuel, crew salaries and expenses, landing fees, and so forth. Indirect operating costs, or fixed expenses, such as maintenance costs, general administrative costs, and the marketing expenses associated with passenger servicing, all must be covered by the revenue generated on flights throughout the system. Thus, in a sense, the production and marketing costs of the carrier represent the floor under the price set for the carrier's product.

The Pricing Process

The basic two-fold responsibility of airline pricing analysts appears to be simple and straightforward. They must:

(1) monitor, analyze, and respond to hundreds, sometimes thousands, of daily fare changes implemented by competitor airlines, and
(2) routinely develop pricing initiatives to strengthen and/or fortify their company's position in the marketplace.

In moving from conceptual responsibility to real-time practice, however, airline pricing becomes quite complex. In broad terms, the pricing process can be characterized as being heavily dependent on automation, having many different fare levels subject to change as a competitive response.

All major airlines participate in the fare filing process via the Airline Tariff Publishing Company (ATPCO), which is jointly owned and funded by 30 U.S. and foreign carriers. ATPCO serves as an electronic "clearinghouse" for fare information and changes. Seven days a week, ATPCO accepts fare changes submitted by all participating airlines, consolidates and processes the changes overnight, then transmits and displays these changes to all carriers by 6:00A.M. ATPCO was established in the 1940s, at a time when airline pricing was still regulated by the CAB. ATPCO's role in pricing was quickly heightened with the advent of airline deregulation, which spawned intense price competition among carriers. Its importance has also grown with the increased role of automation, particularly of computerized reservations sys. At any point in time, because carriers collectively serve tens of thousands of origin and destination (O&D) city-pairs, with each O&D having several different fare levels, the total fare inventory managed by ATPCO exceeds two million individual Ares. Any single airline's share of ATPCO's database may amount to several hundred thousand fares. Each year, ATPCO processes millions of domestic fare changes. An average day may involve over 130,000. For each carrier, this could mean several thousand each workday, which requires some degree of analysis and, in most cases, some type of competitive response.

It is against this backdrop of fast-paced change, fueled by continuing advances in automation, that the pricing staffs of the nation's airlines formulate, and regularly reformulate, their basic pricing strategies and craft daily tactical maneuvers that are part science, part art.

Pricing Strategies and Objectives

The current literature on pricing describes several different strategies or objectives that a firm might pursue, from simple survival pricing for cash, to fighting for market share, to pricing at a premium over competitors to complement a superior product or service quality. Applying these textbook strategies to the airlines is complicated, because carriers don't charge only one price for their services. Instead, they offer a hierarchical array of fares designed to appeal to both price-sensitive leisure travelers and less price sensitive business travelers. Further complications arise from various other factors that characterize the market for airline services. These include:

(1) the predictable seasonal pattern of demand, especially for leisure travel,
(2) the influence of override commissions that many airlines pay to travel agencies,
(3) the dynamic nature of airline schedules and the strong relationship that exists between schedule frequency and passenger demand, and
(4) the tendency for individual carrier pricing strategies and objectives to vary by market and over time.

Despite the difficulties (and subjectivity) of fitting these general strategies to individual airlines, the exercise can be a meaningful one, particularly if a fixed and relatively brief time frame is defined and if strategies are identified for each carrier. American Airlines, for example, tends to be a profit-focused premium prier and a price leader in most markets, whereas United tends to be a quick follower rather than leader. Southwest Airlines represents the extreme case of a low-fare price, strongly focused on obtaining and maintaining market share and on diverting traffic from auto, bus, and rail travel. Also, some of the financially distressed airlines operating under the protection of Bankruptcy laws clearly have priced primarily for survival It is noteworthy as well that despite the differences among airlines, all carriers tend to maintain price parity with their rivals. This is due to the commodity nature of airline service, which may be diminishing somewhat as the supply of air service is controlled by fewer, more financially stable airlines.

Although identifying the fundamental strategies of competing carriers is an essential part of airline pricing, it is every bit as important, and perhaps more so, to understand and execute effectively the day-to-day tactics of pricing.

Pricing Tactics

Pricing tactics can be broadly categorized as (1) fare actions and (2) adjustments to fare rules and/or restrictions. Normally, daily pricing activity involves both tactics. The following discusses some of the more common actions within each category.

Fare Actions. For the most part, fare actions involve changes-increases or reductions-to actual fare levels, in contrast to the rules, restrictions, and/ or footnotes that accompany most fares. Changes can be market-specific, regional, or mass market in scope.

Introductory fares. When a carrier begins service in a new market, it typically offers unrestricted low fares for a period of 30 to 45 days. Key competitors normally match these fares, with restrictions. Provided that introductory fares are not extended beyond the conventional time frame, they usually don't lead to any sort of "upping of the ante" by competitors (for example, extending the period of availability or discounting the fare even further).

System excursion-fare sales. During seasonally weak traffic periods, carriers frequently offer a system wide sale of excursion fares. Sales are conducted, on average, for a period of 7 to 10 days, with travel allowed two to four months into the future. As a rule, provided that the carrier isn't conducting a "fire sale" simply to generate cash, the volume of seats offered in such a sale is limited and controlled on a flight-by-flight basis. American's Super Saver and Max Saver fares are some of the more prominent examples.

System business-fare sales. This type of sale is similar to the system excursion-fare sale, except that it involves higher-level business fares. Common motives are to stimulate demand and brand switching and to provide added value. The typical approach in this case is to introduce a one-way or round-tripfare, between 15 and 30 percent less than the full coach (Y-class) fare, with the requirement that the fare be purchased at least three to seven days prior to travel. Seats offered at this fare tend to be plentiful.

Connect market sales. In markets where an airline offers multiple non-stop flights, the carrier will tend to limit the number of seats sold at discounted fares, because its flights represent a higher-quality service than, for example, connecting-flight service. In these instances, a competing carrier offering only connecting service may periodically attempt to gain increased market presence and steal market share by introducing a low fare in its markets. The business risk faced by the connecting-service carrier is that the competition may attempt the same strategy in the initiator's own nonstop markets.

Target segment pricing. These special fares are lower than normal published fares and are aimed at a well-defined target audience such as military personnel, senior citizens, or students. For passengers to take advantage of these fares; some form of identification is usually required. Because the audience for these fares is small, the risk of diluting current revenues is minimal.

Flight-time-specific fares. To shore up a particularly weak flight in a market or as a basic competitive maneuver, carriers will sometimes offer lower time-specific or flight-specific fares. A common example is "night-flight" fares (for example, after 8 P.M.) that are 20 to 40 percent below comparable fares on earlier flights with higher demand. There is a risk in offering this kind of fare, because the improvement in the night flight's load factor and the increase in revenue may come at the expense of earlier, stronger flights in the same market as passengers alter their normal travel patterns to obtain the lower fare. When such cannibalization occurs, total market revenue may actually decline.

Mileage-based pricing. Although there are almost always aberrations due to competitive pressures, carriers generally attempt to relate price to distance flown, consistent with some price / mileage curve or mathematical function.

Zone pricing. This is a somewhat more streamlined variation of mileage based pricing. From Chicago, for example, destinations might be grouped into one of several regions (for example, Midwest, East Coast, Florida/South, West Coast), with each regional group carrying the same price. Logically, longer-distance regions are priced higher than shorter-distance ones.

Value-added pricing. Because fares can be matched so quickly through the ATPCO system, carriers sometimes seek a value advantage rather than an outright price advantage. Examples of value-added tactics are an offer of first-class seating for coach fares and extra frequent-flier credits for the purchase of higher-level fares. Ultimately, value-added price offerings also tend *to* be quickly matched by all competing carriers.

Adjusting Rules and Restrictions. This second set of tactics involves the periodic adjustment of rules and restrictions that accompany most fares rather than the dollar amount of the fares. Common rules and restrictions tactics include the following.

Advance purchase requirements. Airlines routinely adjust advance purchase requirements on excursion and discounted business fares. Advance purchase cutoffs are one of the key "fences" airlines erect to prevent business travelers from taking advantage of excursion fares. The advance purchase restriction on the lowest excursion fares tends to range from 7 to 30 days, while 3 to 7 days is the norm for business fares. The advance purchase restriction can be likened to a demand throttle: in periods of strong demand, longer advance purchase requirements prevail, on the presumption that higher-fare traffic will materialize as the departure date approaches. Conversely, in times weak demand, advance purchase requirements are less restrictive, that is shorter.

On-way versus round-trip purchase requirements. Excursion fares are usually designed to reamer a round-up purchase, primarily because their dollar value is so low. Conversely, higher-price business fares are usually offered on a one-way basis and typically can be combined with lower one-way fares, if available, to complete an itinerary. In an effort to maximize revenues, airlines will convert one-way business fares to round-trip purchase fares when three conditions exist: (1) the carrier offers a round-trip schedule pattern that will satisfy the passenger; (2) there is a high probability that any resulting fare increase (as passengers are unable to combine a higher one-way fare with a lower one) will more than offset an associated impact on demand; and (3) there is a strong likelihood that key competitors will match the move.

Minimum/maximum stays. Most lower excursion fares carry restrictions such as "requires a minimum three-day or Saturday night stay." The objective is to erect yet another purchase "fence" that business travelers cannot clear.

Fare penalties. These penalties apply to lower excursion fares and are triggered when a passenger cancels a reservation. Common examples are penalties of $25, $50, 50 percent of the ticket value, or even total forfeiture/non-refundability if it involves the lowest excursion fares. The objective is to impose these penalties as a revenue offset to the low fares and, more importantly, to shift seat inventory risk to the passenger. Carriers will periodically try to gain a secondary pricing advantage over one another by relaxing these types of penalties, but competitive matching is usually the end result.

Directional pricing. If an airline's sales are not appropriately balanced at either end of an O&D city-pair, perhaps because it lacks schedule strength in one of the cities, the carrier may attempt to lower fares on a directional basis from the weaker city.

Peak/off-peak pricing. Depending on the seasonality of demand in particular markets, as well as time-of-day and day-of-week patterns of demand, airlines will define certain days of the week and/ or times of the day as *"peak,"* which carry a $20 to $30 premium over "off-peak" prices.

Sales/ticketing/travel windows. As carriers periodically introduce lowest fares, they strive to craft a delicately balanced combination of sale, ticket mix and travel periods. They want a sale period that is long enough for. The advertising message to be heard but short enough to create a sense of purchase urgency 7 to 10 days is the norm. They also want a "ticket" by (date) defined to ensure a degree of control over the pricing initiative, as well as appropriate travel periods for the sale fares. Allowed travel periods usually span 60 to 120 days, during seasonally weak times of the year (for example, January-February and September-October). Travel periods that are too short don't generate the volume of traffic the airlines are seeking. Travel periods that are too long risk dilution of stronger, higher-yield traffic periods.

Pricing Analysis

The decision to use anyone, or a combination, of the tactics described is essentially a decision to raise or lower a fare. For example, increasing the advance purchase restriction from 3 to 7 days on a discounted business fare will force a certain number of passengers to buy the next higher fare. Correspondingly, by relaxing the advance purchase requirements on excursion fares from 21 days to 7 days and/or allowing for more "off-peak" days during the week, more passengers will be able to take advantage of a lower fare.

The proper economic analysis supporting the decision to change fares will differ, depending on whether it involves a fare reduction or an increase. In both instances, "elasticity" expectations are critical, but so are other factors, especially in the case of a fare decrease.

Steps in Analyzing a Fare Decrease. The pricing analyst first calculates the expected revenue gain (or loss) attributable exclusively to elasticity and then does the following:

1. ***Subtract dilution.*** Dilution results from those passengers purchasing the proposed lower fare who would have traveled anyway at the prior higher fare.
2. ***Subtract refunds.*** Airlines normally obligate themselves through the so-called guaranteed-fare rule to refund the dollar difference between a fare / ticket that has already been purchased and a proposed lower fare in the same fare class, provided that the passenger will still be able to travel on the date and flight originally reserved and meet the travel restrictions of the new, lower fare (for example, advance purchase and minimum stay requirements).
3. ***Subtract advertising.*** To the extent that previously unbudgeted funds are: dedicated to a particular pricing initiative, such an expenditure should be deducted as a step in calculating the net revenue gain, or loss, realize from the fare initiative.
4. ***Subtract additional variable passenger costs.*** Certain costs vary directly with passenger volume. Traffic liability insurance, food, and reservations fees are the expenses most commonly identified as truly variable costs. As a final step in estimating the net revenue generated from a fare reduction, the additional variable passenger costs incurred should also be deducted, particularly if the traffic increase is expected to be large.
5. ***Add spill.*** When a newly introduced fare is especially low and is matched by all major competitors in the market, it has the potential to stimulate primary demand to such a high level that certain carriers may benefit by picking up traffic that is "spilled" to them by other carriers that cannot accommodate all of their potential traffic due to excessive high load factors.
6. ***Add rejected demand by other airlines.*** At times, certain airlines will tight restrict the number of seats sold at a particular discount-fare level. On the assumption that they can fill the same seats with higher-fare passengers.

This can result in a "rejected" demand by the restrictive carrier, which can be absorbed by another carrier that is less restrictive in controlling its own discount seat inventory.

Steps in Analyzing a Fare Increase. In the case of a fare increase, there are fewer factors to consider in estimating the net economic impact. The formula becomes simply: revenue gain/ (loss) from elasticity, plus passenger variable costs avoided. With the introduction of a fare increase, spin and rejected demand are irrelevant. Likewise, there is no potential for refunds, and it is highly unlikely that a carrier will choose to advertise a fare increase. The one important nuance is that passenger variable costs will be lowered as a function of each passenger who, facing a higher fare, chooses not to fly or selects an alternate mode of transportation.

Price is an often overlooked marketing strategy, as many tend to focus on promotions or advertising. Pricing strategies, however, can have a large impact on sales and (more importantly) profit.

For clarification purposes, I am defining price as what your customer pays and/or what the end consumer pays for a product or service. In the case of products not sold directly to the end user, pricing is often described as "wholesale" and "retail." When the distribution channel is long (such as when there is a manufacturer, broker/distributor, retailer, and end consumer), multiple mark-ups can occur between the wholesale and the retail price.

Your optimal pricing strategy will depend on more than your costs. Forces within your business environment such as your competitors, your suppliers, the availability of substitute products, and your customers come into play as well. Positioning (how you want to be perceived by your target audience) is also a consideration.

PRICING STRATEGIES

There are a variety of pricing strategies in existence. Each strategy is used in a different set of circumstances. Some of the things to consider when choosing the best strategy for your situation are your costs; both short term and long term sales and profit goals; competitors' activities; and customer lifetime value. While there are others, a few of the more popular pricing strategies to consider are:

Premium Pricing

Use a high price where there is a uniqueness about the product or service. This approach is used where a substantial competitive advantage exists. Such high prices are charge for luxuries such as Cunard Cruises, Savoy Hotel rooms, and Concorde flights.

Penetration Pricing

The price charged for products and services is set artificially low in order to gain market share. Once this is achieved, the price is increased. This approach was used by France Telecom in order to capture the market share. The price is deliberately set at low level to gain customer's interest and establishing a foot-hold in the market. Penetration pricing. This is the opposite of price skimming. Prices are set low in an effort to gain large market share. Because the penetration

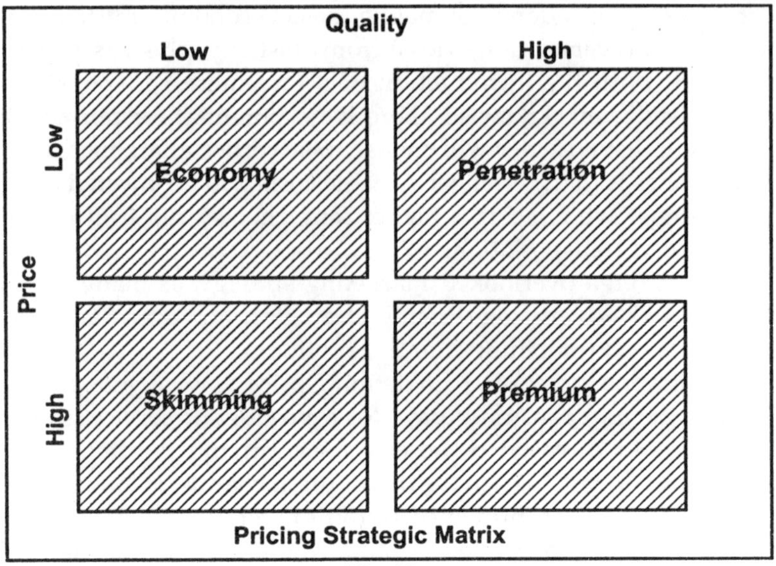

Fig. 23

price does not cover costs, this is also a temporary strategy. For this strategy to be profitable, customers must be willing to pay your normal, higher price later on.

Economy Pricing

This is a no frills low price. The cost of marketing and manufacture are kept at a minimum. Supermarkets often have economy brands for soups, spaghetti, etc.

Price Skimming or Creaming

Charge a high price because you have a substantial competitive advantage. However, the advantage is not sustainable. The high price tends to attract new competitors into the market, and the price inevitably falls due to increased supply. Manufacturers of digital watches used a skimming approach in the 1970s. Once other manufacturers were tempted into the market and the watches were produced at a lower unit cost, other marketing strategies and pricing approaches are implemented. Selling a product at a high price, sacrificing high sales to gain a high profit, therefore 'skimming' the market.

Premium pricing, penetration pricing, economy pricing, and price skimming are the four main pricing policies/strategies.

Competition Based Pricing

Setting the price based upon prices of the similar competitor products. Competitive pricing is based on *three* types of competitive product: Products have lasting distinctiveness from competitor's product. Here we can assume:

1. The product has low price elasticity.
2. The product has low cross elasticity.
3. The demand of the product will rise.
4. Products have perishable distinctiveness from competitor's product, assuming the product features are medium distinctiveness.
5. Products have little distinctiveness from competitor's product. assuming that:

   - The product has high price elasticity.
   - The product has some cross elasticity.
   - No expectation that demand of the product will rise.

When competitive pricing, you look at the prices different competitors are charging and use those prices as a benchmark when pricing your own products. You and your competitors' positioning strategies will determine whether you price at par, slightly below, or slightly above the competition.

The pricing is done based on these four factors.

Cost Plus Pricing

Cost-plus pricing is the simplest pricing method. The firm calculates the cost of producing the product and adds on a percentage (profit) to that price to give the selling price. This method although simple has two flaws; it takes no account of demand and there is no way of determining if potential customers will purchase the product at the calculated price.

Price = Cost of Production + Margin of Profit.

Cost plus mark-up. Here, you decide the profit you need to make before setting the price. Figure out your costs and your selling price is simply your costs plus your pre-determined profit number. This approach helps keep your profitability top-of-mind, but may also result in prices that are out-of-line with customer expectations and worth of your product or service.

Market Oriented Pricing

Setting a price based upon analysis and research compiled from the targeted market.

Price Discrimination

Setting a different price for the same product in different segments to the market. For example, this can be for different ages or for different opening times, such as cinema tickets.

Contribution Margin-based Pricing

Contribution margin-based pricing maximizes the profit derived from an individual product, based on the difference between the product's price and variable costs (the product's contribution margin per unit), and on one's assumptions regarding the relationship between the product's price and the number of units that can be sold at that price. The product's contribution to total firm profit (i.e., to operating income) is maximized when a price is chosen that maximizes the following: (contribution margin per unit) X (number of units sold).

Airlines Try New Pricing Moves

With high fixed costs and perishable products, airlines have long been the poster child for "yield management", "revenue management", and other sophisticated statistical methods for optimizing profit. Or minimizing losses. While travel is up, airlines are still looking for ways to maximize the return on their investment.

One approach is to unbundle products and services that fliers have traditionally consumed in bundled form. In flight meals and soft drinks now cost money on most domestic carriers on most domestic routes. Now Delta sells HBO movies, Northwest charges $15 for exit row seats, and Skybus will charge to check bags and board early. (See the NY Times article, free registration required.) As Skybus says, "Why should your ticket price include your neighbor's dinner?"

While unbundling makes a lot of statistical sense— you can target microsegments of people with different needs and price sensitivity— it adds to the already confusing mess of airline pricing, and to the uneasy feeling that the airlines are taking advantage of you. The article mentions an analogy by Henry H. Harteveldt, of Forrester Research, likening flying to going to the movies. "The popcorn is extra," he notes. However, even if people feel that $5 popcorn is ridiculous, the overall movie experience is pretty good. Flying is not entertainment, especially not these days. If airlines focused more on the customer experience, instead of having disgruntled staff stuffing angry travelers onto dirty planes, people would likely perceive the same pricing model in a different light.

In a less-noticed, but more momentous development, airlines have also started deeply discounting business class fares on routes that tend to leave these seats empty. Business fliers contribute disproportionately to the bottom line on business-heavy routes at certain times. On other flights and at off-peak times, the premium cabins are desolate. Travel expert Joe Brancatelli notes these pricing disparities in a recent column.

- If you need to zip from New York to London tomorrow to close a deal, expect to pay British Airways about 10 grand roundtrip to sit in its newly renovated Club World business-class cabin. But if you want to fly this summer and can book before the seasonal promotion ends this week, the price will be about $2,500.
  - Headed to Tokyo? A flight from San Francisco on Japan Airlines tomorrow will cost you more than $7,300. But book as little as three

days in advance and you may snag one of JAL's midweek "business saver" fares and pay just $4,600.

- Lufthansa normally charges $10,718 (including the fuel surcharge) to fly roundtrip to Frankfurt from Los Angeles. But the German carrier's recent "summer business class" sale cut the price to $2,988 roundtrip.

Not exactly cheap, but much lower than typical business fares. The airlines are betting that many of their well-heeled business fliers will pay a little more to enjoy their typical comforts when going on vacation. As long as the "fences" are good, what do they have to lose?

PRICING AND DEMAND

A fundamental characteristic of demand is that as price falls, the corresponding quantity demanded rises; alternatively, as price increases, the corresponding quantity demanded falls. In short, there is an inverse relationship between price and quantity demanded. Economists have labeled this inverse relationship the law of demand. Upon what foundation does this law or principle rest? Basically, common sense and simple observation. People ordinarily will fly more at lower prices than at higher prices. To passengers, high price is an obstacle that deters them from buying. The higher this price obstacle, the less they will buy; the lower the price obstacle, the more they will buy. Passengers will drive instead of fly; businesspeople will turn to telephone conference calls and the like as fares rise.

This inverse relationship between price and number of passengers purchasing tickets can be presented on a simple two-dimensional graph measuring estimated number of passengers on the horizontal axis and price on the vertical axis he resulting curve is called a demand curve. It slopes downward and to the right because the relationship it portrays between price and estimated number of passengers ticketed is inverse.

The law of demand-people buy more at a low price than they do at a high price-is reflected in the downward slope of the demand curve. What is the advantage of graphing our demand schedule? It permits us to represent

clearly a given relationship-in this case, the relationship between price and estimated number of passengers-in a simpler way than we could if we were forced to rely on verbal and tabular presentation.

Determinants of Demand

In constructing a demand curve, a forecaster assumes that price is the most important determinant of the amount of any product or service purchased.

But the forecaster is aware that factors other than price can and do affects, in our case, of tickets. Thus, in drawing a demand schedule or curve, the forecaster must also assume that other factors remain constant; that is the non-price determinants of the amount demanded are conveniently assumed to be given. When these *non-price* determinants of demand do in fact change *the location of the demand curve will shift to some new position to the right or left* of its original *position*

The major non-price determinants of *demand in* the *air travel market are:*

(1) preferences of passengers,
(2) the number of passengers in a particular market,
(3) the financial status and income levels of the passengers,
(4) the competitors and related travel expenses, and
(5) passenger expect respect to future prices.

Changes in Demand

Let us now examine the effect upon demand of changes in each of the aforementioned non-price determinants, using the same hypothetical example.

1. ***Preferences of passengers.*** A change in passenger preferences favorable to an airline-possibly prompted by advertising-will mean that more tickets will be demanded at each price over a particular time period, shifting the curve to the right. An unfavorable change in passenger preferences will cause demand to decrease, shifting the curve to the left. The airline sells fewer tickets than forecast at all prices offered during that time period. Preferences can include a number of factors, including an airline's image (United's "friendly skies," Delta's "professionalism"), perceived safety record, on-time reliability, in-flight and ground services afforded, gate position, type of aircraft flown, frequency of departure, and many more either real or perceived differences that relate to a passenger's preference for one airline over another.
2. ***Number of passengers.*** An increase in the number of passengers in a market-brought about perhaps by improvements in connecting flights or by population growth-will constitute an increase in demand. Fewer potential passengers will be reflected by a decrease in demand.
3. ***Financial status and income levels of passengers.*** This non price determinant relates to the state of the economy and the level of such things as personal income, disposable income, and profits (in the case of businesses). Air transportation is very sensitive to fluctuations in the economy. If the economy is in a recessionary period, with higher-than-normal unemployment and decreased factory orders, both business and pleasure travelers will be flying less. Conversely, when the economy is booms, businesspeople are traveling extensively and workers are not hesitant to make air travel plans.
4. ***Prices of competitors and related travel expenses.*** An increase in a competitor's price, all other things being equal, will normally prompt some passengers to switch to your airline. The reverse is also true:

if you raise your prices and your competitor doesn't, all other things being equal layout will-lose some business. An increase in the competitor's price will normally shift your demand curve to the right, and, assuming your prices hold and your competitor's prices drop, your demand curve will shift to the left. Economists refer to these as substitute or competing goods.

There are other related travel expenses that complement one another. For example, if motel and rental car rates are falling and these items make up 70 percent of the proposed expenses for a trip, the air fare price on a particular trip may be insignificant, relatively speaking. Thus, if a planned $1,000 vacation is unexpectedly obtainable through a package costing $550, the fact that the air fare went from $150 to $165, a 10 percent increase, becomes insignificant.

5. ***Passengers' expectations with respect to future prices.*** Passengers' expectations of higher future prices may prompt them to buy now in order to beat the anticipated price rises. Conversely, expectations of falling prices will tend to decrease the current demand for tickets.

A *change in demand* should not be confused with a *change in the quantity demanded.* A change in demand is a shift in the entire demand curve, either 10 the right (an increase in demand) or to the left (a decrease in demand). The passenger's state of mind concerning a ticket purchase has been altered because of a change in one or more of the determinants of demand. As used by forecasters, the term *demand* refers to a schedule or curve; therefore, a change in demand must mean that the entire schedule has changed or that the curve has shifted its position. In contrast, a change in the quantity demanded is the movement from one point to another point-from one price-quantity combination to another-on a fixed demand curve. The cause of a change in the quantity demanded is a change in the price of the ticket under consideration. Decide *whether* a *change in* demand or a *change* in *the quantity* de*manded is involved in each of the following illustrations:*

1. Airline B lowers its price on a particular flight, with the result that Airline A, with a flight departing 15 minutes later, loses passengers.
2. Airline C lowers its price on a particular route segment and experiences an increase in the number of passengers carried.
3. Passengers' incomes rise as a result of a turnaround in the economy, resulting in more vacation traveling.

TYPES OF PASSENGER FARES

Several types of fares are included in the passenger fare structure. Normal fares (also called *standard* or *basic fares*) are the backbone of the fare structure in that they apply to all passengers at all times (without restriction) and are the basis for all other fares. Separate normal fares are provided for each class of service: first class, coach, and economy.

Common fares are an unusual application of normal fares in that they apply a specific fare to points other than the points between which the fare is determined.

Joint fares are single fares that apply to transportation over the joint lines or routes of two or more carriers and that are determined by an agreement between them. Joint fares are becoming very popular between the major and national carriers and commuter (regional) lines.

Promotional fares are discounted fares that supplement the normal fare structure. They are always offered with some kind of restriction, such as minimum length of stay, day of the week, or season. Restrictions serve to minimize the risk of diverting full-fare traffic and maximize the generative benefit associated with the fare reduction. Examples include family-plan fares, excursion fares, group fares, and standby fares.

Promotional fares are normally used where load factors are below the optimum level. (Where load factors are above the optimum level, full-fare passengers would be displaced by discounted-fare passengers, thereby reducing revenue.) These discounted fares, because they are lower than normal fares, do reduce revenue yield per passenger. However, this reduction in yield is only undesirable, when the additional traffic generated is not enough to offset the price reduction.

Factors that Transforms Pricing

Aggressive lower cost carriers now drive industry pricing decisions. But in the past few years, the network airlines began working vigorously to approach the low-cost carriers' *cost* levels in the face of emerging passenger growth, lower business fares and higher fuel prices.

Three primary reasons for this transformation within the airline industry:

- **Internet fares:** Near universal pricing transparency has been achieved through individual carrier and independent travel booking entities' websites. These venues have eliminated the network carriers' near-monopoly control of the industry pricing structure.
- **The 2001 recession:** Even before the terrorist attacks on September 11, the 2001 recession sharply reduced the revenue stream for network carriers generated from business travelers willing to pay higher fares. This business downturn forced corporate travel managers to seek lower prices for travel. The increased pricing transparency provided by the internet enabled these businesses to more easily book travel at reduced price levels.
- **The impact of 9/11:** The severe traffic decline following September 11 forced the network carriers to cut flight operations and employee headcount significantly to limit their upward spiraling costs. The more conservatively positioned cost structures of the low-cost carriers enabled them to better withstand the initial revenue fallout from 9/11, and simultaneously, to begin to capture market share that had been voluntarily ceded by the network carriers in their cost reduction efforts.

These factors produced two further changes to industry pricing:

- **New pricing model**: The Southwest Airlines pricing model that established a specific fare ceiling was adopted at differing levels by other low-cost carriers – initially America West Airlines and Frontier Airlines. The ceiling approach reached the network carriers in January 2005 when Delta Air Lines introduced its Simplifares concept nationwide
- **Restrictions relaxed**: The network carriers relaxed travel restrictions, such as Saturday night stayovers, on some of their lower price restricted fares.

Determinants of Elasticity

Competition: Generally speaking, the more competition (the more substitutes and alternatives), the more responsive (elastic) consumers will be. For example, if four carriers are operating flights within 15 minutes of one another to a particular city and one offers a lower fare, a passenger likely will fly with that carrier, all other things being equal.

Distance: Long-haul flights tend to be more elastic than short-haul flights. Thus, vacationers will be responsive to a fare reduction of $100 on a $500 fare even if they have to leave between Tuesday and Thursday. Short-haul fare changes tend to be inelastic. A 10 percent increase on a $30 fare is only $3. A carrier will generally not experience a 10 percent or greater decrease in passengers for such a small amount.

Business Versus Pleasure: Business flyers tend to be less responsive to price changes than vacationers or individuals on personal trips. Why? Most business people are on expense accounts and have to make their trips within a certain period of time. Nor are they generally willing to take a late-night flight to take advantage of a discount. Vacationers can arrange their schedules and be much more elastic (responsive) to price changes if it is worth it to them.

Time: Certainly, if we have time, we can be much more responsive to price changes than if we do not. On the other hand, if we have little time and must be at a certain place at a particular time, we generally will be very inelastic with regard to price changes. For example, fares to Los Angeles may be going up by 20 percent next week, but if niece Kellie is getting married there next month, we cannot be responsive by flying out there now to save the extra 20 percent.

Building Blocks in Airline Pricing Policy

Of all the different facets of airline marketing, none has changed further or faster in recent years than the question of appropriate pricing policies, Today's airline managers are having to learn and apply skills which were either unknown or not needed by their predecessors. It is also a high profile area, where mistakes can result in large losses in a very short time.

Pricing—A Part of the Marketing Mix

In studying the question of appropriate policies for airlines it is first of all necessary to emphasise that pricing decisions cannot be made in isolation they can only be seen in the context of the Marketing Mix model. In particular, product and pricing decisions must clearly be made together. In recent years, many airlines have invested large sums in improving the specification of their First and Business Class products, with costly investments having been made in such things as better seats, higher quality catering and greatly improved in-flight entertainment. At the same time they have generally—and correctly—raised the prices of First and Business Class tickets in real terms, to provide a return on the investment that has been made. Today, though, it id becoming increasingly difficult to maintain these high prices in the face of recessionary conditions and overcapacity.

Deregulation

Until recently, the question of government regulatory policy was a major constraint on airlines' pricing freedom in international aviation. Almost all intergovernmental Air Services Agreements were written in terms which were designed to stop airlines competing on price. The airlines designated under these agreements were required to meet together, agree on what the fares should be, and file these fares with their respective governments for approval. Assuming that this approval was forthcoming—and it normally was—the airlines in question would implement a fare structure based on the principle that all those on a route would change exactly the same prices. Even in domestic markets—notably so in the USA—government regulation was imposed to prevent price competition, presumably in the hope of maintaining a stable industry.

The situation today is totally different. Many domestic markets have been completely deregulated with airlines free to price as they choose. In some international markets, too, a virtual deregulation of pricing has taken place. This is notably so with respect to the Single Aviation Market with the European Union.

Even in markets where the old facade of price regulation nominally remains, the situation today has still changed a great deal from that which prevailed only a few years ago. In these markets, it had been one of the functions of the International Air Transport Association (IATA) to run the Traffic Conferences at which fares are agreed. The machinery of so-called Tariff Co-ordination has become more flexible, with airlines gaining the freedom to innovate with their own promotional fares. Even where fares still fall within the responsibility of the Traffic Conferences it is an open secret that airlines have engaged in a great deal of under-the-counter tariff discounting, with IATA having discontinued what were described as its Compliance efforts. There were designed to ensure that carriers implemented the fares policies to which they had agreed.

It is impossible to exaggerate the significance of the moves towards deregulated pricing. They have allowed some airlines to develop a low cost low fares philosophy, something which they could never have done under the old regulated pricing regimes. This in turn has challenged incumbents to become more efficient and innovative. At the same time, managers responsible for pricing policy have had to develop a completely new set of skills. Under the former regime, the skills required were those of attending often-interminable IATA Tariff Co-ordination meetings and engineering a compromise between supposed competitors. Today, the skills are those of forming an appropriate rapid response to the pricing initiatives of these competitors, and deciding when the airline should lead the market in a change of pricing policy.

Dissemination of Fares Information

Until relatively recently, the pace of change in airline fares was slow. Regulated competition meant that all prices were a compromise, and reaching such a compromise was usually a drawn-out affair. At the same time, the system for disseminating fares information precluded rapid changes. The method for such dissemination was a printed tariff manual. Preparing these manuals ready for a fares change would in itself take many weeks, as would distributing them to the travel agents who needed them (The delivery of the tariff manuals to agents was a task generally undertaken by the airline's field sales executives.) The effect of all these factors was that the fares were only changed once a year or once every two years.

Again, the situation today could not be more different. The development of Global Distribution Systems has meant that almost all travel agents have instant access to a fares database which is up-dated (by the GDS firms) several times a day if necessary. Airlines which own websites also spread tariff information. The result it that the fare structure is now highly unstable at times of active price competition. Such competition will be especially prevalent during recessionary periods, when supply exceeds demand and airlines are fighting to fill otherwise empty seats. It will also break out in the autumn of each year on many routes as the summer peak period comes to an end and airlines compete for their share of the declining market.

At times such as these, millions of fares in the industry's main fares databases may change every day, challenging airline pricing managers not only to get their pricing decisions right, but to make these decisions quickly and under great pressure.

Revenue Management Systems

Clearly, the pricing environment today is a far more challenging one. There is, however, one major change which has made it easier for airline managers to develop sound pricing policies—the advent of sophisticated systems for managing the sale of seats (and, increasingly, of cargo space).

In deciding on pricing policies which will optimise financial returns, carriers must decide on the number of seats they will sell, at what prices and in what currencies. They must also make often difficult decisions about traffic which will be accepted, and which refused on the grounds that the yield obtained from it is too low.

Twenty years ago, there were no tools that would allow this process to be controlled effectively. Today, there most certainly are. Modem airline reservations computers allow the capacity on board each aircraft to be divided up into a large number of booking classes—currently 26 in the most sophisticated systems with larger numbers than this likely to be possible in the future. Decisions can then be made about the number of seats to be allocated to each class, and the time at which these seats will be made available for sale. These decisions will reflect different patterns of demand. For example, for a flight leaving to a business destination on a Monday morning, few if any seats will' be allocated to those classes allowing for early sale at low prices. Almost all of them will be in classes where sale will only be permitted at high fares, with many bookings only being made a relatively short time before flight departure. In contrast, a flight leaving to such a destination early on a Sunday morning will be given a completely different profile. Here, almost all the seats will be allocated to booking classes allowing for sale at low prices (or for their use by people redeeming frequent flyer programme miles) as the airline attempts to obtain at least some revenue from seats which might otherwise remain empty.

A particular problem in airline revenue management at the moment concerns the question of connecting versus point-to-point traffic. Generally, airlines earn a better yield on short-haul routes from passengers who are only flying out and back on the route, rather than from those who are using the short sector to fly to a hub, from where they will connect onto a long-haul service. Unless a revenue management system is monitored carefully, there will be a tendency for long-haul connecting traffic to be turned away, and point-to-point passengers to be accepted. This will improve the apparent financial performance of the airline's short haul routes whilst worsening the carrier's overall financial results because of the loss of so-called network revenue. In terms of the development of revenue management technology, many airlines are now attempting to produce the systems which will allow them to optimise revenue through taking account of the true origin and destination of passengers. This is, though, a challenging and intractable problem of software development.

"Uniform" and "Differential" Pricing

The Principles

Table 4 presents data which describes the present pricing structure of one of the airlines on the Heathrow—Toronto route. This route has not been selected on account of it having any special features. The situation there is a typical one, replicated on thousands of different routes around the world.

Table 4: Fare Structure, Heathrow—Toronto, January 2003

Fare Type	*Fare Level*	*Conditions*
J	£ 3,106 RTN	—
52	£ 1,015 RTN	Point-to-point only
"World Offer"	£ 406 RTN	Saturday night stay required 7 days advanced booking Mid-week travel only Non-refundable

The situation presented is one of considerable complexity. Prices vary enormously from the seemingly outrageous levels of Business Class fares down to the very low so-called "World Offer" fare. They also vary in terms of the conditions attached to each fare, with some fares—the more expensive ones—being fully flexible, and others having tightly restrictive limitations attached to their use.

To some degree, such wide differences in price levels are easy to explain and understand. In particular, the very high prices charged for seats in the First Class and Business Class cabins reflect substantial, tangible differences in the product supplied. As already discussed a modern state of-the-art Business Class cabin will have seats which fold down into full length beds. These will require a Seat Pitch of 70 inches or more. First Class passengers benefit from extravagant standards of in-flight service and entertainment. It is also generally the case that airlines operate their Business Class cabins at low average load factors, with figures of only 60-70% typical. It is clearly correct, therefore, that Business Class passengers should pay both for the seat they occupy, and also for the empty seats in a low load-factor operation.

Overall, whilst Business Class fare levels are very high, it is at least possible for airlines to justify them in terms of differences in the product offered. It is much harder for them to do this for Economy Class fares. Here people paying very different prices will sit in the same part of the aircraft, in the same type of seat. and will experience exactly the same in flight service and entertainment. Not surprisingly, there have been complaints that the existing fare structure is discriminatory. Those people who pay the higher fares argue that they are overcharged in order to subsidize the losses made on "below-cost" cheap fares.

Such arguments appear very convincing, but are incorrect. Both those who pay high fares and those who pay lower fares benefit from a properly applied differential fare structure. This is obvious in the case of low-fare passengers who are able to travel at a price they can afford. It is less obvious, but still the case, that the high-fare payers also gain substantially from differential pricing.

The critic of differential fares might argue that airlines should instead adopt a uniform approach to pricing in the Economy cabin. For example, the data given in Table 6: 1, stated that people in the Economy cabin could be paying a fare somewhere between £1,018 and £406 for a return ticket. A uniform approach to pricing would require that everyone should pay the same. The high fare would be lowered—perhaps to £700, and the lower fares would be raised to the same level.

Whilst such a situation might appear to be an ideal one, this would be far from the case, for two reasons. Firstly, Economy passengers do not all have the same needs, despite the fact that they all sit in the same cabin. In particular, business travellers have a requirement for flexibility which is absent in the typical product needs of the leisure traveller. Those flying on business will often have a requirement to obtain a booking shortly before a flight departs, because of some unexpected business crisis arising. They may also need to cancel a booking once they have made it and re-book on another flight due to their plans changing. Leisure travellers, on the other hand will generally book weeks or months before they fly and will only need to alter or cancel a booking on rare occasions due to factors such as illness.

If an airline is to meet these two sets of needs effectively it must adopt a different philosophy for capacity management in the part of the aircraft given over to business travellers, compared to that occupied by leisure flyers. If business travellers are to be given the flexibility they need, a relatively low year-round load factor will be inevitable. This is because the pattern of demand from such people has a random, unforecastable component to it. If seats are to be available at the last minute for a high proportion of the people who need them, substantial numbers of seats will have to be kept back in the airline's capacity management system—a number well in excess of the average demand for such seats. This will, of course, result in empty seats at take-off on days when the actual demand is low.

Overall, an airline successfully offering last minute seats and full ticketing flexibility to those of its customers who need them will do well to achieve a year-round load factor of 65-70% in the part of the aircraft allocated to this segment of the market. In contrast, an airline not seeking to give an on-demand product will be able to operate at much higher load factors, often in excess of 90%. Indeed, charter airlines in Europe which are certainly not in the "on-demand" business, do achieve these very high load factors consistently.

These differences in load factor give a first, important clue as to why fares have to vary in the Economy cabin, despite all the passengers there experiencing the same tangible product features. The tangible features are indeed the same, but the intangible one of flexibility is not. Prices must reflect the costs of providing these different degrees of flexibility.

Some of the arguments in favour of differential pricing can thus be based on questions of costs. Others, and ones of greater importance still, can be derived from the nature of airline market segmentation.

The advocate of a uniform approach to pricing might argue that such an approach would be an optimal one because people currently paying high prices would pay substantially less. This, however, is a quite false view, They would actually in the long run end up paying more, for an inferior product.

If we return to the data given in Table, the suggestion is that uniform pricing would see the fares charged to those paying the higher fare fall from the current level of over £1000 down to, say, £700. They would no doubt be pleased by this, arguing that this represents the amount by which they are now being overcharged. The situation would be less happy, though, for those passengers who are currently paying the lower fares. The proposition for these people is that their fares would have to rise to the uniform level, reflecting the end of the existing cross-subsidy of their fares by those currently paying higher prices.

In such a situation, it is most unlikely that the people concerned will simply pay the extra in order to continue travelling with the airline concerned. Most leisure air travellers have a high price-elasticity, reflecting the fact that they are paying fares out of their own pocket. Because of this, a sudden steep increase in ticket prices would result in some not travelling at all. A much greater number will continue to travel, but will choose an airline which is continuing to offer attractive low fares as part of a differential fare structure. Overall, an airline changing over from such a fare structure to one of uniform pricing might easily find that the number of passengers it carried fell by 40% or more.

The first reaction of business travellers to such a development might be to welcome it. They might argue that their air trips will be more enjoyable without revelling holidaymakers. They might also see it as a vindication of their arguments about cross-subsidy. Once the over-charging of business travellers to provide such cross-subsidy ceased, large numbers of leisure travellers could no longer afford to fly. Such an attitude would be foolish. There is a synergy available to airlines which carry significant numbers of both business and leisure travellers, and the business flyer is a major beneficiary of this. In particular airlines which participate in both the business and leisure markets are able *to* maintain a much broader network, with a better flight frequency than those which do not. Network and frequency are two of the prime product requirements of the business traveller. Also, such airlines are able to maintain frequencies whilst using larger aircraft. Aircraft show economies of scale whereby lower seat-kilometre costs can be obtained from larger planes. These cost advantages can in turn be passed on to passengers in the form of lower fares. Finally, all airlines have a proportion of their costs which must be regarded as fixed overheads. Expenses such as those associated with the reservation and revenue accounting systems, and brand-building advertising come into this category. Larger and larger numbers of passengers permit these costs to be spread more widely, again allowing fares to be lowered. On the other hand, a substantial fall in the numbers of passengers carried would not be followed by a pro-rata fall in overheads. If passenger numbers fell by *40%*, an airline might do very well to reduce overheads by, say, *20%*. The result would be that the remaining passengers would each have to cover a higher proportion of overhead costs if the airline is to achieve a profit. This will in turn lead to higher, rather than lower, fares.

Overall, uniform pricing will result in business travellers paying still higher prices for a worse product than they currently receive. It is not at all in their interests that such a pricing policy should be adopted, despite its superficial attractions.

An airline decision to adopt a differential pricing system should not be taken lightly. It may lead to anger amongst business travellers who think, that they are being overcharged. It will also inevitably lead to pricing structures which are very complex. This will in turn result in a costly database management task as fares information is stored and up-dated. It will necessitate a high training expense as staff have to be trained to understand and use the complex tariffs. Finally, it will result in a time-consuming point-of-sale task as the different fares have to be explained to often bemused passengers, and limit the build-up of Internet sales. It will, though, if correctly applied, bring significant benefits both to the airline in terms of its profit performance and to its customers. Interestingly, this is a view taken not only by most airlines, but also by other modes of transport. Railway operators, in particular, are now are major exponents of differential pricing principles.

Management of Discount Fares

Given the necessity for a differential rather than a uniform pricing structure, there are still difficult decisions for airline pricing managers to make regarding both the structure and level of prices. The offer of discount fares must be carefully controlled. Otherwise, passengers with a low price elasticity will take advantage of discount fares, causing a high degree of so-called "revenue dilution". Also, decisions about price levels must be made in an increasingly deregulated market, where airlines must both respond to the pricing initiatives of their competitors and decide when they should lead the market by a pricing initiative.

Control of discount fares is exercised in two ways. Firstly, and to an increasing degree, the revenue management system is used to decide on tre number of low-fare seats which are available on different flights. On off-peak flights, a large number of seats will be made available at low prices, reflecting the low marginal costs of seats, which would otherwise be flown empty. On peak-time flights, however, few if any low fares will be offered, forcing people who need to travel on these flights to pay higher prices.

The second way in which control is exercised is through the setting of restrictive conditions on discount fares, conditions which make them unattractive to the business traveller who is generally the person in a position to pay more. Some of these conditions, but by no means all of them, also help airlines by enabling them to carry low fare passengers at lower costs. We will now review each of the major types of discount fare condition:

1. Minimum Stay Conditions

Many discount fares require passengers to spend a minimum amount of time at their destination. On short-haul, routes, a Saturday night stay is often specified. This means that passenger cannot make return journeys earlier than the Sunday morning following their outbound trip. On longer routes, a minimum period of days—usually seven—which must be spent at the destination is sometimes defined. In both cases, passengers can return early if they wish to do so: However. they will have to pay the full fare.

These conditions, whether set as a Saturday night stay or a period of days, all have the same purpose. They are designed to restrict the business travellers' freedom-of-action. The Saturday night stay condition means that they must use the full fare to spend the weekend at home. Also, business trips usually last for only a few days in anyone place. Indeed, a salesperson on a sales tour may visit several countries on a two or three week business trip. The minimum stay conditions on the cheaper fares will ensure that they have to buy a full fare ticket in order to obtain the flexibility they need.

Generally, minimum stay rules are amongst the most effective of the conditions designed to protect airlines' high yielding traffic, providing they are strictly applied. It is, though, becoming more difficult to retain them on short-haul routes as traditional airlines face competition from "Cost Leader" players.

2. Maximum Stay Conditions

Maximum stay conditions define a maximum length of time that passengers can stay at their destinations and still return home using a cheaper discounted fare. If they stay longer than the stipulated maximum—45 or 60 day periods are often allowed—they will have to pay the full fare to return.

Generally, maximum stay conditions are a less effective way of controlling discount fares and their usage by airlines has declined in recent years. They may, though, have some effect in controlling dilution in that sometimes someone who is travelling to a destination and staying for several months may not be on holiday. Instead, they may be travelling on a business contract, in which case their employer will be paying the fare. They may be able to pay a higher price as a result.

3. Advanced Purchase

Advanced purchase rules are still sometimes applied to discount fares. They mean that passengers must book and pay for their ticket a defined minimum period in advance. They must also accept that there will be a substantial penalty if they wish to alter or cancel their booking once they have made it.

Advanced purchase conditions bring airlines a number of advantages. They improve cash flow. They also ease the task of capacity management in that they force low yielding demand to come forward at an early stage. Their most telling advantage, though is again that they make it difficult for the business traveller to use a lower fare. Many business trips arise in response to last minute emergencies and cannot be planned far in advance. Even where they can be, business executives often cannot accept the limits on their flexibility that a cancellation or rebooking penalty will cause.

4. Standby

Standby fares can be booked at any time. They do not, though, guarantee the passenger a seat on a particular flight. Instead, the passenger must report for a flight and wait. If there is an empty seat, they will travel. If there isn't, because the flight is full with higher yielding demand, the Standby passenger will not be given a seat. Instead, they will have their money refunded, or will have to wait for a later flight.

Standby fares bring a number of advantages. They are a genuinely cost-related lower fare, in that they are profitable as long as the fare paid exceeds the passenger-related costs of filling an otherwise empty seat. Also, they are often sold at the airport or at an airline's downtown ticket offices. Therefore, no' commission has to be paid on them. They penetrate the airlines to exploit a market for last minute, unplanned leisure travel decisions. Advanced booking requirements do not allow this. Of most importance, though, is the fact that, if properly managed, Standby fares protect airlines from revenue dilution. Except in the circumstances discussed below, a business traveller who has to attend an important meeting is unlikely to use a Standby fare to reach it, in view of the uncertainty involved.

Despite these advantages, the use of Standby fares remains controversial, and many airlines have backed away from them in recent years. They ate certainly unpopular with airport operators, because of the risk they carry that airport terminals will become crowded with people holding Standby tickets waiting for many hours—perhaps days—for flights on which they can be offered a seat. Also, a passenger holding a Standby ticket for a particular flight has an incentive to phone the airline to make extra bookings using false names, addresses and contact phone numbers. Finally, business travellers may find it surprisingly easy to take advantage of a Standby ticket. All they need to do is to buy a full economy ticket in advance of their flight. On arrival at the airport they check to see if the flight is fully booked. If it isn't, they then buy a Standby, fully confident that they will be offered a seat. The full-fare ticket is, of course, refundable. They would merely keep this ticket to claim their refund at a later date. Had they found the flight full, they would have used their full. fare ticket in order to get on it.

A final point about Standby fares is a particularly important one. Airlines should not offer Standby fares on their off-peak flights. This is apparent contradiction. Off-peak flights are those with the greatest number of empty seats, which the Standby fare can help to fill. If, though, Standbys are allowed on off-peak flights, the deflationary effects of doing so will be severe. Passengers who need to take the flight in question will still have a very high probability of getting it, despite the fact that they only hold a Standby ticket. In contrast, Standbys bought at the peak season will carry with them a significant risk that a seat will not be available. Business travellers in particular may not therefore be able to use them.

5."Preferential"

Fares Airlines today still offer many types of cheaper fare which are only available to named groups of passengers. These fares f can be divided into two types. First, what are known as *stage-of-life* fares. Examples include the special low fares offered to children, young people and to senior citizens. Second, airlines offer many *occupation-related* cheaper fares. Special fares are, for example, often given to seamen, to military personnel and to diplomats.

These "preferential" fares (they are sometimes, and better, described as "discriminatory" fares) give preference to named groups. Unfortunately, it is impossible to support them as a form of pricing for airlines. Those carriers that use them often find that they are offering an increasing number of discounts to a wider and wider range of their passengers. The reason is, of course, that once a discriminatory discount has been offered to one group, there are no reasons of principle to deny it to others. Airlines will therefore be subject to constant lobbying, to some of which they may eventually have to give way. Also, after a discriminatory discount has been introduced, it will be very difficult for airlines to withdraw it. Once a particular group has known the privilege of cheaper fares on a preferential basis, they will fight hard to retain this right.

6. Fares Only Available as Part of a Tour Package

These conditions limit the sale of fares to wholesalers, who are then supposed to add in the accommodation and other features which make up a packaged holiday. Only these complete holidays should then be retailed. If these rules are complied with, again the proposition becomes an unattractive one to the business traveller.

Pricing Response and Pricing Initiatives

Today, in price-competitive markets, pricing managers will be constantly faced with situations where they have to decide whether or not to respond to the pricing initiatives of their rivals. This may involve questions of responding—or not doing so—to the fares discounts that a competitor introduces. There may also be opportunities to lead the market either in terms of discounts, or in the raising of prices to improve yields.

In all these situations, it can, of course, be stated that every case is unique. Whilst this is undoubtedly true in principle, it is an unhelpful proposition in terms of airlines deciding on what their pricing policy should be. Instead, it can be argued that there is a series of questions which should always be asked. The answers to these questions will ensure that there is at least a consistency in an airline's pricing philosophy.

If we begin with the question of a rival airline coming into a market with discounted fares, the most fundamental question of all is to decide why they are doing so. There is a wide variety of possible reasons for an airline to offer discounts, reasons which will explain whether or not the initiative may be limited and short-term—in' which case it may be possible, to ignore it—or substantial and long-term, demanding action from competitors.

In terms of possible reasons for lowering fares, by far and away the most common is that the airline is suffering from an overcapacity problem It may have taken delivery of an aircraft type which is too big for the prevailing demand, or over-ordered in terms of the number of planes entering its fleet. Such mistakes may be exacerbated by the trade-cycle entering a downswing, so that forecast increases in demand—which might have filled the new capacity do not materialise.

In such a situation, other airlines will have little alternative but to respond to the challenge with which they are being faced. By responding, they will risk running into a loss-making situation. By not doing so. though, the fall in their market share may cause even worse problems.

Closely related to price discounting caused by overcapacity is the situation where an airline cuts fares in order to raise cash in the short term A carrier on the edge of bankruptcy will need to find the cash in order to payoff its most demanding creditors. If it cannot do so, these creditors may insist on the liquidation of the company, seeing this as the best hope of securing at least some of the money they are owed.

This type of pricing is often characterised as the "Dash-for-Cash." It poses an awkward problem for other airlines challenged by it. Their first reaction might be to respond fully by matching or even undercutting the lower prices of the failing airline. By doing so, they would hope to speed its decline into bankruptcy, resulting eventually in the removal of the competitor from the market altogether.

Today, such a reaction might be seen as over-hasty. If an airline disappears, it may be replaced by another, stronger carrier. The long-term result of a weak airline going into bankruptcy may therefore be that a favourable competitive situation is replaced by an unfavourable one. It is often better to allow a weak airline to raise sufficient cash to stay in business, by not fully responding to any desperate pricing initiatives it may undertake. Such a conclusion may be especially true in the USA where Chapter 11 of the bankruptcy code may allow an insolvent airline to survive for a considerable time using the expedient of court protection from its creditors. Whilst it does so. it may be able to price in a cavalier and destructive fashion because it knows that only its short-term creditors (in order to persuade them to continue to forward necessary supplies) rather than its long-term creditors will need to be paid.

There are other reasons why an airline may offer lower prices. A stan-up airline may do so, in order to gain useful publicity and to persuade people to try its services. Equally, a mature airline might do so when launching a new route serving a market where it is not well-known. In both cases, established players will have difficult decisions to make. If they match, or even undercut the newcomer they will undoubtedly make life very difficult. They will, though also dilute the yield obtained from the large number of passengers who would have continued to fly with them any way, despite the newcomer's presence.

They may also (within the European Union at least) risk court action being taken against them, with the accusation that they have abused a dominant position under the terms of Article 82 of the Treaty of Rome.

Once a view has been taken as to why a competitor is engaging in fare discounting, other questions then come into play.

The question of appropriate action will be very different in the situation where the price leader is a dominant player rather than a minor market participant. A large airline in its home market will have sufficient power to ensure that whatever pricing initiatives it takes, these will almost certainly have to be followed by its rivals. A minor player, though, may well be left alone if its overall impact on the market is small.

A further question is that of the number of seats made available at discounted prices. Modem revenue management systems allow a precise control to be kept not only on the prices which are offered, but also of the number of seats available at each price in an airline's differential pricing structure. There have been accusations from time to time that some carriers use advertisements describing attractive offers of lower prices in an unscrupulous way. These offers are designed to encourage people to contact the airline seeking the very low prices described in the advertisements. In fact, the airline ensures that very few seats are available for sale at these prices. Those making enquires are told that all the very low-priced seats have already been sold, but that seats are still available at a significantly higher fare. The aim is to "bait and switch" these people into buying higher-priced tickets.

Whilst the morality of such tactics are open to question, their implications for pricing policy are clear. Rival airlines should not over-react to the prices placed in newspaper advertisements. Rather, they should base their reaction on the number of seats being made available at the different fares. This can easily be checked by calling the airline in question and making enquiries about seat availability or logging on to its website.

A final issue with the question of response to a discounting competitor is the need to study past situations where price discounting has occurred in a particular market. Such discounting often has a seasonal component to it. It commonly breaks out at the end of the summer peak season as airlines position themselves for the quieter winter period. Careful study of the effect on market share and yield of past decisions to match or not to match rival's fare initiatives will certainly have a bearing on the question of appropriate responses to any current challenges being laid down by competitors.

The other major question airlines need to address in managing pricing and when they should take the risk of leading the market in terms of a price increase.

Sometimes, it will be possible to do this in consultation with rival airlines. In some international markets, it is still possible for competitor carriers to meet together at the Traffic Conferences organised by IATA These conferences can be used to discuss the levels of the higher, fully flexible, fates with hopefully (from the airline's point-of-view) agreement being reached that these fares should be raised in tandem. In other situations, all the different airlines serving a market may unite in a so-called Yield Improvement Programme (YIP), with again the questions of reduced availability of discount fares and fare increases on the agenda.

Today, the evidence is that such multi-airline approaches to tariffs management are only effective in situations where capacity and demand are in some sort of equilibrium. When they are not, one or two airlines will always break ranks in pursuit of their own commercial objectives. Once they have done so, any agreement will quickly break down due to the pressures of market forces. This is an especial problem in the difficult market conditions prevailing today.

In a situation where airlines are under pressure to raise their prices, it will often be the case that the requirement to do so is dictated by poor profitability. In turn, low profits or losses may be caused by cost increases. If they are, it will be vital to decide whether these increases are in "controllable" or "uncontrollable" costs.

"Uncontrollable" costs are those which airlines can do little or nothing to influence. Examples are the price of aircraft fuel and the level of en route navigation charges. If these rise, they will affect all airlines more-or-less equally. Presumably all airlines will then welcome the opportunity to raise prices on order to, hopefully, allow their financial position to recover.

"Controllable" costs are those which are within the control of airline management. By far the largest component of them for almost all airlines is that of labour costs. Typically, 30% of a carriers total costs will be made up of these costs. In pricing terms a very worrying situation is that where an airline fails to control its labour costs effectively by conceding an over-generous wage and salary settlement, or by allowing changes in work rules which damage productivity. Then, rival, better-managed carriers will not be affected to the same degree. They may in turn see competitive advantage in not matching any fare increases which might be put in place to cover higher costs, instead seeking to improve market shares on the basis of sustainable cheaper prices. Beyond any question, in a market where active price-competition is taking place, the effective control of these controllable costs is one if the central tasks which management must address.

Other factors to be taken into account is deciding whether or not to lead the market with a price increase, are the questions of the stage of the trade cycle, and the degree of market dominance which a carrier has. Generally, it is possible to raise prices much more easily in the up-swing period of the trade cycle when demand is recovering and deliveries of new aircraft comparatively small (due to airlines only ordering small numbers of planes during the preceding recession).

With regard to market dominance, generally it is a strong airline in its home market which will decide when prices will rise in that market. Smaller players will often have little choice but to follow the initiatives taken by their stronger rival.

All-in-all, the questions of pricing response and pricing initiatives illustrate the enormous changes which have come about in the skills required to manage pricing in the airline industry. Today, it is a question of judging, quickly, the pricing decisions which need to be made, in the ever-present knowledge that mistakes will result in large financial losses.

Revenue Management

Revenue Management is a technique to optimize the revenue earned from a fixed, perishable resource. The challenge is to sell the right resources to the right customer at the right time.

Revenue Management implements the basic principles of supply and demand economics in a tactical way to generate incremental revenues. There are three essential conditions for revenue management to be applicable:

1. That there is a fixed amount of resources available for sale.
2. That the resources sold are perishable. This means that there is a time limit to selling the resources, after which they cease to be of value.
3. That different customers are willing to pay a different price for using the same amount of resources.

Revenue Management is of especially high relevance in cases where the constant costs are relatively high compared to the variable costs. The less variable costs there are, the more the additional revenue earned will contribute to the overall profit.

For example in the passenger airline case, capacity is regarded fixed because changing what aircraft flies a certain service based on the demand is the exception rather than the rule. If the aircraft departs, the unsold seats cannot generate any revenue any more and thus can be said to be perished. It's finally trivial that a businessman is willing to pay more for a seat when booking late than a leisure traveller is willing to pay for a trip due in several months.

If the resources available are not fixed or not perishable, the problem is limited to logistics, i.e. inventory or production management. If all customers would pay the same price for using the same amount of resources, the challenge would perhaps be limited to selling as quickly as possible, e.g. if there are costs for holding inventory.

One way of achieving a different willingness to pay is to achieve effective market segmentation. A firm may repackage its basic inventory into different products to this end. In the passenger airline case this means implementing e.g. purchase restrictions, length of stay requirements and requiring fees for changing or cancelling tickets.

Price and/or availability of these products may be manipulated to maximize the expected future revenue based on detailed statistical demand forecasts and mathematical optimization. The passenger airlines achieve this by implementing either demand based pricing or extremely sensitive and dynamic availability controls, or both, on their reservation systems.

Revenue is often 'left on the table' by firms that do not effectively segment their market. Although the exact mechanisms used to implement price and availability controls vary between industries the underlying business process and mathematical techniques have a remarkably broad applicability.

Revenue Management has significantly altered the travel and hospitality industry since its inception in the mid 1980s. It requires analysts with detailed market knowledge and advanced computing systems who implement sophisticated mathematical techniques to analyze market behavior and capture revenue opportunities. It has evolved from Yield Management which the airlines invented as a response to deregulation and quickly spread to hotels, car rental firms, cruise lines, media, and energy to name a few. Its effectiveness in generating incremental revenues from an existing operation and customer base has made it particularly attractive to business leaders that prefer to generate return from revenue growth and enhanced capability rather than downsizing and cost cutting.

Revenue Management "... the single most important technical development in transportation management since we entered deregulation...".—Robert Crandal, Chairman and CEO of American Airlines Revenue Management is most effective in a high capital cost, low marginal cost environment. This is because it focuses on maximizing expected marginal revenue for a given operation and planning horizon. It optimizes resource utilization by ensuring inventory availability to customers with the highest expected net revenue contribution and extracting the greatest level of 'willingness to pay' from the entire customer base. Revenue Management practitioners typically claim 3% to 7% incremental revenue gains due to revenue management activity. In many industries this can equate to over 100% increase in profits. A competent revenue management analyst with good decision support tools can generate $10,000 per hour.

Deregulation is generally regarded as the catalyst for RM in the airline industry, but this tends to overlook the role of Global Distribution Systems (GDS's). It is arguable that the fixed pricing paradigm occurs as a result of decentralized consumption. With mass production, pricing became a centralized management activity and customer contact staff focused on customer service exclusively. Electronic commerce, of which the GDS's were the first wave, created an environment where large volumes of sales could be managed without large numbers of customer service staff. They also gave management staff direct access to price at time of consumption and rich data capture for future decision-making.

Although Yield Management had been a common practice in the airlines in the early 1980s, Revenue Management may reasonably assigned an inception date of January 17, 1985 when American Airlines launched Ultimate Super Saver fares in an effort to compete with low cost carrier PeopleExpress. Donald Burr, the CEO of PeopleExpress, is quoted in the book "Revenue Management" by Bob Cross saying "We were a vibrant, profitable company from 1981 to 1985, and then we tipped right over into losing $50 million a month...We had been profitable from the day we started until American came at us with Ultimate Super Savers." The Revenue Management systems developed at American Airlines were recognized by the Edelman Prize committee of INFORMS for contributing $1.4 billion in a three year period at the airline.

Revenue Management spread to other travel and transportation companies in the early 1990s.

Airline Revenue Management

Key Capabilities of Airline Revenue Management:

1. Forecasts demand, cancellations and no-shows for each of your market segments.
2. Forecasts customers' demand sensitivity to price.
3. Offers optimization solutions for setting optimal selling prices or optimal inventory allocation depending on business requirements.
4. Tailors quotes to each specific competitive situation.
5. Allocates inventory so you do not turn away the most valuable customers or fly with empty seats when demand exists for them.
6. Quickly responds to competitive changes in the marketplace.
7. Manages overbooking of inventory to balance the risk of displacing passengers against the risks of flying with empty seats.
8. Monitors the overall revenue performance of the controls in order to explain results and guide future decisions.

Airline Revenue Management helps airlines maximize revenue and profits by accurately forecasting future demand, optimizing price plans and optimally allocating capacity, based on passenger price sensitivity as a key driver. It runs frequent optimization of prices and controls based on price-sensitive demand, available capacity and airline business rules, and provides optimization of overbooking along with powerful reporting and data exploration capabilities.

The solution is scalable to the requirements of airlines of almost any size. As the nature of the airline business changes with increasingly price-sensitive passengers, new competitors and more diverse distribution, JDA's next-generation price-sensitive Revenue Management solutions provide airlines with the ability to optimize every transaction in every individual market segment. These leading-edge solutions support frequent and accurate calculations of optimum prices and inventory controls that reflect and exploit the changing demand conditions in order to deliver increased profitability.

Cargo Revenue Management

Key Capabilities of Cargo Revenue Management:

1. Generates enhanced revenue and profit throughout your trading network.
2. Provides reliable demand forecasts.

3. Optimizes routings for each request.
4. Supports sales by providing rapid responses to booking requests.
5. Supports operations by checking loadability at booking acceptance time.

"An accurate demand forecast is a vital step in maximizing revenue and cargo capacity utilization for each flight. JDA's Cargo Revenue Management solution provides more accurate forecasting with a longer horizon that allows us to plan budgets, forecast revenue and optimize prices with better information."

In the cargo environment, business is often dominated by relationships, which means that transactions need to be evaluated in context. For each transaction you must consider several factors: the total business offered by the customer, the multiple dimensions of capacity and any erratic customer-tendering behavior. In such a setting, where market conditions are dynamic and the issues complex, Cargo Revenue Management offers a rich opportunity for your company to enhance revenues and profits.

Cargo Revenue Management routinely considers the complexities surrounding your decision process – late bookings, shifting capacity and demand, competitor actions, variable and opportunity costs, market share objectives, and other conditions. Based on these criteria, the system provides critical business decision support for a variety of markets, products, customer segments and distribution channels – every day.

The solution's transaction manager is designed to help you make the best possible business decision based on the most important criteria. Using advanced statistical methods and algorithms, Cargo Revenue Management forecasts customer demand for your products and your available capacity. Based on this forecast, it then determines the optimal price to assign capacity in each market according to origin and destination – helping you make the most of every transaction to enhance your system-wide profit.

AIRLINE DISTRIBUTION PLANNING

Distribution (also known as the *place* variable in the marketing mix, or the 4 Ps) involves getting the Airline product from the operators to the ultimate consumer. Distribution is often a much underestimated factor in airline marketing. Many marketers fall for the trap that if you make a better product 7 better services, consumers will buy it. The problem is that Travelling agents may not be willing to devote shelf-space to new offers. Ticket sellers would often rather use that shelf-space for existing offers of the other airlines have that proven records of selling.

Although many Airlines advertise that they save the traveller's/customers money by selling direct and "eliminating the middleman," this is a dubious claim. The truth is that intermediaries, such as Travel agents like IATA, tend to add efficiency because they can do specialized tasks better than the consumer or the airlines. Because customer can buy conveniently and as per his requirement the tickets are available. Thus, Booking agents or direct airline agents add efficiency by:

- *Retail sale*—the consumer can buy small quantities at a time.
- *Availability of tickets-the consumer can buy any time (Subject of airline confirmations).*
- *Carrying authorizations.*
- *Discounts and Financing*—Some time.

For a service to be of value to consumers, it must be available when and where they want it. The place element in the marketing mix includes all institutions and activities that contribute to delivering the product at the times and to the places consumers desire-in other words, convenient facilities or sales outlets where customers can purchase the service.

Channel structures vary somewhat by the nature of the product. Jet aircraft are custom made and shipped directly to the airline. Automobiles, because they are difficult to move, are shipped directly to a dealer. Other products are shipped through a wholesaler who can more efficiently handle, and combine, products from many different suppliers. Several layers of wholesalers may exist, depending on the product. Occasionally, agents may also be involved. Agents usually do not handle products, but instead take care of the business aspect of negotiating with distributors, which manufacturers may feel uncomfortable or ill prepared for doing themselves.

Manufacturers of different kinds of products have different interests with respect to the availability of their products. For convenience products such as soft drinks, it is essential that your product be available widely. Chances are that if a store does not have a consumer's preferred brand of soft drinks, the consumer will settle for another brand rather than taking the trouble to go to another store. Occasionally, however, manufacturers will prefer selective distribution since they prefer to have their products available only in upscale stores.

Parallel distribution structures refer to the fact that products may reach consumers in different ways.

Most products flow through the traditional manufacturer → retailer → consumer channel.

Certain large chains may, however, demand to buy directly from the manufacturer since they believe they can provide the distribution services at a lower cost themselves. In turn, of course, they want lower prices, which may anger the traditional retailers who feel that this represents unfair competition. Firms may also choose to utilize factory outlet stores. To allay concerns held by conventional stores, however, these factory outlet stores are usually located in areas where they are not easily accessible.

We must consider what is realistically available to each firm. A small manufacturer of potato chips would like to be available in grocery stores nationally, but this may not be realistic. We need to consider, then, both who will be willing to carry our products and whom we would actually like to carry them. In general, for convenience products, intense distribution is desirable, but only brands that have a certain amount of power—e.g., an established brand name—can hope to gain national intense distribution.

Note that for convenience goods, intense distribution is less likely to harm the brand image—it is not a problem, for example, for Haagen Dazs to be available in a convenience store along with bargain brands—it is expected that people will not travel much for these products, so they should be available anywhere the consumer demands them. However, in the category of shopping goods, having Rolex watches sold in discount stores would be undesirable—here, consumers do travel, and goods are evaluated by customers to some extent based on the surrounding merchandise.

In general, a brand can expect lesser distribution in its early stages—fewer retailers are motivated to carry it. Similarly, when a product category is new, it will be available in fewer stores—e.g., in the early days, computer disks were available only in specialty stores, but now they can be found in supermarkets and convenience stores as well. Certain products that are not well established may have to get their start on "infomercials," only slowly getting entry into other types out outlets. (Please see PowerPoint chart).

Different parties involved in the marketing of products tend to have different, and often conflicting, interests:

- *Full service retailers* tend dislike intensive distribution.
- *Low service* channel members can "free ride" on full service sellers.
- *Manufacturers* may be tempted toward intensive distribution—appropriate only for some; may be profitable in the short run.

Market balance suggests a need for diversity in product categories where intensive distribution is appropriate. Service requirements also differ by product category.

Diversion occurs when merchandise intended for one market is bought up by a distributor that then ships it to a different market. Sometimes, a manufacturer will run a promotion in one region but not in another, and speculators will then buy extra quantity in the promoted area and ship it another area. The speculator will then sell it to local retailers or distributors for a price slightly lower than what is being charged through the regular channel but at a price that still allows a nice profit. Certain products sell for different prices in different countries. As we discussed in the unit of international marketing, a gray market occurs when a product is bought in one country and exported to another where the price is generally higher.

Distributing the Airline Product

In all areas of marketing links must be made between the customer and the product. These links are known as Distribution Channels. Airlines use a variety of these channels. All of them are giving rise to particularly intense debate at the present time, because the different channels result in different costs, and because they vary in the extent to which they allow airlines to exercise proper and necessary control of the channel. The purpose of this chapter is to consider these controversies, and to analyse current developments in the field of airline distribution.

Distribution Channel Strategies

Types of Distribution Channel

In any industry, firms can choose from different types of distribution channel. Some may opt for the *direct* route. This is where the producer makes direct contact with the final customers for its product, without any intermediaries being involved at all. This channel philosophy is normal in the industrial marketing of big-ticket capital goods. It certainly has been usual in the field of aircraft manufacturing, though the rise of the specialist operating lease companies has provided an intermediary between tbe aerospace firms and their final customers, the airlines. In marketing activities involving less costly items a direct approach might still be adopted. For example, some firms choose to deal direct by selling their goods through mail order, backed by extensive advertising aimed at final customers, or increasingly, over the Internet.

Direct channels bring the advantage that no mark-ups or commissions have to be paid to channel intermediaries. They also allow producers to keep complete control of their marketing activities. The problem is that they may make it difficult for the producer to achieve sufficient geographical coverage, though in some areas (notably so, insurance), this is being overcome as a result of peoples' increasing willingness to buy over the telephone or on-line.

In many industries, producers make use of *wholesalers*. These are the firms which buy in bulk from a range of producers, using their buying power to gain appropriate discounts. They then in turn sell on the goods, either by adopting a direct sell policy themselves, or by in turn using *retailers*. Retailers buy from wholesalers, and sell to the final customer for the product.

The essence of both wholesaling and retailing from the producer's point of view is risk-taking. Discounts will have to be given to allow an opportunity for mark-ups to be added and profits to be made by the intermediaries. In turn, though, the producer's risks are reduced because once the goods have been sold to a wholesaler or retailer, unsold goods cannot normally be returned.

The remaining type of channel relationship is that of the *agency*. Such a relationship is common in service industries where there is only an intangible rather than a tangible product offered for sale. In such industries, producers often require wide geographical coverage, but find it costly or impossible to provide this in their own. They therefore use agents, who are paid a commission each time they sell on behalf of a particular firm. The agent is able to make a living by selling a variety of products on behalf of many firms, in what should be a mutually beneficial relationship. The problem, of course, is that because agents are selling on behalf of many firms, they may be tempted to use their market leverage by working harder to sell the products of the firms which pay them higher commissions. Firms in turn may leapfrog each other's commissions in an attempt to secure agent's support, resulting in an inexorable rise in commission costs. Exactly this process was prevalent in airline marketing in the 1990s.

The aviation industry illustrates all of these different forms of channel relationship. In many ways, the role of the aircraft leasing company is that of a wholesaler. Firms such as ILFC and General Electric Capital Aviation Services buy large numbers of aircraft from the manufacturers and are given substantial price discounts for doing so. They then lease out these aircraft to their customer airlines. and in buoyant times make substantial profits as a result. They do, though, assume significant risks. In a market downturn, large numbers of aircraft may be returned to them by lessees, and, due to a glut of capacity in the market it may be difficult or impossible to place these aircraft with new customers or sell them in order to realise their second hand value. Indeed, in the major recession of the early 1990s, the then-largest operating lease company, GPA, could not survive and was taken over on the edge of bankruptcy.

Another example of a producer/wholesaler relationship is that between charter airlines and tour operators in the European holiday industry. The principle here is that the airlines produce plane-loads of capacity which are then sold to tour operators. In turn, the operators add in accommodation, surface transfers and. other features of a holiday such as cultural tours or sporting opportunities, to make up a complete package. The tour operators are then responsible for retailing these packages to the final customer.

Scheduled carriers may also adopt a wholesaling approach by selling seats to tour operators, though when they do, the tour operators often have a greater freedom to return unsold seats than they have in their dealings with charter carriers.

In terms of agency relationships, it is of course the travel agency system which has been dominant distribution channel for airlines. The percentages are declining, but many airlines still find that over 80% of their tickets are sold by travel agents. The trend until recent years was in fact for this percentage to rise, with the forces of deregulation allowing the travel agency industry to cement its position as the industry's dominant distribution channel. Deregulation often means rapid changes in airlines' schedules and fares. Often, the bemused consumer has been forced to turn to an agent in order to find up-to-date information without the chore of contacting each of the airlines serving a route individually.

In recent years, direct selling has become significant as traditional airlines have supplemented direct selling through sales shops and call centres with an increasing emphasis on web-based business. New airlines have appeared which largely or totally ignore the travel agency industry.

The Concept of "Super-Profits"

The reason is simple: control of distribution channels is one of the most powerful drivers of profits in any industry, and this is especially the case in the airline business.

The concept of the control of distribution channels is a straightforward one. In any channel where wholesaler, retailers or agents are involved. producers must ensure that they are in a position to control the rewards received by these channel intermediaries. If a wholesaler, retailer or agent is in a powerful position, they will not be able to do so. Instead, the intermediaries will be able to play one producer off against another, only supporting those who outdo the others in terms of their offer of mark-ups or commissions. In turn, producers will receive only the rewards needed to keep them in the business from year to year. The "Super-Profits"—profits over and above these basic rewards—will accrue to the intermediaries who are able to exercise control.

There are a number of danger signals which indicates a probability that producers will lose effective channel control. One is that each intermediary, controls a significant share of the market. For example, in the UK grocery market, the scene is dominated by three giant supermarket chains, Sainsbury's, Tesco and Walmart. Today, any producer of grocery products has to ensure that it goods are stocked by these firms. If they are not, then they will not be able to reach something like 70% of the UK market. The supermarket firms are thus in an extremely strong bargaining position, a position emphasised by their robust profit performance in recent years.

The other worrying indicator of problems for producers is that their product is perceived as a "commodity" rather than a "brand". The subject of brands management is now a crucial one in airline marketing and the whole of the next chapter is devoted to it. Briefly, though, a commodity situation is one where customers perceive the products of competing suppliers to be identical. The brands case is the opposite of this, where customers see significant differences between the products of alternative suppliers.

The commodity case is the ideal one for wholesalers, retailers and agents seeking to establish and retain control of a distribution channel. This is because customers have no strong preference as to which firm's products they buy. Therefore the intermediaries will be in a perfect position to play one supplier off against another, because it will be irrelevant from the customer's point-of-view as to which producer is supported.

In some industries, commoditisation of the product has become so complete that the only way forward for producers wishing to protect their "Super-Profits" is to own, or at least franchise, their own distribution channel. This is the case, for example, in the petrol (gasoline) industry where in most countries the firms which refine petrol also own a network of filling stations. It is very difficult indeed for a stand-alone refiner of petrol to earn a reasonable return, given the clear perception of many people that petrol is a commodity. One's car run exactly the same whichever type of petrol is put into it.

Another sector where ownership of the distribution channel by producers has become the norm is in that of the European package holiday/charter airline area. Seats on charter airlines are often perceived as a commodity by vacationers, in the sense that very few will specify the airline with which they wish to travel when booking their holiday. Indeed many people do not know the identity of their airline until they arrive at the airport on their day-of-departure. Because of this, it is difficult for independent airlines which have no links to their distribution channels to survive. Such airlines can often make reasonable profits when demand is buoyant and capacity limited, as will generally be the case during the up swing period of the trade cycle. They will find life much more difficult in a recession, when capacity will exceed demand and where market power will swing strongly to tour operator intermediaries. These firms will easily be able to play the independent charter airlines off against each other because passengers have no great preferences as to with which airline they fly. The result will be strong profits for the tour operators and weaker ones for the airlines, to the point where some of the airlines may not be able to survive. A case-in-point was the UK airline Dan-Air, which disappeared (through a take-over by British Airways) in the recession of the early 1990s, for exactly the reasons described.

A better situation in the market of airlines and tour operators is where the airline either owns, or is owned by, its distribution channel. For example, the UK's biggest charter airline, Britannia, Thomson Holidays (Britain's largest tour operator) and Lunn-Poly, the travel agency with the biggest high-street presence, are all subsidiaries of the same parent company (the German firm TUI). The airline therefore knows that it has guaranteed outlet for its production even at times when market conditions are difficult.

One final point needs to be made about distribution channel management. In almost all sectors of the economy there are very substantial differences in the capital invested by producers I and by intermediaries. This is certainly the case in the field of travel.

Airlines have to invest truly vast amounts in aircraft in order to grow and develop their businesses. For example, the purchase of just one wide bodied aircraft, will involve an outlay of perhaps $180—$200 million. A fleet of these planes will involve a risky investment of billions of dollars. In contrast, investments made by tour operators and travel agents will be tiny by comparison. It is absolutely essential that airlines should be control of their distribution channels so that they can earn the "Super. Profits" which will give their shareholders a fair return on their money.

The Travel Agency Distribution System

Advantages and Disadvantages

Having established the general principles, it is now necessary for us to look in more detail at the particular issues raised by the past general reliance on the travel agency distribution channel in the airline industry. In this context, it cannot be emphasised too strongly that this reliance always brought airlines very important benefits. Exactly as one would expect with an agency relationship, one of these was geographical coverage. An airline would find it prohibitively expensive to have its own sales shop in every high street and shopping mall around the world. Yet some passengers like a personalised source of tickets, and someone they can turn to for advice and help. A travel agent provided such a presence by selling tickets on behalf of all airlines and tour operators, and by also offering services such as hotel, car rental and theatre bookings. Agents could—and still can—identify and explore specialist niche markets such as those dealing with hobbies like golf and winter sports, and those focussing on particular ethnic groups.

A second advantage of agency relationships is that they were not a heavy overhead burden on the airlines. It is true that all airlines had to incur the costs of agency support in the form of such things as training for agency staff and special telephone lines to deal with agents' enquiries. The principle though of the agency relationship was that the airline only had to reward the agent when the agent concluded a piece of business on the airline's behalf. This was in contrast, say, to an airline owned and operated sales shop in a city centre, which was an overhead cost burden on the carrier at all times, whether or not any business was actually being transacted.

A final point about the airline/agency relationship is that agents have undoubtedly relieved airlines of a great deal of the costly administrative work associated with air travel. For example an agent would issue tickets, assist with visa applications and deal with passengers' queries about airport check-in times, baggage rules etc. If they had not done so, carriers would have had to employ extra staff and resources. Generally, too, airlines paid their staff higher salaries than the poor levels of pay which were generally prevalent in the travel agency sector. Travel agents could therefore probably carry out this work at lower costs than would prevail if airlines had done it themselves.

Despite these obvious and strong advantages, the airline/travel agency relationship was the subject of increasing disquiet during the 1990s, and has now seen revolutionary reform.

Table 5 presents data on the commission costs of British Airways between 1986 and 1996. It is especially valuable data, because it separates out commissions from other selling costs. Normally, it is not possible to do this, as many industry data sources only present as an aggregate cost category of "Ticketing, Sales and Promotion" which includes reservations and advertising costs alongside those of commissions.

The picture painted by the table is a disturbing one, and was typical of almost all airlines. During this time commissions increased in absolute terms of monetary payments. They also rose sharply as a proportion of the airline's operating costs (admittedly, partly because other costs fell, especially the costs of aircraft fuel).

Table 5: British Airways: Commission Costs 1986-96

YEAR	*BRITISH AIRWAYS*		
	Total Operating Expenses £m	*Commission £m*	*Per cent*
1986	2,644	223	8.43
1987	2,947	269	9.12
1988	3,559	332	9.32
1989	4,029	391	9.70
1990	4,373	467	10.67
1991	4,444	506	11.38
1992	4,772	563	11. 79
1993	5,289	650	12.28
1994	5,580	768	13.76
1995	5,878	821	13.97
1996	6,612	916	13.85

Source: CAA Annual Statistics.

There were a number of reasons why this should have happened. As has already been stated, the period covered by the table was a time when the proportion of tickets written by agents rose still further, as the travel agency industry was able to use the confusion associated with deregulation to further cement its control. Also, this was when more and more tickets were being paid for using credit cards, and carriers were having to payout increasing commissions to credit card companies. Nonetheless, we are safe to draw a conclusion that for UK airlines at least, the travel agency distribution system had become very expensive. The same conclusion could be reached for the US domestic market, another where disaggregated data were available. It was also strongly suggested by the actions taken elsewhere to control commission costs, to which we will turn shortly.

Rising commission costs were in themselves worrying. They might have been justified, though, from an airline viewpoint, if they had resulted in investment going into improving the distribution channels so that carriers were being better served by these. Unfortunately, one's suspicion was that this was not the case, or at least that the level of investment by the travel' agency industry was inadequate to sus1ain such a conclusion. Increasing commissions were often used by travel agents to finance an intensive market share battle between themselves rather than for investment to provide airlines with better distribution channels. Such competition took on two forms. Firstly, in pursuing market share of the business travel market, agents were often prepared to pass on a proportion of the commission they earned to their retail customers in the form of discounts, either to build the loyalty of their existing clients, or to buy that of the clients of other agencies. Secondly, with sales to the leisure market, the manifestation of higher commissions came in the form of a proliferation of sales outlets as firms have opened more and more retail shops to strengthen their geographical presence in the market relative to that of their rivals.

In both cases, airlines' money, through higher commissions, was used to finance agents' battle for market share. This was not an acceptable situation, especially bearing in mind the huge investments (mainly through aircraft purchases) made by airlines in the future of the industry, and the comparatively small investments made by agents.

All in all, the situation of airlines with respect to their distribution channels was a very mixed one by the end of the 1990s and was ripe for reform. The travel agency distribution system brought them important advantages, advantages emphasised by the domination of travel retailing which the system achieved. There were, though, significant problems too. The question for airline business strategy was therefore very clear. How could distribution channels be developed so that the advantages were retained, whilst the problems and shortcomings were alleviated?

Today's Distribution Channels

The situation regarding distribution channels today can be traced to a process of reform which dates back several years. In 1996, some airlines began to make radical changes. Market conditions at the time were very buoyant, something which is always likely to favour producers at the expense of intermediaries. At the same time, it began to become clear that the Internet held out the promise of being an alternative distribution channel which could challenge the dominance of the travel agency system. It was already being used by some of the new entrant Cost Leader airlines, which were achieving substantial cost savings as a result, further increasing the pressure on traditional carriers.

The first signs of change came when Delta Airlines announced that for domestic ticket sales in the USA, payments of commission would be capped at a maximum of $50, whatever the percentage calculation of the fare might be. The effect of this was to significantly reduce the amount of commission paid on expensive First Class and Flexible Coach tickets, Within a very short time, Delta's initiative was followed by all the other major airlines in the USA, and, despite many predictions, it has stood the test of time. Indeed, the process of reform has been both strengthened and widened. Commissions have been reduced or eliminated in many markets today. Where travel agents are still being rewarded directly by airlines, this is now often done using the so-called "Task-Based" approach. With this, agents are not paid a percentage of the price of the ticket they sell. Instead, flat rate payments are made for each task the travel agent has undertaken so much for making the booking, for issuing the ticket and for dealing with payment. The effect of such policies has been to reduce the travel agents' rewards significantly, again especially on First and Business Class tickets, and on Flexible Economy fares, where high prices had meant especially high payments to agents.

The overall effect of such reforms has been little short of revolutionary.

The proportion of airline tickets being sold by traditional travel agents has fallen, as airline websites have become more popular and a new breed of on-line travel agents has appeared. At the same time, the relationship between airlines and travel agents has changed fundamentally, as agents have had to seek new sources of revenue.

This has been especially the case in the business air travel market. Here, in many markets, travel agents have changed their role into being one of a travel consultant for their clients, rather than an airline sales agent. They have argued that they have specialist skills in booking travel, in negotiating corporate deals with airlines and other travel suppliers, and in tracking and tracing travel spending to ensure that the finn gets the best value-for-money from its travel expenditure. In return for such skills, travel agents have asked for, and have been paid, management fees by their commercial clients.

The changeover from commission-based rewards to management fees paid by clients has had mixed results for airlines, but on balance it has proved to be a correct policy. It is true that agents are no longer the airlines' ally in selling higher yielding tickets. Any form of reward for intermediaries based on commissions can be annoying for those who pay them, with often a feeling that the commission does not accurately reflect the work done. Commissions do, though, give a common interest to both principal and supplier to secure the highest possible revenue. Management fees can have the reverse effect. In order for a travel agent to justify their work, and to ensure that they retain their travel accounts, they must show their commercial clients that they have managed the travel budget well, and that they have achieved the greatest possible cost savings. This may mean that they encourage booking on low yielding promotional fares, even if restrictive conditions apply to them, or book people on Cost Leader airlines via these airlines' websites, even though they receive no commissions for doing so.

Despite this possible adverse consequence, changing the basis for the rewarding of travel agents has been a necessary and long overdue reform. It has saved airlines large sums of money which they otherwise would have lost to the travel agency industry, and has given them a better control over their distribution channels than would have been the case had the reforms not come about.

The Future of Distribution

Despite the changes of recent years, the question of distribution channels for airlines is one which is still in a state of flux. Can we yet forecast what the mature situation will be?

It is already clear that the future is going to see a greater proportion of airline seats sold using direct distribution channels. Airline call centres, sales offices and airport ticket desks will remain significant, though the growth in direct sales is unlikely to be explained by them. Clearly, most of this growth will come from the increased use of airline websites. Internet access is spreading rapidly around the world, and regular use of the Internet is now a regular part of daily life for hundreds of millions of people. These people are, of course, drawn disproportionately from groups who are likely to be regular air travellers. Also, airlines are increasingly adopting the simpler reservations and ticketing procedures, which are necessary to make Internet booking commonplace. The newer Cost Leader airlines have always done this, and the "Legacy" airlines that they are threatening are increasingly responding.

Having said this, it is not the case that the future will see an end for the travel agents' role in airline distribution. Many better-managed agents will be able to defend their position by adopting policies, which their clients will perceive as adding value. We have already looked at the business travel agents who are repositioning themselves as travel consultants rather than airline sales agents. On the leisure side, the better agents may be able to find niche positions by specializing in particular activities such as winter sports, golf, trekking etc. Clients may then continue to support them because they value their expertise. The best opportunities for the travel agency industry in the future will.. "stem from the one advantage that they will continue to hold over airline websites. When a passenger consults an airline site, they will only be told about travel options and fares on that airline. In order to find out the best option out of the many that are available, they may have to spend a considerable amount of time looking M the websites of all the competitor airlines in the market. If, however, their consult a good travel agent, the travel agent will be able to display all the flight and fares options that are available and make a "best-buy" recommendation.

This is a service which a traditional off-line travel agency can offer in some form, but it becomes an even more powerful one if it can be made available over the Internet. Recent years have seen the rapid growth of a number of very large and well-capitalized on-line travel agencies such as Travelocity (begun by American Airlines, but subsequently sold) and the Expedia service pioneered by Microsoft. This has in turn raised disturbance, possibilities for airlines. Their websites have allowed them to loosen the formerly very tight hold that large travel agency chains held over them, but the rise of firms such as Expedia and Travelocity has raised the specter of a new domination, this time by on-line rather than off-line agencies. Such a threat has induced airlines to respond. In both the USA and Europe, consortia of airlines have set up what amounts to their own on-line travel agency, branded Orbits in the US and Epode in Europe. Though both are at an early stage of their development, the plan presumably is that they will rival and preferably outdo the new on-line agencies.

Overall, it is possible to reach a more optimistic conclusion about airline distribution (at least on the passenger side of the industry) than would have been possible only a few years ago. The use of the Internet and the reform of the reward systems for travel agents have both made useful contributions to the correcting of what was formerly a totally unsatisfactory situation.

Global Distribution Systems (GDSs)

For nearly twenty years, the subject of so-called Global Distribution Systems has been a controversial one in the airline industry, and it remain so today.

Until the early 1970s, contact between airlines and their distribution outlets was mainly by telephone. As the 1970s proceeded, the first, pioneering carriers set out to automate airline/travel agency contact. In order to do so, direct links were provided from each agency location into the airline's reservations computer. Instead of phoning, agents could use the keyboard of a Visual Display Unit to make bookings direct with the airline concerned. Besides saving a great deal of time, this also gave the agent visual confirmation that the required reservation had been made.

In the USA, the leading airlines behind this move were United Airlines with its Apollo system, and American with SABRE. By the end of the 1970s these airlines had been joined in Europe by carriers such as Lufthansa (with START) and British Airways (with BABS).

By today's standards, these systems were extremely basic. They were, though, accompanied by controversy almost from the beginning. It was soon learnt that they provided a cast-iron way for the airlines which owned them to increase their market share at the expense of their rivals. The reason was that travel agents had a clear tendency to book their clients if they could from the first screen of information about the flight options in a given city-pair market. Indeed, booking was made from the first screen on over 90% of occasions. Over 50% of the time, the booking made would be that of the flight at the top of the first screen.

Given these facts, the option for the owner of the system was obvious. They needed to make sure that their own flights were the ones which were displayed most prominently. By doing so, they could obtain a handsome return on their investment through an increased market share. Generally, therefore, they were prepared to provide the systems free, or for a nominal rental, to the agents who used them. Also, though the flights of other airlines were shown, generally bookings were made on these airlines in small numbers, and little or no charge was made for such bookings. Indeed, other airlines' flight were only included because of the agent's requirement for a comprehensive system which would enable then to book all their client's requests on one system.

By the mid-1980s, the question of these early, biased systems was becoming a controversial one. In the USA in particular, the airline industry had by this time been deregulated, and complaints were made by some airlines that bias in Computer Reservation Systems was significantly hindering the operation of the supposed free market in aviation. This complaint was, of course, raised most vociferously by the airlines which did not have a significant presence in the GDS industry. At the same time, those that did have such a presence—notably American Airlines—argued that the returns they were getting through biased displays merely reflected the investment they had made and the risks they had taken.

The outcome of the debate was that GDS displays—ironically in a supposedly deregulated industry—became subject to regulation by the US government, a move subsequently followed by the European Commission in respect of GDS operations within the European Union. The regulator regime in both cases had essentially the same purpose, though there were differences in detail to ensure display neutrality. This purpose has largely been achieved. Though the question of the fairness of the rules continue to be debated, any residual bias in the systems today is at a far lower level than was the case during the 1980s.

Once displays became regulated, it was inevitable that a further issue would arise. Airlines which had invested heavily in GDSs—and American Airlines was by this time claiming that it had spent more than a billion dollars on SABRE—expected to get a return on their investment. If biased displays were ruled out, how was this return to be obtained? The answer soon became clear. The system owners began to charge other airlines substantial booking fees for every booking made, at an initial level of about $2.80 per Passenger Name Record created.

The effect of booking fees was dramatic. Suddenly, Global Distribution Systems were transformed into highly profitable businesses, with American Airlines in particular soon conceding that its involvement in GDS was the most lucrative of all its activities—much more so than the airline itself. At the same time, booking fees provided American with the resources it needed to continue to invest in SABRE. At that time, more than 40% of the travel agents in the USA were using SABRE, giving the system considerable power in that market. There were rumors circulating of American's intention to achieve such dominance on a global basis. Had they done so, their ability to levy higher and higher booking fees would have been immense.

To address the perceived threat of SABRE, it was necessary for other airlines to make counter moves, and in Europe two groups of carriers carne together to form consortia, each with the aim of setting up a system with I the functionalities and customer base necessary to compete with SABRE, I The result was the formation of the AMADEUS and GALILEO consortia in 1987. Both these systems were up and running by the early 1990s, when, a series of mergers and acquisitions finally lead to the emergence of a I mature industry structure. As one would expect in an industry where there are very large economies of scale, this structure was an oligopolistic one, SABRE was a dominant player, as were GALILEO and AMADEUS, both having strengthened their position through mergers with US-based systems in the early 1990s. The fourth and smallest player was WORLDSPAN, a system jointly set up by three US airlines, Delta, Northwest and TW A.

The most recent developments have seen changes in the ownerships of the GDS industry. Airline enthusiasm for the Internet as a distribution channel—brought about in part because of the high charges they were incurring in GDS booking fees—has resulted in a lower proportion of bookings coming through the traditional travel agency/GDS channel. This, accompanied by the fall in traffic characteristic of today's difficult industry environment has ended what might be called the "golden age" of GDS profitability. At the same time, airlines having an ownership stake in one of the GDSs have been under pressure to raise cash in order to maintain liquidity. The result has been that these stakes have almost all been sold off. In some cases, this has been through an Initial Public Offering (for example, with the American Airlines holding in Saber), or through a trade sale (Galileo is now a wholly-owned subsidiary of the US-based Decant Corporation).

The selling off of airline stakes in the GDS has given the industry a degree of unity of purpose about them. Before, those airlines which had an equity stake in a GDS (and which were therefore benefiting from the substantial dividend income they were then providing) took a different attitude to the question of booking fees than those who did not. Today, almost all airlines have a common interest in lowering booking fees to achieve more cost-effective distribution.

Current Issues

Though the subject of bias in Global Distribution Systems is now less controversial than it was, there are still some substantial debates in progress.

Amongst the most contentious of these is the question of funding of the GDSs. Airlines now argues that they pay, through their booking fees, a disproportionately high level of total costs, whilst the travel agency industry pays far too little.

In principle, both airlines and travel agents benefit from the availability of a GDS. Airlines certainly gain from the wide distribution of their product, but agents also find that their costs are significantly reduced because of the much greater staff productivity they can achieve. The original suggestion was that GDS costs should be met to an equal degree by airlines and agents, reflecting these mutual benefits. This has not turned out to be the case. With the economics of a GDS so dependent on the volume of throughput, the GDS firms have every incentive to try to steal market share from their rivals. In order to do so, it has become a common tactic to allow travel agents the use of the system for a very low rental or, in some cases, if throughput in terms of the number of bookings made is sufficient, free of charge. The result has, in many countries, been an intense market share battle, with agents being offered bigger and bigger incentives to switch from one firm's system to another. In turn, a larger and larger share of GDS costs have in practice been paid by airline through booking fees—current estimates are that more than 90% of GDS income is being derived in this way.

The dominance of airline funding of Global Distribution Systems has in turn led to two further controversies. The travel agent will often have a deal which seems that the GDS will be made available free of charge, or for a nominal rent providing a sufficient number of bookings are made. Then the agent with a sense of humour will have a clear incentive to make false and fictitious bookings if the number of true bookings they have insufficient to reach the relevant break-point. Not surprisingly, such practices have provoked outrage on the part of those airlines that have been the victims of them, for the booking fees levied by the GDS companies have been based on the Passenger Name Records (PNRs) created, not on the number of passengers carried. Because of the controversy, the GDS firms have had to divert significant resources to policing false and passive bookings and, because they have done so the problem now seems to be more under control.

The same certainty cannot be said for the second major problem associated with GDS funding. We have already seen how the travel agen9 system dominates airline distribution channels, and that in recent years the system has been costing airlines more and more. Because of this, it has become an unsaid policy objective for many carriers to reduce their sales through travel agents. The use of the Internet, and the development of electronic ticketry are the technical developments which have made this possible.

As we have seen, in responding to this challenge to their dominance. better-managed travel agency firms are making what is, for them, an entirely logical move. They are repositioning themselves as travel management firms, able to assist corporate customers not only in the making of bookings, but in the negotiation of deals with airlines and other principles, and in the subsequent policing of expenditure to make sure that those who travel using the firm's money abide by its corporate travel policies.

Such a repositioning requires the travel agent to have a number of tools available in the form of computer systems to aid effective travel management. The GDS firms have been only too willing to develop these tools, hoping that by doing so they will be able to cement their relationship with their existing travel agency customers and also hopefully attract some new ones from rival GDSs. By a supreme irony, though, these system developments have largely been funded by airline booking fees, with the actions of the GDS firms helping travel agents to retain their dominance of airline distribution channels at exactly the time airlines have been seeking to reduce it.

A final issue for the CRS firms reflects the emergence of the so-called "Cost Leader" airlines. Airlines such as Southwest in the USA and Ryanair and Easy jet in Europe have grown significantly in recent years. Their strategy had been based on a low cost low fares proposition. In order to lower their costs to the level which will make their low fares profitable, they have tried to simplify the product they have offered. In particular, they have generally use simple fares and reservations procedures, and have not offered interline or transfer services to their passengers, working purely on a point-to-point basis.

In the strongest contrast, the GDS firms have been proud to point to the sophistication of the services which through the travel agent, they can provide to the passenger. A passenger today can contact their travel agent and make a very complex multi-sector booking on any number of different airlines, dealing at the same time with issues such as seat selection and special meal requirements. They can be given information about any fare which is on offer, as all the GDS firms maintain enormous fares databases. Finally, they can book any extra requirements they may have for such services as car rental or hotel accommodation.

Of course, the GDS firms argue that such sophistication comes at a price and they would claim that the booking fees charged represent very good value for money given the range of services on offer. The problem is that the customers of the low fares airlines do not need this level of sophistication yet are being asked to pay for it, because booking fees are levied on a fiat-rate basis. Worse still, the booking fee, were it to paid, would represent a very significant component of their fare.

The upshot of this controversy is that, as we have seen, the GDS industry had been shunned by the low fare airlines. The oldest of them, Southwest Airlines, pays only for a low level of participation in one of the GDSs, SABRE and has no relationship with the others. It also tries to actively encourage bookings which allow it to avoid booking fees completely, through its own call centers or the Internet. In Europe, Easy jet is an example of a direct-sell airline, avoiding completely the travel agency distribution system. Through doing so, it has also avoided any need to be displayed in the databases of the GDS firms and has been able to add the elimination of GDS booking fees to the savings on commissions which it had achieved.

Distribution Channels in the Air Freight Market

The question of product distribution is no less controversial on the freight side of airlines' activities—indeed it could be argued that airlines are further away from finding a solution for their freight distribution problems that they are for those on the passenger side.

We have seen that the equivalent to the travel agent in air freight is the air freight forwarder. Forwarders provide the same sales agency function as the travel agent does. They also have an important role to play in the handling and consolidation of freight.

Forwarders have only a small role in the so-called "Express" market of small urgent packages. The Integrated Carriers that dominate Express have built powerful retail brands and have invested large amounts in ground handling systems, which largely negate the role of the forwarder. In the remaining markets of so-called "Heavy Freight", though, the domination of the forwarding industry is almost total. The proportion of heavy freight in the hands of forwarders is well over 90%.

Such a reliance on a single channel of distribution would be unhealthy in itself, but the structure of the forwarding industry makes it worse still. Forwarding appears to be an industry where there are substantial economies of scale, and where important advantages accrue to the largest firms. Fewer than 15 global forwarders now dominate the market, with this number tending to reduce steadily through time as a result of merger and takeover activity amongst the leading players.

The result of airline reliance on a single channel of distribution is entirely as one would expect. Profits in the airline sector of the air freight industry have been under tremendous pressure in recent years. A serious market downturn in 2000 and 2001 has been followed by overcapacity and falling yields on many routes. In the strongest possible contrast, reported profits of publicly-quoted air freight forwarders during this time have never been better. Overcapacity amongst the airlines benefits them as they are able to play one carrier off against another, lowering the rates that they pay Iand in turn increasing the profits they make on their consolidations.

Rather than getting less, forwarders ability to play one airline off against another may be increasing. A number of airlines are now forming consortia, the aim of which is to streamline the process of booking in the air freight industry by the use of the Internet. At the moment, booking is mostly an archaic process using the telephone and appears ripe for reform Internet platforms such as the recently formed GFX are revolutionary. They are certainly achieving a streamlining of the process, though the charges rendered by GFX promise a controversy comparable to that generated by Global Distribution Systems on the passenger side of the industry. The charges made by the GFX organization on the airlines that use it have been high enough to discourage many carriers from joining, whilst the question of the display which each carrier's flights are given in the system is likely to be controversial. Most seriously of all, GFX may complete the commoditization of the air freight product, with forwarders able to make an immediate comparison between the rates on offer from the different competitors in the market. Great power will then accrue to the lowest-pricing airline, giving an endemic tendency towards rate cutting, especially in an over-supplied market.

It is easy to conclude that the present situation with regard to distribution channels for air freight is unsatisfactory. Airlines have too little market power despite making the bulk of the capital investment in the industry. They have also failed to make the progress seen on the passenger side in recent years, where the situation today is a good deal better than it was in the late 1990s. Unfortunately, arriving at solutions to the problem will not be easy.

In the past, some airlines have attempted to address matters by buying into the forwarding industry, or by setting up subsidiaries to compete with forwarders in such areas as off-airport ground handling. These attempts have generally not been successful. Whatever benefits they may have brought in terms of improved market control have been outweighed by the fact that remaining independent forwarders have generally reacted angrily, regarding such moves as an invasion of their territory. The commercial damage that they have been able to inflict has generally outweighed the benefits.

A more promising initiative has been taken in recent years, most notably by Lufthansa and Air France. These airlines appear to have learnt from the computer chip industry, and the strategies of Intel. Intel does not manufacture its own computers, but maintains a powerful position with those who do by investing a great deal in the development of a powerful brand for its microprocessors. Both Air France and Lufthansa have developed brands in air freight based on time-definite deliveries and different segments of the market. They clearly hope that these brands will be requested more when shippers and forwarders are contemplating which airline to use.

Overall, questions of distribution strategies are today amongst the most contentious in the whole field of airline marketing. It is essential that airlines should control their distribution channels as it is largely their money that is at risk through these channels. The problem is that safeguarding long-term channel control may conflict with short-term objectives to maximise revenues, especially given the powerful positions that the industry's wholesalers and retailers have been able to build.

AIRLINE PROMOTIONAL PLANNING

A major goal of promotion is to let customers in target markets know that the carrier's services are available at the right time, place, and price. The calls for selecting the right blend of promotional activities are the combinations that best suits the particular market. Promotion is the communication between carrier and customer. This communication can be achieved in various ways, but the two most important forms of promotional communication are *advertising* (sometimes referred to as mass selling) and *personal selling*. Other promotional activities include trading stamps, two-for-the-price-of-one air travel, and free giveaway items.

The broad goal of an airline's promotional activities is to increase revenues and profits. To accomplish this, a carrier must engage in activities that in-form, persuade, and remind customers in the target market about its services.

The principal task in promoting a new item is often simply to inform prospective customers about the existence of the service, to demonstrate its superiority over potential alternatives, and then to encourage customers to try the service and form their own opinions. When a product faces competition from close substitutes, such as competing carriers, the promotional objective IS generally-to *persuade* customers to buy the carrier's services rather than another carrier's services. If more competition arrives in the marketplace, the promotional effort is directed toward *reminding* customers of their favorable experience with the service and encouraging them to continue to use it or to return to it if they have switched to another carrier.

Advertising is another important element in the promotional scheme of an airline. Other promotional activities include the literature provided to Travel agencies to inform them of the latest specials, such as promotional areas and tours that are available. Much of this activity is carried out by the carrier's sales personnel that service a particular agency.

We are nearly at the end of our survey of marketing principles and their application to the airline industry, but one crucial step remains for analysis. The subjects addressed so far show how airlines can analyze their markets and their marketing environment, plot a sound strategy, and, following on from this, put in place correct product, branding, pricing and distribution policies. In order to be successful, though, they must convince and persuade potential customers to buy from them rather than from their rivals. The early stages of marketing should certainly make this process easier. It will always be more straightforward to persuade people to buy value-for money products which will meet well-understood customer needs, rather than those which do not. In no sense, though, is the sales task an easy one. A great deal of planning and hard work will be needed, and this chapter will discuss the necessary skills.

Integrated Marketing Communication and Promotion

Integrated Marketing Communication (IMC) involves the idea that a firm's promotional efforts should be coordinated to achieve the best combined effects of the firm's efforts. Resources are allocated to achieve those outcomes that the firm values the most. Promotion involves a number of tools we can use to increase demand for our products.

The most well known component of promotion is advertising, but we can also use tools such as the following:

- ***Public relations*** (the firm's staff provides information to the media in the hopes of getting coverage). This strategy has benefits (it is often less expensive and media coverage is usually more credible than advertising) but it also entails a risk in that we can't control what the media will say. Note that this is particularly a useful tool for small and growing businesses—especially those that make a product which is inherently interesting to the audience.
- ***Trade promotion***. Here, the firm offers retailers and wholesalers temporary discounts, which may or may not be passed on to the consumer, to stimulate sales.
- ***Sales promotion***. Consumers are given price discounts, coupons, or rebates.
- ***Personal selling***. Sales people either make "cold" calls on potential customers and/or respond to inquiries.
- ***In-store displays***. Firms often pay a great deal of money to have their goods displayed prominently in the store. More desirable display spaces include: end of an aisle, free-standing displays, and near the check-out counter. Occasionally, a representative may display the product.
- ***Complementary.***

Generally, a sequence of events is needed before a consumer will buy a product. This is known as a ***"hierarchy of effects."*** The consumer must first be aware that the product exists. He or she must then be motivated to give some attention to the product and what it may provide. In the next stage, the need is for the consumer to evaluate the merits of the product, hopefully giving the product a try. A good experience may lead to continued use. Note that the consumer must go through the earlier phases before the later ones can be accomplished.

Promotional objectives that are appropriate differ across the Product Life Cycle (PLC). Early in the PLC—during the introduction stage—the most important objective is creating awareness among consumers. For example, many consumers currently do not know the Garmin is making auto navigation devices based on the global position satellite (GPS) system and what this system can do for them. A second step is to induce trial—to get consumers to buy the product for the first time. During the growth stage, important needs are persuading the consumer to buy the product and prefer the brand over competing ones. Here, it is also important to persuade retailers to carry the brand, and thus, a large proportion of promotional resources may need to be devoted to retailer incentives. During the maturity stage, the firm may need to focus on maintaining shelf space, distribution channels, and sales.

Different promotional approaches will be appropriate depending on the stage of the consumer's decision process that the marketer wishes to influence. Prior to the purchase, the marketer will want to establish a decision to purchase the product and the specific brand. Here, samples might be used to induce trial. During the purchase stage, when the consumer is in the retail store, efforts may be made to ensure that the consumer will choose one's specific brands. Paying retailers for preferred shelf space as well as point of purchase (POP) displays and coupons may be appropriate. After the purchase, an appropriate objective may be to induce a repurchase or to influence the consumer to choose the same brand again. Thus, the package may contain a coupon for future purchase.

There are two main approaches to promoting products:

- The ***"push" strategy*** is closely related to the "selling concept" and involves "hard" sell and aggressive price promotions to sell at this specific purchase occasion.
- In contrast, the ***"pull" strategy*** emphasizes creating demand for the brand so that consumers will come to the store with the intention of buying the product. Hallmark, for example, has invested a great deal in creating a preference for its greeting cards among consumers.

There are several ways that a Airline can budget for advertising. The strategy used depends on the firm's policy and internal politics. Some of the methods commonly used are:

- ***Percentage of sales.*** Here, the firm decides to base its advertising budget on how much has been sold. This appears to be an "objective" way to make the budget decision and to "reward" performing brands and products with resources. However, this method is quite arbitrary. A firm may find it worthwhile to invest heavily in advertising up-front—before the product has begun to sell significantly— so that a promising product can achieve its potential. When a product is performing well, staying with a fixed percentage may also result in spending more than is cost-effective.
- ***Percentage of profits.*** This is similar to the above, but takes into

consideration that some products may have larger margins than others. Thus, a product with lesser sales but high margins may be a better investment than one with high sales but low margins. Still, however, this method is arbitrary and questionable because of the factors listed above.

- *Competitive parity.* This entails setting the budget to match competitors. Note, however, that different brands may have different needs. Coke and Pepsi may be competing "head-on," and competitive parity may be appropriate. In contrast, some firms may be targeting customers who are relatively brand loyal while others target "switchers." The firm that targets loyal customers may be better off spending money on product quality than on promotion.
- ***Affordability.*** This entails budgeting based on the resources that the firm has available. Smaller firms obviously do not have the same resources as larger ones. However, the firm should still evaluate how effective such a budget will be in meeting the brand's needs. A firm may be able to afford to spend more than is appropriate. In contrast, other firms may not be able to spend what is needed to adequately influence consumers. In such cases, it may be more appropriate for the firm to try to sell of this brand rather than fighting a losing battle.
- *Objective and task.* This method sets the budget based on what is needed to achieve what the firm has set out to accomplish. The ultimate budget may then have little relation to the factors discussed above.

There are several types of advertising. In terms of product advertising, the "pioneering" ad seeks to create awareness of a product and brand and to instill an appreciation among consumers for its possibilities. The competitive or persuasive ad attempts to convince the consumer either of the performance of the product and/or how it is superior in some way to that of others. Comparative advertisements are a prime example of this. For instance, note the ads that show that some trash bags are more durable than others. Reminder advertising seeks to keep the consumer believing what other ads have already established. For example, Coca Cola ads tend not to provide new information but keep reinforcing what a great drink it is.

Developing an airline advertising program entails several steps:

- *Identifying the target audience.* Market reports can be bought that investigate the media habits of consumers of different products and/or the segments that the firm has chosen to target.
- *Determining appropriate advertising objectives.* As discussed, these objectives might include awareness, trial, repurchase, inducing consumers to switch from another brand, or developing a preference for the brand.
- *Settling on an advertising budget.*

- ***Designing the advertisements.*** Some commonly used approaches:
  - ***Information/persuasion.*** Comparative ads attempt to get consumers to believe that the sponsoring product is better. Although these are frequently disliked by Americans, they tend to be among the most effective ads in the U.S. Comparative advertising is illegal in some countries and is considered very inappropriate culturally in some societies, especially in Asia.
  - ***Fear appeals*** try to motivate consumers by telling them the consequences of not using a product. Mouthwash ads, for example, talk about the how gingivitis and tooth loss can result from poor oral hygiene. It is important, however, that a specific way to avoid the feared stimulus be suggested directly in the ad. Thus, simply by using the mouthwash advertised, these terrible things can be avoided.
  - ***Sex appeals*** are more common—and more explicit—in some cultures than in others. Their effectiveness depends a great deal on how well such ads are designed for the specific product category. In many cases, sex appeal is used more to get the consumer's attention than for actual persuasion.
  - ***Humor appeal.*** The use of humor in advertisements is quite common. This method tends not to be particularly useful in persuading the consumer. However, more and more advertisers find themselves using humor in order to compete for the consumer's attention. Often, the humor actually draws attention away from the product—people will remember what was funny in the ad but not the product that was advertised. Thus, for ads to be effective, the product advertised should be an integral part of what is funny.

Numerous media are available for the advertiser to choose from. Each medium tends to have advantages and disadvantages.

It is essential to pretest advertisements to see how effective they actually are in influencing consumers. An ad may have to be redesigned if it is found not be to be as effective as targeted. Note that selecting advertisements is often a "numbers game" where a lot of advertisements are created and the ones that "test" best are selected.

The effectiveness of advertising is a highly controversial topic. Research suggests that in many cases advertising leads to a relatively modest increase in sales. One study suggests, for example, that when a firm increases its advertising spending by 1%, sales go up by 0.05%. (The same research found that, in contrast, if prices are lowered by 1%, sales tend to increase by 2%). In general, it appears that advertising is more effective in selling durable goods (e.g., stereo systems, cars, refrigerators, and furniture) than for non-durable goods (e.g., restaurant meals, candy bars, toilet paper, and bottled water). Also, advertising appears to be more effective for new products. This suggests that advertising is probably most effective for providing information (rather than persuading people). Note that many advertising agencies make a large part of their money on commissions on advertising sold. Thus, they have a vested interest in selling as much advertising as possible, and may strongly advise clients to spend excessive amounts on advertising.

Research suggests that advertising effectiveness follows a sort of "S-" shaped curve. Very small amounts of advertising are too small to truly register with consumers. At the medium level, advertising may be effective. However, above a certain level (labeled "saturation point" on the chart), additional adverting appears to have a limited effect. (This is comparable to the notion of "diminishing returns to scale" encountered in economics).

There are several potential ways to measure advertising effectiveness. Two main categories include:

- **"Field" based studies.** These studies look at what happens with real consumers in real life. Thus, for example, we can examine what happens to sales of a company's products when the firm increases advertising. Unfortunately, this is often a misleading way to measure advertising impact because we live in a "messy" world where other factors influence sales as well. For example, a soft drink firm could conclude that there is very little correlation between advertising and sales because another, much more powerful factor is at work: temperature. That is, the firm may find that although a great deal of advertising is done in the winter, sales are greater in summer months because people drink more soft drinks in hot weather. Note that the choice of brand of soft drink purchased in the summer may very well be influenced by advertising heard at other times.
- **Laboratory studies**. To get around the confounds imposed by nature, advertising researchers often use artificial situations to evaluate advertising. This sacrifices the use of real consumers in real settings, but allows the marketer to control sources of influence. An advertising firm may hire people to come in and participate in research. The consumers may come in and be asked to view some television and respond to a questionnaire about the programming later. Half of the subjects can then see a version which includes an ad to be tested (the other half is known as the "control" group, which will serve as a basis for comparison). We can now compare the two groups on factors such as attitude toward the brand, purchase intention, and preference.

A significant objective of advertising is attitude change. A consumer's attitude toward a product refers to his or her beliefs about, feeling toward, and purchase intentions for the product. Beliefs can be both positive (e.g., for McDonald's food: tastes good, is convenient) and negative (is high in fat). In general, it is usually very difficult to change deeply held beliefs. Thus, in most cases, the advertiser may better off trying to add a belief (e.g., beef is convenient) rather than trying to change one (beef is really not very fatty). Consumer receptivity to messages aimed at altering their beliefs will tend to vary a great deal depending on the nature of the product. For unimportant products such as soft drinks, research suggests that consumers are often persuaded by having a large number of arguments with little merit presented (e.g., the soda comes in a neat bottle, the bottle contains five percent more soda than competing ones). In contrast, for high involvement, more important products, consumers tend to scrutinize arguments more closely, and will tend to be persuaded more by high quality arguments.

Celebrity endorsements are believed to follow a similar pattern of effectiveness. For trivial products, a popular endorser is often effective regardless of his or her qualifications to endorse (e.g., Bill Cosby endorses Coca Cola and Jell-O without having particular credentials to do so). On the other hand, for more important products, consumers will often scrutinize the endorser's credentials. For example, a basket ball player may be perceived as knowledgeable about athletic shoes, but not particularly so about life insurance.

Direct Marketing

Direct marketing involves bypassing the retailer in reaching the consumer. Generally, this is not cost-effective, but exceptional situations may make it so. For example, certain customers may buy in very large quantities. Others may be spread over large geographic areas and require specialized products (e.g., beekeepers).

Direct marketing provides exceptional opportunities for segmentation. An excellent tool is the so-called "merge-purge" technique. Marketers can buy lists of names and addresses of consumers from numerous sources (e.g., vehicle registrations, college enrollment, magazine subscriptions, catalog purchases). One can then combine different sources (e.g., surfers are likely to live in areas indicated by coastal zip codes, may subscribe to surfing magazines, and may have made purchases from surfing goods catalogs) and eliminate the overlaps (those people who appear on more than one list). Thus, we can target our potential buyers more closely than we could by advertising in newspapers (which are not read by many surfers and also reach a large number of non-surfers who are not interested in our products).

A great deal of interest has arisen in recent years on the potential for marketing on the Internet. While the jury is still out on this medium's ultimate potential, sales so far have been limited, although a large potential may exist. It should be noted that a large segment of the population in the U.S. is still not "connected," with numbers being even lower in even many developed countries. Many consumers are also reluctant to provide credit cards and other personal information on the Net, although attitudes in this area may change with. Note that the Internet may serve purposes other than direct sales. For example, the Internet is a good way to provide information to consumers, and this can be done at a relatively low cost.

Electronic Commerce

Online marketing can serve several purposes:

Actual sales of products

- *Promotion/advertising*: Customers can be quite effectively targeted in many situations because of the context that they, themselves, have sought out. For example, when a consumer searches for a specific term in a search engine, a "banner" or link to a firm selling products in that area can be displayed. Print and television advertisements can also feature the firm's web address, thus inexpensively drawing in those who would like additional information.
- *Customer service:* The site may contain information for those who no longer have their manuals handy and, for electronic products, provide updated drivers and software patches.
- *Market research*: Data can be collected relatively inexpensively on the Net. However, the response rates are likely to be very unrepresentative and recent research shows that it is very difficult to get consumers to read instructions. This is one of the reasons why the quality of data collected online is often suspect.

There are many obstacles to the growth of e-commerce:

- *Reach*: Although the majority of U.S. households now have computers connected to the Internet, a very large minority does not, and penetration rates are considerably lower in some countries. In foreign countries, even those households that have computers may be reluctant to spend time online due to per minute charges, which discourage the more leisurely "browsing" American style.
- *Concerns about privacy*: A number of consumers are concerned about giving up information to marketers that can easily be collected electronically. Naturally, few consumers would like information about their medical status widely collected by firms, but many consumers are even reluctant to have marketers know the ages of their children and past book purchase records.
- *Reputational issues*: Although not as much of a problem as before, firms operating online or through direct mail have often been viewed with suspicion since consumers may question whether they will be around if they do not deliver satisfactorily.
- *Costs*. During the "boom," Internet firms were not expected to be efficient and thus developed bad habits. Although shipping and handling charges can help cover costs of shipping and administration, these often take away the attractiveness of Internet shopping. The most successful e-commerce firms turn out to be the ones that have been successful doing other kinds of direct marketing (e.g., catalog sales) before and have developed the discipline and efficiency

required there. For products that have relatively high absolute margins—e.g., computers—there is more money to cover administrative costs.

- ***Language.*** Since the Internet reaches around the world, it is often difficult to match viewers with their preferred languages. Because U.S. firms and individuals tended to predominate among those first to occupy the Web, most sites are in U.S. English. British speakers of English generally do not perceive American English as American—they tend to perceive spelling such as "color" rather than their "colour" as misspellings. French consumers do not like to have to click to get from an English language to a French language site. It is estimated that by the year 2007, the majority of web surfers will not be comfortable in English and will want sites in their own languages.
- ***Government regulations***: In the U.S., the government has tried to keep its hands off the Net as much as possible to foster its growth as a trade area, and a recently expired moratorium on new sales taxes was even instituted to make Internet shopping more attractive. However, governments in many other countries are more forceful in their regulations. In countries such as China, where sites can be used to spread "subversive" ideas, there is a great deal of government scrutiny and suspicion.
- ***Cultural obstacles.*** The whole purpose of the web is to make information readily available. In countries where information is closely guarded, that is a frightening idea. There is often also a desire for personal interaction, which may be required to establish the trust needed to secure a deal.
- ***Payment issues.*** U.S. consumers exposed to credit card fraud have very limited liabilities, but these protections do not exist to the same extent in Europe or Asia. In China, much of the purpose of the Internet is defeated with some 80% of transactions being completed off-line, usually with funding instruments other than credit cards.

There are a number of problems in running and developing web sites. First of all, the desired domain name may not be available—e.g., American Airlines could not get "American.com" and had to settle for "AmericanAir.com." There is also a question having your site identified to potential users. Research has found that most search engines have a great deal of "false hits" (sites irrelevant that are identified in a search—e.g., information about computer languages when the user searches for foreign language instruction) and "misses" (sites that would have been relevant but are not identified). It is crucial for a firm to have its site indexed favorably in major search engines such as Yahoo, AOLFind, and Google. However, there is often a constant struggle between web site operators and the search engines to outguess each other, with the web promoters trying to "spam" the search engines with repeated usage of terms and "meta tags." The fact that many computer users employ different web browsers raises questions about compatibility. A major problem is that many of the more recent, fancier web sites rely on "java script" to provide animation and various other impressive features. These animations have proven very unreliable. Sites may "crash" on the user or prove unreliable, and many consumers have found themselves unable to complete their transactions.

There are a number of legal issues associated with the Internet:

- *Reach across borders*. Web sites transcend country lines and thus, a firm may be subjected to legal standards of different countries. It may be difficult to create advertising that simultaneously complies with rules for each country.
- *Taxation.* There is a great deal of ambiguity as to which state and local governments may collect taxes on merchandise sold on the Internet. There is also a question as to who has the responsibility for making the payment—the seller or the buyer?
- *Privacy issues*. Many foreign governments prohibit the collection of personal information of consumers (as Amazon.com does), which greatly reduces the customization opportunities online.

Web site design: The web designer must make various issues into consideration:

- *Speed vs. aesthetics*. As we saw, some of the fancier sites have serious problems functioning practically. Consumers may be impressed by a fancy site, or may lack confidence in a firm that offers a simple one. Yet, fancier sites with extensive graphics take time to download—particularly for users dialing in with a modem as opposed to being "hard" wired—and may result in site crashes.
- *Keeping users on the site.* A large number of "baskets" are abandoned online as consumers fail to complete the "check-out" process for the products they have selected. One problem here is that many consumers are drawn away from a site and then are unlikely to come back. A large number of links may be desirable to consumers, but they tend to draw people away. Taking banner advertisers on your site from other sites may be profitable, but it may result in customers lost.
- *Information collection*. An increasing number of consumers resist collection of information about them, and a number of consumers have set up their browsers to disallow "cookies," files that contain information about their computers and shopping habits.

Cyber-consumer behavior. In principle, it is fairly easy to search and compare online, and it was feared that this might wipe out all margins online. More recent research suggests that consumers in fact do not tend to search very intently and that large price differences between sites persist. We saw above the problem of keeping consumers from prematurely departing from one's site.

Sales Planning

The Sales Budget

Given the challenging and complex nature of the sales task in the airline industry, sound planning will be essential if it is to be accomplished successfully.

Such planning will need to take place at different levels. An overall sales and marketing plan will be needed for the airline as a whole, and preparing this will be the responsibility of the Executive Vice-president for Marketing working with the other senior managers of the company. Amongst the crucial issues that this will settle is the total budget that will be available to underwrite the sales effort.

At a lower level, comparable sales and marketing plans will be needed for each sales region in the airline's network. These will, amongst other things, decide how the overall sales budget should be allocated between the regions, and how each region will spend the available funds. The latter will require decisions on the so-called "Communications Mix", the ways in which the different forms of marketing communication are brought together to make up, hopefully, an integrated and successful policy.

Any form of budget setting is likely to involve a difficult and contentious internal debate. Such debate, though, is likely to be especially intense when it involves decisions about the money to be spent on the sales and marketing effort. No-one, presumably, would dispute the point that some cash will be needed to support sales and marketing. The problem is that measuring the return obtained on such spending is notoriously difficult. It also does not produce a tangible result in the way that spending the same money on a fixed asset such an aircraft would. It is therefore important that sales and marketing managers should be able to make the case for the money they need in a persuasive and credible way.

Traditionally, one can find three ways in which this case can be made. Two of these are simple and straightforward, but unfortunately wrong. The third is much more difficult, but is the one most likely to lead to a positive outcome.

Of the incorrect methods, it still happens that budget requests are made using the so-called Percentage of Revenue method. This is where the request is made for a promotional budget based on a fixed percentage of the revenue which the sales and marketing team have achieved in the last year or which they will be expected to produce in the next one.

This concept certainly has the merit of speed and simplicity, but it is fundamentally incorrect. It ties spending to the prevailing market conditions. If the market is buoyant, revenue will rise naturally and promotional spending with it. If market conditions deteriorate, there is a risk that revenues will fall and that promotional spending will therefore follow. The worst possible situation could then result, with a downward spiral of falling revenue leading to a smaller promotional budget which will in turn cause a further loss of revenue.

The promotional budget should actually follow exactly the opposite pattern to the one which will result from the Percentage of Revenue method. When the market is growing strongly, an airline operating in that market will be able to increase its own revenue in line with the market for only a small promotional spend. When the overall market is stagnant or declining, success for the individual firm can only come by it increasing its share of the market. Growth through increasing market share is notoriously difficult, and will only come about through a determined, and costly, marketing communications effort.

The second common way for a promotional budget to be settled is for it to be based on what was agreed for the previous year with an adjustment for inflation. Whilst such an approach may be inevitable in the real world of corporate politics, it results in the promotional budget being at roughly the same level year after year without the necessary questions ever being asked as to whether it is correctly pitched or not.

This last point leads us on to the correct way to set a promotional budget, which is known as the Task-Based Method. Under this, the budget is set by first asking and answering a series of questions about the money which will be needed if the target revenue and profit for the year is to be achieved. Whilst there can be no precise answer to these questions, the fact that they are asked at all means that a sound approach to sales budgeting is more likely.

Of these questions, the first has already been mentioned, but its influence on decision-making should be the reverse of that implied by the Percentage of Revenue concept. If a market is stagnant or declining this is an indicator that higher promotional spending will be needed.

It will also be necessary to take account of the spending of the airline's competitors. Whilst in principle it may not be necessary to exactly match the budget of a high-spending rival, there will at least need to be a reasonable relationship with the expenditure of others. If there isn't, the airline's efforts will simply be swamped.

The problem, of course, in the airline industry is that airlines have to compete both in their home market, where they should be dominant, and at the other end of the routes they fly, where the home airline is likely to be in a similarly strong position. Therefore, it is often the case that in overseas markets even airlines with a large promotional spend are being heavily out-spent. They therefore have a particular need to ensure that every dollar they have is made to work as hard as possible.

Besides the question of the promotional spending of competitors, the number and quality of these competitors will be of obvious importance. A carrier fortunate to have only a small number of poor 'quality competitors in a particular market should not spend a great deal on persuading people to fly with them who will do so anyway. Instead, the money should be used in other, difficult markets or kept for the time when conditions become more challenging.

The nature of the marketing task in any particular year will also need to be considered. It may be a year in which new routes are to be launched, or when a major product upgrade is to take place. If it is, substantial extra cash will be needed to ensure that these new developments are explained and promoted to actual and potential customers.

A further, important question will be that of brand positioning. Airlines sometimes attempt a fundamental repositioning of their brand. A case in point was the Canadian carrier Wardair which attempted—unsuccessfully—to change from being a leisure travel airline to one with a substantial presence in the business travel market. Something as ambitious as this will only stand any chance of being successful if it is underwritten by a substantial promotional budget.

Other airlines may not be attempting a major brand repositioning. They do, though, need to strengthen their brand. They may, for example, have carried out attitude studies which show that the airline is perceived in a poor light by potential customers in terms of such crucial issues as punctuality and customer service. If they have, some honest assessment of the situation will be required. It could be that these attitudes are a legacy of a time when the carrier thoroughly deserved a poor reputation, with today's situation much better. If they are, then investment in marketing communications will be justified because this can be used to persuade customers to give the airline another chance and to experience today's improved product standards. If, on the other hand, today's standards are as bad as ever, it is a delusion to think that marketing communications expenditure can rescue the situation. It will probably make things worse. There will be a temptation to embark on a communications campaign aimed at getting people to try the airline again. When they do, and find that things are the same, they will feel betrayed and tricked by the messages that have been put out to them. In such a situation, any available funds should be spent on addressing the product and service weaknesses which are at the heart of its problems, with investment in marketing communications a much lower priority.

A final and inevitable factor will be the cost of the different forms of marketing communication. Generally, media buying costs have risen in recent years. In the future they may fall as the advent of, in particular, digital television increases competition to attract advertising and promotional spend. The problem then will be that the fragmentation of the different media will make it harder and harder to reach a target audience effectively, indeed this is already the case. Overall, it is likely that the cost of marketing communications will rise at least as fast as the rate of inflation, and any bid for a promotional budget should reflect this.

The "Communications Mix"

Once a budget has been obtained, the airline marketing manager's task is to decide how to spend the budget in the most effective way. In doing so, 16 For more detailed coverage see P.R. Smith, J. Taylor, "Marketing

Communications An Integrated Approach", Third Edition, Kogan Page, 2003 and P. Smith, C. Berry, A. Pulford, "Strategic Marketing Communications", Kogan Page, 1999. they have a clear problem: the number of ways in which money can be spent is now a bewildering one. Choosing between them will therefore require a great deal of thought and analysis. It is possible to spend money on sponsorships, database marketing, media relations, trade entertaining, on various forms of advertising (including, now, through the Internet) and through personal selling through investment in a field sales team.

Each of these will have different advantages and disadvantages. Our next task is to discuss them in turn, and also to consider the ways in which each technique should be used to ensure that it provides the best value-for-money. Once we have done so, it will become clearer as to how the different methods can be combined into an optimum Communications Mix.

Marketing Communication Techniques

Sponsorship Policy

The term "Sponsorship" is used to describe a situation whereby a firm has its name associated with an event, a team or a competitor, in exchange for money.

In recent years, sponsorships have become increasingly important in marketing communication generally. They have certainly done so in the airline industry. It is not difficult to see why. A successful sponsorship can result in a firm's name becoming widely known, very quickly. This can be especially valuable for a new airline, or for an established operator opening a new route into a market area where it has had no previous presence. Sponsorships can also help in building and reinforcing brand values. They can provide useful opportunities for corporate hospitality and trade entertaining. They can sometimes produce directly increments of new business, especially if an airline is nominated as the "Official Carrier" for an event, as part of a deal to sponsor it. Lastly, they address problems associated with the fragmentation of media advertising opportunities.

Despite these advantages, the question of sponsorship remains a controversial one. It is notoriously difficult to measure and quantify the benefits obtained from a sponsorship, and the suspicion will therefore always remain that a great deal of the resources put into them are wasted. This is an especially serious point because airlines everywhere find that they are inundated with sponsorship requests. Many carriers are identified as national representatives, and many people in the countries where they are based see sponsorship activities as the airline's patriotic duty. Also, there is a perception that air tickets are available to airlines free-of-charge, and that giving away tickets in a barter deal associated with a sponsorship costs them nothing. The problem here is that when a carrier agrees to a sponsorship in return for free tickets, they have seats left to sell to revenue passengers. They must accept that there will be a significant cost associated with a free ticket, if this results in a potential revenue passenger being denied a seat on the flight of their choice, and such tickets must therefore be seen as a form of currency. Only if such tickets are truly offered on a subject-to-Ioad basis can they be seen as having a negligible cost. There are a number of rules which must be followed to ensure a successful use of sponsorship. Crucial amongst these is that the airline must decide what are the values which underlie its brand, and must only undertake sponsorships which reinforce them.

For all airlines, the cornerstone of their brand is safety. The sponsorship rule which flows from this is absolutely clear. No airline should have anything to do with any event which is dangerous. The risks of a catastrophic accident giving as association between the airline's name and danger and death is simply not worth taking. It is remarkable how many airlines have ignored this fundamental rule in recent years with, for example both Air Canada and Qantas sponsoring Formula One motor racing and Emirates having its name associated with power-boating.

For many airlines, a reputation for quality is also crucial to their brand development. They should not, therefore, sponsor down-market events with a poor public image. They have to be very careful, too, to be perceived as a "winner." This will help them in turn to penetrate the business travel market where people who are themselves successful will want to be seen to be travelling with the airline which is a market leader. It might be thought that the best way to be seen as a winner would be to get involved in sports sponsorship and to pick competitors and teams that do well—ideally to pick those that win the events in question. Whilst this is undoubtedly true in principle, it is also extremely risky. It may not matter a great dealfishes selected teams or competitors do not win, but still perform well. It will certainly matter if they are humiliated. A more cautious, but much safer option is therefore to sponsor an entire event, rather than one of the individuals or teams in that event, and this is normally the policy which should be adopted.

A final, but important value underlying all airline brands is that of caring. Carriers should not get involved in any activities which have an adverse effect on the environment. They should at the same time be especially attracted by activities which are associated with charities and other good causes.

Once a decision has been made in principle as to the activities with which the airlines wishes to be associated, steps must be taken to ensure that the maximum value-for-money is obtained from them. Here, it is first of all important that the airline should if possible be the sole sponsor certainly no other airlines should be involved. Too many sponsors can result in the identity of each individual firm being lost. Also, the event should be one where substantial media exposure can be guaranteed, exposure in which the sponsor's name will feature prominently.

In terms of assessing whether or not a sponsorship provides value-for money, its likely full costs should be should be quantified. This costing must include items such as any client hospitality provided, and any promotional back-up offered through special giveaways etc. Then, at least for a major sponsorship, research should be commissioned, related to its objectives. If the principal objective is to raise awareness, the research task will be an easy one. A study will be needed in the relevant market area of awareness levels before and after the sponsorship, with, hopefully, a significant positive change being the result. Where the objective is to improve the image and perception of the airline, the required research will be more complex and will almost certainly involve a quantitative study, and also some qualitative, focus group-based, research.

Database Marketing

Like sponsorship, database marketing has been increasing quickly in importance in airline marketing communication. Today, storing and processing database information is cheaper than it has ever been. At the same time, carrier are seeking to make better contact with their retail customers as a component of their strategy to secure greater control of their distribution channels and they have seen database marketing as a way of doing so. The subject remains, though, controversial and we have to look at both the advantages and disadvantages which database marketing brings, and the decisions which will have to be made to ensure that it brings the best possible results.

With advantages, beyond question the main one is that, if it is properly applied, database marketing will allow for finer market segmentations and better targeting of marketing messages, in a way that media advertising, for example, cannot. We have now moved away from a proposition that airlines' markets can be divided into just "business" and "leisure" travellers. In business travel, customers can be divided up by the routes they fly and the class of service which they (or their employer) choose. A tactical advertisement announcing, say, an increase in frequency on a particular route will be seen by many people who never fly that route. One which describes a relaunch of Business Class will be seen by many people—and may irritate them—who are forced to travel in Economy and who will merely learn what they are missing. Database marketing avoids this problem.

In leisure air travel, there is an increasing need to recognise discreet market segments, especially amongst discerning, up-market travellers. People vary, for example, in their stage-of-life and personal circumstances. Travel needs will also be distinctly different for families with young children compared with couples or singles. Preference may vary according to age. Also, hobbies and interests form an increasingly useful basis for market segmentation. People who travel, for example, for winter sports, golf, fishing etc all form distinct and potentially valuable market segments.

Database marketing allows for fine segmentations, and pennies messages to be prepared and communicated which demonstrate an airline's ability to meet a precise set of needs. Traditional media advertising cannot offer the same opportunities.

Other features of database marketing are that it permits tactical messages to be communicated quickly, and only to those people that the airline wishes to tell. Buying advertising space may involve delay if the space has to be booked in advance. It will also mean that offers of, say, discounted fares become generally known, rather than knowledge of them being confined to those people whom it is in the airline's interest' to approach.

Despite these very significant advantages, the use of database marketing in the airline industry remains controversial. If the selected medium for using a database is the telephone, many people still regard an unsolicited telephone call as an invasion of their privacy. The same may apply to a mails hot, fax or Email, albeit to a somewhat lesser degree. With these latter media, though, the problem is one of over-use. The modem executive's in-tray or in-box is awash with database marketing communications. Many of these will be ignored and thrown straight into the waste paper bin or deleted. Only the most professional of messages will be seen and acted upon.

A further, important point with database marketing is that it must be viewed as n expensive form of marketing communication. The costs of a database marketing campaign might at first appear to be small in comparison with one based on, say, media advertising. The relevant cost, though, is not the total cost but a unit cost measure expressed in cost-per thousand terms. Using such measures, database marketing is a high-cost solution.

Putting all these points together, the conclusion is clear. Database marketing campaigns must be executed with the utmost professionalism. If they aren't, the only result will be a costly waste of time and money.

To achieve such professionalism, there are a number of rules which must be followed:

Responsibilities and Timescales Successful database marketing requires a proper definition of objectives and a sound action plan is which is properly formulated and communicated. This should be made the responsibility of one individual.

"Integration" Database marketing should never be implemented on its own, without proper consideration being given to its integration into the finn's wider marketing communication activities. At a narrow level, this may mean a simple, but very necessary co-ordination between the breaking of a media advertising campaign, and the sending out of a mailshot based on it. More broadly, though, it will be necessary to ensure that no contradictory messages are sent out. An airline seeking to position itself as a premium brand, aiming at the business air traveller should not put out advertising targeted at that market segment whilst at the same time sending out mailing material of poor quality emphasising the wide availability of cheap fares.

Databases Sound information in a convenient-to-use form is absolutely essential for successful database marketing. A great deal of attention may be devoted to the production of attractive mailing material, but if this material is then sent to the wrong people, a campaign based on it has no chance of success. Indeed, poor material sent to exactly the right people will achieve more.

In some senses, database management is now less of a problem that it once was, because computing power and the relevant software is now cheap and widely understood. However, problems associated with obtaining the necessary data and processing it are increasing through time rather than easing.

In searching out database information, some fundamental divisions of the data can be made. Firstly, it will be necessary to obtain ***demographic*** details about the target audience for a campaign. This will obviously include names, addresses and titles. It is important that names should be correctly spelt and titles accurate. If a job title is to be used, this should reflect a person's status with the organisation they work for.

A further requirement with demographic data is that it should be reduplicated. It might be thought that duplicates in a database are a minor problem, resulting in a small increase in mailing costs as the same communication is sent to one recipient twice. Duplicates are much more serious than this, because they give the impression that the company sending out the mailing is incompetent and inefficient. Few people will buy from a firm when this is their perception of it. Fortunately, modem database management software generally includes a de-duplication package and the use of this can eliminate many of the problems.

In seeking out demographic information, by far the best sources are those based on situations where people volunteer to be included in a database. Besides addressing to a large degree invasion of privacy issues, cases where people offer their names voluntarily are generally much easier to deal with under the terms of the relevant data protection laws in different countries.

People can be asked when joining a programme to provide all necessary information about themselves. They will then keep this information up-to-date for all the time that they are a programme member, because they will be anxious to ensure that their mileage statements are sent to the right address.

Another possible source of database information is to invite people to join a travel club. As we have already seen, the leisure travel market is changing, with significant numbers of people now searching for individually-tailored holidays, often centered around their hobbies and interests. They are also prepared to spend regularly and heavily to obtain these holidays. This development gives a classic opportunity for database marketing, and it may well be worthwhile to form a club which will enable database information to be collected and regular communication to be maintained with members.

A final opportunity to obtain database information which people have volunteered comes with the question of low fares offers. A number of airlines invite people to volunteer their Email addresses. Once they have done so, they are regularly sent information about flights where there are substantial numbers of empty seats and where the airline is able to offer them particularly attractive low prices.

Despite the attractions of databases for which people have volunteered, it will often be necessary to go beyond them. In particular, "volunteer" databases can only include people who currently fly with the airline concerned, or who at least are reasonably well-disposed towards it. They do not give opportunities for increasing market share by enabling people to be reached who are currently flying with other carriers.

Where the aim is to reach a competitor's customers, it will generally be necessary to buy in lists. Today, these lists are generally based on geographical principles, with addresses being obtained from the Electoral Register and classified according to the neighborhoods in which people live. The proposition is that people who live near to one another will have income levels and spending patterns which are to a significant degree similar. The problem with these lists is that they go out-of-date very quickly. The Electoral Register is only up-dated once a year, and by the time the information is in a form ready to be used in database marketing campaigns it may no longer be accurate enough.

Much the same applies to magazine circulation lists and trade directories as sources of database information. In principle, these can be useful in business-travel orientated campaigns. Databases founded on them may, though, go out-of-date quickly, particularly those derived from lists *for* free-circulation trade papers.

Once the necessary demographic data has been obtained, this must then be combined with the relevant activity data. Airlines need to know where people fly, in what class of service and how often. They need also to be able to capture this data, and marry it to the demographic information they are carrying in their databases. Only then can they produce effectively targeted marketing campaigns.

A final requirement in database management is that the database should be properly integrated with an airline's customer relations activities. We have already seen that someone who complains, with a justified grievance, provides carriers with an important opportunity. If the complaint is dealt with well, it can result in a strengthening, rather than a weakening of the relationship between that person and the airline. Having said this, it will be particularly annoying if someone complains, *for* example, about a delayed flight and then receives a mails hot shortly afterwards in which the airline boasts of its fine punctuality performance. They should not do so, if there is a proper integration between the marketing and customer relations databases. Indeed, if there is, this may result in an important opportunity because someone who complains will also at the same time be providing information about themselves. If their complaint is handled sympathetically, they will then be well-disposed towards the airline in question and may respond to future database marketing messages. Therefore, those who complain and express satisfaction at the way in which their complaint has been dealt with should be added to the airline's marketing database.

Copywriting The subject of copywriting for database marketing remains extremely controversial. What is certainly true is that the investment made in building and maintaining a database can be leveraged substantially if is used well through the production of good material. With decisions about copywriting, the first requirement is clearly that a statement should be made as to the objectives which a particular campaign should meet. These objectives can vary substantially. It may be that the intention is simply to give information to an airline's existing customers on a particular route about, say, a change in flight timings. Another possible objective is that the campaign should encourage these existing customers to fly more through, for example, the offer of bonus frequent flyer miles or a move to a higher status in the airline's loyalty programme. A third, and much the most challenging, possible objective is that the campaign should be targeted at people who are currently flying with other airlines, with the objective being to change their choice-of-carrier decision.

Alongside decisions about objectives, a choice will have to be made about the medium to be employed. A first possibility is that the database will be used for a telemarketing campaign, in which case the copywriter's task will be to help to prepare the script which those working the telephones will use. This will have the benefit of immediate impact, but as previously mentioned may be resented by those who are called. Secondly, the mail may be used. This will allow for the preparation of attractive mailing material but, as we have already seen, this material may be put into the waste paper bin without even being opened. Email provides a newer choice, but it may be difficult to obtain a suitable database of Email addresses and emails are easily deleted without being read.

With decisions made about objectives and medium, the copywriting process can begin. It should follow a series of easy-to-state, but difficult to apply, principles. The flrst of these follows the AIDA model. All material should aim to catch people's attention through a bold headline promising them a worthwhile benefit. It should interest them in the proposition to be made through showing an understanding of their problems. A solution should be presented in a persuasive and credible way, with every effort being made to anticipate possible objections and to deal with these. Finally, a course of action should be proposed, with clear information being presented as to how to follow this.

In using the AIDA model, there is a never-ending debate over the length of copy that should be employed. It is certainly the case that people are becoming busier and busier, and that their willingness to read long copy is lessening all-the-time. Because of this, communications which are designed simply to impart information should certainly be kept short and to-the-point. It is less clear, though, as to whether or not a 'short-is-best' conclusion will always be appropriate where the objective of a campaign is to radically change people's buying behavior.

Here, it should be born in mind that any database, no matter how well prepared, will consist of two groups of people. The first are those who should not, in fact, be on it at all because they have no interest in the propositions being made and never will buy the products or services in question. In history, there has been no example of a perfectly-targeted database. The second group of people are those who do potentially have such an interest.

In copy writing for database marketing, no time should be spent worrying over the fact that mailing material has not been read by people who will never buy the product anyway. The tragedy of the campaign will be if people with a genuine potential interest cannot be persuaded to act upon this and buy the product.

For these people, it is unlikely that a major change in their buying behavior will be achieved by short copy. They have to be thoroughly convinced that the firm seeking their business has an understanding of their problems, and that it can solve these problems better than the existing firms from which they are currently buying. It is most unlikely that they will be so convinced by a few words.

If long copy needs to be employed—and there will be cases where is essential—the style adopted can go a long way to ensuring that resistance to reading it is overcome. Short sentences and paragraphs will be needed, broken up by frequent sub-headings. It will also be necessary to talk in plain, rather than flowery, language. "Correctly co-ordinate schedule" may put people off reading further whereas "right timings" will not.

A particularly useful tactic may be to employ a P.S. at the end of a letter. If this is well written, it can deal with any dissonance people may feel about carrying out the actions proposed in the main body of the letter. It may also be the first thing that they see when looking at a letter and may persuade them to go back and read the earlier body-copy.

In terms of the style and quality of the material to be sent out, this should reflect the objectives of the campaign. An airline re-Launching its Business Class service and seeking to persuade potential passengers the new product is of the highest possible quality, will be unlikely to do so by the use of cheap and shoddy mailing material. On the other hand, a mailing may have the purely tactical purpose of informing customers about a forthcoming fares increase. If it has, it would be a mistake to dress up such a mailing with extravagant expenditure on high quality production.

A final, very important rule with copy writing is that, wherever possible, it should be made interactive. Effective campaigns are generally based on encouraging potential customers to respond to an attractive offer. This might be in order to obtain a free giveaway or to participate in a prize draw for free tickets or bonus frequent flyer miles. Making an offer may overcome people's dislike of the "invasion of privacy" aspect of database marketing. It may also be a means of obtaining from them further, useful. database information about their travel patterns and service preferences.

"Gatekeeping" Today, in most countries, the post is reasonably reliable and the services which back up fax and Email both very efficient. It is therefore possible to ensure that a database marketing message reaches the home or the office of the target recipient. This, though, is the beginning and not the end of the task, because it will be an altogether bigger challenge to ensure that a marketing message is read and acted upon. Many people will simply throwaway what they perceive to be direct mail into the waste paper basket without even bothering to open it, whilst in the office situation, a secretary may be told to throwaway any direct mail items without even putting them into their boss's in-tray. There is an active debate in the literature on direct mail as to how it is possible to ensure at an envelope will be opened and the contents read.

In addressing the problem, there are two possible approaches. One is to employ subterfuge. In extreme form, this consists of writing "Private and Confidential" on the outside of an envelope. This should at least ensure that the envelope is placed in the relevant in-tray. A similar approach, though less extreme, is to make a direct mails hot look exactly like an ordinary business letter. This at least ensures that the letter will be opened as the receiver will hope that there will be an important business communication inside or, better still, a cheque.

As a general rule, deceit can be rejected as a way of getting envelopes opened. It is true that both these methods will succeed in a narrow sense, but they will fail to assist in getting the recipient to act on what they find inside the envelope once they have opened it. They will realize that they have been tricked—the so-called "Betrayal Factor"—and because they have been, they are unlikely to respond in a positive way.

The second approach to addressing gate keeping problems is much to be preferred. This consists of putting a message on the outside of the envelope saying to the recipient that there is a very good reason for them to open it and, if they do, they will be pleased with the offer contained inside. Preparing such a message should be easy. After all, if there is nothing inside the envelope which will make someone pleased they have opened it, why is it being sent in the first place?

Media Relations

It is impossible to over-estimate the importance of a sound approach to media relations in airline marketing communication. Air transport is regarded as immensely newsworthy by editors of newspapers, magazines and television and radio programmes. Because of this, an airline which fails to cultivate strong media relations can suffer a great deal of bad publicity when things go wrong. One which does will not only head off this kind of trouble. It will also be well-placed to obtain favorable coverage when positive things happen such as new route introductions or product and brand re-Launches.

Sound media relationships require in turn a systematic approach to achieve them. Every effort must be made to cultivate the goodwill of journalists through trade entertainment and the offer of free travel on the airline's network. At the same time, helpful background information must be produced. This will include well-written press material, containing quotes from the airline's most senior management.

Poor media relations will result from any attempt to treat journalists with contempt—a sometimes-understandable emotion which must be firmly resisted. Cover-ups should also be avoided. If for example, an airline has an emergency landing of one of its aircraft, nothing will be achieved by denying that such an incident has occurred. Instead, emphasis should be placed on the skill with which the airline's staff handled the situation, and the fact that the carrier has been able to maintain its strong safety record.

The Field Sales Team

Of all aspects of airline selling and sales planning, none generates greater controversy than the question of the management of the airline field sales team. Disagreements occur over the role the field sales executive should play and the recruitment and motivation policies which should be employed. *The Role* Until relatively recently, the role of an airline field sales executive was a straightforward one. The fact that competition in the industry was highly regulated meant that the pace of change was slow. Regulation also meant that all airlines charged the same fares. There was therefore no need for sales executives to seek out customers and negotiate deals with them. Instead, the job was essentially a flag-waving one, with a heavy emphasis on trade entertainment and hospitality and—in many markets—on the consumption of large quantities of alcohol.

Today, the situation could not be more different. As deregulation has come about, so the pace of change in the industry has accelerated. In turn, sales executives now have to accept the challenge of keeping their knowledge up-to-date in a rapidly-changing marketplace. They also have to collect—and communicate to those who need to know—market intelligence data about the activities of competitors. Crucially, they have to negotiate deals with the business houses and travel agencies for which they are responsible. The nature of marketing to the business air traveller changed fundamentally during the 1990s. Instead of the "customer" being business travellers themselves, increasingly firms sought to use their bargaining power to negotiate deals with airlines whereby discounts were demanded in return for loyalty. Negotiation of these deals is today a normal part of the work of the airline field sales executive. Likewise, today travel agents remain important customers of airlines, but few, if any, are satisfied with the standard 9% commission that they have traditionally been paid. They are normally looking for over-ride commissions where bigger commissions are paid for higher volumes of business. Again, the field sales executive will be expected to negotiate these deals, and to monitor agent's performance relative to them, whilst under great pressure to reduce, rather than raise, commission payments.

Besides important market intelligence and sales negotiation roles, the airline field sales executive is today expected to carry out an important customer relations role. One of the challenges of their job is that they are not selling a tangible product. Rather, they have to sell a long-term relationship with a relatively small number of demanding clients. They can only do so if they work hard to support their clients in the jobs that they in turn have to do. Today, the supply of information is not usually the problem, in that modem Global Distribution Systems such as Galileo, SABRE and Amadeus make available almost limitless quantities of information about schedules and fares. Rather, the challenge is to use this information in a creative and imaginative way to build sales, and the sales executive must be prepared to work with their travel agency accounts in particular to ensure that this is done.

Recruitment Criteria—It is clear from the above that the airline sales executive is now required to do a professional selling job. The question of recruiting the right person is a crucial one which all airline sales managers' will have to address from time-to-time.

There are, of course, a number of basic requirements. The person selected must be articulate and persuasive, something which can be tested at an interview. A person who cannot convince an interviewing panel that the firm should take them on is unlikely to be able to persuade a travel agency to increase its sale of the airline's tickets. They should also be of a clean and tidy appearance, as scruffiness will be taken by clients as a sign of a cheapskate company. A current clean driving license will also be needed.

A much more contentious question is the previous experience that should be required. Carriers have a number of possible recruitment sources for their field sales executives. They can aim to hire people with a proven selling track record, even it this has been obtained from outside of the aviation industry. They can simply approach experienced airline sales executives who are currently working for other airlines. They can recruit from the travel agency industry. Lastly, they can transfer people who already work for them, but in non-sales jobs.

Hiring people from other industries is an especially interesting option. It can certainly be argued that true salespeople are born and not made, and that the great sales success stories have often been achieved by insecure people who are driven to sell as they seek reassurance that they are likeable. In that sense, someone who has a proven selling track record is saying a great deal about themselves, despite their lack of airline industry experience. Even here, it can certainly be argued that, generally, airlines are likely to be better at training people in airline industry familiarization rather than in the skills of selling.

Despite this, the issue is not a clear-cut one. The problem is that, airlines do not generally reward their sales people on a basic-plus-commission principle fasted, a reasonable salary is paid, together with perhaps a relatively small bonus if the annual target is reached. This therefore begs the question as to why someone who has achieved success in commission-based selling should want to come and work for an airline, where they certainly will not starve but neither will they have an opportunity to achieve very high earnings. The answer often is that they are burnt out and are looking for an easier life with a steady monthly salary. If they are, they should be rejected out-of-hand.

Hiring—or rather, poaching—fully trained and experienced sales executives from other airlines might seem in many ways to be the ideal solution. These people will have industry knowledge and—hopefully—proven selling skills. They will also have established industry contacts and perhaps will bring some useful inside information about a competitor.

In many situations, airline will have little choice but to use this recruitment source as they will not have the training budget available to spend on appropriate staff development. This will be especially the case for small airlines, or at the minor stations of larger carriers. The dangers of poaching, should, though, be emphasized. Someone who brings market intelligence with them may be disloyal enough to move in a year or two's time, giving away in turn the trade secrets of the airline they have joined. Also, people who move from one airline to another in quick succession begin to lack credibility with their trade contacts, especially if the different carriers they work for are also competitors.

The travel agency industry may give some attractive recruitment opportunities. People with work experience as travel agents should have a good understanding of the travel business. They will also have seen airline sales executives at work, and will know of examples of the job being done badly.

With the final possible recruitment source, the airline's own staff should be looked at seriously. There will almost certainly be people who are doing other customer contact jobs who have the qualities which will be needed to do well as a field sales executive. They will already have a knowledge of the airline, and can be expected to bring a greater degree of loyalty and commitment compared with those brought in from outside.

The ideal age for an airline sales executive is a final, interesting recruitment issue. The person hired has the difficult task of ensuring that they get on well with the young people who generally make up the clerks who work in travel agencies, whilst at the same time being able to present themselves as credible company negotiators with senior management both in travel agents and business houses. Because of the negotiation role, there is probably a minimum age of early to middle twenties—few people will warm to the idea of being asked to complete a deal with a child. At the same time, an older person applying for a job as a junior sales executive should be viewed carefully. They may have many qualities which will make them exactly right for the job, but one's concern would be that they lack ambition and are simply looking for an easy ride towards a well deserved retirement.

Motivation of Airline Field Sales Executives

This is a very difficult question. In many industries money is used as the prime motivator for a sales team. Members of the team are paid a small retainer, and then a substantial commission on everything they sell. Generally, airlines have found a basic-plus-commission reward structure difficult to devise and implement. Airline salespeople are not selling a specific product to a clearly identifiable customer in the way that, say, someone selling double-glazing is. Rather their task is to build a long-term relationship with a group of clients, and, in the case of relationships with travel agents, to encourage the agent to sell rather than doing the selling themselves. Also, there are complications in deciding who has been responsible for a sale being achieved. A common situation is for a business house to use a travel agent, but for different members of the airline sales team to be responsible for the relationship with the business house and the travel agent. If this is the case, both will claim any commission that might be available. The person responsible of the business house will argue that they have done all the persuading, with the travel agent being simply presented with a fait accompli with regard to choice-of-airline decisions. The person calling on the travel agent is unlikely to see things in the same way.

The difficulties associated with commission-based reward structures mean that few, if any, airlines are able to use them. Instead, salespeople are generally paid a reasonable salary, with a relatively small bonus on offer if they reach their annual sales target. In turn, because of this, a wide range of policies will be necessary to ensure the a high level of motivation in the members of the sales team, because the cutting-edge that commissions might provide will not be available to the sales manager.

Of these motivation methods, the annual salary on offer will be an obvious starting point. Here, it is important that the salary should be comparable to that paid to salespeople working for rival airlines. It is very demotivating to realize that others are being paid more for doing exactly the same job. The annual bonus should also be a worthwhile one, with the salesperson involved in the setting of the targets which must be achieved in order to earn it.

Training will be an important part of the motivation process. The point was made in that airline salespeople are now expected to take on a challenging, professional selling role. They cannot do so successfully unless they are equipped with the necessary knowledge and skills. Training must therefore encompass both product knowledge and selling skills, and it must be on a continuous basis given the pace of change which is now characteristic of the industry.

Career progression and advancement will also be an important factor in maintaining the interest and commitment of the most capable people. Providing a clear way ahead may be difficult or impossible for a small airline, or at an outstation of a major carrier. In other situations though, members of the team must feel that if they perform well the necessary training and development policies are in place to allow them to advance to sales management positions.

Questions of expenses and corporate hospitality are often a festering sore in many sales teams. What is important is that salespeople should be able to give their clients a comparable level of hospitality to that on offer from their competitors. It is very demotivating if only the basics can be given when rivals can offer generous treatment.

A very important general heading with sales force motivation is that of the tools to do the job. If a firm has high expectations, it should be prepared equally to invest heavily in resources. For airline salespeople, these resources will include a modem, reliable car and a management information system which allows them to be fully up-to-date both with what is going on within the airline and what business is being obtained from the accounts for which they are responsible. A final requirement is for there to be an adequate level of office back-up and support, with meeting rooms available when necessary.

The last, but perhaps the most contentious question in a motivation policy is the part to be played by fear. It is most certainly true that an element of fear must always be present. If the members of a sales team know that however poorly they perform and however lazy they are they will always have a job, it will be almost certainly impossible to obtain high levels of performance from them. At the same time, though, the role of fear should not be overdone, and it should not be seen as a substitute for other motivational methods. It may from time-to-time be necessary to for people for laziness or dishonesty, but dismissing people for incompetence raises questions about who is incompetent and who therefore should be fired. A person who is dismissed because they cannot do the job may have been wrong for that job in the first place. In that case they should not have been hired and the incompetent person is the one who did the hiring. A second, still worse possibility is that they did have the potential to make a success of the difficult job of being an airline sales executive, but the manager responsible for them could not provide an environment in which they could give of their best. The necessary skills and qualities are relatively rare, and for an airline to lose someone with potential in these circumstances should be seen as a case of criminal negligence. It is their manager, and not them, who should be fired.

Airline Advertising

Advertising is, of course, no more than another marketing communication method available to airlines. It is, though, so important, and so controversial, that it needs a special section of its own. The purpose of this part of the book is to look at what advertising can and cannot do for airlines, and to discuss the decisions which have to be made in preparing and implementing an advertising policy.

The Functions of Advertising

No advertising campaign will be successful unless clear objectives are set for it, and the performance of the campaign monitored against these objectives. In turn, it is necessary to decide what advertising can do, so that any objectives which are set are achievable ones.

Clearly, advertising can be expected to promote corporate image and corporate brand values. It will also playa role in building sub-brands such as those which airlines have built around cabin classes or service concepts. With shorter-term objectives, advertising can be used to provide tactical information about service changes such as the introduction of a new route or a new type of aircraft. It can also sell special offers such as those associated with discount fares or bonus frequent flyer miles.

More controversially, airlines may see advertising as a way of influencing policy-makers and opinion formers so that their policy objectives are achieved.

No carrier can operate independently of the political process. They may rely on this process for favorable treatment with regard, for example, to the award of international route rights. Increasingly, too, they are having to lobby over environmental questions of noise and pollution in order to ensure that limitations on their freedom of action are kept to a minimum. Advertising may be able to playa subtle but useful role in positioning an airline as a good corporate citizen.

A final function of advertising which some would claim and many dispute is that advertising can help in a staff motivation policy. Motivating customer contact staff to give outstanding service is a notoriously difficult task, especially in large mature airlines. The fact that staff members see their airline advertising in newspapers or on the television may help them to feel part of a team. If in these advertisements they see role models providing warm and friendly service to customers, this may in turn subtly affect their behaviour when dealing with customers in real life. Unfortunately, this theory only works in situations where motivation is already high and service standards already good. Where morale is poor, using advertising as a form of brainwashing will only make matters worse, with the added problem that the airline's customers will see claims being made in the advertising which their experience of the product will not match. This will add significantly to their anger and disenchantment.

Advertising Decisions

Setting the Brief

All good advertising campaigns start with a clear decision about what the campaign should achieve. This in turn can only be decided in the context of an overall marketing communications policy, with a proper integration of any advertising which is undertaken with other forms of communication such as sponsorships or database marketing.

The brief itself should be as detailed as possible, and should include a statement of the objectives that a campaign should meet and the criteria which will be employed to decide whether it has succeeded or failed. It is also important that the brief should be agreed to and signed by the airline's most senior management at the earliest possible stage. It is a peculiar, but vitally important feature of advertising that everyone regards themselves as an expert about it, especially CEOs. In practice, no campaign will be implemented without the Chief Executive's approval, and it is always a costly disappointment if a great deal of work is done, only for the resulting advertising to be vetoed shortly before it is launched. Such occurrences can never be prevented entirely, but their frequency can be minimized by. ensuring that the Chief Executive at least agrees with the brief before work begins.

Agency Selection

Choosing an advertising agency is a very important decision, where mistakes will prove very costly. As a first point, advertising should be recognized as a professional discipline where outside help from a specialist agency will be needed. Some low fares airlines have in recent years attempted to produce their own advertising as a cost saving measure, but the results have generally looked very amateurish. Also, even for cost-saving, the policy is of doubtful value, because agencies will be paid commission by the media where they buy advertising, whereas firms booking their advertising space themselves generally will not be.

Once it has been decided that an agency will be appointed, the question arises as to which one to choose. The good news here is that in the advertising industry, airline accounts are perceived as very attractive ones, Besides being seen as fun to work on, they give an agency a great deal of prestige. Therefore, when it becomes known that an airline is seeking to appoint an agency, or to replace one they already have, there will be no shortage of firms willing to pitch for the account.

For many international airlines, a crucial question will be whether or not the agency can give a true global coverage. It is important that, in particular, brand-building advertising should be consistent across all markets. It may therefore be better to choose an agency with a large number of offices in different countries. This will, though, restrict choice to the comparatively small number of agencies which can credibly claim a global presence. If a smaller agency is selected, then it will have to be one which has well-established links with other agencies located in the overseas markets which the airline serves.

When choosing an agency, an overwhelming emphasis should be placed on its record of being able to produce original, imaginative and exciting work. Still, far too much airline advertising is hackneyed and stereotyped. It consists of pictures of blissfully happy passengers being served wonderful food by beautiful girls. If an agency's initial proposals include any variations around this tired theme, they should be shown the door with the utmost speed.

Once those agencies with the necessary creative skills have. been isolated, other issues may come into play. There may be an attraction is the idea of appointing an agency which can supply a wide variety of services under one roof. These may include a media planning and media buying unit—most agencies would expect to provide this service. It may also be helpful if the agency can provide direct mail and sales promotion expertise and—increasingly important today—a unit able to deal with so-called "new Today, the fashion is rather away from this "one-stop-shop" principle. An agency may be strong on one area and weak in others, and it may be better for clients to put together their own group of experts by calling in people from smaller, specialist agencies. This will, though, impose a major management task as the proper integration of the different forms of marketing communication will be a vital requirement. It would be a serious mistake if, for example, the firm's advertising was putting out different messages compared with its direct mail material.

One final point is that the appointment of an advertising agency should be seen as a strategic, long-term decision. Some firms may feel that it is a smart move to change their agency very frequently, because this keeps their current agency on its toes and also allows them to benefit from a flow of new ideas every time a new agency is appointed. This view is a mistake. Besides being very costly—substantial fees will be charged by each new agency to finance their initial work on the account—frequent changes of agency are unlikely to result in consistent and successful advertising. It will take time for the agency to fully understand their client's business and for the necessary personal relationships to be established. The essence of brand-building is that the brand values which should underlie a firm's advertising must remain consistent on a long-term basis. Whilst a determined client might ensure such consistency when working with a succession of agencies, achieving it will be much easier if agreement can be reached with one agency at an early stage as to what these brand values are, with the same agency charged with communicating them over a long period of time.

Media Buying

Once an agency has been selected, there are then a large number of decisions which will be made using the agency's professional advice. It is important, though, that the airline should maintain an independence of thought, otherwise it risks merely becoming a slave to the agency's whims. Media buying choices will decide where the airline's advertising will be seen, by whom, at what cost, and in what form advertising messages can be communicated. In making them, it will always be necessary to decide first on how best to spend the available budget. No airline will have the money to spend limitless amounts on advertising. Also, for carriers away from their home base, they will always be wrestling with the problem that locally-based airlines will be able to outspend them, often by a factor of several times. Their task will therefore be to make an impact against a competitor with far greater resources—always advertising's most difficult challenge.

In attempting to achieve this impact there are two possible approaches. Firstly, advertising expenditure may be spread evenly throughout the year. This ought to ensure that the airline will not be forgotten, but the difficulty will be in making a worthwhile impact. Secondly, advertising may be put out in short, concentrated bursts in the hope that, if it is memorable enough, this will carry the airline through the times when, because of budget limitations, it is doing no advertising at all. Of these two possibilities, the second is to be very much preferred. In today's world, it is hard enough to get noticed, given the proliferation of different advertising media and the way in which people are becoming increasingly bombarded with advertising messages. Making a strong investment, even if it has to be over a short time, is the best way of ensuring that you are.

Media buying choices will, of course, be decided by the objectives of a campaign, in terms of both its target audience and whether or not the campaign has a strategic or merely a tactical objective. To reach the business air traveller, there are now a well-established number of possible media choices. These will include business-orientated newspapers such as the Wall Street Journal and the Financial Times, and news magazines such as Newsweek and The Economist. In terms of television advertising, then commercial breaks in the main evening news programmes and some sporting events may bring a suitable audience profile.

With leisure air travel, weekend newspapers will prove useful, as will specialist magazines such as those aimed at enthusiasts for particular sports.

The Internet, too, provides an increasingly exciting medium as it allows a destination to be sold in an attractive and interesting way, alongside messages about the best way to reach the destination in terms of a choice of-airline decision.

With questions of strategic campaigns, a long-term brand-building objective may well justify investment in the time and money to make TV commercials. These allow messages to be put across using sound and pictures in a way which print media cannot match. There may well, though, be a gap of months between an ad. being planned and it being ready to launch. This is often too long in the rapidly-changing world of today's deregulated aviation market. Newspaper advertisements, on the other hand, should be quick to produce and also usually can be placed at short notice with little or no advanced booking of space being required. They are often the most effective way of communicating messages about, say, a seat sale in a market which suddenly and unexpectedly turns down.

The cost of the different media will obviously be a crucial question when deciding between them. Here, it is important not to be misled by the up-front, invoiced costs. Rather, a Cost-per-Thousand (CPT) measure should be used. Thus, for example, the media buying costs of television advertising can appear very high. If, though, this expenditure allows a large audience to be reached in the right way at the right time, it can represent good value-for-money.

Creative Strategies

Successful creative strategies are, of course, at the heart of all worthwhile advertising. One is often tempted by a rule which states "There is only one rule—there are no rules." There are certainly examples of airline campaigns which seem to fly in the face of all logic yet appear to have been very successful, and others which looked soundly-based at the outset which have proved to be disastrous. Such a conclusion, though, is not helpful. There have to be some basic guidelines, even if it will always be possible to quote exceptions to them.

For a start, all campaigns where the budget is sufficient should be research-based. Common sense, intuition and past experience are all important aspects in the evaluation of an agency's creative proposals. They cannot, though, always prevent mistakes being made. Advertising proposals should be researched through well-structured market studies using representative members of the campaign's target audience. Continuing research will also be needed as a campaign runs, research which should be related to its objectives and to measurement of the extent to which these objectives are being achieved.

Secondly, airlines should invest in decent quality-of-production of all their advertising, even if this means that within a given budget, less money will be available for media buying. All airlines have to base their appeal on the fundamental proposition that they are safe, whilst many are attempting to build brands which position them as quality up-market producers. Cheapskate advertising will soon be associated in passenger's minds with a poor quality company. If there isn't the money available for reasonable production quality, it is better to do nothing.

As a further proposition, all airline advertising should be fundamentally honest. "If you cannot say it honestly, shut up and talk about something you can say honestly" is a sound dictum. Passengers particularly regular business travellers—are not misled or fooled by false claims in airline advertising. Rather, they are angered and alienated by them. Besides the problems the offending airline may run into with the bodies that regulate advertising content, it will also increase many times over the anger of those caught up in its service failings. People take a long time to forgive a firm if they feel that they have been tricked into buying its product through deceit.

In deciding on the creative content of their advertising, airlines and their advertising agencies are usually faced with a difficult dilemma. Should they aim to include many arguments in an ad. as to why the airline should be chosen, or should they merely try to say one thing in a persuasive and convincing way?

The proposition in favour of including many arguments is, at first sight, easy to make. If an ad. succeeds in capturing somebody's attention, a prime selling opportunity is being lost unless a substantial number of arguments are put forward to persuade them to buy. The risk is, though, that no message is communicated effectively, in the enthusiasm to put across a great many. A better approach is to try to say some thing, using individual arguments to support a single proposition in a memorable way. If this is done well (in the case of, say, a television commercial), only a relatively short one will be needed. Further commercials can then be made within a given budget, to make up an overall campaign in which all the required messages can be communicated.

The balance between long-term, corporate brand-building advertising and short-term tactical campaigns poses a significant, and increasing dilemma, in the airline industry. Deregulation is in turn leading to instability, where tactical messages will often be needed to communicate changes in prices or product to customers. At the same time, airline sales managers are under increasing pressure to achieve their end-of-year sales targets and they often worry that they will be fired if they fail to do so. They will always therefore be lobbying that a high proportion of advertising spend should be directed towards the tactical campaigns that they hope will help them. It is a great mistake, though, to merely consider tactical questions when setting advertising objectives.

A significant amount of advertising expenditure must therefore be directed at the brand, and great care must be taken to ensure that frequent tactical messages—which are inevitable today—do not undermine fundamental brand values.

A final question with creative strategies is the difficult one of the balance between local and global advertising approaches. Perhaps more than in any other industry, airline brands need to be global, and it will be a problem if people travel around the world and see the airline they are flying with putting forward totally contradictory messages in different markets. This might lead to a conclusion that all advertising should be controlled centrally, with creative work carried out by one agency in the airline's home country. This will also allow the advertising production budget to be spent in a concentrated way, with, in particular, quality work being done on expensive television commercials. The problem is, of course, that there are substantial market-by-market and culture-by-culture differences in what is acceptable and what is not.

In a difficult area, the best approach is probably to appoint a lead agency, with overall responsibility for brand positioning and brand values in the airline's most important home-base market, and to in turn appoint sub-agencies in the airline's overseas markets. These agencies should then be given clear, but limited opportunities to adapt or change centrally produced material in order to make it suitable for local markets.

Monitoring Success/Advertising Life Cycles

It is essential that thorough procedures are in place to decide whether or not an advertising campaign is meeting its objectives. No matter how well initial research is done, disasters do occur, and without a formal monitoring process, the fact that a campaign is failing may not be picked up. Even successful campaigns, though, eventually fun out-of-steam because of Product Life Cycle effects. They then need to be replaced with new approaches. Deciding on the moment to do this will be difficult. Those with the task of doing so need to be helped by having available quantitative data from a monitoring programme.

The monitoring methods which should be used will vary with a campaign's objectives. The easiest case will be with advertising designed to make people respond to an offer. For example, an advertisement may offer a "golden hello" of free miles in the airline's frequent flyer programme for those applying to join the programme before a deadline date. If it also contains a cut-out coupon or special free-phone number, it will be possible to precisely measure the response, or the lack of it.

Other advertising will have a longer-term, more strategic objective. The airline may, for example, have gone through a difficult period with failing product standards. Its advertising might then be designed to persuade people that things are now improving and that the time has come to try the airline once again. If it is, a significant boost to bookings once the campaign has begun would be taken as an encouraging sign. Also, it might be possible to test people's attitude towards the airline by talking with members of its sales team who regularly meet travel agents and corporate customers.

For advertising with a purely brand-building objective, precise measurement of the results is notoriously difficult. It will be necessary to invest in initial market research designed to define levels of awareness of potential customers and the attitudes they adopt towards the airline. As the campaign is implemented and develops, more will have to be invested to repeat this research, and also to ask people if they remember seeing the airline's advertising and, if they do, what they recall about it. Successful campaigns will show a growing awareness, a positive move in attitudes and a high level of recall of the content of the advertising.

What are the Features of "Good" Airline Advertising?

Of course, good research data will be particularly valuable in deciding whether advertising is working or whether it isn't. There will be many occasions, though, when such data is simply not available. This will especially be the case when area sales managers have to decide whether or not centrally-produced advertising will be valuable in the market areas for which they are responsible. In such situations, a checklist will at least result in the right questions being asked prior to a decision being made.

The basis of such a checklist will be a judgment as to whether or not the ad. is likely to attract and hold attention. If it will, it must also be professionally produced, with no accusations being possible that it is a cheapskate effort. It must certainly be credible, as damage will result if it is not. It must also be persuasive, showing an understanding of the customer's true needs, and demonstrating the ways in which the airline can meet these needs. The degree to which the ad. is likely to persuade will be increased if it can demonstrate that the airline can credibly offer a unique selling proposition to the customer (for example, "First Flight of the Day"). Finally, it will be necessary to study the ad. very carefully to make sure that it is compatible with the airline's long term development of its brand values.

Selling in the Air Freight Market

With air freight consistently growing faster than the passenger side of the business, the question of effective marketing communication with its freight customers is one of growing important to many airlines. Some of the issues are the same as on the passenger side and some are unique to air freight.

The Sales Task in the Air Freight Market

One of the major differences between air freight and air passenger marketing is the degree of existing market penetration. It is true that on the passenger side, airlines face competition on short-haul routes from buses, private cars and especially from rail services. On medium and long-haul routes, though, their penetration is almost total. Virtually everyone who travels now flies, with surface transport restricted to the specialist market for cruising (even here, airlines often benefit by flying people to their port of embarkation).

With freight, things could not be more different. Surface transport provides formidable competition on all routes, either in the form of trucking and roll-unroll-off ferries (in short haul markets) or deep-sea container services on long-haul routes. This competition is especially difficult for airlines to deal with because it is almost always based on the proposition of cheaper freight rates than those which are available from air transport.

Given this competitive scene, the most straightforward selling task is that based on the need to secure a high share of the existing air freight market. Here, airlines mainly aim their efforts at the air freight forwarding industry. Still, a very high proportion of this traditional market (over 90% in many cases) passes through the hands of freight forwarders. Also, because much of the traffic consists of smaller consignments which are consolidated into larger consignments by forwarders, they, rather than the shippers who provide the original shipments, have the dominant role in deciding which airlines will be used. Marketing efforts, therefore, need to be concentrated on the senior management teams of large forwarding firms in pursuit of long-term relationships and also on the clerks in these firms who are responsible for routing and carrier-choice decisions for individual consignments.

A far more difficult, but more exciting opportunity comes with the task of converting existing surface transport traffic flows into air freight. Air freight's market penetration when calculated on a weight basis is very low. On most routes, still only 2 or 3% of the goods that move do so by air. The remaining traffic is transported by much cheaper surface modes. This is not to suggest, of course, that all such traffic is potentially available to airlines—much of it is too low in value for air freight to make any sense. It is still true, though, that if air freight could double its market penetration from 2 to 4%, this would in turn double the size of the air freight market.

In carrying out this market development work, those airlines that attempt it have to use a fundamentally different approach. These are little point in approaching the forwarding industry. Most major forwarding firms have a substantial presence in both air and surface traffic. Therefore, they are unlikely to see a worthwhile incentive to convert surface traffic into air freight, as this will often merely be moving traffic from one part of their business to another. Instead, approaches have to be made to the firms which are the originators of the traffic. These approaches have to be at a high level of management. The task of making the case for air freight is a challenging one. It involves arguing that there are tradeoffs to be made between the higher transport costs (brought about by the fact that air freight's rates are generally more expensive), and the savings that can be made in packaging, insurance, stockholding and warehousing costs. These tradeoffs can generally be made only by senior managers with a wide span of responsibility over all the relevant areas.

There is one final area of air freight marketing which is potentially the most interesting of all, because air freight gives opportunities for firms to do things which they simply cannot do if they employ slower surface transport. This is the most obvious in the case of perishable goods, which, if surface modes are used, can only be sold in local markets. These in turn will often be saturated with the product in question, with only low prices therefore on offer. Use of air freight allows them to be flown to much more distant markets where prices will be much higher and profits potentially greater.

Even for non-perishable goods, air freight may give firms the chance to open new markets. Use of air freight allows firms to begin to sell in overseas markets with the minimum of delay once they have made a decision to enter. They can do so without a large and inflexible investment in overseas warehouses. This is because the speed of air freight allows stock to be held in a single centralized warehouse and then to be shipped to customers once orders have been placed. In a very true sense, air freight allows marketing to be carried out on a global basis.

Because of the new opportunities which it gives, the most promising kind of air freight marketing consists of generating entirely new traffic flows by persuading firms to take advantage of them. This approach is in principle an especially appealing one because the resulting traffic will not be vulnerable to poaching by surface transport operators. It will, though, place high demands on an airline's field sales team, because it will require them to perform a consulting role with a firm's senior managers.

Marketing Communication Methods

For all the different tasks in the air freight market, personal selling by a team of freight sales executives is generally very important, and more so than is the case in the passenger business.

This is especially the case for the many airlines which restrict their ambition to competing for their share of the existing air freight market. To do so, they will need a sales team which calls regularly on the major forwarding firms, both at their head offices and at regional branch offices. They will need in turn to offer generous corporate hospitality, as well as opportunities for key decision-makers to travel on overseas familiarisation trips. With advertising and promotion, most airlines see a role for some advertising, usually placed in the trade magazines which circulate amongst the forwarding community. This advertising usually merely describes the benefits of using one airline rather than another, with a dull and repetitious emphasis on the quality of ground handling.

For the more challenging tasks of converting surface traffic into air freight and of building entirely new flows of air freight business, a personal selling approach will again be needed. It will, though, be of a very different kind. Airline salespeople will have to aim to make contact with high level managers, and be prepared to run a sales campaign which may take months or years to bring to fruition. During this time, they will have to carry out extensive studies to prove that airfreight can be a cost-effective way forward. Such studies will need to be backed up by advertising messages, with these placed in locations such as the Financial Times and Wall Street Journal which are read by senior management.

Brands Management in Airline Marketing

An essential issue in product management is branding. Different firms have different policies on the branding on their products. While 3M puts its brand name on a great diversity of products, Proctor & Gamble, on the opposite extreme, maintains a separate brand name for each product. In general, the use of brand extensions should be evaluated on the basis of the compatibility of various products—can the same brand name represent different products without conflict or confusion? Coca Cola for many years resisted putting its coveted brand name on a diet soft drink. In the old days, available sweeteners such as saccharin added an undesirable aftertaste, implying a clear sacrifice in taste for the reduction in calories. Thus, to avoid damaging the brand name Coca Cola, Coke instead named its diet cola Tab. Only after Nutrasweet was introduced was the brand extension allowed. Research shows that consumers are more receptive to brand extensions when (1) the company appears to have the expertise to make the product [McDonald's was not thought as credible as a photo-finishing service], (2) the products are congruent (compatible), and (3) the brand extension is not seen as being exploitative of a high quality brand name [e.g., one should not use a premium brand name like Heineken to make a trivially easy product like popcorn].

Co-branding involves firms using two or more brands together to maximize appeal to consumers. Some ice cream makers, for example, use their own brand name in addition to naming the brands of ingredients contained. Sometimes, this strategy may help one brand at the expense of the other. It is widely believed, for example, that the "Intel inside" messages, which Intel paid computer makers to put on their products and packaging, reduced the value of the computer makers' brand names because the emphasis was now put on the Intel component.

Certain "peripheral" characteristics of products may "signal" quality or other value to consumers. For some products, packaging accounts for a large part of the total product manufacturing cost. Long warranties often signal to consumers that the product is of good quality since the manufacturer is willing to take responsibility for its functioning.

There is no clear distinction between a "pure" tangible product and a service. Most products contain some of both. A computer, for example, is a tangible product, but it often comes with a warranty and software updates.

Brands management is receiving increasing attention in airline marketing today. There is optimism that by adopting branding concepts developed in other industries, carriers will be able to both add value to their product (and thereby reverse the long-term trend of declining average yields), and secure better control of their distribution channels. The author's experience is, though, that the subject is one where there is a great deal of misunderstanding in the industry. This chapter's aim is to clarify the issues, and to set out the ways in which airlines can make the best use of branding techniques.

"Brands" and "Commodities"

What is a "Brand"?

In terms of understanding the concept of a brand, it is best to think in terms of a spectrum. At one end of the spectrum, there are products which customers perceive as pure "commodities". At the other, there are situations where they recognise the existence of powerful brands.

A "commodity" can be defined as any situation where customers do not perceive significant differences in the products of competing suppliers. Such situations are common. As has already been noted, in the UK at least, the petrol (gasoline) market is a good example. Few qrivers have strong preferences as to the type of petrol they put in their car. Instead, they take into account a range of factors when deciding which filling station to use, none of which are related to the qualities or lack of them in the different types of petrol on offer. Many people will pull into the next garage they see after deciding they need to fill up. Others will choose the garage where the petrol is cheapest. Some—especially those with company cars where the petrol is being paid for by their employer—will select the garage with the best loyalty scheme where payments for petrol can be translated into gifts through an awards programme.

Commodity situations are fundamentally unhealthy from a marketing viewpoint. Because buyers have no strong preferences they can be attracted only by price discounts or incentives. Commodity markets are thus ones characterised by intense competition and often, low profit margins.

The aviation industry has one classic commodity market—the aeroplane seat included in packaged holiday arrangements. This is especially the case in Europe, where the industry is dominated by charter airlines, few, if any of which have a significant brand presence. Most people when booking their holiday specify the destination they would like to visit. If a brand is quoted, it is normally the brand of the tour operator organising their holiday. It is almost never that of the airline that will fly them there.

It is possible for producers in commodity markets to make satisfactory profits, but those that do are almost always those that are vertically integrated with their distribution channels, either owning or being owned by the firms that make up these channels. This is certainly the case in the petrol market, where as we have discussed, the firms refining the petrol from crude oil generally also own or franchise a network of filling stations, They are able to earn significant profits from such outlets. A concern for them, though, is the increasing proportion of petrol being sold through supermarket filling stations, with now about a third of the UK market in the, hands of these outlets. They have no formal links with the refiners of petrol, but have substantial and increasing bargaining power with them. As a consequence the refiners are finding it much more difficult to achieve acceptable profits in the supermarket-controlled sector.

If commodity situations bring significant problems, it is clearly better in many cases for firms to aim at "brand" rather than "commodity" status, A brand is defined as any situation where customers do perceive significant differences in the products of competing suppliers. The reasons why they do are of vital importance in understanding the concept of brands management.

For many products, some of the reasons for their brand status can he found in so-called tangible brand differentiators. These are features of a product that can actually be experienced through the senses of taste, appearance, smell etc. For example, someone might have a preference for a particular type of soup because it is thicker than other brands, or for a make of car because they believe it has a superior air conditioning system.

Tangible brand differentiators are important for almost all brands. Indeed, those that lack them, or possess them to an insufficient degree, often have to face problems of counterfeiting. (This is because it is all too easy to reproduce the product and sell counterfeit items in competition with genuine ones.) It is rarely possible, though, to build powerful brands on the basis of tangible differentiators alone. The reason is that a tangible brand differentiator may produce only a transient marketing advantage, because it can often be matched or over-ridden very easily by the firm's competitors. The manufacturer of thicker soup may obtain some short -term growth in its sales, if consumers prefer thick soup to thin. The very fact that they do will force rival firms to thicken up their own soups, something they will be able to do very easily by a slight adjustment to the recipes they use.

The airline industry certainly has its share of easily-matched tangible brand values. This is especially so in such areas as seat comfort and catering standards. Recent years have seen a steady stream of airlines relaunching their Business Class products. The cornerstones of such relaunches are normally better seats with a greater seat pitch and improved catering. Providing the airline's investment is large enough, a short -term improvement in market share can often be obtained. The fact that it can, though, forces other airlines to respond with their own product up-grades which normally surpass, rather than just match, the standards achieved by the innovating carrier. The end result is higher costs for all the competitors, without a significant long-term change in market shares.

The fact that tangible brand values are often easily matchable means that powerful brands cannot be based soley on them. Brand power is normally dependent on psychological brand values, which cannot be quickly matched by rivals. If they are to be matched, this can only be done after the expenditure of a great deal of time, money and effort.

With psychological brand values, very common and very powerful ones relate to the pride, status and aspirations of those that use a particular brand. In many markets, BMW or Mercedes cars have exactly this appeal. The BMW driver does, of course, benefit from tangible brand values relating to such things as engineering excellence and interior comfort, and would no doubt point to such factors as the dominant ones in their decision to buy the car. They may also feel, though, that driving a BMW is a sign that they have made a success of their lives, and that they are someone to be looked up to and admired by those less prosperous than themselves. Similar aspirational brands are Rolex and VanCleef and Arpel.

Another, increasingly common psychological brand value is that of fun. In many ways, the success of McDonalds as a fast food brand can be attributed as much to its customers' perception that McDonalds stores are fun places to go as to the food and drink actually on offer there. Disney is a fun brand in the entertainment industry, with the Virgin brand having a similar strength, though it has now been stretched to encompass a much wider range of products than was the case in its original base in the entertainment industry.

Some brands attempt to position themselves as being trustworthy. This is especially so with long-established firms such as Marks and Spencer. For them, trustworthiness is a powerful psychological brand differentiator because it allows them to defend their strong position against the attacks of newer rivals. A perception of being trustworthy can only be established and sustained after a long period of customer-friendly trading. It is not usually a credible claim when made by a new entrant.

A final, interesting, example of a psychological brand value which grew in importance during the 1990s was that of greenness and environmental awareness. The UK cosmetics firm Body Shop has been an example of a brand built on the proposition that it trades ethically, with a proper concern for issues such as the environment and animal welfare. The US ice-cream firm Ben and Jerry's achieved a similar positioning.

This discussion of the fundamentals of branding has been a necessary one. It shows that branding is a complex and difficult subject. The fact that it is raises the question of why brands can be useful to airlines, and the methods that should be used to build and position brands.

Why Brands?

Strong brands bring firms two benefits. Firstly, they can add value to the product, allowing branded products to be sold at a premium price compared with those that are merely perceived as commodities. Secondly, they assist firms in establishing and maintaining control of their distribution channels.

The ability of brands to add value is substantial and still, despite some threats which have arisen in recent years, beyond dispute. For example, BMWs sell at a substantial price premium compared with other cars with a comparable product specification. People pay very much more for trainers with a strong brand associated with them than for those without such a name. As airlines wrestle with the problem of a continuing decline in their average yields, they can reasonably expect that emphasis on brands management will at least make a contribution to arresting this trend.

The contribution that brands can make towards securing control of distribution channels is less clear, but still of vital importance. To understand it, we need to revisit the concept of "Super-Profits". These are the profits earned which are over and above the "normal" profits needed to keep a firm in business. They accrue to the firms which are able to establish and maintain control of a distribution channel through the exercise of market power. Generally, such control is disputed between manufacturers, wholesalers, retailers and agents.

In many markets today, it has been wholesalers and retailers who have been able to establish distribution channel control, at the expense of manufacturers. This has been especially so in fields such as grocery retailing, where as we have seen retailers such as (in the UK), Tesco, Sainsburys and Asda dominate the market. As they have done so, they have invested a great deal in the development of "own-brand" products, whereby goods are bought in from outside manufacturers and the retailers own-brand labeling added prior to sale in the supermarkets and hypermarkets which now constitute most of the grocery retailing scene.

Own-brand goods can be sold at relatively low prices (helping the firms to defend and expand their market share), whilst still permitting high profit margins. The reason for this is that the retailers are in an excellent position to play one supplier off against another, enhancing their own profit margins through "Super-Profits" whilst restricting the profits of the suppliers to the levels necessary to keep them in business. In this regard, it is instructive to note that the early 1990s were a period of serious recession in the UK, with profit margins of most firms significantly affected by poor trading conditions. During this time, Tesco and Sainsburys, the two largest supermarket retailers, continued to make record profits at a time when their suppliers' returns fell significantly. This is because they had successfully established control of their distribution channels.

Despite the widespread dominance of "own-label", there have been significant sectors where its advance has been successfully resisted. A notable case of this has been in the retailing of cigarettes. The major supermarket chains have each launched "own-brand" cigarettes, presumably of acceptable quality and at prices well below those of the manufacturer-based cigarette brands. The penetration achieved by own brand cigarettes has remained small, and very much lower than has been the case in most other sectors of supermarket retailing. The reason, of course, is that the cigarette market is occupied by some of the world's most powerful brands, with brands such as Marlboro, Camel and Lucky Strike still overwhelmingly dominant. Because of the strength of these brands, they are asked for by name at supermarket tobacco counters. The supermarkets therefore have no choice but to stock them, but they cannot achieve the same profits from them as they do in the own-brand sector because they do not have the same degree of distribution channel control.

Battles to take control of distribution channels are very prevalent today in airline marketing. Such control is disputed between the airlines themselves, tour operators and other wholesalers, and the travel agency sector. It is absolutely essential that airlines should establish and maintain control of their distribution channels because, overwhelmingly, it is their money which is at risk. If an airline can ensure that when people go to a travel agent, they demand to be booked with that carrier and no other, they will have taken a significant step towards proper channel control. This is because the agents' ability to play one supplier off against another in searching for the best deal for themselves, will have been eliminated.

Overall, investment in brands can bring airlines very worthwhile advantages, and make a real contribution to the achievement of satisfactory profits.

Brand-Building in the Airline Industry

Foundations for Brand-Building

In developing a brand-building strategy, airlines must first of all decide on the basis which will be used for brand development. Here, it is useful to distinguish between corporate and sub-brands.

Corporate brands are those which are based on a firm's principle trading name—Ford cars, Philips vacuum cleaners etc. The extent to which they are emphasised varies from industry to industry. In some—the airline business is a good example—almost all of the brand-building activity is carried out around corporate brands. In others, corporate brands are of little or no significance. For example, in the cigarette market, smokers are often unaware of which company has actually manufactured the cigarettes they are smoking. It is, for example, unclear as to which of the major brands are Philip Morris brands and which are from RJ Reynolds or BAT Industries.

Sub-brands are those which exist under a corporate umbrella. In the car market, for example, some of the brand values are corporate, but some relate to individual models under the corporate umbrella. Ford is in itself a major corporate brand, but models such as Mondeo, Focus and Fiesta (to use UK brand-names) are aimed at different segments of the market and each has different brand values associated with it.

In the airline industry, there have been few successful developments of sub-brands. Many airlines have tried to launch sub-brands based on cabin classes, particularly on their business classes, but few of these have made a real impact. Exceptions are the British Airways Club World brand and also the Upper Class brand developed by Virgin Atlantic.

Another attempt at sub-branding in the airline industry has been to build such brands on the basis of a service concept. "Shuttle" became a well-recognised brand both in UK domestic markets and in the north-east of the USA, whilst the Air France "La Navette" service and Air Canada "Rapidair" concepts are similar both in the nature of the operation they describe and the way in which the attempt has been made to build a sub-brand around the concept of high-frequency short-haul services. At the opposite end of the market, Concorde was an example of a sub-brand until it was withdrawn from service in the autumn of 2003.

An early, and very impressive example of sub-branding in the airline industry was that of the "Sky train" brand developed -by Laker Airways for North Atlantic services in the late 1970s. Laker Airways was lost to bankruptcy in 1982, but whatever faults there were lay outside the area of brand-building. "Sky train" was a powerful and well-recognised brand, backed by a strong mixture of both tangible and psychological brand values. The successors to Sky train are now the brands which some airlines are developing around low fares subsidiaries such as Delta's Song and SAS's Snowflake.

At the time of writing, the relationship between corporate and sub-branding in the airline industry may be undergoing significant change. The trend towards airlines to come together in a small number of large global alliances. If these alliances are to stay together and to achieve what the airlines which are members hope will come from them, branding may have a crucial role to play. Until now, airlines' names have tended to form the corporate brands, with, as we have seen a very limited development of sub-brands under the corporate umbrella. In the future, the brands of individual airlines might come to be perceived as the sub-brands, under the umbrella of an alliance-based corporate brand. The first alliance to move in this direction was the one pioneered by United Airlines and Lufthansa, where a significant investment was made in brand-building through the brand name of the Star Alliance. It is a major point of controversy as to the extent to which alliance-based brands should subsume the brands of individual airlines within an alliance.

Positioning Brands

Once a decision has been taken as to the basis for brand building, airlines must decide on the values that will position their brand. These must encompass a proper mixture of tangible and psychological brand values, so that the brand is both powerful and defendable.

The starting point in the brand positioning process is, of course, the airline's business strategy. Some airlines target mainly the business air traveller. Others are more leisure-market orientated, or operate purely in the air freight business. Many carriers aim at a presence in all the major market segments, a strategy which carries with it especial brand positioning problems which we will discuss shortly. The correct brand positions for these different types of airline will themselves be very different.

This point becomes especially clear when we introduce the next factor that should be taken into account—the needs of customers in the airline's selected target market segments. The question of customer needs, and laid especial emphasis on the difference between "apparent" and "true" needs. "Apparent" needs were defined as the needs which the person concerned will willingly admit to if asked. "True" needs are deeper, and represent the true motivation for the customer's buying behaviour.

In terms of customer needs, there is one that all of them have in common, that of safety. It can be said that all passengers are frightened of flying. There is simply a spectrum stretching from those who are mildly concerned about it to those who are terrified of the whole experience. Because of this, all airlines have to build their brands on the basis of a brand value of safety, and those that do anything to compromise this (for example, by becoming involved in the sponsorship of a dangerous sport such as motor racing) make a serious mistake.

Once the fundamental value of safety has been accepted the variety of customer needs give airlines significant choices when positioning brands. For example, an airline targeting the business air traveller will have to focus on tangible brand values such as punctuality, reliability and frequency. In terms of psychological values, it is known that many business flyers are prestige and status-conscious. An airline seeking to attract them must in turn position its brand in such a way as to suggest that it is the carrier of choice for successful people, who know the sort of airline they like to be seen to be flying.

Airlines targeting the leisure market, they will know that many of their customers will have the price of the ticket as a prime factor in making their choice-of-airline decisions. Therefore, airlines have to position themselves as the value-for-money choice, offering the cheapest fare possible whilst maintaining safety standards and giving acceptable levels punctuality and passenger amenities. Southwest Airlines illustrates perfectly exactly this positioning.

With regard to passenger needs, the most difficult brand positioning problems are faced by the many airlines which are seeking to be well represented both in business travel (because of its high yields) and in leisure travel (because of its higher-than-average growth rates). The e carriers have to position themselves as the airline of choice for the status conscious business traveller, and as the value-for-money solution for the leisure flyer looking for a cheap fare. These two positions represent a contradiction, one that has not often been dealt with successfully. British Airways has perhaps been as successful as any with the launch of its "World Offers" sub-brand. This has enabled cheap-fare offers to be separated from advertising, promotion and brand-building aimed at the business traveller.

As in many other aspects of airline marketing, the question of the trade cycle has to be brought into discussions about brand positioning. People's sentiments about spending money tend to be very different in the up-swing times of the cycle compared with times of recession. In prosperous periods, spending in an extravagant, conspicuous way may be commonplace. It will not be during recessions. Some poorly-positioned brands have brand values which are suitable for up-swing periods, but leave the brand badly exposed when things get tougher. Examples might be some of the car and jewellery brands which suffered during the recession of the early 1990s, and are doing so again in the early years of the new century.

The question of market gap analysis is a crucial one in successful brand positioning. The essence of a brand is that it is perceived as being unique and different from the offerings of rival suppliers. Such a perception is unlikely if customers believe that all features of competing products are similar. In positioning brands, firms need to carry out studies into the ways in which rivals are perceived, and to position their brand in such a way that it is focused on areas where they are seen as strong and their rivals weak. One can assume that this was the thinking behind the brand positioning adopted by the airline Lauda Air when it was set up by the former racing driver Nikki Lauda. Lauda positioned itself as a light-hearted "fun" brand, in strong contrast to the rather stolid image of its main rival Austrian Airlines.

A final factor to be considered in the correct positioning of a brand may be that of the national interest. This will be of obvious importance to a state-owned airline which may be in need of continuing financial support from taxpayers. Even for privately-owned airlines, however few can operate successfully without a measure of favourable support from governments. This may be needed in such areas as the granting of international route rights, or in favourable access to capacity at a congested airport. Branding messages that the airline is behaving patriotically, or providing substantial benefits to the national economy may then be especially useful.

Whatever criteria are used, the proper positioning of an airline brand will be a complex and demanding process. It is certainly a process that should be based on proper research and analysis, rather than hunch and guesswork.

The Brand-Building Process

One of the greatest misconceptions is that brand building is a simple task. and that it provides an easy panacea for a firm's problems. Once agreement has been reached on the values that will position the brand, it is essential that the process concentrates on the delivery of the promises which are implicit in the positioning of the brand.

This crucial requirement is most obvious with the question of tangible brand values. Clearly, it will be a brand-building disaster if an airline has a fatal accident, or, worse still, a series of such accidents. All airlines have to make absolute safety the cornerstone of their brand, and failure to deliver this product feature will be very serious. Punctuality is also a good example. Many carriers have tried to position themselves as the "on-time airline", yet, punctuality is one of the most difficult product features to deliver in practice, and many fail to do so.

With product weaknesses in the area of tangible brand values, it should be born in mind that their effect will not be a neutral one. An airline with a poor punctuality record will always alienate its customers every time a flight is late. The effect on customer perceptions of the airline will though be especially serious if the carrier has been attempting to get across a branding message with a media advertising campaign based on a slogan such as "Europe's most punctual airline."

With psychological brand values, delivery, or the failure to do so, may be more subtle, but still important in the building of a brand. For example, an airline might choose a positioning based on the proposition that it is a "winner"—a successful company with which successful people will want to be associated. It would then be a significant mistake to get into a sponsorship deal with an unsuccessful football team that lost every game played.

Once, and only once, an airline is confident that it can deliver on the values that will position its brand, it can then proceed to the next stage of brand-building, that of marketing communication. For the moment, though, it should be emphasized that almost all marketing communication work can playa role in brand-building, and that very substantial spending will almost certainly be necessary if a powerful brand is to be built and sustained. Media advertising must be developed which contains messages that reflect consistent, underlying brand values, as will any database marketing activity the airline carries out. Sponsorship policy can be an especially powerful component of brand-building, but it must be used in the right way. If it isn't, it will have a negative rather than a positive impact on a brand of an airline's marketing communications activity will be that of media relations. The airline industry is regarded as especially high profile by media owners and editors. Bad news will often be played up, and will have a potentially disastrous impact on an airline's brand if media attacks are sustained on a long-term basis. Positive stories will have a strongly beneficial effect, and the maintenance of strong relations with the media will be of great importance in getting the coverage to aid long-term brand building.

A final point about brand-building is that strong brands are rarely built quickly (though they can be destroyed quickly). It is of vital importance that firms adopt a stick-with-it principle of emphasizing strong, core brand values on a very long-term basis. One only has to look at the power achieved by the Marlboro brand, where the core values have been unchanged now for nearly 40 years to see the truth of this statement. In the airline industry, until recently Singapore Airlines gave an equally good illustration of the importance of consistency in successful brand development.

Brand Strategies

The discussion has now reached the point where we have covered the fundamentals of positioning and building brands. All firms have to make strategic decisions about managing their brands.

A first area of debate in many industries is whether investment should be directed towards. the development of new brands, or the purchase of existing ones from other firms. Development of a new brand allows the firm to start with a clean sheet of paper, and to use the b and values which exactly match their business strategy and capabilities. It may also be that the end result of the process is a significant asset, which might in turn be sold at a later stage. The problem is that brand building is a risky, time-consuming and expensive business. For all the new brands that are introduced and eventually become valuable successes, there are many others which turn out to be costly failures.

Building new brands is so risky that in many areas of the economy, established brands are bought and sold, rather than new ones being developed. This may occur as a specific transaction, or it may be the driving force behind merger and take-over activity. An example was the take-over of Rolls-Royce cars by BMW of Germany in 1999—a clear case where the price paid by BMW was significantly above the value of Rolls tangible assets. This extra payment essentially represented the value placed by BMW on the Rolls-Royce brand.

Such activity is rare in the airline industry. There are few examples where a brand owned by one airline has been sold to another as a standalone transaction. This reflects the emphasis in the industry on corporate rather than sub-brands. A case where this might be said to have taken place was in 1988 when Pan American, desperate for cash and in a near-bankrupt condition, sold its Shuttle routes in the north-east of the USA USAirways. The price paid was significantly above the value of the tangible assets transferred, with it being possible to argue that the extra payment was for the Shuttle brand.

With merger and take-over activity driven by brand acquisition, the ownership rules which still dominate the aviation industry mean that mergers and take-over are in any case much less common that in a "normal" industry. Where mergers and take-over do occur, they only do so on the basis of airlines from the same country merging (or, in the case of the European Union, carriers within the same trading bloc).

When airline mergers and take-over do occur, it is certainly not generally the case that they are driven by the desire of the bidder to acquire the brand of the airline it is attempting to take over. Indeed, the commonest situation is for the brand of the airline being taken over to be dumped, and all trace of it to disappear in the shortest possible time. This was certainly the case, for example when USAirways took over Piedmont Airlines in the USA in the late 1980s. The Piedmont brand was abandoned completely, despite the fact that its reputation had been a good one—probably better than that of USAirways.

The buying and selling of brands in the airline industry may be rare, but we have seen a number of examples of *brand repositioning*. The most extreme example of this has been when airlines with a significant presence in the leisure air travel market try to reposition their brand to help them achieve penetration of the business travel segment. There are certainly factors which might lead them to attempt this. Business travel yields are much higher, and it also tends to be a year round activity—with resultil1g cash-flow advantages—rather than showing the acute seasonality normally characteristic of leisure travel. Generally, though the problems of doing so have been insuperable, with questions of brand positioning amongst the most intractable.

Two well-known airlines which attempted such a transition at almost exactly the same time were the Canadian airline Wardair and the British-based carrier Air Europe. Both had built a strong presence in the leisure market with their emphasis on charter flying for the holiday traveller. Both in 1987 made announcements that they were going to radically re-position themselves, with the business traveller the future target market. In each case, the move was a disastrous failure. Wardair was soon taken over in a near-bankrupt condition by Canadian Airlines whilst Air Europe went into receivership in 1991. (A former franchise partner still survives in Italy and uses the Air Europe name.)

Amongst the problems both airlines had was the enormous investment required to make the transition. They recognised—correctly—that they would need a new fleet of smaller aircraft so that they could boost frequencies to the level required by the business traveller. Ironically, both selected the Fokker 100 and made a large commitment to acquire new aircraft from Fokker. Unfortunately, this required a huge cash outflow before the products could be introduced which would make the airlines attractive to the business traveller. At the same time, they were handicapped by a brand which was perceived as leisure-orientated and, in the case of Air Europe, associated with young, rowdy and poorly-behaved holiday travellers. Their brands were unlikely to appeal to status conscious business flyers, and in truth it came as no surprise that they were overwhelmed by their financial difficulties before the brand repositioning could bring its hoped-for rewards.

Brand strengthening obviously needs to be a constant strategy in any sound brands management process. Many brands run into difficulty from time-to-time, because of the inability of the firms that own them to deliver on the brand values consistently. When this happens, the delivery problems must be addressed, and then, and only then, marketing communication work to bring the brand back to its former strength must be undertaken.

Two interesting issues in brand strategy are those of brand stretching and co-branding. A brand stretching strategy is one where the brand values developed around one product are used to market others. Such strategies have become increasingly common in recent years, notably so in the cigarette industry where brands originally developed for cigarettes are now being used to market such things as outdoor clothing and travel.

In the airline industry, the use of brand stretching has so far achieved only mixed results. Three airlines—Virgin·Atlantic, Virgin Express and Virgin Blue—are in fact itself an extension of the Virgin brand which began life in the entertainment industry. Many carriers have attempted to stretch their own brand into travel-related businesses, such as hotels and tour operations. There are currently some suggesting that lucrative areas for investment might be in travel-related financial services products such as travel insurance and traveller's cheques.

The potential benefits of brand stretching are clear, in that it leverages, investment made in the brand. The problems, though, are equally telling.

A brand stretching exercise amounts to a giant house of cards where if the essential values related to the core brand are undermined, the whole house collapses. Also, brand stretching runs the risk that management time and the financial resources will be diluted, by businesses about which the firm knows little and where there are few synergies between the new -activities and the core business. Where such synergies may be argued to exist—between an airline and, say, a chain of hotels—the value of the synergy may be reduced by the fact that both the businesses are vulnerable to the same downswings in the trade cycle.

In some ways, a better approach to the leveraging of brand investment is that of brand franchising. Franchising has a long history in the airline industry, having begun in the USA in the 1970s. It did, though, become much more common in the 1990s, and can be seen as part of the trend towards consolidation and the emergence of global alliances.

The essence of franchising relationships as they have developed in the airline industry is that a smaller airline contracts with a larger one by renting its brand. This buys the small carrier respectability, in that passengers are likely to perceive it in a better light with regard to technical aspects such as safety and punctuality. The small airline also benefits because it is able to join the frequent flyer programme of the major carrier, and share its GDS code (so that it can appear to offer on-line service to its connecting passengers). Finally, the small airline benefits too because its partner will act as its global General Sales Agent and a substantial increase in bookings should be the result.

For the large airline, the advantages are also clear. It will be able to charge substantial franchising fees, and such fees will constitute useful incremental revenue. Even more significantly, it will gain important feed into its long-haul traffic system, without the costs of providing such fee-j itself. Large airlines generally find it difficult to achieve competitive costs on thin routes, mainly because these routes require small aircraft which in turn do not allow high operating costs to be spread over a large number of seats. Smaller airlines, with lower pilot salaries in particular, will be much better placed to do so.

Despite these advantages, franchising brings disadvantages, to both the small and the large airlines who engage in it. The smaller airline has to accept the payment of franchising fees, and a loss of a great deal of its independence. Its larger partner will dictate such decisions as aircraft livery, staff uniforms, seating comfort and service standards. For the larger airlines, the issues mainly centre around the question of brand integrity. If someone books with a major airline, they expect the service to be provided by that airline, using a jet aircraft. With franchising, they may arrive at their report to find that they are actually flying with the commuter partner, on a turbo-prop. However wrong it may be, turbo-props are still regarded by many people as being slow and old-fashioned, and they may feel that the brand promise has not been kept if they have to travel in one.

Overall, it is impossible to exaggerate the contribution which can be played by sound brands management in airline marketing today. Brands can add value, and give carriers the best possible opportunity to establish and sustain control of their distribution channels. It is a subject that should be given the greatest possible emphasis.

CHAPTER 5

Airport Marketing

ABOUT AIRPORTS

A definition of marketing is described by Philip Kotler, a well-known author in the field of marketing, as: "All activities which are aimed at the satisfaction of buyers' needs and wishes by means of trading processes". Airport marketing is a niche from this perspective. The traditional airport concept offers core trading products, namely transfer of passengers and goods. Today, airports have become commercial enterprises with value propositions, specifically designed to target specific market segments. As in any enterprise the ultimate goal is long-term profit generation that can both sustain independent development and reward stakeholders.

An **airport** is a facility where aircraft such as airplanes and helicopters can take off and land. An airport minimally consists of one runway or helipad (for helicopters), but other common components are hangars and terminal buildings.

Additionally, an airport may have a variety of facilities and infrastructure, including fixed base operator services, air traffic control, passenger facilities such as restaurants and lounges, and emergency services. A military airport is known as an airbase or air station. The terms **airfield**, **airstrip**, and **aerodrome** may also be used to refer to airports of varying sizes. In some jurisdictions, the term airport is used where the facility is licensed as such by the relevant government organization (e.g. FAA, Transport Canada). Elsewhere the distinction is merely one of general appearance. Yet other areas define an air*port* by its having the necessary customs offices etc expected of a port.

Attributes

Airports vary in size, with smaller or less-developed airports often having only a single runway shorter than 1,000 m (3,300 ft). Larger airports for international flights generally have paved runways 2,000 m (6,600 ft) or longer. Many small airports have dirt, grass, or gravel runways, rather than asphalt or concrete.

In the United States, the minimum dimensions for dry, hard landing fields are defined by the FAR Landing And Takeoff Field Lengths. These include considerations for safety margins during landing and takeoff. Typically, heavier aircraft require longer runways. The longest public-use runway in the world is at Ulyanovsk Vostochny Airport, in Ulyanovsk, Russia. It has a length of 5,000 m (16,404 ft). At 105 m (344 ft), it should also be the world's widest paved runway. As of 2006, there were approximately 49,000 airports around the world, including 14,858 in the United States alone.

Airport Structures

Airports are divided into *landside* and *airside* areas. Landside areas include parking lots, public transportation stations, tank farms and access roads. Airside areas include all areas accessible to aircraft, including runways, taxiways and ramps. Access from landside areas to airside areas is tightly controlled at most airports. Passengers on commercial flights access airside areas through terminals, where they can purchase tickets, clear security, check or claim luggage and board aircraft through gates. The waiting areas which provide passenger access to aircraft are typically called concourses, although this term is often used interchangeably with terminal.

The area where aircraft park next to a terminal to load passengers and baggage is known as a *ramp* (or, to the media and uninitiated, "the tarmac"). Parking areas for aircraft away from terminals are generally called aprons.

Both large and small airports can be towered or non-towered, depending on air traffic density and available funds. Due to their high capacity and busy airspace, most international airports have air traffic control located on site.

Airports with international flights have customs and immigration facilities. However, as some countries have agreements that allow travel between them without customs and immigrations, such facilities are not a definitive need for an international airport. International flights often require a more conspicuous level of physical security, although in recent years, many countries have adopted the same level of security for international and domestic travel.

Modern engineers and architects are developing "floating airports" which could be located several miles at sea and which would utilize designs such as Float Incorporated's Pneumatic Stabilized Platform (PSP) technology.

Shops and Food Services

Airports have a captive audience, and consequently the prices charged for food is generally higher than are available elsewhere in the region. However, some airports, such as JFK's Terminal 8, guarantee prices comparable to those outside of the airport. Airport fees are fees commonly paid for use of services of airports, such as in the Subic Bay International Airport, known for charging airport fees. However, some airports now regulate food costs to keep them comparable to so-called "street prices". This term is a bit misleading as prices often match the MSRP but are almost never discounted.

Premium and VIP Services

Several mid-large size airports also have facilities for premium passengers. In the United States, these lounges are typically for international or long-haul first and business class passengers, paid members, and elite-level frequent fliers on long haul flights (regardless of what class they are in). In the rest of the world, the lounges are not open to purchase, but can be used by all premium passengers and most elite frequent fliers. Some lounges are comparatively Spartan and only offer a quiet place to sit and work; other lounges include meals and massage services.

Cargo and Freight Services

In addition to people, airports are responsible for moving large volumes of cargo around the clock. Cargo airlines often have their own on-site and adjacent infrastructure to rapidly transfer parcels between ground and air modes of transportation.

Support Services

Aircraft maintenance, pilot services, aircraft rental, and hangar rental are most often performed by a fixed base operator (FBO). At major airports, particularly those used as hubs, airlines may operate their own support facilities.

Some airports, typically military airbases, have long runways used as emergency landing sites. Many airbases have arresting equipment for fast aircraft, known as Rotary Hydraulic Arrester Gear—a strong cable suspended just above the runway and attached to a hydraulic reduction gear mechanism. Together with the landing aircraft's arresting hook, it is used in situations where the brakes would have little or no effect.

Airport Access

Many large airports in the world are located next to or even above railway trunk routes, for instance Frankfurt International Airport, Amsterdam—Schiphol Airport, London Heathrow Airport, London Gatwick Airport and London Stansted. For local access, many airports have local train lines, rapid transit, light rail lines or other mass transit systems, for instance the AirTrain JFK at John F. Kennedy International Airport in New York and the Silver Line T at Boston's Logan International Airport by the MBTA (Massachusetts Bay Transportation Authority). These systems are usually directly connected to the main terminals. Large airports usually have access also through freeways from which cars fed into two access roads, designed as loops, one sitting on top of the other. One level is for departing passengers and the other is for arrivals. This road concept was pioneered at Los Angeles International Airport.

Airport Security

Airports are required to have safety precautions in most countries. Rules vary in different countries, but there are common elements worldwide. Airport security normally requires baggage checks, metal screenings of individual persons, and rules against any object that could be used as a weapon. Since the September 11, 2001 attacks, airport security has been dramatically increased worldwide.

Outside the terminal, there is a large team of people who work in concert to ensure aircraft can land, take off, and move around quickly and safely. These processes are largely invisible to passengers, but they can be extraordinarily complex at large airports.

Air Traffic Control

The vast majority of the world's airports are non-towered, with no air traffic control presence at all. However, at particularly busy airports, or airports with other special requirements, there is an air traffic control (ATC) system whereby controllers (usually ground-based) direct aircraft movements via radio or other communications links. This coordinated oversight facilitates safety and speed in complex operations where traffic moves in all three dimensions. Air traffic control responsibilities at airports are usually divided into at least two main areas: *ground* and *tower*, though a single controller may work both stations. The busiest airports also have *clearance delivery*, *apron control*, and other specialized ATC stations.

Ground Control is responsible for directing all ground traffic in designated "movement areas," except the traffic on runways. This includes planes, baggage trains, snowplows, grass cutters, fuel trucks, and a wide array of other vehicles. Ground Control will instruct these vehicles on which taxiways to use, which runway they will use (in the case of planes), where they will park, and when it is safe to cross runways. When a plane is ready to take off it will stop short of the runway, at which point it will be turned over to Tower Control. After a plane has landed, it will depart the runway and be returned to Ground Control.

View of apron from top floor observation room, Halifax International Airport

Tower Control controls aircraft on the runway and in the controlled airspace immediately surrounding the airport. Tower controllers may use radar to identify and accurately locate an aircraft's position in three-dimensional space, or they may rely on pilot position reports and visual observation. They coordinate the sequencing of aircraft in the traffic pattern and direct aircraft on how to safely join and leave the circuit. Aircraft which are only passing through the airspace must also contact Tower Control in order to be sure that they remain clear of other traffic and do not disrupt operations.

Traffic Pattern

All airports use a traffic pattern (often called a *traffic circuit* outside the U.S.) to assure smooth traffic flow between departing and arriving aircraft. Generally, this pattern is a circuit consisting of five "legs" that form a rectangle (two legs and the runway form one side, with the remaining legs forming three more sides). Each leg is named (see diagram), and ATC directs pilots on how to join and leave the circuit. Traffic patterns are flown at one specific altitude, usually 800 or 1000 ft. above ground level (AGL). Standard traffic patterns are *left-handed*, meaning all turns are made to the left. Right-handed patterns do exist, usually because of obstacles such as a mountain, or to reduce noise for local residents. The predetermined circuit helps traffic flow smoothly because all pilots know what to expect, and helps reduce the chance of a mid-air collision.

At extremely large airports, a circuit is in place but not usually used. Rather, aircraft (usually only commercial with long routes) request approach clearance while they are still hours away from the airport, often before they even take off from their departure point. Large airports have a frequency called *Clearance Delivery* which is used by departing aircraft specifically for this purpose. This then allows airplanes to take the most direct approach path to the runway and land without worrying about interference from other aircraft. While this system keeps the airspace free and is simpler for pilots, it requires detailed knowledge of how aircraft are planning to use the airport ahead of time and is therefore only possible with large commercial airliners on pre-scheduled flights. The system has recently become so advanced that controllers can predict whether an aircraft will be delayed on landing before it even takes off; that aircraft can then be delayed on the ground, rather than wasting expensive fuel waiting in the air.

Navigational Aids

When flying, there are a number of aids available to pilots, though not all airports are equipped with them. A Visual Approach Slope Indicator (VASI) helps pilots fly a perfect approach for landing once they have found the airport. Some airports are equipped with a VHF omnidirectional range (VOR) to help pilots find the direction to the airport. VORs are often accompanied by a Distance Measuring Equipment (DME) to determine the distance to the VOR. VORs are also located off airports, where they serve to provide airways for aircraft to navigate upon. In poor weather, pilots will use an Instrument Landing System to find the runway and fly the correct approach, even if they cannot see the ground. The number of instrument approaches based on the use of the Global Positioning System (GPS) is rapidly increasing and may eventually be the primary means for instrument landings.

Larger airports sometimes offer Precision Approach Radar (PAR), but these systems are more common at military air bases than civilian airports. The aircraft's horizontal and vertical movement is tracked via radar, and the controller tells the pilot his position relative to the approach slope. Once the pilots can see the runway lights, they may continue with a visual landing.

Guidance Signs

Airport guidance signs provide direction and information to taxiing aircraft and airport vehicles and assist in safe and expedient movement of aircraft. Smaller airports may have few or no signs, relying instead on airport diagrams and charts.

There are two classes of signage at airports, with several types of each:

Operational Guidance Signs

1. Location signs—yellow on black background. Identifies the runway or taxiway currently on or entering.
2. Direction/Runway Exit signs—black on yellow. Identifies the intersecting taxiways the aircraft is approaching, with an arrow indicating the direction to turn.
3. Other—Many airports use conventional traffic signs such as stop and yield signs throughout the airport.

Mandatory Instruction Signs

Mandatory instruction signs are white on red. They show entrances to runways or critical areas. Vehicles and aircraft are required to stop at these signs until the control tower gives clearance to proceed.

1. Runway signs—White on a red. These signs simply identify a runway intersection ahead.
2. Frequency Change signs—Usually a stop sign and an instruction to change to another frequency. These signs are used at airports with different areas of ground control.
3. Holding Position signs—A single solid yellow bar across a taxiway indicates a position where ground control may require a stop. If a two solid yellow bars and two dashed yellow bars are encountered, this indicates a holding position for a runway intersection ahead; runway holding lines must never be crossed without permission. At some airports, a line of red lights across a taxiway is used during low visibility operations to indicate holding positions.

Lighting

Many airports have lighting that help guide planes using the runways and taxiways at night or in rain or fog.

1. On runways, green lights indicate the beginning of the runway for landing, while red lights indicate the end of the runway. Runway edge lighting consists of white lights spaced out on both sides of the runway, indicating the edge. Some airports have more complicated

lighting on the runways including lights that run down the centerline of the runway and lights that help indicate the approach (an Approach Lighting System, or ALS). Low-traffic airports may use Pilot Controlled Lighting to save electricity and staffing costs.

2. Along taxiways, blue lights indicate the taxiway's edge, and some airports have embedded green lights that indicate the centerline.

Wind Indicators

Planes take-off and land into the wind in order to achieve maximum performance. Wind speed and direction information is available through the ATIS or ATC, but pilots need instantaneous information during landing. For this purpose, a windsock is kept in view of the runway.

Safety Management

Air safety is an important concern in the operation of an airport, and almost every airfield includes equipment and procedures for handling emergency situations. Commercial airfields include one or more emergency vehicles and their crew that are specially equipped for dealing with airfield accidents, crew and passenger extractions, and the hazards of highly flammable airplane fuel. The crews are also trained to deal with situations such as bomb threats, hijacking, and terrorist activities.

Potential airfield hazards to aircraft include debris, nesting birds, and environmental conditions such as ice or snow. The fields must be kept clear of debris using cleaning equipment so that loose material doesn't become a projectile and enter an engine duct. In adverse weather conditions, ice and snow clearing equipment can be used to improve traction on the landing strip. For waiting aircraft, equipment is used to spray special deicing fluids on the wings.

Many airports are built near open fields or wetlands. These tend to attract bird populations, which can pose a hazard to aircraft in the form of bird strikes. Airport crews often need to discourage birds from taking up residence.

Some airports are located next to parks, golf courses, or other low-density uses of land. Other airports are located near densely—populated urban or suburban areas. In the 1980's, a conflict arose in San José, California, when a plane attempting to land at Reid-Hillview Airport (built in the 1930's) collided with a Macy's department Store at the Eastridge shopping mall. Many local residents tried to get the airport shut down, even though it had been there for fifty years: their neighborhoods (and the mall) were about a decade old.

Depending on their configuration, an airport can have sections of their pavement where collisions between airplanes on the ground can tend to occur. Records are kept of any incursions where airplanes or vehicles are in an inappropriate location, allowing these "hot spots" to be identified. These locations then undergo special attention by transportation authorities (such as the FAA in the US) and airport administrators in order to reduce accidents.

During the 1980s, a phenomenon known as microburst became a growing concern due to accidents caused by microburst wind shear. (For example, see Delta Air Lines Flight 191) Microburst radar was developed as an aid to safety during landing, giving two to five minutes warning to aircraft in the vicinity of the field of a microburst event.

Some airfields now have a special surface known as soft concrete at the end of the runway that behaves somewhat like styrofoam, bringing the plane to a relatively rapid halt as the material disintegrates. These surfaces are useful when the runway is located next to a body of water or other hazard, and prevent the planes from overrunning the end of the field.

Airport Ground Crew

Most airports have ground crew handling the loading and unloading of passengers, crew, baggage and other services. Some ground crew are linked to specific airlines operating at the airport.

Equipment

- passenger stairs
- fuel tankers
- aircraft tow tractors
- baggage carts and tow tractors
- lift loaders
- lavatory service trucks and/or carts
- airport fire tender
- airport fire foam truck
- passenger boarding bridges
- airport crash tender
- airport fire foam truck
- catering trucks
- service vans
- generators
- converters
- deicing machines
- belt loaders
- snow plows
- security vehicles

Environmental Concerns

The traffic generated by airports both in the air and on the surface can be a major source of aviation noise and air pollution which may interrupt nearby residents' sleep and produce other noise health effects. The construction of new airports, or addition of runways to existing airports, is often resisted by local residents because of the effect on the countryside, historical sites, local flora and fauna. As well, due to the risk of collision between birds and airplanes, large airports undertake population control programs where they frighten or shoot birds to ensure the safety of air travellers.

The construction of airports has been known to change local weather patterns. For example, because they often flatten out large areas, they can be susceptible to fog in areas where fog rarely forms. In addition, because they generally replace trees and grass with pavement, they often change drainage patterns in agricultural areas, leading to more flooding, run-off and erosion in the surrounding land.

Military Bases

An airbase, sometimes referred to as a *military airport* or *airfield*, provides basing and support of military aircraft. Some airbases provide facilities similar to their civilian counterparts. For example, RAF Brize Norton in Oxfordshire, England has a terminal which caters to passengers for the Royal Air Force's scheduled Tristar flights to the Falkland Islands. Military airbases may also be co-located with civilian airports, sharing the same tower/air traffic control facilities, runways, taxiways and emergency services, but with separate terminals, parking areas, hangars and shelter areas. Examples of this are Bardufoss Airport/Bardufoss Air Station and Gardermoen Airport/ Gardermoen Air Station, both in Norway. A special variant of a military airfield is the Aircraft Carrier.

Aircraft Carriers

An aircraft carrier is a warship that functions as a floating airport for military aircraft. Aircraft carriers allow a naval force to project air power great distances without having to depend on local bases for land-based aircraft. After their development in World War I, aircraft carriers replaced the battleship as the centrepiece of a modern fleet during World War II. Unescorted carriers are considered vulnerable to missile or submarine attacks and therefore travel as part of a *carrier battle group* that includes a wide array of other ships with specific functions.

Entertainment

Airports have occasionally played major roles in motion pictures and television shows due to being transportation hubs, but also because of their unique characteristics. One such example of this is the movie *The Terminal*, a film about a man who becomes permanently grounded in an airport terminal and must survive only on the food and shelter provided by the airport. Movies such as *Airplane!*, *Airport*, *Die Hard II*, *Jackie Brown*, *Get Shorty*, *Unaccompanied Minors*, *Soul Plane*, *Flightplan*, and *The Langoliers*, as well as television series like *Lost* also have significant parts of their story set within airports.

Also, several computer simulation games were created in which the player is in charge of an airport. Names include Airport Tycoon and the sequels; Airport Tycoon 2 and Airport Tycoon 3.

Airport Types

A **domestic airport** is an airport which handles only domestic flights or flights within the same country. Domestic airports don't have customs and immigration facilities and are therefore incapable of handling flights to or from a foreign airport.

These airports normally have short runways which are sufficient to handle short/medium haul aircraft and regional air traffic. They have in many countries not had any security check/metal detector, but such checks have been added in recent years.

Most municipal airports in Canada and the United States are of this classification. At international airports in Canada, there are domestic terminals that handle flights within Canada (flying from one Canadian city to another).

Several small countries do not have any public domestic airports, or even not any public domestic flights, e.g. Belgium.

Regional Airport

A **regional airport** is an airport serving traffic within a relatively small geographical area. Contrast with international airport. A regional airport usually does not have facilities to process traffic between countries, such as customs. In Canada regional airports usually service connections within Canada and some flights to the United States.

Aircraft using these airports tend to smaller business jets, private aircraft and regional jetliners.

A **Civil Enclave** is an area allotted at an airport belonging to the armed forces, for the usage of civil aircraft and civil aviation related services. Civil enclaves are common in countries like India, Sri Lanka, and Pakistan where a part of an Air force base, almost invariably a legacy of World War II vintage, is allotted for domestic air traffic instead of building a new civilian airport. They are rare in the United States where the term joint use is applied. These airports usually have a curfew (mostly after sunset) during which civil aircraft are not permitted to operate. Many reserve morning hours for military flight training. Some civil enclaves adopt an altitude restriction i.e. one below which a civilian aircraft cannot descend while over-flying the enclave. The curfew system results in airport congestion (and higher air fares) while the altitude restriction results in long detours (and greater fuel consumption). Both constitute economic waste which is acceptable on security grounds provided the latter is not exaggerated. The Air Traffic Control at civil enclaves is usually entrusted to the armed forces while security is often the responsibility of paramilitary personnel. It is generally accepted that the military receives revenues from ATC services. However it is not clear as to whether capital expenditure such as for runway expansion is for the account of the military or civilian authorities.

Goa's Dabolim Airport is an example of the interface between civilian and military operations at an airbase. Meanwhile Ahmedabad's Sardar Vallabhbhai

Patel International Airport is an example of the obverse of a civil enclave, namely a military enclave at an airport.

An **international airport** (or **airport of entry**) is an airport typically equipped with customs and immigration facilities to handle international flights to and from other countries. Such airports are usually larger, and often feature longer runways and facilities to accommodate the large aircraft commonly used for international or intercontinental travel. International airports often host domestic flights (flights which take place inside only one country) in addition to international flights. In many smaller countries most airports are international airports, so the concept of an "international airport" has little meaning. In certain countries however, there is a sub-category of *limited international airports* which handle international flights, but are limited to short-haul destinations (often due to geographical factors) or are mixed civilian/ military airports.

Many airports with regularly scheduled international service have the word "International" in their official names, but others, including such major airports as London Heathrow Airport, do not. Conversely, some airports which call themselves *international airports,* especially in smaller United States cities, in fact have no scheduled international airline passenger service but do have customs and immigration facilities serving charter, cargo and general aviation flights. At many of these airports customs and immigration services are only available with several hours advance notice. Examples of such airports include Gerald R. Ford International Airport in Grand Rapids, Michigan, Gary/Chicago International Airport in Gary, Indiana and Portland International Jetport in Portland, Maine.

Other airports which previously served international flights now serve primarily domestic flights (international traffic having been redirected to a newer, larger airport in the area) but retain the "international" designation in their name. Examples of these are:

- Tokyo International Airport (Haneda), in Tokyo, Japan, relieved by Narita International Airport.
- Taipei Songshan Airport in Taipei, Taiwan (which retains its name as "Taipei International Airport" in Chinese), relieved by Taoyuan International Airport.
- Gimpo International Airport in Seoul, South Korea, relieved by Incheon International Airport.
- Shanghai Hongqiao International Airport in Shanghai, People's Republic of China, relieved by Pudong International Airport.

Many international airports also serve as "hubs," or places where non-direct flights may land and passengers switch planes. International airports often have many airlines represented, and many of these are often foreign.

Passengers connecting to domestic flights from an international flight generally must take their checked luggage through customs and re-check their luggage at the domestic airline counter, requiring extra time in the process. In some cases in Europe luggage can be transferred to the final destination even if it is a domestic connection.

In some cases, travelers and the aircraft can clear customs and immigration at the departure airport. As one example of this, the United States has customs and immigration officials at certain Canadian airports. This allows flights from those airports to fly into US airports that do not have customs and immigration facilities. Luggage from such flights can also be transferred to a final destination in the U.S. through the airport of entry.

Table 6: Passengers Services and Facilities

Airport Passengers Services	Airport Passengers Facilities
Information & Customer Service Counter	Telephone
Immigration & Customs department	Foreign Exchange & ATM
Postal services	Baby Nursery/Diaper Change room
Wireless Broad band Services	Facilities for the disabled
Porters Services	Flight information Display System
Connectivity Services	Prayer room, Security system, Parking
Police Station	Locker Services
Car Rental Services	Smoking Lounge & Restaurant services
Transport Services	Gifts shops & custom free retail shops
—Shuttle Vans; Mini Coaches	Shoe shining, Beauty Parlor, Saloons
Boarding Services	Sky cap—Luggage assistance, wheel chair
Business Services	Insurance
—Copier, Work Station, Modem-hook—UP's	Hotel & Tourism Facilities
—Electrical outlets, Phone Services,	Facilities for airlines operators
—Internet & Ethernet Connection	–Fixed based operations
	–Private Chartered Services
	–Aircraft Maintenance

AIRPORT MARKETING PLAN

Turbulent competitive dynamics in the airport business are forcing all players to reengineer their strategies as the only way to maintain long-term viability. Start-up of greenfield airports or the conversion of former military ones; deregulation processes in former monopoly 'cash-cows', like ground handling; growing competitive pressures from the likes of high-speed trains as well as videoconferencing; all of these combined elements mean that today market-based ingenuity has become crucial for airport enterprises. The adoption of a 'customer-centred' approach is capable of creating more satisfied customers which may be considered an effective basis to counteract both intra-industry and inter-value chain attacks.

This, however, does not mean that airports on a widespread basis are actually adopting a full-scale, marketing-based approach to manage their intermediate and final relationships. Most of the time, in fact, airports remain passive in both negotiations and market interactions. With their target audiences, this position being a direct consequence of the historic lack of managerial know-how. What airports need today, is a cultural change in management practices, to move airport managers away from the pure exploitation of natural-monopoly rents towards a proactive viewable to construct a solid competitive advantage in a turbulent scenario.

One of the main pillars of this new approach lies naturally in the planning of all strategic and operational duties to be implemented. Dealing specifically with marketing, the definition of an airport marketing plan is a fundamental step for establishing new 'rules of conduct' and later implementing them in a consistent way. We may define the contents of an airport marketing plan into four phases:

- An assessment of the firm's macro and micro competitive position;
- Definition of the main goals and objectives for the airport enterprise;
- Implementation of the chosen objectives;
- Auditing of actual performances achieved.

Assessment

A first goal of the diagnosis phase lies in the analytical evaluation of each product-market combination in which the airport enterprise operates. Moreover, it also aims to map the nature and intensity of current relationships with intermediate and final customers. On completion, this phase should provide a good picture of the airport's past and current competitive position. Understanding macro and micro boundaries should help managers to adopt a consistent package of operational decisions and improve the airport's position by removing weakness, while reinforcing existing key success factors.

The assessment can be split into two different viewpoints:

- how did the airport's market position change since the last period of observation?
- what is the airport's current market position?

Main Drivers of Change which have Occurred in Recent Years

Here the main aspects to be considered refer to macro environmental changes that have impacted on the business performance during the time period in question. For instance, we may think of the SARS epidemic or the post-September 11 environment, or the Iraqi and Afghanistan wars, not to mention Euro-dollar exchange rate fluctuations and OPEC's decisions about oil production levels. Managers have to check if all past economic and commercial goals have actually been achieved. Some key performance indexes (KPIs) that should be taken into consideration refer, for instance, to the amount of forecasted passengers or to the percentage of connecting passengers, if we are referring to a primary hub airport.

This kind of analysis, which should be conducted on a broader scale to include all strategic business units (SBUs), must involve financial figures, too. In this case, each SBU's ROI must be compared with internal past figures (internal benchmarking) or by matching airport data with both best-in-class intra-industry performers and with zero-risk financial activities, like State bonds (external benchmarking).

One of the main problems concerning external benchmarking lies in how to gather this critical information. Industry associations would be an initial source, even if this data is usually old and manipulated. Some other field tactics, like the 'mystery shopper' approach, could follow. Finally, alliances may provide a good platform for data exchange between partners.

Later on; a portfolio analysis will be conducted on the overall airport's B2B and B2C relationships. This tool will evaluate the quality levels of market links by measuring loyalty achieved on intermediate and final customers, the latter one being possible only in the case of an existing Airport Loyalty Program (ALP).

Moreover, in the case of B2B transactions, airport managers will have to fully understand the reasons behind any kind of market transaction's breakdown. The reason is that such an unfavourable condition could be due to some exogenous factors, like September 11, but also to an incorrect behavioural approach by the airport enterprise. A detailed map of these situations of ineffectiveness will be crucial not only to drive shortterm4 recovery strategies but also improve managerial skills and portfolio efficiency in the long term.

Finally, a competitive analysis will be considered to fully map competitors' moves, both direct and indirect ones, in the market. This will assume different scopes according to the market positioning that the airport enterprise wants to achieve. For instance, a primary hub will be interested in tracing competitive moves only within its own cluster and will not take into consideration what regional airports have done over the last year.

The Airport's Current Market Condition

To complete the picture we must look at the firm's current position. The same aforementioned categories of analysis will have to be used in this case.

A typical tool used to illustrate an airport's current competitive situation is the Boston Consulting Group (BCG) matrix designed for each Strategic Business Unit involved.

Definition of Goals

This second phase asks airport managers to explore, and later adopt, one of the main available strategic marketing options, like:

- the 'fight option', that promises to increase an airport's market share;
- the 'retrench option', that work to protect the current market share in a highly turbulent environment;
- the 'streamlining option', that looks at divesting unprofitable SBUs;
- the 'abandon option', that sees a company exiting a current business.

Fighting for Acquiring New Market Power

This is always the preferred option by both airport managers and political stakeholders, as it is linked to positive and rather successful policies. This option seems, however, to require a high level of stability in both macro and micro scenario drivers. In fact, an airport's market growth is due not only to successful internal KPls, but also to both a growing primary demand and a stable competitive environment as well. An airport management may define this goal through a bundle of operational activities:

- by fostering the effectiveness of actual market relationships with served customers. Improving their loyalty indexes will provide a good chance to make these players concentrate a larger slice of their activity on a single airport platform;
- by maximising the quality of business development processes through the use of dedicated intelligence and IT supports. This could be the result of an excellent aviation-related marketing campaign, where the airport succeeds in attracting new airlines thanks to the scope of its value proposition in terms of information and marketing support packages;
- by diversifying the range of services offered and targeting both current and potential customers. In the case of current customers, providing extra retailing comers in the terminal building will be a good trick to improve both customer satisfaction and the length of time spent in the terminal building, with an associated effect on the average expenditure level. In the case of potential customers, a more radical innovation in the non-aviation activity, like the launch of discotheques and supermarkets, will attract new non-passenger cluster targets and extend the power of commercial influence.

Hyper competition and stagnation in demand levels, as a consequence of economic recession, requires airports to focus on a less aggressive and more conservative strategy. This option suggests that airport managers identify similar target goals to those of the previous year. Thus, in a hyper-turbulent environment, maintaining the current financial and competitive position should be considered a significant success. The retrench tactic will permit the airport to act and focus on its core competencies and, thus, reinforce its drivers of competitive advantage. At the end of the downturn, the players who survive would be able to turn once again to a growth strategy.

Divesting

A negative economic climate may require airports to take much more drastic decisions. One of these is the need to cut unprofitable business units as a means to rationalise the portfolio of offer and improve overall efficiency. This activity is frequently implemented by giving away a slice of the current business to a third party concessionaire. In the case of aviation-related activities, this could involve the practice of outsourcing handling services and dismantling the internal production, while conserving the marketing-related activities concerning scouting for new carriers. In the non-aviation business, airport managers could instead decide to give away to a third-party specialised concessionaire the management of properties to improve the market performance that may be gained from this business.

In the case of airlines, divesting is *common in the case of frequency reductions on a certain route or eventually to an entire route cut. Airlines typically act like this to reduce their burden of losses, even if the carrier's overall visibility* is *also negatively impacted in terms of being less attractive for passengers, especially business ones.*

Abandon an Entire SBU

This option is the most painful one for any company as it causes severe socio-economic consequences, like job redundancies and possible interference by political actors. It tends to be cautiously used in the airport business and may deal with the non-aviation business only, as aviation-business practices remain the technical core of the airport enterprise. In the case of non-aviation related businesses, this decision could be represented by a management contract, in which all terminal activities III are given to a concessionaire that will pay some royalties or fixed income to the landlord. Clearly, an airport management will have to choose between one of these four paths and then implement it on a consistent basis.

Implementation of Objectives

This phase will typically deal with:

- timing of activities to be followed and achieve desired goals;
- assignment of responsibilities;
- definition of the budget of economic resources.

Timing of Activities

This operational practice aims to define a schedule for all operations that will be taken and achieve the desired results. On the one hand, this kind of timetable will be correlated to a number of endogenous constraints, like:

- infra structural constraints, that could pose a limit to a projected upgrade of retailing facilities, requiring, for instance, an extension of terminal spaces to firstly be implemented;
- organisational constraints, referring to a lack of flexibility in job positions, leading to longer execution and response-to-market times;
- financial constraints, related to negative cash-flows that would necessitate borrowing money on the market with inherent delays in operating procedures.

On the other hand, timing decisions will be correlated with exogenous factors, like aggressive moves by competitors. This will clearly force an airport enterprise to compress its timing steps so as not to lose market share and frequently to borrow extra capacity on the market, especially labour capacity, on a short-time basis. A quieter environment will instead mean that airport managers can structure their schedule of activities more accordingly with endogenous constraints.

Assignment of Responsibilities

This phase seems consistent with a 'management by objectives' logic of conduct. In this case, a project manager is identified and he/she will become responsible for all coordination duties of the group of peers and provide stakeholders with the expected sound economic results as well. Some best-in-class airport companies are already abandoning a strict functional organisation and adopting more complex divisional and mixed solutions that take into account the tool of project managing.

Budgeting

Assigning the correct amount of resources seems a crucial step on the path to reach some sort of company goal. For instance, a limited budget could force managers to use only second—best tools in communicating their value proposition to the market. Over-budgeting might instead create some internal 'islands of ineffectiveness', with employees proving to be less committed in reaching challenging results and, therefore, leading to chronic weaknesses.

Auditing of Financial Results

The fourth and last part of the airport marketing plan deals with performance auditing. It maintains some distinctive elements, the first one related to its timing. This activity, in fact, logically follows on from the first three planning phases.

Nevertheless, the results of the auditing phase will be critically helpful in suggesting some milestones to be included in the next plan's diagnosis. This interdependence emphasises the circular, long-term view that links each marketing plan of the airport enterprise, as each covers a short-term perspective (usually 1-2 years) but is directly linked to the previous one.

The two subparts that compose the auditing phase are:

- gap analysis,
- definition of corrective hypotheses to smooth, in the next plan, the kind of gaps identified and targeted.

Gap Analysis

Here each SBU's actual and budget values and all airport's internal and external processes are identified. Regarding competitive data, market share is the main parameter to be taken into account. A negative gap may be ascribed for a number of reasons. First, these difficulties may be due to a rapid and unforeseeable change in the 'rules of the game' of the industry: like in the case of the introduction' of governmental decrees that limit the daily range of operations, or the attack by new competitors or, eventually, some random events.

Nevertheless, a negative result could be explained by an error in the budget planning. This often occurs when managers choose to fix too many challenging goals, which cannot actually be achieved due to some organisation or structural weaknesses or because a competitors' role had been underestimated. A practice like this has to be kept under strict observation, because it can produce some negative behaviour in the mind of airport employees, when they perceive them as impossible to be reached.

Corrective Hypotheses

An airport management, on the basis of the figures described above, will have to define some corrective actions to be implemented in the next diagnosis. This kind of qualitative contribution appears crucial because it forces managers to make a hierarchy of priorities by identifying the most relevant ones.

The bundle of changes that airports are now being faced with are too relevant and will certainly take them, at the end, to rather different industry boundaries than the existing ones. This increasingly complex microenvironment tends to extend the scope of marketing planning and its implementation in both analytical and professional terms. In other words, the later an airport improves both managerial skills and knowledge capabilities, the higher will be the risk of market marginalization and, thus, to be able to survive only in a niche perspective. No more protectionist barriers will be able to prevent this situation, either at a domestic or global scale.

The example of London City Airport, a private airport that has passed from 35,0006 to more than 2 million passengers per annum in a rather short space of time, proves that passive conducts may be dangerous even in the case of first-tier performers. This kind of marketing lesson, however, should provide a positive stimulation as well for all new comers in the new Millennium's airport industry. Market-rents may not exist in hypercompetitive territories; only a purely reactive and fearful behaviour may justify them. But it's also true that to successfully win, airports have to deeply reengineer their value proposition according to the paradigms of a 'customer-centred view' and offer the target market an offer which is consistent with their expectations.

London City Airport: A Best-in-Class Provider in the Airport Business

London City Airport (LCA) was inaugurated in 1987. Nowadays, it probably represents the world's best-in-class example of a private airport enterprise.

Looking back to the early 1980s, the core of LCA's strategic design was the idea that a new infrastructure could become a primary catalyser for the outgoing and incoming business community in the Docks area. There were however significant technical obstacles which had to be overcome before aircraft operations could commence on the new site.

Firstly, available space for ground movements was scarce, as the taxiway was to be built on a strip of land reclaimed from the river Thames. This situation would provide a limit to the number of yearly slots that was initially fixed at 10 per hour. It was also impossible to build a parallel taxiway.

Secondly, the limited runway length—only 800 meters!—would require airlines to operate small turboprop aircraft, like 50-seater Dash7s, this model being the only one to be fully compliant with a steep 7.50 approach instead of an usual 30 descent. Finally, air space congestion and nearby obstacles, like the Canary Wharf building, would impose, in any case, an upper slot cap of 12 per hour.

Based on these figures, LCA's inauguration actually introduced very limited additional capacity to the congested London area, with a small chance of becoming a head-to-head competitor with the much larger airports at Heathrow, Gatwick, Stansted and Luton. LCA, however, could exploit its favorable geographic location to attract high-yield O&D passengers flying between London and some main business centers.

Early economic and competitive results, when compared with an initial investment of 15 million pounds, were discouraging. In 1990, LCA reached only 200,000 passengers: difficulties in accessing the airport (no Subways were available) and longer flying times, due to turboprop operations, were preventing a lot of potential customers from choosing LCA.

In 1991, however, LCA was able to attract 50% of English business traffic and 30% of foreign business traffic flying between London and Brussels, Paris and Rotterdam. 70% of these passengers were paying full fares, when' compared with. only 27% in the case of Heathrow. 1991 saw also the decision to extend the airport's runway length to 1199 meters. These improvements would mean an additional investment of 41 million pounds. This decision, however, would enable the landing and take-off of Bae146 regional jets at LCA. Bae146s also named 'whisper jets' were able to carry around 100 passengers on a much longer range than turboprops while significantly upgrading on-board comfort, too. In the same period, a new weekly slot cap was fixed at 130.

From that moment onwards LCA's story has been paved with many successful milestones. In 1995 the airport managed 550,000 passengers, while in 1997 this figure reached 1.16 million and in 2000 1.6 million passengers.

Today LCA is served-by all the main European carriers, either directly or, more often, by their regional franchisees or associates. These airlines look for the opportunity to collect premium connecting volumes for their hubs, like Paris or Frankfurt, or focus on point-to-point traffics only, as it is the case of VLM, a Belgian carrier operating 7 times per day on the LCA-Rotterdam route.

LCA, which has since been sold by Mowlem, an engineering company, to an Irish entrepreneur, represents today a formidable competitor for BAA's Heathrow, Gatwick and Stansted. BAA was forced to establish a new high-speed connection between Heathrow and Paddington Station to counteract this threat and protect its share of high-yield passengers. LCA is also considered an icon of the 'city airport' concept, as its management was able to turn structural weaknesses into competitive points of strengths.

LCA's airport management approach may be broken down into four main pillars. The first one has been the creation of a permanent joint committee between the airport authority and citizens' representatives, with the goal of discussing both occasions of growth for the airport and the pace of negative externalities generated by aircraft operations. This kind of cooperative approach between the various airport shareholders has contributed to nearby residents accepting both the runway extension and a progressive increase in the number of weekly slots to reach the current level of 260.

Second, LCA has strictly cooperated with regional aircraft manufacturers to reach full operational ability and certification to land their various types of aircraft at LCA. We already mentioned the inauguration of Bae146 operations as a key element for the increase in passenger numbers, thanks to their superior capacity compared to turboprop models.

Third, LCA management has strongly believed in an airport-related marketing strategy aimed at extending the number of connections and attracting new operators to its airport. This activity has been implemented by using market research studies on a large scale and by formulating innovative value packages for prospect carriers.

Fourth, the terminal building has been designed to provide excellence in the most significant processes for its business target audience. The Minimum Check-in Time (MCT) now is ten minutes prior to flight departure. Baggage delivery times have—also been compressed.

In April 2000 LCA management presented a new expansion plan, which, once realised, should allow the airport to manage 3.5 up to 4 million passengers per year with employees more than doubling from a Current level of 1,300 to 2,800. A new remote aircraft parking site will be built and the existing apron will be extended, with an extra office building, a connecting taxiway, car park and a holding point for departing aircraft also to be added. This bundle of upgrades, with an estimated value of 20 million pounds, should all be completed within 2004, when the Dockland Light Railway, linking LCA and the Docks area with downtown London, should be operational, too.

[The Airport Marketing Plan was adopted by City Council in 1995]

MISSION STATEMENT

To further identify and develop convenient and specialized future airport facilities and services for the residents and businesses of Fayetteville, Northwest Arkansas, and the aviation community.

GOAL

To actively pursue business opportunities which will optimize airport revenues, expand economic development and positively impact Fayetteville, Northwest Arkansas, and the aviation community.

OBJECTIVES

I. Maintain Drake Field as a Viable Regional Air Carrier Airport

(a) Consult current regional air carriers to determine how best to serve them and their customers (passengers). [Invite the presidents of each air carrier corporation serving Drake Field to an appreciation luncheon with the Mayor and aldermen in order to show our commitment to their needs and hopes for their continued business.]

(b) Survey commercial passengers to determine destination, purpose of trip, how to increase their satisfaction with Drake Field (needed improvements, etc.).

(c) Consult the remainder of airport tenants (restaurant, car rental agencies etc.) to determine how best to serve them and their customers.

(d) Hold quarterly planning and discussion sessions (maybe luncheons) with air carriers and all other tenants to obtain input and to provide prompt response to new problems or concerns.

(e) Develop Fly Fayetteville promotional campaign to maintain customer base for Drake Field.

II. Identify and obtain needed improvements required to compete in the regional aviation market

Action Plans

(a) Inventory of existing Fayetteville Municipal Airport assets.

(b) Determine area/regional competition and identify the extent of their resources.

(c) Survey area/regional aviation related business to determine their needs.

(d) Research and investigate airports that are in a similar situation as FMA.

(e) Research and list possible incentive plans, tax abatements, incubation start-up grants, and funding sources from government agencies for attracting aviation businesses.

(f) Research and list possible state and federal agencies that can help with marketing information and/or assistance.

(g) Determine the business projections for the FMA for the next 5-10 years.

III. Increase general aviation use

Action Plans

(a) Develop separate collateral pieces of marketing information for each target market segment; i.e. general aviation, commercial aviation and industrial aviation.

IV. Expand existing aviation uses that will increase revenues

Action Plans

(a) Conduct survey of existing users to determine needs.
(b) Conduct inventory of area / regional aviation related industries.
(c) Develop separate collateral pieces of marketing information for each target market segment; i.e. general aviation, commercial aviation and industrial aviation.

V. Attract new Aviation Industries

Action Plans

(a) Conduct inventory of area/regional aviation related industries.
(b) Investigate cargo shipping and industrial uses.
(c) Explore opportunities for spin off industries from the Northwest Arkansas Regional Airport development.
(d) Explore possible marketing campaigns for mass mailing, trade shows, etc. [*sic*]
(e) Develop separate collateral pieces of marketing information for each target market segment; i.e. general aviation, commercial aviation and industrial aviation.
(f) Research and list possible incentive plans, tax abatements, incubation start-up grants, and funding sources form government agencies for attracting aviation businesses.

VI. Explore new opportunities and uses.

Action Plans

(a) Develop regional/area partnerships and alliances.
(b) Explore linkages and connections between FMA and the City of Fayetteville South Industrial Park.
(c) Explore University of Arkansas/aviation related opportunities.
(d) Investigate cargo shipping and industrial uses.
(e) Research and investigate airports that are in a similar situation as FMA.
(f) Explore opportunities for spin off industries from the Northwest Arkansas Regional Airport development.
(g) Develop separate collateral pieces of marketing information for each

target market segment; i.e. general aviation, commercial aviation and industrial aviation.

VII. Develop an identity for the FMA and increase community awareness and support within the aviation field

Action Plans

(a) Develop strong working relationships with the City of Fayetteville, the Fayetteville Chamber of Commerce, and community members.
(b) Develop partnerships with travel agents with incentive to book FMA.
(c) Establish an Airport Support Group that will raise the level of awareness of the FMA.

AIRPORT PERFORMANCE MEASURES

It is easier to adopt normal business accounting methods to establish the financial performances of airports. Some of the common ones are:

1. *Operating Ratio*—operating and maintenance expenses divided by operating revenue. The ratio measures the share of revenues absorbed by operating and maintenance costs. A relative low operating ratio indicates financial strength, since it signifies that only a small share of revenue is required to satisfy operating requirements. A high ratio (Close to 1) indicates that relatively little additional revenue is available for capital spending.
2. *Net Take-Down Ratio*—gross revenue minus operating and maintenance expenses, divided by gross revenues. This similar to the operating ratio, but it also includes non-operating revenues (e.g. Interest income). It is a slightly broader measure of the share of airport revenues remaining after payment of operating expenses.
3. *Debt-to-Asset Ratio*—gross debt minus bond principal reserves, divided by net fixed assets plus working capital. This measures the fraction of total assets provided by creditors. Creditors prefer low debt ratio because each rupee of debt is secured by more rupee of assets.
4. *Debt Service Safety Margin*—gross revenue less operating and maintenance expenses and annual debt services, divided by gross revenues. This ratio measures both the percentage of revenues available to service new debt and the financial cushion to protect against unexpectedly low revenues.

Some researchers have used all of the indicators in Table 7 for research purposes. As it turns out the actual situation is rather simpler. In 2000, a survey of 200 of the world's largest airports was undertaken by Loughborough University and the UK Open University to investigate how they measured their performance (Francis et al, 2001). Some of the most popular measures used were

Table 7: Other Measures include

• Aeronautical revenue per ATM • Aeronautical revenues as a % of total costs • Aeronautical revenues as a % of total revenues • Aeronautical revenue per 1000 ATUs • Aeronautical revenue per passenger • Staff costs as a % of operating and staff costs • Staff costs per 1000 ATUs • Staff costs per passenger	• Total revenue per ATM • Total revenue per 1000 ATUs • Total revenue per passenger • Total revenue per employee • Total costs per ATM • Total costs per passenger • Total costs per 1000 ATUs • Total assets per passenger • Return on capital employed, • Return on shareholders' funds	• Commercial revenue per passenger • Commercial revenue as a % of total revenue • Operating costs per passenger • Operating profit • Operating profit per passenger • Passengers per employee • Passengers per ATM • ATUs per employee • Equity ratio • Liquidity ratio	• Assets per employee • Capital expenditure per passenger • Capital expenditure as a % of turnover • Taxation effect • Net cash generation per passenger • EBITDA as a % of turnover

found to be cost per passenger and total, aeronautical and non-aeronautical revenue per passenger, whilst revenue per WLU, for example, was less commonly used. Here we have used the most popular measures of economic performance are used, e.g. cost per passenger and total revenue per passenger.

ICAO suggests the following indicators for measuring performances—

- Income per passenger
- Expenditure per passenger
- Aeronautical income per passenger
- Non-aeronautical income per passenger
- Passenger per employee
- Income per employee
- Value added per employee
- Capital expenditure per passenger
- Net assets per employee

Airport Economic Performance

Airports are an essential part of the air transportation system. They play a vital role not only within the macro environment of transportation, but also in the process of increasing the quality of life of their regional economies and direct participation in wealth creation.

Historically, publicly owned and generally strictly controlled airports have been treated as "Public Utilities," with public service obligations (Doganis, 1992). Consequently, the economic performance of airports was not given top priority. With widespread airline privatisation and commercialisation, progress toward airport commercialisation and economic performance has grown in importance. Increasingly airports are real enterprises, their goal being long-term profit generation to both sustain independent development and reward stakeholders.

For most airports their application of Internet Technology is a Web site. However this is limited to a marketing presence, or a simple electronic brochure. Most sites are static, incapable of supporting online commerce. A very small number of airports use the Internet to manage internal operations – maintenance, scheduling, billing, purchasing, accounting, and personnel, and still fewer airports are connected electronically to their suppliers and business partners. Overall the Internet's contribution to airport economic performance is insignificant.

The objective of this paper is to discuss the improvement of airport economic performance through Internet Technology. It starts with consideration of airport business models, followed by airport revenue and cost structure, and then analysis of airport economic performance measurement, finally, it provides some solutions for airports and future Internet applications.

In the current turbulent environment, large airport development and management is a significant strategic issue. Managing a modern airport is like managing a town, it is very complicated. Some airports have over 50,000 employees such as Hong Kong International airport and Amsterdam Schiphol airport, together with a huge number of users such as airlines and passengers (in some cases over 70 million per year).

With airport privatisation and commercialisation, improving an airport's economic performance is increasingly important for airport managers. Other industry issues such as terrorism and soaring fuel prices make this harder than ever.

To enhance employee productivity and business performance airport managers are turning to technological solutions such as the Internet. Some airports such as BAA (British Airport Authority) plc have already demonstrated that Internet Technology can increase revenue and significantly reduce operational costs, while other operators still struggle to break-even.

Internet Technology could play in helping airports improve their economic performance. First, some basic issues such as airport models, airport revenue and structure, and methods of measuring airport economic performance need to be introduced.

Operating Revenues vs. Operating Expenses Performances

Airport revenue provides for the operations, maintenance, and capital improvements of the Pierce County Airport – Thus Field. The 3-year goal is for airport operations to be self-supporting through user fees and tenant charges.

The operating expenses associated with the airport include maintenance

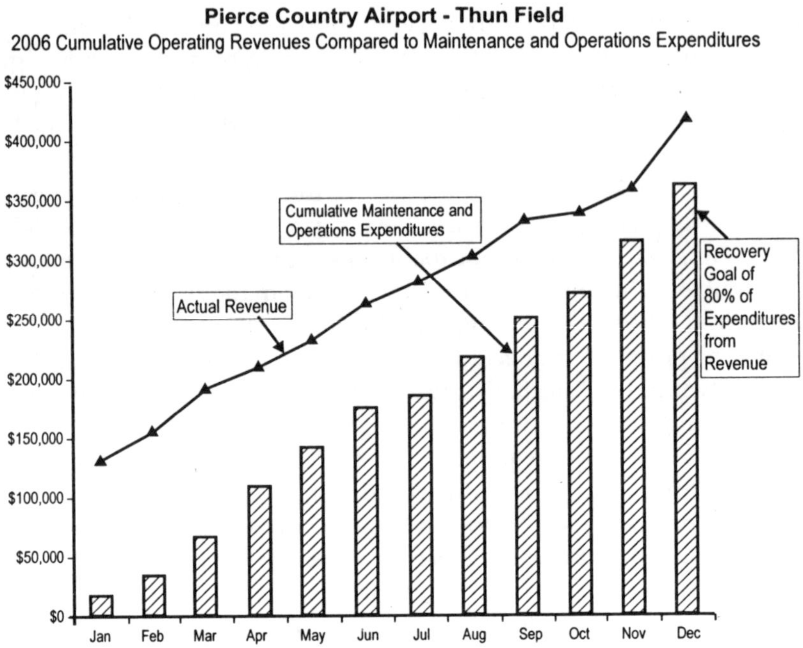

Performance Goal: The Airport Operating Revenues will cover at least 80% of Operating Expenses (excluding depreciation).

Data Note: Operating expenses do not include expenses such as improvements or preservation costs for runway maintenance or other physical assets associated with the Airport.

Fig. 24

of airport systems and facilities, power and other utilities, and supplies and administration. The operating revenues come from leases and rental charges for land, hangers, tie-downs, and other facilities at the airport and a share of concessions.

The graph above shows that all four quarters of actual Airport operating revenue compared to cumulative operating and maintenance expenses data easily exceeds the 80% recovery goal. This information has prompted us to change our 2007 goal to state that "Operating revenues will cover all operating expenses (excluding depreciation)." Recent efforts to bring leases up to market rates is the primary reason for the increase in operating revenues.

Airport decision makers face frequently complex decisions related to airport planning, design, and operations. These decisions are highly complicated since they involve a variety of entities processed through the system, a number of different airport elements, and a large variety of airport performance measures like capacity, delays, safety, security, noise, and cost-effectiveness.

Existing airport modeling capabilities suffer from:

(i) fragmentation between the various airport elements, entities, and their operations,

(ii) the isolated manner in which the airport performance measures are assessed and modeled, and

(iii) lack of user-friendly modeling capabilities and decision support systems adopting a problem-oriented approach for airport decision making and planning. Advanced airport modeling capabilities should be deployed with the aim to integrate domain knowledge with tool expertise in assisting airport decision makers to answer frequently arising airport planning questions in an integrated, user-friendly, and problem-oriented environment.

The objective here is:

(i) to introduce the operational concept for an integrated, problem-oriented modeling approach for total airport performance analysis,

(ii) to describe the development of a Decision Support System for airport performance assessment and capacity management, and

(iii) to demonstrate the modeling and decision support capabilities of the system.

Airport Revenue and Cost Structures

Regardless of whether a traditional or commercial airport model is applied, airports' revenue and cost structures are very similar, the difference lies in the percentage of each revenue and cost component.

Revenue Structure

Airport's income comes from both aeronautical/traffic-related activities (aeronautical revenues) and non-aeronautical/commercial sources (non-aeronautical revenues).

Aeronautical Revenues

- Landing fees
- Passenger fees
- Aircraft parking fees
- Handling fees, such as aircraft handling and freight handling fees (if handled by airport operator)
- Other aeronautical fees (air traffic control, lighting, airbridges etc.)

Non-aeronautical Revenues

- Concessions
- Rents
- Direct sales (shops, catering and other services provided by the airport operator)
- Car park
- Recharges (for gas, water, electricity etc.)

- Other non-aeronautical revenue (consultancy, visitor and business services, property development etc.)

Cost Structure

Unlike with revenues, there is no industry standard for the reporting of airport operating costs. From published accounts, however, it is usually possible to identify the three separate cost items associated with:

- labour,
- capital, and
- other operating costs.

How to measure Airport Economic Performance

Traditional Airport Model

Airports operating under the traditional model assess their performance using criteria based solely on traffic growth. This is in spite of a growing awareness by airport management of the financial and commercial implications of operating an airport.

Commercial Airport Model

There are 15 to 20 indicators commonly used to measure airport performance such as cost-efficiency, labour and capital productivity, revenue generation and commercial performance, and profitability (Doganis, 1992; Ashford and Moore, 1999; Humphreys and Francis, 2000). Table 1 presents the most popular of these. Some have been used for analysis of specific markets such as France (Assaily, 1989), Australia (Doganis et al., 1994), the UK (CRI, 2002) or more generally to compare airport performance within Europe (Graham, 2003) and around the world (TRL, 2002).

By considering total revenue generated, since most airports handle both passengers and freight, this suggests the use of an output measure which combines the two, such as the WLU (Work Load Unit). The WLU originated from the airline industry and uses a weight criteria for combining these two types of traffic (i.e. one WLU = one passenger or 100kg of freight). Some argue, however, the focus should be passenger numbers since freight handling at airports is very much an airline activity and has little impact on an airport's economic performance.

Performance indicators commonly used to assess economic performance (Graham, 2003)

1. Cost Efficiency

- Costs excluding depreciation per WLU
- Costs including depreciation per WLU

- Depreciation costs per WLU
- Labour costs per WLU
- Depreciation share of operating costs
- Labour share of operating costs

2. Labour Productivity

- WLU per employee
- Revenues per employee

3. Capital Productivity

- WLU/total assets
- Revenues/total assets
- Total assets per employee

4. Revenue Generation

- Revenues per WLU
- Aeronautical revenues per WLU
- Non-aeronautical revenues per WLU
- Aeronautical share of total revenues

5. Commercial Performance

- Concession plus rental revenues per passenger
- Concession revenues per passenger

6. Profitability

- Revenues: costs ratio
- Operating profit excluding
- Depreciation per WLU
- Operating profit including depreciation per WLU
- Operating profit including/excluding depreciation/total assets
- Net retained profit after interest and taxation per WLU

How can Internet Technology Improve Airport Economic Performance?

As noted before, greater attention has begun to be placed on the commercial aspects of running an airport such as financial management, non-aeronautical revenue generation and airport marketing. The application of Internet Technology can help airports achieve these goals and improve their economic performance by:

- Increasing revenue per passenger
- Reducing cost per passenger

Increasing Revenue Per Passenger

Revenue per passenger can be generated by using Internet Technology in two main areas: improving service and Internet marketing.

Improving Service and Customer Relationship

Information included on airport websites, which have been set up by most airports, display various degrees of sophistication. Typical information includes airport location details, car parking, and local transport details, with opportunities for pre-booking car parking spaces or buying public transport tickets online. Tourist and other information about the airport's services area might be included. Nearly all airport websites, even the most basic, include terminal maps and a facilities list, such as shops and catering available. Major airports sites now include real-time flight information and flight-delay details. This information will soon appear on those sites of smaller operators (Hoevel, 1999).

Clearly, the Internet can play a much greater role than simple travel information. Airports can strengthen relationships with existing customers by allowing them to access—via its Web site—previously inaccessible decision-support information, such as detailed research reports, or environmental protection documents. Shareholders can track performance of their shares and have instant access to the airports' financial reports, e.g. Melbourne Airport in Australia.

Research has shown increased customer service levels can improve customer relationships and in turn increase revenue per passenger. The following case study demonstrates this.

Using Internet Marketing

Historically the airport industry has been rather passive towards marketing, only responding to customer needs when absolutely necessary. The more businesslike approach to airport management, coupled with a more commercially driven and competitive airline industry, has encouraged airports to take a more dynamic and proactive role. In the United Kingdom, for example, many airports have set up marketing departments, started to use pricing tactics and promotional campaigns to attract new customers, and begun to undertake market research (Humphreys, 1999).

The Internet offers many marketing and revenue opportunities, and increasingly airports are taking advantage of this. For example, customer profile and preference information can automatically be collected from website users. Pre-ordering purchases, online shopping, and advertising can also increase non-aeronautical revenues. Airports are beginning to experiment. For example, BAA plc in co-operation with the travel company expedia UK provides online reservations for many airlines and hotels, last-minute travel details, weather updates, health advice, travel plans, and destination profiles. Furthermore, in 2000, BAA plc invested in lastminute.com. It also has airport upgrade packages available on the net. In turn Amsterdam Schiphol airport uses the Internet to further its concept of an AirportCity. It defines the Internet as the virtual AirportCity and customises information for specific groups such as business, leisure, and transfer passengers. It also provides information to customers interested in Schiphol real-estate properties and online purchases from the See Buy Fly shopping centre can be made. In September 2001, Schiphol launched its virtual travel agency, Schiphol Travelport, which allows passengers to book online airline tickets, rentals car, airport taxis, and other travel products. It also has the Schiphol Travel Update service, which uses SMS or e-mail to update passengers and others on arrivals and departures times, check-in counters, gates, or baggage carousel.

Airports advertise to the public through the Internet as with all other usual media channels such as television, radio, newspapers, magazines, and posters. The choice of media, as with all marketing, depends on relative costs, target audience, and message the organization wants to put across. Most commonly, airports try to increase consumer awareness of flights and closeness of the airport by listing destinations on offer or focusing on the convenience of public transport links. More specific messages may relate to a certain service or facility at the airport—a notable example being the advertising various airports have undertaken to recover some of their lost retail trade since the loss of EU duty and tax-free sales. The advertising may be targeted at certain market segments, particularly business travelers. For instance, Abu Dhabi's airport marketing campaign 'Start at the Heart' was based around a heart logo designed to inform business travelers that they could check in at the 'heart' of the city and take a luxury car to the airport (Graham, 2003).

Web-based marketing programs offer incredibly cost-effective methods of creating customised versions of information and products. Development of these systems requires careful profiling of both product and prospect and then carefully mapping these needs to relevant products and offerings.

Reducing Cost per Passenger

Application of Internet Technology for airports can also significantly reduce airport operation cost. A good example of the application is e-Business, Figure 25 shows that an airport may be involved in both B2B (Business to Business) and B2C (Business to Customer).

Airport facility B2B market provides one stop for the airport industry, and it can cut airport procurement costs significantly (e-procurement). For example, both http://www.airfield—lighting.com/b2b/catb2b.html and htp://www.thirtythousandfeet.com/b2b.htm provide B2B portals for airports.

The retail B2B market enables airports to contact retailers worldwide directly which also cuts airport outsourcing fees. For instance, BAA plc established its own retail B2B platform including UK Airports Retail, World Duty Free, and International Retail, ensuring retail becomes an important element of the airport experience.

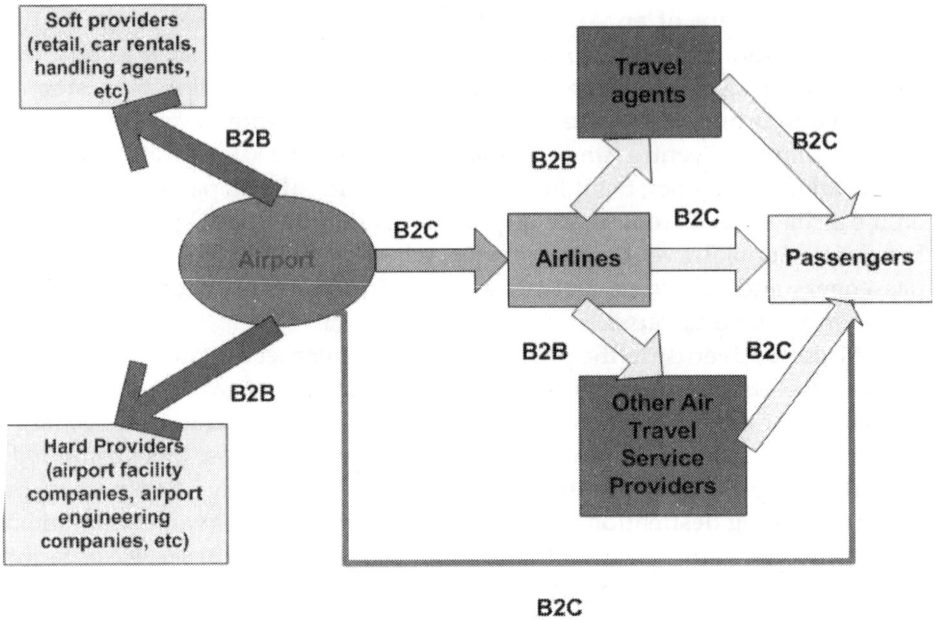

Fig. 25: Airport e-Business System

Airport B2C can also integrate Internet and Intranet together and provide 24/7 services for airport customers, which can lower airport operational costs. Figure 26 gives an example of B2C used at The Kuala Lumpur International Airport (RMS—Retail Management System, developed by AMC Company).

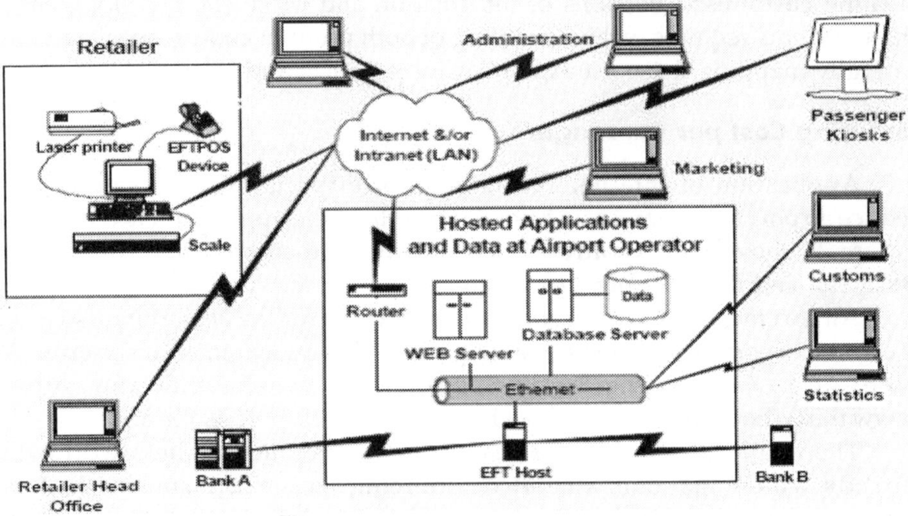

Fig. 26: Example of RMS Airport Solution (Source: AMC Company, 2003)

There are vast opportunities and challenges in the application of Internet

Technology to the airport environment. Clearly it is time to focus on Airport B2B, B2C and Internet Marketing to improve airport services and economic performance. It is also important to develop business solutions based on the SPT (Simplifying Passenger Travel) concepts and to tighten the customer relationship to improve non-aeronautical revenues. The old business model was flawed and key to improving passenger logistics was the provision of information ahead of the logistical flow. New technology, including Internet and wireless communication, enables airport processes to be effected earlier in the travel chain without a physical service desk. This could increase processing capacity of the terminal whilst reducing costs of passenger processing.

This work clearly shows Internet Technology and its application can assist the airport industry to improve its economic performance.

AIRPORT MODELS

Traditional Airport Model

The traditional strategy of government-owned airports, operated and managed by a Ministry of Transport or Department of Civil Aviation is to meet basic and essential needs of passengers, airlines, freight forwarders and other direct airport customers such as retailers. Such a strategy will have significant implications for airport planning and design. In particular, the airport will be primarily oriented to facilitating passenger handing and throughput; with all extraneous or unnecessary activities kept to a minimum and with relatively little space allocated to them. Within imposed design and space constraints, airports following this traditional strategy can still try to maximise commercial revenue. Clearly they will be severely constrained in what can be done, particularly within the terminal, both by a lack of space and the priority given to meeting passengers' primary needs. This traditional airport model can be seen in over 100 airports in China, most airports in Canada before 2000, and all airports in Papua New Guinea.

Commercial Airport Model

In contrast a 'commercial airport' will exhibit critical differences in both its strategic mission and its inherent marketing implementation, when compared to the 'traditional airport' concept (Jarach, 2005).

The aim in this case is income maximisation from any airport activity. This also means that one regards the airport as a business opportunity, which not only serves its direct and traditional customers—airlines, passengers, cargo shippers and so on—but also a wider range of potential customers including airport and airline employees, visitors, people meeting passengers, local residents in surrounding communities as well as local businesses and industries (Doganis, 1992). This strategy has several design implications. While every effort is made to facilitate movement of passengers and cargo through the

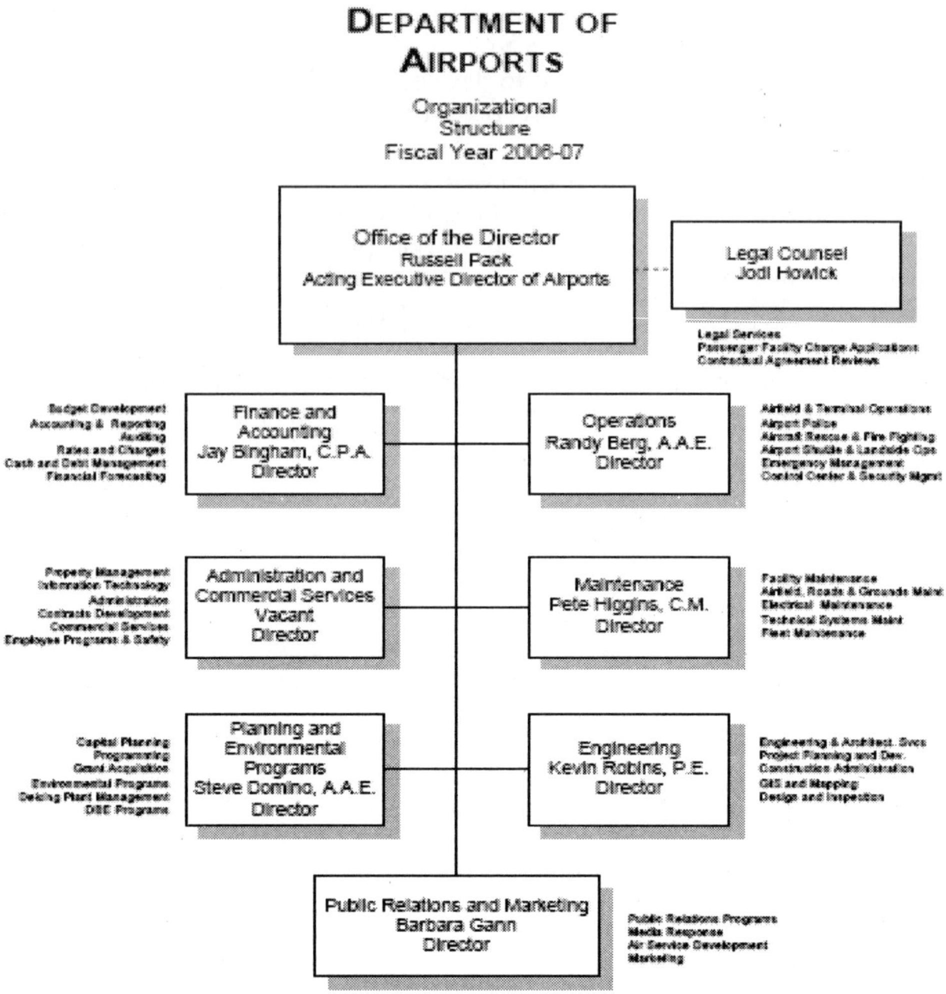

Fig. 27

airport; every effort is also made to maximise opportunities for additional commercial income generation even from activities indirectly related to air traffic—such as light industry or even leisure complexes. To be most effective, such a strategy requires abundant and flexible space both in- and out-side various airport terminals and buildings. Examples of the commercial airport model include Frankfurt airport, Amsterdam Schiphol airport in Europe and Melbourne airport in Australia. Figure 28 best illustrates the enriched service package offered by a modern airport enterprise.

Main elements involved in Airport Choice

- Width, density and potential market growth of the catchment area;
- Slot availability;
- Presence or absence of direct competitors;

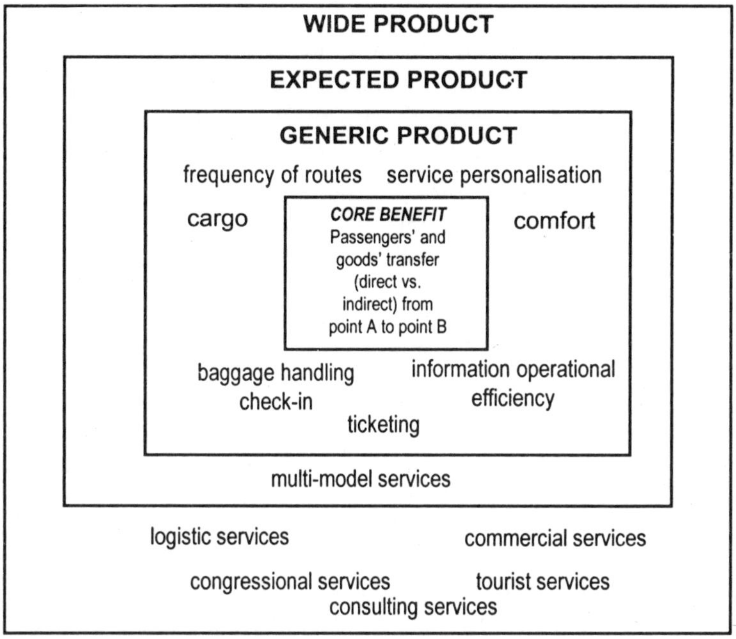

Fig. 28. The enriched service package offered by a modern airport enterprise (Jarach, 2005)

- Network and operational consistency;
- Airport charges (landing and handling fees plus fuel prices);
- Minimum guaranteed turnaround times;
- Presence of economic and commercial incentives at start-up of operations;
- Width and availability of airport infrastructural facilities; Availability of a range of intermodal solutions for accessing and leaving the airport;
- Absence of environmental restrictions (fundamental in the case of overnight cargo services);
- Availability of maintenance centres at the airport;
- 24 hrs. non-stop opening times (again, critical in the case of cargo);
- Presence of upgrade projects for terminal expansion;
- Low historical rate of accidents on apron caused by handling operations.

The large urban hinterland area of London today hosts seven airports, each one struggling to attract extra passengers or cargo on the basis of a specific positioning. ***Heathrow*** competes as a global primary hub, ***Gatwick*** is more of a leisure-oriented, charter airport; whilst ***Stansted*** is home to the main low-cost operators. ***London City Airport*** provides business access to the financial district of the British capital, whilst ***Luton*** is transforming itself to host a growing range of point-to-point, LCC traffic. Biggin-Hill is one of the UK's best-known airports, having been one of the main RAF stations during the Battle of Britain and home to the annual air show. Over the last 40 years it has also undergone a gradual metamorphosis into the busy commercial airport it is today. ***Biggin Hill,*** which is only 12 miles from the centre of London, can cope with aircraft up to the size of a B737 and has a number of private charter operators based there. ***Manston Airport*** offers some maintenance and technical facilities and seems focused on cargo traffic, with MAS (Malaysian Airlines Cargo) as one of its core customers.

AIRPORT'S MARKET POSITIONING

This kind of strategic decision seems today to be at the core of the commercial policy of the airport-enterprise. On the basis of the distinctive features of each individual airport, a consistent positioning strategy is a preliminary step in the design of all operational airport marketing tools, such as:

- *definition of the level and content of the value proposition,* or, in other words, of the offer that will be presented to the potential audience by the value chain's intermediate customers and end consumers;
- *identification of the price level,* or of the price band, that an airport-enterprise will charge its intermediate customers for the bundle of services produced;
- *implementation of the communication campaign* that an airport-enterprise will launch to capture the attention of operators or political stakeholders;
- *Level of distribution of the value proposition,* this element referring to the coverage and penetration levels that an airport will choose to reach in its primary catchment area and, eventually, attacking the competitive field controlled by other industry players (the so called secondary catchment area).

To achieve the correct market positioning, an airport-enterprise will need to implement an exploratory market research study, aimed at understanding both the quantity/quality of current traffic values and the potential purchase intentions of its catchment area. This path seems fundamental to generate a consistent v lue system which matches the target's needs. Each geo-commercial area will show different trends due to a stronger business—industrial or leisure—tourist element; for example, the different quantity and quality of traffic that influence movements in Verona, Italy (mainly an industrial area) or Palma de Majorca, Spain (a typical sunshine destination) are clearly visible. Nevertheless, airports may decide to differentiate their offer system and abandon local demand connotations. This process, however, seems much more risky and is likely only to be activated in the case of dramatic market growth by a new offer cluster, like LCCs.

On the basis of this analysis, an airport will have to choose between *three different positioning strategies.*

The first one refers to a competitive market positioning, in which an airport is in open and direct competition with other airports, on the basis of parameters like geographical proximity or the type of operations hosted, e.g. point-to-point vs. hubbing activities.

The second strategy refers to a niche market positioning, that aims at avoiding an open confrontation with other players. This option will be adopted when financial and management resources are lacking. It will be successfully implemented when technical or infra structural weaknesses can *ex ante* impede airport activities on a competitive arena, as in the case of London City or Dusseldorf City airports.

A third and final option may see airports gaining a specific market positioning as a result of their association with an airport alliance. This positioning strategy will have to be a complementary and synergic one to those of to the ones of other allied partners.

Referring to the possible types of positioning that an airport may adopt within a chosen positioning strategy, we may count five different alternatives.

Primary Hub

Here the airport enterprise aims to operate as a hub focusing on facilitating passengers and goods travelling on a transnational level. This goal will be best achieved by first attracting one or, possibly, a couple of airlines that will develop their main base of operations4 at the airport.

In this sense, it's critical to note that the role, strategies and performance of the hub carrier arti key in terms of the growth potential and long-term economic viability of the primary hub airport. Network rationalisation, when accompanied by severe flight cuts, will drastically impact on the hub's attractiveness to the market, whilst a steady increase in served destinations will improve its market visibility, especially for connecting traffic.

Munich airport, although located in a smaller and less wealthy area than Milan Malpensa airport, has seen ready passenger growth for the last few years thanks to the significant capacity growth of Lufthansa, the hub carrier. In contrast, Alitalia' s network cuts, especially after September 11, have drastically reduced the chances for Malpensa to become a primary player in the Southern European region.

Primary hubs have historically been developed at major political and business locations. In these locations, the hub carrier will be able to count on a significant base of O&D (Origin & Destination) traffic. The airline will create opportunities for growth in connecting and transit traffic due to its links with spoke destinations.

Some airports, however, have reinforced their position as primary hubs, not only through online traffic by the hub carrier, but also due to huge interlining traffic agreements between non-partner carriers.

This is the case of London Heathrow, for instance, which is historically considered by US travellers as the main European gateway, thanks to the unmatched level of frequencies along US-UK city-pair destinations. Many American travellers choose to fly with a US carrier and then stop in London and board another operator to reach their destination.

The primary hub formula targets both business and leisure, thanks to the large amount of system capacity offered to and from the airport by the hub carrier. Nevertheless, some airports have stretched their role of primary hubs by including cargo traffic. For instance, Amsterdam, London Heathrow, Frankfurt and Paris CDG are the main players in the cargo business even if their primary focus remains passenger traffic. The development of cargo as a complementary activity is possible thanks to the availability of belly—offer on passenger and combi flights, as well as dedicated cargo—only flights to some of the main destinations.

Secondary Hub

An airport enterprise with a secondary—hub objective acts within a smaller geographical and commercial horizon than that of primary hubs. In fact, this kind of airport aims to manage, almost exclusively, connecting traffic on a regional basis.

The location of secondary hubs is similar to that of primary hubs, that is in regional business or leisure centres with strong O&D inbound and outbound traffic: as is the case of Barcelona, Clermont Ferrant, Basel, Seattle, St. Louis? Mumbai and Nairobi. Frequently secondary hubs emerge at airports where a previous primary hub project has collapsed, due to insignificant local demand or to the hub carrier's bankruptcy, as in the case of Zurich and Brussels.

The commercial success of secondary hubs can be related to lower congestion levels that permit smoother transfer times, as is the case of Clermont Ferrant in France. This tiny airport, established to serve Michelin's travel needs, has operated for several years as a secondary hub, competing with Paris CDG to attract business connecting traffic. This was possible thanks to the lower number of aircraft operations, with a positive impact on the efficiency of technical hubbing procedures, and to a strong partner carrier, Regional Airlines. When this airline was bought by Air France, the French national carrier decided to limit hubbing operations in Clermont Ferrant to reduce cannibalisation with Paris CDG.

Regional Airport

These airports usually manage 10-15 million passengers per year. They do not host any hub carrier as they traditionally play the role of spokes within major airlines' networks. Regional airports promote a significant offer of regional carriers, the latter acting independently or through a bundle of different partnerships with network airlines. Regional airports tend to focus on point-to-point traffic, with very little connecting traffic.

The commercial success of a regional airport relies mainly on the chance to exploit a favourable geographic location and proximity to a city's downtown area. Some best-in-class examples from this category are Turin and. Venice in Italy, Valencia in Spain, Dusseldorf and Stuttgart in Germany, Nice in France, and La Guardia in New York.

A subcategory of the regional airport model is provided by city airports. These operate inside city boundaries and, for this reason, are usually subject to some operational limitations in take-off and landing procedures or in the type of aircraft permitted. City airports serve exclusively business targets that are willing to pay a premium for a closer-to-city departure point, faster handling services and a huge number of point-to-point services to the main regional financial centres.

Traditionally, city airports are secondary airports, close to city boundaries or within them, that have a lower number of movements and passengers than other airports in the same area for the following reasons:

- current constraints in the infrastructural package, like short runways, or tiny terminal and apron spaces.
- technical limitations, due to obstacles that may impact on takeoff and landing procedures;
- operational and environmental regulations that are aimed at preserving the quality of life of neighbouring residents.

Due to these constraints and limitations, these airports have played for decades a marginal role in the market. In the last decade, however, some of these players have been able to turn these elements of competitive disadvantage into critical factors of success, thanks also to the growing congestion of the primary sites. First of all, city airports have identified regional carriers as their main partners. These carriers usually manage small aircraft, turboprop or jet ones, and are primarily interested in providing point-to-point connections between regional and main business locations. Their target customers are typically business travellers, willing to pay higher tariffs in exchange for non-stop air links rather than having to stopover at hubs.

The strategic profile of today' s best-in-class city airports, however, sees a significant differentiation of the whole value proposition to the customers. For instance, business travellers usually like to shorten their staying times at terminal buildings to maximise their work time. At London City Airport, thus, passengers may check-in up to 10 minutes before departure. Again, another perceived KPI (Key Performance Index) by the customers, like baggage delivery times to incoming passengers, will be much shorter than at hubs, thanks to efficient cooperation between the airport authority and ground handling operators.

City airports do not provide customers with a different package of routes and air services than other airports they have, instead, reengineered their value proposition around KPls to stay in touch with the expressed needs of their target audience. Of course, this should be a fundamental rule of airport management.

A second subcategory of regional airports is represented by charter airports, which host the seasonal traffic of charter carriers. Here the target cluster becomes a purely leisure one and the range and bundle of services offered will De reduced to stay in touch with the strict economic requests by airline operators. Many airports included in this category are now evolving themselves into the paradigm of low-cost airports.

A typical example of a charter airport is Crete's Heraklion airport in Greece. This airport has a complete reversal of operations from winter to summer. In the latter case, take-off and landings are separated by just a couple of minutes! This creates a lot of pressure on the terminal and apron infrastructures, and new buildings are now being constructed to cope with peak demand. However, there is a problem concerning the inefficient utilisation of infrastructures during winter seasons, which increases the annual management costs of the airport.

All-Cargo Airport

The main distinctive feature of this cluster of airports is that they are fully dedicated to the cargo business, thanks to a package of state-of-the-art inter modal solutions (rail, road and sometimes, water). By exploiting a favourable location, which is usually far from cities to avoid environmental limitations, 11 this kind of infrastructure may be able to operate on a 24-hour basis.

There are still a few examples of all-cargo airports in the international arena. One of them is Euro port', located 150 km. from Paris, that entered into service in 2000. In Asia, Subic Bay in the Philippines, a former USAF base, now acts as an all-cargo airport for FedEx.

More Positioning Criteria

The above framework which categorises airport positioning strategies into five main areas is, of course, a simplification of the actual situation which exists in the airport industry. In fact, there exists much higher variance, due to the combination of both endogenous and exogenous factors. Table shows 19 different market positioning, that have been identified on a basis of worldwide empirical research.

Table 8: Airport Positioning Criteria

	Market positioning	*Examples of airports located in the described category*
1	Airports integrated into a city's marketing plan	Manchester
2	Airports integrated into a region's (or federal state's) marketing plan	Munich
3	Airports with growth potential, although limited by physical constraints	Brussels, San Francisco, Amsterdam

4	Airports integrated within a system and where the same hub carrier is dominant	Paris Orly and CDG London Heathrow and Gatwick
5	Airports integrated within a system by the will of a regulator	Milan Linate and Malpensa Tokyo Haneda and Narita, Washington Dulles and Reagan
6	Airports operating within the same catchment area, although with different value propositions	Chicago O'Hare and Midway Stockholm Arlanda and Bromma Milan Malpensa and Orio
7	Airports attracting overflow traffic	London Biggin Hill Paris Le Bourget Rome Ciampino
8	Airports with an alternative (low-cost) proposition	London Luton and, Stansted Paris Beauvois, Brussels Charleroi Milan Orio, Frankfurt Hahn
9	Airports implementing cooperative policies with neighbouring residents and counties	Frankfurt, Amsterdam, Tokyo Narita
10	Airports with technical limitations (city airports)	London City Airport, Florence, Toronto City, Courchevel Chambery Dusseldorf Express, Aosta
11	Airports under reengineering, due to abandonment by the hub carrier	St.Louis, Raleigh-Durham London Gatwick, Geneva
12	Airports designated as national or pan regional gateways (primary and secondary hubs)	Wien, Miami, Toronto, Johannesburg Dubai, Los Angeles, Bangkok New York JFK
13	Airports with a cargo focus (all-cargo airports)	Vatry, Rotterdam (scheduled), Memphis, Louisville, Luik
14	Greenfield airports	Munich, Oslo, Seoul, Athens
15	Upgraded airports, on the basis of previously existing infrastructures	London Heathrow Milan Malpensa, Doha, Dubai Bahrain, Madrid, Paris CDG
16	Airports with limitations in the range of air services offered, due to infrastructural constraints	New York La Guardia Tokyo Narita Washington Reagan
17	Airports acting as a country's sole gateway	Singapore, Hong Kong, Malta Larnaca/Nicosia
18	Airports undergoing conversion from military to civil operations	Torrejon (Spain), El Toro (California) Grazzanise (Italy)
19	Dominant airports (not the sole country's gateway, but controlling most of the market)	Helsinki, Copenhagen, Tel Aviv Wien, San Juan, Dublin

CHAPTER 6

Air Cargo Marketing

ABOUT AIR CARGO

Carrying cargo has been far more important than carrying passengers for almost every mode of transportation ever used by humankind. This was true of beasts of burden, water-borne carriers, and wheeled vehicles, including railroads. The only exception so far has been aircraft. Many people believe that aircraft will always be primarily passenger carriers. Others believe that aircraft will be carrying more cargo than passengers by the next century. But there is no doubt that cargo volume has been increasing more rapidly than passenger volume for the past two decades.

Air cargo got its start on May 28, 1910, when Glenn Curtiss flew a sack of mail from Albany to New York City for the Post Office Department, covering the 150 miles in two and a half hours. Or you could say it all started on November 10, 1910, when the Wright Company flew 65 miles from Dayton to Columbus, Ohio, with five bolts of silk cloth strapped into the passenger seat of the plane for a department store that wanted to sell strips of the cloth as mementos of "the first air shipment."

These were interesting events, but they did not mark the start of any regular air cargo service. Actually, there are three separate elements of air cargo services-air mail, air express, and air freight-and therefore three histories to trace. Air mail is self-explanatory, but "air express," as originally used, included what we now call "air freight," a term that did not come into use until the first all-cargo aircraft were introduced. Today, air express refers to small packages that usually have a higher priority of carriage than air freight. Until the mid-1970s, air express was also distinguished from air freight by the fact that it was a cooperative effort among airlines, using a separate ground operator, the Railway Express Agency (REA). The REA accepted shipments from customers and distributed them over the available routes of the associated carriers so as to give the customer the most expeditious service.

Air freight, on the other hand, has always been marketed independently by airlines in competition with one another. In recent years, the lines of distinction between air express and air freight have become less clear. In 1989, Federal Express, the pioneer of overnight small-package air service and now the largest carrier in that business, acquired Flying Tiger, the world's largest all-freight carrier. The weight limit on express shipments was removed, causing some industry analysts to conclude that the boundaries between freight and express are blurring and may soon disappear.

Air mail service, the first of the air cargo services, was an important factor in the formation of air transportation in the United States. The first air mail service, which its founders hoped would be permanent, started with an experimental service between Washington, D.C., and New York. During the three-month test, the Post Office Department moved 193,021 pounds of mail, collected $159,700 from the sale of its 24-cerit air mail stamp; and showed a profit of $19,103. This experiment marked the real beginning of air mail service, because it convinced the Post Office Department that air service was feasible.

For the next nine years, the Post Office Department completely controlled air mail service-even the operation of the airplanes-using both Army Air Corps and civilian pilots. In 1925, Congress ordered the government out of the business of flying the mail and established procedures for contracting with private operators. By 1927, the government had ceased aircraft operations for mail services completely. Air mail began to grow more rapidly after the Post Office Department turned operations over to private contractors.

It is difficult to overemphasize the importance of air mail to the early aircraft operators. The first commercial aircraft were built primarily to transport mail, and mail was the principal revenue source for the operators for many years. Air mail was responsible for the beginnings of the U.S. airline system as we know it today. Mail continued to be the dominant revenue source for the airlines until the arrival of the DC-3 in 1935. This craft could carry 21 passengers across the country in 15 hours, but more importantly, it was the first aircraft that could be operated profitably on passenger revenues alone. The introduction of the DC-3 began to shift the focus away from air mail and toward passenger operations. Although air mail would continue to be a significant revenue source to the airlines, it would gradually slip in relative importance. Today, mail accounts for less than 3 percent, of the airlines' revenues.

AIR EXPRESS

Whereas mail had its greatest impact on air transportation in the early days of the industry air express has only recently begun to fulfill its promise. Air express service was inaugurated at Hadley Field near New Brunswick, N.J on September 1, 1927, by National Air Transport, a predecessor of United Airlines, created specifically for the purpose of carrying air express, and by the American Railway Express Agency (REA). Three other carriers joined the effort to provide a comprehensive express service: Colonial Airlines, Boeing Air Transport, and Western Air Express.

The carriers affiliated with the REA tried to persuade other air carriers to join them in this enterprise, but American, Eastern, TWA, and several others were concerned over the choice of the REA as the ground operator. They were afraid that the REA's rail operations would be in conflict with the air service and preferred a more neutral operator. These airlines decided instead to organize General Air Express. Established in August 1932, General Air Express claimed to provide "the largest and most complete air express service in the world, serving 125 cities directly by air and offering connections to Canada, Mexico, the West Indies, and Central and South America. But the REA's head start was too much for General Air Express to overcome; General Air Express folded at the close of 1935, and the REA became the sole express agent for the US Air Carrier industry

Even with the REA acting as coordinator for all the carries, air express was a small part of the airlines income. When the mail contract was canceled in 1933, United Airlines was earning almost 60 percent of its revenues from the carriage of mail and 40 percent from passengers. Its express business accounted for only a little over 1 percent of the gross—some $133,000 a year

Air express did not become the important revenue source the carriers hoped it would. While airline managements concentrated on winning passengers away from the railroads, the REA and the airline cargo staffs struggled with air express, often at odds over who should control the product and how revenues should be shared. On November 12, 1975, the REA declared bankruptcy. In place of the coordinated joint effort, each carrier introduced its individual air express service, foregoing the nationwide coverage they were able to provide with the REA.

Overnight Air Express on April17, 1973, Frederick W. Smith begins his Federal Express operations at 13 airports. Smith's concept was to provide a door-to door overnight service for small packages. The new key element the overnight feature. Up till then, air express service relied almost entirely on passenger flights that operate during daylight hours. Packages tendered after the close of business generally sat at the origin airport until the next morning and were not delivered until the second day. By trying dedicated aircraft, FedEx was able to fly at night and deliver packages the next business day.

Operationally, Fred Smith revolutionized the air industry by introducing the hub-an spoke system, routing all packages and aircraft through a hub in Memphis. A large portion of FedEx's work force was made up of college students who performed the sorting and loading functions at Memphis each night.

In 1975, its third year of operation, FedEx was grossing $173 million in revenues but still losing money. 'What helped turn FedEx profitable was the demise of the REA. By then, Smith's company was big enough to enable it to pick up the pieces from the REA, his fleet having grown to 30 Falcon 20 mini freighters, each with a capacity of 350 to 400 packages.

And so the banner was passed from the passenger carriers to FedEx. And FedEx has carried it very high indeed. From an average of fewer than 500 packages handled per night in 1973, FedEx has grown at a phenomenal rate, to garner half of the express traffic in the United States and become a significant factor in international service.

The Arrival of Jumbo Jets

In January 1970, the Boeing 747 jumbo jets began operating as passenger liners. They proved to be both a boon and a bane for the cargo business. They were a boon because as all-cargo aircraft they provided the capacity to carry containers as big as 8 × 8 × 40 feet and to lift over 100 tons per trip. In November 1971, Boeing finished construction of the first 747 freighter. Delivered to Lufthansa German Airlines on March 9, 1972, it was put into service on the Frankfurt-New York route. On February 21, 1974, Sabena World Airways marked another important first in the jumbo jet era by introducing the 747 combo in scheduled service-an aircraft that divided the main deck so that 8 × 8 × 10-foot cargo containers could be carried aft of the passenger compartment.

The jumbo jets were also a bane, however, because the bellies of passenger aircraft could accommodate most of the air cargo tonnage available and by virtue of the byproduct nature of the space at considerably less cost than dedicated freighter aircraft. The combination of expanded belly capacity and lower air freight rates permitted under the CAB's liberalized pricing policies following deregulation in 1978 proved to be the death knell for freighter operations by the U.S. passenger airlines. TWA operated its last freighter in December 1978, and in subsequent years, American, United, and Pan Am all got out of the business. Today, Northwest is the only one of the originally certificated combination carriers to operate freighter aircraft. Flying Tigers, acquired by Federal Express in 1989, was the only surviving all cargo carrier from those originally approved by the CAB in 1948.

After most US certificated carriers phased out their operation of freighters, the promotion of air cargo devolved upon the freight forwarders, who had been the airlines' best customers. Some of the largest forwarders, such as Emery, Burlington Air Express, and Airborne, later began to fly their own aircraft to provide the cargo lift they needed, at the times of day they needed at the times of day they needed it, and became major cargo carriers in their own right.

Foreign-flag carriers, which continue to operate cargo services with dedicated freighters and Combo aircraft, have been far more aggressive than US. carriers in promoting air cargo.

Types of Carriers

The air cargo industry includes three types of carriers: integrated carriers, passenger airlines, and conventional all-cargo carriers. Integrated carriers, also called express carriers, operate door-to-door freight transportation networks that include all-cargo aircraft, delivery vehicles, sorting hubs, and advanced information systems. These carriers operate their own aircraft to ensure adequate capacity and service reliability, although they also use the belly cargo space of passenger aircraft to supplement their own capacity and to provide international service. The U.S. express carriers include FedEx, United Parcel Service (UPS), and Airborne Express, DHL Airways, Emery Worldwide, and Burlington Air Express.

A second major type of cargo carrier is the combination carrier that carries passengers and cargo. These carriers primarily offer point-to-point service on a wholesale basis, relying on freight forwarders for pickup and delivery sales to shippers, and customer service. Because the passenger plane belly space that represents much of their cargo capacity is a co-product of passenger service, combination carrier cargo services have a low marginal cost and thus usually offer much lower prices than express carriers. Although virtually all passenger airlines handle some cargo, the importance of the cargo business varies substantially from airline to airline. Many large Asian and European carriers, including Korean Air, Cathay Pacific Airways, Lufthansa German Airlines, and Air France, operate fleets of freighter aircraft to supplement their belly cargo capacity. Cargo accounts for a large share of total revenue for most major non-US. air carriers, but it plays a much less prominent role for many other airlines including most major U.S. passenger airlines.

The third type of cargo carrier is the all-cargo airline; which operates a variety of cargo services: Some, including American International Airways, Challenge Air Cargo, and Polar Air Cargo, provide point-to-point service for air freight forwarders, either as common carriers or under guaranteed-space agreements. Others, like Atlas Air and Air Transport International, primarily operate aircraft on a contract basis for other airlines. Two of the conventional carriers, Atlas and Polar, specialize in international 747 freighter service and are among the fastest-growing cargo carriers in the world.

AIR CARGO TODAY

Air cargo traffic continues to grow at a healthy rate, but it has not yet achieved the status envisioned by the air cargo pioneers of the 1930s and 1940s. They fully expected that air cargo would in time be the most important revenue source for the airlines. After all, every known form of transportation had earned more money from the carriage of freight than of people. Thus, the only real question for the airlines was how soon air freight would overtake passenger revenues. Most experts felt it would happen within years or 10 YEARS at the most. So what has happened? Why is it that the time frame for the ascendancy of air cargo keeps being pushed into the future? And why do many experts suspect that air cargo may never be the top money maker?

A fundamental reason for air cargo's inability to surpass passenger revenues is that air is a premium-cost transportation mode compared to any surface system. It costs far more to operate an airplane than to run a truck, ship, or railroad car. Thus, there has to be a compelling reason for customers to use air services. Computer companies regularly ship by air, for example, because the added cost of air transportation is more than offset by getting the product to market and into service earlier. Shippers of perishables-such as fresh fruits, flowers, and fish-use air transport because they have no other way to reach their worldwide markets. But shippers of most commodities find surface delivery times acceptable and therefore choose the lower transportation costs associated with surface modes.

Another reason freight lags behind passenger traffic is that aircraft being produced today, and on which air cargo has relied in the past, have been designed primarily for the carriage of passengers and are not particularly well suited for freight. Nor are we likely to see, any time soon, the research and development funds needed to produce a vehicle better suited to the carriage of cargo.

The unprofitable operations of freighter aircraft through the years also took a toll on air cargo's reputation. The fact that freighters lost money somehow translated to the belief among senior management of the leading US carriers that air cargo was an unprofitable business-certainly not a valid conclusion when you look at the profits that are made by the carriage of cargo in combination aircraft. In any, event, the perception that cargo was a loser has convinced many passenger airline managements not to invest their scarce capital in any more freighter aircraft.

Although air cargo has failed to achieve the preeminent position that was expected of it, and in spite of the limitations imposed by the marketplace and the 'design of aircraft, air cargo is alive and well. More and more companies are using air cargo services as they experience the inventory reduction benefits that air transportation can provide.

Table 9: Freight and express Ton-miles and Revenues for US Air Carrier Scheduled Services, 1975-95

Year	*Ton-Miles (Thousands)*	*Revenues (thousands) $*
1975	4,795,308	1,309,779
1980	5,741,567	2,431,926
1985	6,030,543	2,680,715
1990	10,546,329	5,431,627
1995	14,568,416	8,480,085

Air cargo has grown very rapidly during the past two decades, as shown in Table Freight and express ton-miles have tripled while revenues have increased more than six fold during this period. Although cargo accounts for only 5 to 10 percent of total revenues for most of the combination carriers in the United States, it is a considerably more important revenue source for many of the foreign-flag carriers, which continue to operate jumbo freighters and Combi aircraft on international routes. Some of them-such as Lufthansa, Japan Airlines, and Air France-earn as much as one-third to one-half of their gross revenues from cargo on some routes.

The four largest markets-the North Atlantic, transpacific, Europe-Far East, and U.S. domestic-account for nearly three-quarters of air cargo shipments, with traffic divided almost equally among them. In recent years, international traffic has grown more quickly among than US domestic business

The composition of the U.S. domestic market changed dramatically during this time, as the integrated all-cargo carriers captured virtually all of the growth and became the industry leaders. Today, the express carriers hold a two-thirds market share and earn over 80 percent of domestic air freight revenues.

The integrated carriers have successfully followed the strategy of offering superior service at a premium price. By providing time-definite, guaranteed, door-to-door service supported by real-time shipment tracking service', they are able to generate a yield of about $2.00 to $250 per pound for domestic shipments. Their leading competitors, the combination carriers, supply airport-to-airport service primarily on a space-available basis, usually provide no service guarantees, offer little or no tracking capability and typically earn $0.30 to $0.40 per pound for domestic freight.

The combination carriers appear to have little chance of reversing the trends of the past 20 years and capturing a larger share of the domestic freight market. By offering a consistently high level of service, the integrated carriers. Have raised the expectations of freight shippers. The passenger airline freight product has changed little over the past 20 years, and the gap between the level of service they can support and the level demanded by the market is widening. Recent changes designed to improve the profitability of passenger service, including grounding wide-body aircraft and scheduling faster turn times, further limit cargo opportunities for combination carriers. In addition, the integrated carriers have developed a variety of lower-cost second-day and deferred service options through increased use of trucking. These services options reduce the combination carriers' price advantage: while preserving shipment tracking and other integrated-carrier service advantages.

The most important competitive response by U.S. combination carriers is the trend toward contracting out airport cargo services. This may increase airline cargo profitability by reducing labour costs, but it will not help the combination carriers regain market share and may cause a further drop in share if it lowers their service quality.

If current trends continue as expected, the volume of domestic traffic handled by the integrated carriers will continue to grow rapidly. This will have important implications for U.S. airports. Because almost all integrated-carrier domestic traffic moves in all-cargo aircraft, the number of all-cargo operations will rise. This will increase the demand for cargo aircraft parking positions, particularly at spoke airports, where many cargo aircraft remain parked from early morning until late evening. Integrated carriers have more flexibility in locating cargo warehouses than do combination carriers, which need access to passenger aircraft, so the demand for on-airport cargo warehouse space will grow less rapidly than the demand for cargo aircraft parking. Parts of the airport that do not have good access to passenger terminals and are not' well suited for combination-carrier freight warehouses may be suitable for integrated-carrier facilities. The noise impacts from cargo may also increase e, because most integrated-carrier flights are operated at night, although the shift to quieter, Stage 3 aircraft will offset the increase in the number of cargo operations in many cases.

The growth in U.S. airport freighter activity primarily reflects the development of integrated-carrier flight routings. Most of the airports with the greatest activity and growth are the integrated-carrier hub/gateway airports: Memphis, Indianapolis, Anchorage, Oakland, Newark, and Dallas Fort Worth for FedEx; Louisville, Anchorage, Newark, Dallas-Fort Worth, Philadelphia, and Ontario for UPS; Dayton for Emery Worldwide; and Toledo for Burlington Air Express. Because the integrated carriers have established major facilities, cargo usually receives sufficient attention at these airports. Where cargo may not always receive enough attention, and where the increase in freighter activity makes it an important issue, is at the large airport that are not integrated-carrier hub, such as, Atlanta, Chicago, Denver, Honolulu, Phoenix, and Boston.

The Future

Although air mail was the first of the air cargo products, it now accounts for only about 7 percent of the revenues for cargo carried by the world's air, lines. Mail growth has been steady but slow, advancing an average of about 4 percent a year but eclipsed by the faster growth in express and freight. Mail will probably continue to grow at a leisurely pace, aided on the one hand by the expansion of international commerce and beset on the other by the rapid growth of fax services and small-package carriers. The real potential for air cargo growth lies with air express and air freight. In the short term, most projections place air cargo growth on the order of 6 to 8 percent a year.

Two primary factors influence freight growth: economic conditions and rate levels. The outlook for both is positive for cargo. Moderate economic growth is expected to continue into the future, with only a minor slowdown in the short term. Cargo rates should also remain low as several factors serve to keep the lid on prices.

A large number of new aircraft have been introduced in recent years. This new capacity will help keep prices down. Labor costs for the world airlines should continue to move downwards due to better utilization of the labour force to continued industry consolidation. In addition, the formation of an integrated European economic community should result in increasing traffic to Europe from all areas of the world. The European market will consist of some 330 million people, exceeding by half the size of the United States. Furthermore, to the extent that trade barriers are removed, customs procedures simplified, and carriers given more t1exible operating rights, air cargo traffic growth will be stimulated.

FedEx and UPS, the two major US express operators, are expanding their international services so that they can offer worldwide distribution. But they face some formidable competition from well-established international operators, notably DHL and TNT, both of which provide global service. The competition promises to keep the small-package express market lively for a while.

The globalization of the world economy-the production of parts and the assembly of products half a world away from where they will be placed in service-will also provide a major stimulus to air freight. Rather than rely on ocean transportation, which can take as much as two or three weeks shippers can transport the goods by air within a couple of days. For products with a short shelf life-be they magazines or fashion goods or fresh fish—air freight is the only real choice shippers have, and they are realizing it more and more.

All in all, the future of air cargo should well exceed its past. Air cargo revenues may not overtake passenger revenues in the next 5 to 10 years, but the gap between them will undoubtedly be narrowed. The blend of additional capacity (air cargo people simply can't accept unused capacity); the continued explosion of traffic in the competitive express package market, and the customers' interest in quick and reliable delivery will fuel air cargo's accelerated growth.

AIR FREIGHT MARKET

Air Freight

If we accept the original definition of air freight as traffic carried in all-cargo aircraft, then the birth of air freight operations would date back to 1931 when Transcontinental & Western Air began overnight air freight service between New York and Kansas City. It used "specially constructed freight planes cruising over 100 miles per hour." The planes were unscheduled; they departed in the evening whenever a full cargo load became available. They made six intermediate stops-in Philadelphia, Harrisburg, Pittsburgh, Columbus, Indianapolis, and St. Louis. Customers could ship between any two of the points served for the same "astonishingly low price" of $11 per 100 pounds. As part of the promotion for "the first air freight service," TWA introduced a new shipping document, the air freight waybill, and offered a souvenir copy to any customer who requested one. The first regularly scheduled all-cargo service was started by United Airlines in 1940 between New York and Chicago. The flight left New York at 11:30 P.M. and arrived in Chicago at 3:40 A.M.

Air freight received a big boost at the end of World War II with two landmark decisions by the Civil Aeronautics Board. The first, in April of 1948, legitimized air freight forwarders as middlemen between shippers and airlines, giving them the right to consolidate individual shipments and tender them to the airlines at the carriers' volume rates. Although opposed by most or the air carriers, the official recognition of the forwarder added a new dimension to air freight, greatly increasing marketing and sales efforts and stimulating new traffic.

The second CAB decision gave operating-rights to three all-cargo carriers: Slick, U.S. Airlines, and Flying Tigers. The last-named airline had been formed by Bob Prescott in 1945 under the name National Skyway Freight Corporation. But it soon came to be known by its slogan, "The Line of the Flying Tigers," because it was equipped with surplus military transports, flown by pilots who had served with Prescott under General Chennault, defending the Burma Road. It was the first of the three all-cargo carriers to be certificated, on September 21, 1949.

The halcyon days of air freight began in the 1960s. In October 1962, American Airlines ordered its first 707 freighters, and United followed suit in 1964 by ordering 727-QCs (for "quick change"). These planes had removable passenger seats so that they could be flown in the daytime as passenger aircraft and at night as freighters. By 1969, American was operating a fleet of 39 of the 707 freighters; United had 15 DC-8 freighters plus 30 QCs; and TWA was flying 12 of the 707s and 8 QCs. Even with all this dedicated lift, however, cargo still accounted for only 10 percent of the revenues for these carriers.

A review of the major commodities shipped by air, according to data supplied on an annual basis by the Air Transport Association, gives a good idea of the major markets for air cargo. These commodities include the following:

- Auto parts and accessories Machinery and parts
- Printed matter
- Electronic/electric equipment and parts, including appliances
- Fashion apparel
- Footwear
- Tools and hardware
- CDs, tapes, televisions, radios, and recorders
- Computers and software Fruits and vegetables
- Sporting goods, toys, and games
- Live animals
- Chemicals, elements, and compounds
- Machines for electronic data storage and processing
- Metal products
- Photographic equipment, parts, and film
- Cut flowers and nursery stock
- Plastic materials and articles
- Medicines, pharmaceuticals, and drugs
- Instruments-controlling, measuring, medical, and optical
- Food preparations and miscellaneous bakery products

Shipping commodities by air is the most desirable form of distribution when one or more of the following characteristics is present:

1. When the commodity is:

A. Perishable
B. Subject to quick obsolescence

C. Required on short notice
D. Valuable relative to weight
E. Expensive to handle or store

2. When the demand is:

A. Unpredictable
B. Infrequent
C. In excess of local supply
D. Seasonal

3. When the distribution problems include:

A. Risk of pilferage, breakage, or deterioration
B. High insurance costs for long in-transit periods
C. Heavy or expensive packaging required for surface transportation d, Special handling or care needed
D. Warehousing or stocks in excess of what would be needed if air freight were used

For commodities that are perishable, subject to quick obsolescence, or required on short notice, the speed of air transportation becomes advantageous. Timing is important for products such as recordings, fashion apparel, and novelty items. When the market is seasonal or demand fluctuates for any reason, air freight allows an immediate response without the penalty of costly fixed overhead-being out of stock or overstocked. A manufacturer that offers a wide selection of styles, sizes, colors, or accessories in a product line and whose market covers a wide geographic area is usually faced with the dilemma of carrying costly inventory and obsolescence or long delays in filling orders. Air freight can eliminate the cost of carrying inventory. Customers can select freely from the entire line of products and they can be assured of delivery from a central warehouse as quickly as from a local warehouse.

Air freight is premium service. It projects an image of premium product and company progressiveness. The retailer who advertises "flown in from ..." and the salesperson who assures the client that "we'll fly it in from our main office" understand the value of such an image. The various modes of transport represent great differences in quality. Air freight can add a new competitive edge to the marketing effort. Superior service adds value to any product and generates a quality image for the shipper.

Air freight can stimulate growth in existing markets, and it allows firms to enter new markets without making a commitment to large, fixed investments in warehousing and inventories. Test markets supplied overnight by air allow adjustment to market response as readily as to the demands of a local market.

The risk of pilferage, breakage, or deterioration is minimized through the use of air transportation because of the lack of en-route handling and exposure of goods to long periods under minimum security. Insurance charges tend to be substantially lower for air freight than for surface freight, because there is less risk by air and because the transit time is shorter. Insurance represents a considerable expenditure for many companies.

Packaging for air freight is usually of minimal cost. Because air transport reduces the risk of jolts and shocks, cardboard cartons usually will suffice, whereas heavy wooden crates may be required for surface transportation. Ground handling is done on a more individual basis than is the case for most other modes of transportation. Risk of exposure to the elements is slight, and for commodities for which containerization is used, there may be no need to package at all.

The total costs associated with carrying inventory are high; it includes the cost of capital tied up in warehouse facilities and in stock, insurance, and taxes. In addition, stocked items may become obsolete, and the cost of labour and multiple handlings is a major consideration. With each handling, loss and damage is a factor. Air freight can often bring about drastic reductions in the cost of carrying inventory. Businesses that use regional warehousing supplied by surface transportation can reduce safety stocks and perhaps eliminate some warehouses. Even when air freight costs more than surface freight, the tradeoff in reduced costs has made it profitable for many businesses to substitute overnight distribution by air from a central warehouse.

AIR FREIGHT RATES

General Commodity Rates

The air freight rate structure is similar to the passenger fare structure in that there is a normal or basic price applicable to all commodities in all markets.

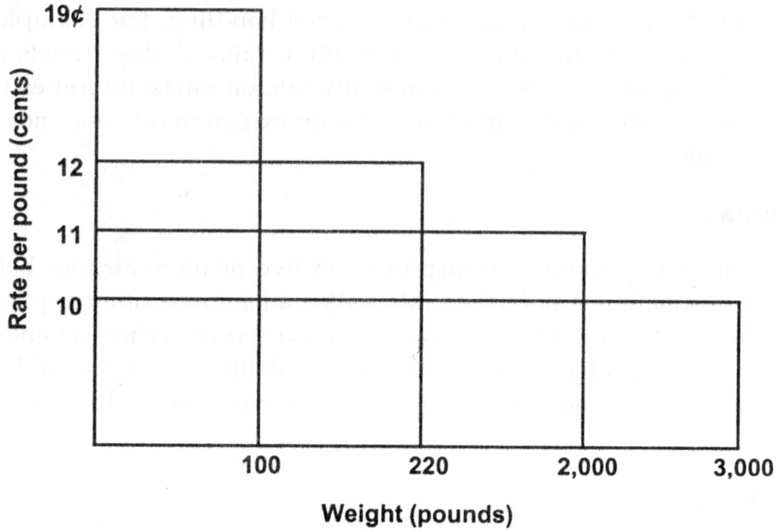

Fig. 29: General Commodity rates by weight of the shipment. The greater the weight, the lower the rates (hypothetical example)

This is called the general commodity rate. General commodity shipments are rated by weight. (Dimensional weight is used if the shipment is of very low density; this will be discussed shortly.) As the weight of a shipment increases, the per-pound rate decreases, as Figure illustrates. There is generally a minimum charge, depending on the city-pairs between which the shipment takes place.

Dimensional weight is computed by finding the cubic measurement of a shipment (length × width × height) and charging the rate for one pound for each 194 cubic inches. There are exceptions. For example, cut flowers and nursery stock being transported to domestic cities take a charge of one pound for each 250 cubic inches. In this way, if a cargo compartment were filled with, say, 20 pounds of Styrofoam cups, the charge would be based on a weight that represented a minimum density in relation to the space occupied.

Specific Commodity Rates

Specific commodity rates are established for unusually high-volume shipping of certain products between certain cities, such as fish from Anchorage; Alaska, to certain points in the continental United States; recording tapes, athletic goods, and musical instruments from Denver to San Francisco; and flowers, decorative greens, furs, fruits, and vegetables between Seattle/ Tacoma and Minneapolis-St. Paul in most cases, the specific commodity rate is lower than the general commodity rate to reflect the benefit to the carrier of regular high-volume shipments.

Exception Rates

Exception rates are higher than the usual air freight rates and apply to certain types of shipments that require special handling. For example, live animals and uncrated furniture take exception rates. A dog travels at 110 percent of the applicable general commodity rate on interstate routes within the continental United States. In some cases, an exception rate does not apply on certain routes.

Joints Rates

For domestic shipments transported on two or more airlines between origin and destination, a published rate, called a joint rate, often applies. The joint rate is usually the same as the rate for direct service. Where a joint rate is published, the shipper has the advantage of availability of a number of different routings at the same rate. This is especially advantageous if direct service is limited.

Priority Rates

Priority reserved air freight is designed to serve shippers of heavy or bulky freight who need the advantage of reserved space on a specific flight.

For example, if an oil-drilling company has stopped production because it needs some drill bits, space can be reserved on the next flight. Knowing exactly when the drill bits will arrive, the drilling company can plan accordingly. Because special handling is required for this type of service, the rate is higher than the normal general commodity and specific commodity rates.

Speed Package Service

SPS is a small-package fast-delivery service, airport-to-airport, with certain carriers on their own systems. Packages are accepted at the airport passenger terminal, at the passenger baggage check-in position, or at the air freight office. They are delivered to the baggage claim area at destination. Speed package service is handled like passenger baggage, but because there is no accompanying passenger, the sender must make arrangements for someone to pick up the package on arrival.

Speed package service is designed for situations in which even a few hours are important. For example, critically needed small machinery parts often are shipped by this method. There is generally a flat rate based on distance between city-pairs for any speed package service shipment.

Container Rates

Container rates are low rates charged by the carriers to shippers using containers to ship air cargo. There are many types of containers designed for air freight, suitable for shipping quantities from 400 pounds to 5 tons. Some types are owned by the airline and made available to the shipper on request. Other types are purchased by shippers for regular use or rented from various sources (see Figures 30 and 31). There are many advantages to containerizing air freight shipments:

1. Transportation charges are lower when a shipper has a large-enough shipment to fill, or nearly fill, the container used. This is true even when the airline supplies the container.
2. Packaging costs can be reduced, because the container provides protection against handling mishaps.
3. Shippers can seal containers to prevent pilferage.
4. Shipments arrive as one complete unit; there are no delayed or missing parts.
5. Counting and checking the pieces of the shipment at destination is simplified.
6. Transportation costs for high-density freight shipments in containers often are lower than for surface transportation.

Shippers can use carrier-owned containers, for which they are generally charged a flat fee that includes both the use of the container and the transportation of its contents. Sometimes, the weight of the contents allowed

Type: A1 Dom. SAB-UAB Intl. Int. Capacity: 399 Cu. Ft. Ext. Dimensions: 88×125×87 In. Max. Gross Weight: 13,300 Lbs. Cube Displacement: 425 Cu. Ft. 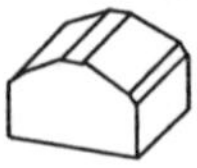	**Type: LD6 Dom./AWC-AWF Intl.** Int. Capacity: 316 Cu. Ft. Ext. Dimensions: 25×60.4×64 In. Max. Gross Weight: 5,680 Lbs. Cube Displacement: 339 Cu. Ft. 
Type: A1,A3 Dom. AAA-SAA Intl. Int. Capacity: 440 Cu. Ft. Ext. Dimensions: 88×125×87 In. Max. Gross Weight: 12,500 Lbs. Cube Displacement: 475 Cu. Ft. 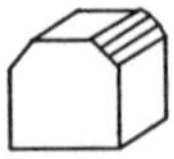	**Type: LD7,LD9 Dom./AAP-AAR Intl.** Int. Capacity: 355 Cu. Ft. Ext. Dimensions: 125×88×64 In. Max. Gross Weight: 13,,300 Lbs. Cube Displacement: 401 Cu. Ft. 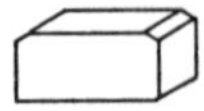
Type: FTC Dom./= Int. Capacity: 151 Cu. Ft. Ext. Dimensions: 81×60.4×62.75 In. Max. Gross Weight: 4,500 Lbs. Cube Displacement: 174.5 Cu. Ft. 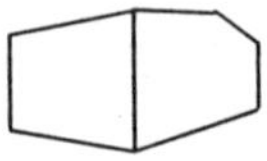	**Type: LD8 Dom./ALE Intl.** Int. Capacity: 253 Cu. Ft. Ext. Dimensions: 196×60.4×60 In. Max. Gross Weight: 5,400 Lbs. Cube Displacement: 280 Cu. Ft. 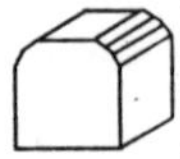
Type: LD2 Dom./ APA Intl. Int. Capacity: 120 Cu. Ft. Ext. Dimensions: 47×60.4×64 In. Max. Gross Weight: 2,700 Lbs. Cube Displacement: 134 Cu. Ft. 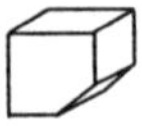	**Type: LD10 Dom./AWR-AWS Intl.** Int. Capacity: 246 Cu. Ft. Ext. Dimensions: 125×60.4×64 In. Max. Gross Weight: 5,680 Lbs. Cube Displacement: 257 Cu. Ft. 
Type: LD3 Dom./AVE-AKE Intl. Int. Capacity: 150 Cu. Ft. Ext. Dimensions: 79×60.4×64 In. Max. Gross Weight: 3,500 Lbs. Cube Displacement: 166 Cu. Ft. 	**Type: LDW Dom./=** Int. Capacity: 70 Cu. Ft. Ext. Dimensions: 98×42.2×41.6 In. Max. Gross Weight: 1,700 Lbs. Cube Displacement: 76 Cu. Ft. 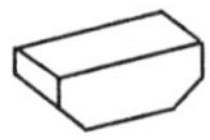
Type: LD4 Dom./DLP-DLF Intl. Int. Capacity: 193 Cu. Ft. Ext. Dimensions: 96×60.4×64 In. Max. Gross Weight: 5,400 Lbs. Cube Displacement: 215 Cu. Ft. 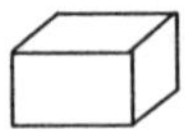	**Type: M1 Dom./ARA Intl.** Int. Capacity: 572 Cu. Ft. Ext. Dimensions: 125×96×96 In. Max. Gross Weight: 15,000 Lbs. Cube Displacement: 666 Cu. Ft. 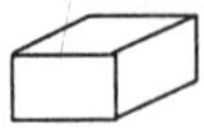
Type: LD5, LD11 Dom./AWB-AWB Intl. Int. Capacity: 399 Cu. Ft. Ext. Dimensions: 88×125×87 In. Max. Gross Weight: 13,300 Lbs. Cube Displacement: 425 Cu. Ft. 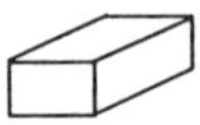	**Type: M2 Dom./ASE-ASG Intl.** Int. Capacity: 1,077 Cu. Ft. Ext. Dimensions: 240×96×96 In. Max. Gross Weight: 25,000 Lbs. Cube Displacement: 1,286 Cu. Ft. 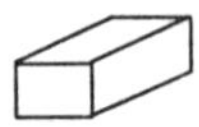

Fig. 30

Containers provided by airlines, these containers are owned by the airlines and are certified as an integral part of the aircraft. These units are available from the carrier for shipper use. The specifications may vary slightly by owner; this information is provided as a guide only. (Source: Air Transport Association of America, *Air Cargo from A* to Z [Washington, D.C.: Air Transport Association, 1979].)

at the flat fee is a specified maximum. An *excess pound rate* is applied to weight that exceeds the amount allowed at the flat rate. (The weight of the container is not considered in these calculations.) In many cases, there are different rates for day and night. Airlines can also provide one or more containers for the

Type: B Dom. / Intl. = Int. Capacity: Varies (Insert for A) Ext. Dimensions: 84×58×76.45 In. Max. Gross Weight: 5,000 Lbs. Cube Displacement: 1,97.7 Cu. Ft. 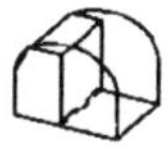	**Type: EH Dom. / =** Int. Capacity: Varies (Insert for A) Ext. Dimensions: 35.4×21×21 In. Max. Gross Weight: 250 Lbs. Cube Displacement: 9.03 Cu. Ft. 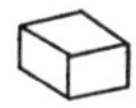
Type: B2 Dom. /= Int. Capacity: Varies Ext. Dimensions: 42×58×76.45 In. Max. Gross Weight: 2,500 Lbs. Cube Displacement: 98.85 Cu. Ft. 	**Type: LD-N Dom. /=** Int. Capacity: Varies (LD-3 insert) Ext. Dimensions: 56×55×57 In. Max. Gross Weight: 3,160 Lbs. Cube Displacement: 1,016 Cu. Ft. 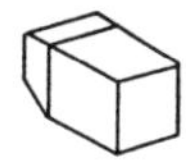
Type: D Dom. / = Int. Capacity: Varies Ext. Dimensions: 58×42×45 In. Max. Gross Weight: 2,000 Lbs. Cube Displacement: 63.44 Cu. Ft. 	**Type: Q Dom. / =** Int. Capacity: Varies Ext. Dimensions: 39.5×27.5×21 In. Max. Gross Weight: 400 Lbs. Cube Displacement: 12 Cu. Ft. 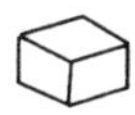
Type: E Dom. /= Int. Capacity: Varies Ext. Dimensions: 42x29x25.5 In. Max. Gross Weight: 500 Lbs. Cube Displacement: 17.97 Cu. Ft. 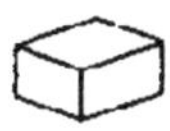	

Fig. 31

Containers offered by shippers. These containers are shipper owned and are available from many commercial sources and from the airlines. Most carriers offer container incentive rates when used. Specifications may vary slightly; is information is provided as a guide only. (Source: Air Transport Association of America, *Air Cargo from A to* Z [Washington, D.C.: Air Transport Association, 1979].)

shipper that has many items going to the same city and charge the shipper less for the total shipment while reducing packaging costs and providing the benefits of decreased handling and protection from weather. Carriers have specially built containers for heavy items, such as machinery parts.

Shippers often purchase their own containers or else rent them. These containers also qualify for special rates that are lower than the general commodity rate. Most shipper-owned containers are small enough to be moved through factory assembly lines. Thus, goods can be loaded and the container sealed at the plant. An airline normally will charge a container rate to a shipper that can stack its boxes on a pallet and secure them with a cargo net, provided that the overall dimensions do not exceed the dimensions for the type of container on which the rate is based.

FACTORS AFFECTING AIR FREIGHT RATES

Costs of the Service

A basic consideration in rate making is that the rates should cover the costs of service and yield a reasonable profit. In air transportation, where air freight is carried in the cargo compartments of passenger aircraft as well as in all-cargo aircraft, the costs that must be covered generally are the same as those of an all-cargo aircraft operation. This approach is usually followed for two reasons: (1) the allocation of costs in a combination aircraft is difficult, and (2) the maximum development of an air cargo industry requires the operation of all cargo aircraft whose costs must be met. As was pointed out earlier in the chapter, freight rates have considerably less profit potential than passenger fare because the advantages of air over surface modes of transportation are less apparent.

Volume of Traffic

Numerous pricing considerations affect rates. One of these is the volume of new traffic a carrier can achieve at any particular rate. Volume is significant, because traffic potential is a key factor in determining the maximum net revenue that can be derived from any commodity. Thus, the rate structure contains reduced rates for larger shipments.

Directionality

Whereas most passenger travel is round-trip, freight traffic is all one-way. Historically, domestic air freight has tended to move in larger volumes in a westbound direction than eastbound, and in larger southbound than northbound volumes within the eastern United States. Consequently, rates have been set at lower levels in the off-direction as a means of filling up space to equalize the flow of traffic and put aircraft to more efficient use.

Characteristics of the Traffic

Air carriers also consider the transportation characteristics of the commodity as an important element in the rate-making process. The major transportation characteristics are the density of the commodity (the relationship of weight to measurement), the size (weight or volume) per average piece, and the average weight of the shipment (whether 10, 20, 40, 100, 1,000 or 10,000 pounds makes up one shipment at one time).

In cargo aircraft, utilization of available space and available lifting capacity must be optimized. The density of the load must be related to the capability of the aircraft in determining freight rates. A cargo aircraft fully loaded with a particular commodity should produce sufficient revenue to cover the full cost of operation and earn a profit. For example, suppose an all-cargo aircraft has a practical volume capacity of about 7,700 cubic feet and a lifting capability of almost 92,000 pounds:

$$\frac{92{,}000}{7{,}700} = \text{About 12 lb per cubic foot (optimum density for traffic)}$$

When individual shipments are loaded on an aircraft, unavoidable losses in the utilization of space occur due to the irregular shapes of the shipments. These are called *stacking losses.* To achieve the optimum density, the average density of shipments tendered to our example aircraft must be greater than 12 pounds per cubic foot to compensate for stacking losses. If the loaded density of the commodity is 12 pounds or more, the revenue-producing load will be' 92,000 pounds in this aircraft. Basically, the total cost of the operation plus the profit margin, divided by the pounds of the commodity on board, will give the approximate air freight rate for that commodity. The character of the commodity also includes whether it is dangerous, hazardous, perishable, or susceptible to damage or pilferage; what packing and packaging is needed; whether it is easily loaded and stowed aboard aircraft; and, whether it will readily ensure safe transportation with ordinary care in handling. When utilized or containerized shipments are involved, the importance of some of these rate-making factors may be reduced.

Value of the Service

Value of service is frequently an important factor in establishing a specific commodity rate. In theory, a specific commodity rate should allow the commodity to move in a volume that yields the maximum revenue in excess of the added costs of carrying the commodity. Taking revenue dilution' into consideration, the principal factors that reflect value of service include the speed and reliability of air freight service, the value of the 'commodity, and the profit margin of the consignor or consignee. The consignor, usually the shipper, is the party that designates the person to whom goods are to be sent. The consignee is the person named as the receiver of a shipment-one to whom a shipment is consigned.

Market demands, possible obsolescence of stock, cost of inventory, the necessary lead time in placing orders for surface shipments, and the possibility of reduction of warehouse expenses are all factors that may influence the shipper's acceptance of a rate level for an air shipment.

Competition

Competition is, of course, also a major factor in determining air freight rates. Where capacity exceeds demand, there is considerable pressure to lower rates. Rate reduction can be introduced by the least successful competitor to improve its market share or possibly by the principal carrier to generate new traffic.

Competition from other modes of transportation, especially trucks and railroads, may help determine the rate that can be charged on any commodity. The competitive impact of shipping via other routes, shipping via nonscheduled air carriage, or using shipper-owned vehicles also may be pertinent.

AIR FREIGHT SERVICES

Assembly Service

Airlines will consolidate packages from a shipper, or group of shippers, and base the transportation charge on the total weight of all the pieces, which allows a price break on heavy shipments. When numerous shipments are sent to the same address, the use of assembly service can result in real savings to the shipper. The assembly time can begin at 12:01 A.M. and end the following day at 12:00 A.M. During the 24-hour period, a shipper that asks for assembly service can dispatch any number of packages to the carrier's air freight office and the airline will assemble the parts until the shipment is complete or the assembly time has expired (see Figure 32).

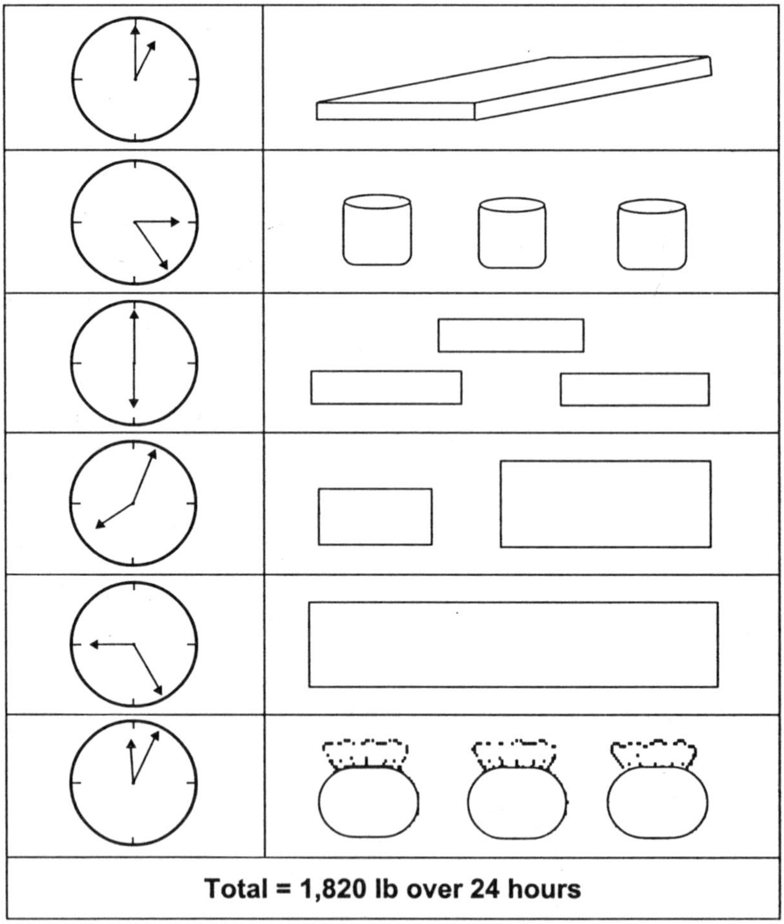

Fig. 32: Assembly service charge by total shipment weight over a 24-hour period

Distribution Service

Another service provided by airlines that fly air cargo is accepting one shipment from a shipper and, at destination, separating it into its parts and distributing them to different customers. The advantages are the same as those for assembly service in that a shipper with many customers in the same city can take advantage of the rate break for heavy shipments. However, carriers generally do not provide assembly and distribution service on the same shipment. A variation of this service is for the carrier to deliver a shipment to the main post office at the destination city, where 'the shipment is sorted by zip code. Rather than ship thousands of items from the home office, large retailers and wholesalers who mail catalogs, magazines, and so forth frequently use this service because of the substantial savings involved.

Pickup and Delivery Service

Air freight pickup and delivery service is performed by independent local truckers under contract to act as the carrier's local agent. They are governed by Air Cargo, Incorporated (ACI), an organization owned jointly by the major airlines whose major function is to negotiate contracts. with local truckers, ACI truckers generally make two regular pickup and delivery runs daily within a 25-mile radius of the airport. Rates for services performed at ship docks or outside the 25-mile radius are generally higher.

Other Specialized Services

Airlines provide a number of other specialized air freight services, including armed guards for shipments of highly valuable goods, such as furs, precious gems, watches, jewelry, negotiable securities, bills of exchange, bonds, and currency. Generally, such items are not accepted by the carrier until three hours before scheduled departure time of the flight on which they are to be transported, nor can they be held for more than three hours after arrival at destination. Because many of these items are small, carriers generally require a minimum sized container to be used. For example, coins must be shipped in a 1,500-cubic-inch container.

Shipments of human remains' are arranged for by a mortuary and are consigned to another mortuary at the destination city. The shipping mortuary must provide a death certificate and burial certificate to accompany the shipment.

Commodities called *restricted articles* range from those that are accepted without limitation but that must have an identifying label (magnetized materials, for example) to such things as poison gas, which cannot be made safe enough for commercial air transportation under any circumstances. Most restricted articles are materials that can be shipped safety when packaged according to DOT specifications for hazardous material and that are limited in terms of allowable quantities per container and p aircraft. All restricted-article shipments must be conspicuously labeled by the shipper, using authorized labels, so that all airlines participating in routing can observe special loading arrangements and advise flight crews of any potentially hazardous materials on board. Accurate labeling is also essential so that the carrier can deal appropriately with leakage or spillage of materials that are hazardous to humans and animals, to aircraft structure, or in combination with other materials being shipped in the same cargo compartment. Most restricted-article shipments require a shipper's certificate.

Many products have various degrees of hazard, depending on their components. Aerosol products, for example, may be classified as all inflammable gas or as poison or may have no restrictions, depending on both the contents and the propelling agent used. Paint is another product classified in various ways, depending on its composition.

Some airlines accept certain restricted articles not accepted by other airlines. Some restricted articles may be carried on all-cargo aircraft but not on the passenger-carrying aircraft of any carrier. And, again, some highly dangerous material cannot be made safe enough to carry on commercial air carriers under any circumstances.

The Air Cargo Guide

The *Air Cargo Guide* (2000 Clearwater Drive, Oak Brook, IL 60521) is a basic reference publication for shipping freight by air. It contains current domestic and international cargo flight schedules, including pure-cargo, wide-body, and combination passenger-cargo flights. Each monthly issue also contains information on air carriers' specialized services, labeling requirements, airline and aircraft deco dings, air carrier and freight forwarders, cargo charters, U.S. and Canadian city directory small-package services, interline air freight agreements, aircraft loading charts, and a great deal more information regarding air cargo services.

Index